Sustainable Consumption

Sustainable Consumption

Multi-disciplinary Perspectives In Honour of Professor Sir Partha Dasgupta

Edited by
Dale Southerton and Alistair Ulph

OXFORD
UNIVERSITY PRESS

OXFORD
UNIVERSITY PRESS

Great Clarendon Street, Oxford, OX2 6DP,
United Kingdom

Oxford University Press is a department of the University of Oxford.
It furthers the University's objective of excellence in research, scholarship,
and education by publishing worldwide. Oxford is a registered trade mark of
Oxford University Press in the UK and in certain other countries

First Edition published in 2014

Impression: 1

Published in the United States of America by Oxford University Press
198 Madison Avenue, New York, NY 10016, United States of America

British Library Cataloguing in Publication Data
Data available

Library of Congress Control Number: 2014932824

ISBN 978–0–19–967935–5

Printed and bound by
CPI Group (UK) Ltd, Croydon, CR0 4YY

Dedication to Professor Sir Partha Dasgupta

In our Preface to this book we will explain how Professor Sir Partha Dasgupta initiated the process that led to the publication of this book by exploring how insights from other disciplines can enrich the economists' model of consumer behaviour. Partha has built a reputation as one of the world's leading economists, spanning a range of sub-disciplines in economics, including the area of environmental and resource economics. But he has also been active in drawing on ideas from different disciplines both to enrich his analysis and to extend economists' models where their formulations have been too narrow. It is for these abilities that the SCI was delighted to appoint Partha to a part-time position, and for which it is appropriate that we should dedicate this volume to him.

Partha's first undergraduate degree was in Physics at the University of Delhi and his second in Mathematics at Cambridge followed by his PhD in Economics. In his subsequent academic career, spanning over 40 years, he spent 13 years at LSE, where he was promoted to a chair, before returning to Cambridge where he was Fellow of Trinity College and Frank Ramsey Professor of Economics until retiring from that chair in 2010. Since 2008 he has also been a Professorial Research Fellow at the Sustainable Consumption Institute. He has held numerous visiting professorships at leading universities in the US and India.

Partha has published more than twenty books and 240 articles covering a huge range of economics, most notably core economic theory, industrial economics and innovation, public economics, welfare economics and the two areas for which he is perhaps best known—environmental and resource economics, in which he published the seminal book *Economic Theory and Exhaustible Resources* with Geoff Heal (1979), and development economics in which he published the book of which he says he is proudest: *An Inquiry into Well-Being and Destitution* (1993).

What is distinctive about Partha's work is not just its high intellectual quality, but his concern to build the intellectual links between these, often separate, fields of economics and, more importantly, to build links with other disciplines, such as philosophy, medical sciences, social anthropology and ecology, to the enrichment of them all.

Partha's academic distinction has led to his appointment to the editorial boards of more than ten leading journals, the presidency of the leading economics and environmental economics learned societies in the UK and Europe, and invitations to present distinguished named lectures all round the world.

As well as being an outstanding academic, Partha has been heavily involved in ensuring that his research feeds into policy-making at the highest levels. For example his first book was *Guidelines for Project Evaluation* written with Marglin and Sen for the United Nations (1972), which translated the latest thinking from economic analysis into clear advice to help policy-makers in developing countries undertake project appraisal. In addition to his work for the UN and its various bodies, such as UNEP and UNESCO, he has been a member of advisory boards for the World Health Organization, the World Bank, and numerous university research centres and independent think tanks.

As an important recent example, Partha and Professor Karl-Goran Maler have developed a theoretical framework for measuring sustainable wealth, an aggregate measure of the progress of an economy which goes well beyond the narrow measure of economic output that is captured in Gross National Product (GNP) to measure the extent to which a society is becoming better off. But not only has Partha contributed to the theoretical underpinnings of this measure but he has helped countries implement this measure, most recently being appointed by the Prime Minister of India to lead a commission which has applied this framework to Indian data.

A further insight into Partha's commitment to practically help people in developing countries is provided by his establishment of the South Asian Network for Development and Environmental Economics (SANDEE). Partha had noted that it was often difficult for environmental and development economists from developing countries to get their papers accepted for presentation at leading international conferences. So in the 1990s he set up SANDEE, which held summer schools involving himself and the world's leading environmental and development economists to help young economists from that region develop their skills in writing academic papers. The SANDEE model has since been extended to Africa. With colleagues he also set up a new journal, *Environment and Development Economics* to give more attention to environmental problems outside the developed world, and these young scholars were encouraged to publish in this journal.

Not surprisingly Partha has been the recipient of numerous honours and awards, most notably Fellowship of the British Academy in 1989, Fellowship of the Royal Society in 2004, and in 2002 he was knighted for his services to economics.

Although we said Partha retired from the Frank Ramsay chair in Economics at Cambridge in 2010, he remains extremely active. In the past two years he has accepted five new appointments to chair or be a member of various international advisory committees, been given five awards and honours, presented eight named lectures, and published over twenty papers.

From all that we have said it will be obvious why we were so delighted that Partha accepted an appointment at the SCI, and why we have sought to honour him by dedicating this book to him.

Dale Southerton
Alistair Ulph

Preface

It is clear that if global society is to address the many environmental and other sustainability challenges that confront us in the twenty-first century, it will be necessary to make significant changes in our patterns of consumption, production, and distribution. There is a growing realization that while changes in production and distribution are formidable, the proposed solutions may not succeed unless it is possible to persuade individuals and households to change their patterns of consumption, both directly in the many activities that constitute consumption (from purchasing through to disposal) and indirectly through the role of individuals as voters.

Consumption forms the bedrock of modern economics and many of the empirical economic models used by policy-makers in international agencies, governments, and businesses to underpin policy advice. Yet it is conceptualized in a way that is at variance with findings in anthropology, sociology, history, politics, psychology, neuroscience, and other disciplines. To understand how consumption can be made more sustainable it is vital that we try to develop a conceptualization of consumption that draws on the insights from these different approaches, to seek new ways of empirically testing this conceptual framework, and hence to consider what might be the most appropriate policies for making consumption sustainable.

This broad objective is central to the mission of the Sustainable Consumption Institute (SCI) established in The University of Manchester in the United Kingdom in 2008 with generous financial support from Tesco Plc. When Professor Partha Dasgupta joined the SCI he ran a series of cross-disciplinary workshops in which he began the process of pulling together insights from different disciplines. We decided to build on this work by holding a conference titled *Sustainable Consumption: Multi-Disciplinary Perspectives* at the SCI on 8 and 9 March 2012, to which we invited world-leading experts from neuroscience, psychology, economics, politics, history, sociology, and anthropology to share their perspectives on sustainable consumption. Alongside the invitation we sent invitees a short paper Partha wrote entitled 'Reflections on Consumer Behaviour from Different Disciplinary Perspectives'. The papers presented at this conference form the basis of the chapters in this book. Partha further developed his short paper to form the basis of a public lecture he gave as part of the conference. The discussion of his and other papers that took place at the conference led to further elaboration by Partha into what now appears as Chapter 2 of this book. As we explain in the Dedication, it is for his groundwork leading up to this volume, but more generally for his career in developing cross-disciplinary thinking, that we dedicate this volume to Partha.

We have been keen to emphasize the attempts to build links across the different disciplinary approaches to understanding consumption. As organizers of the conference we sought to stimulate this building of linkages by selecting as discussants of each paper a conference contributor from a different discipline. This ensured a lively discussion at the conference, and all the contributors said they had found the conference to be a stimulating experience. This was followed through in the refereeing process we used for preparing the final versions of the chapters in the book. Perhaps most importantly, we felt that as editors of this volume we had a key responsibility for trying to strengthen cross-disciplinary links, and we have done that in Chapter 1 by (i) providing a framework within which we can locate the approaches of the authors of the different chapters; (ii) writing a rather more detailed account of the content of each chapter than is found in some introductions to help readers see the differences and similarities in disciplinary approaches; (iii) providing our suggestions for how the work reported in this book might be further developed in terms of conceptual underpinnings, empirical testing, and policy design.

We are not naïve enough to believe that we should be striving to achieve some overarching grand theory of sustainable consumption which will embrace all disciplines. But we do think some progress is possible, and, in the light of the sustainability challenges we outlined at the beginning of this Preface, it is incumbent upon social scientists to seek to make further progress.

Dale Southerton
Alistair Ulph

Acknowledgements

We would like to acknowledge the support of a number of colleagues in the Sustainable Consumption Institute (SCI) for their help in both organizing the conference and the preparation of the material for this book. Susan Cooper led the team who helped organize the conference, kept track of invitations and their responses, chased authors for their revised chapters, and organized meetings. This team included Lynda McIntosh, who produced the publicity material, Susan Huzar, Jane Raftery, and Richard Seeley, who made sure the conference ran smoothly and helped attendees with their travel and accommodation inquiries. Dan Welch has played an important role in the production of the book, compiling the index, proof reading all the chapters, and liaising with authors over detailed matters such as illustrations. We thank all of these people for their terrific support.

Dale Southerton
Alistair Ulph

Contents

List of Figures

List of Tables

Notes on Contributors

Geoff Beattie is Professor of Psychology at Edge Hill University, UK, and formerly a Professorial Research Fellow of the Sustainable Consumption Institute at The University of Manchester. He is best known for his analyses of nonverbal communication, in works such as *Talk: An Analysis of Speech and Non-Verbal Behaviour in Conversation* (Open University Press, 1983) and *Visible Thought: The New Psychology of Body Language* (Routledge, 2004). He is also author of *Why Aren't We Saving the Planet? A Psychologist's Perspective* (Routledge, 2010). He is a Fellow of the British Psychological Society (BPS) and was awarded the prestigious Spearman Medal by the BPS for 'published psychological work of outstanding merit'.

Ricardo Correia is a Portuguese PhD student of Economics at ISCTE Business School (Instituto Universitário de Lisboa), who holds a Master degree in Finance from ISCTE-IUL and received a merit scholarship for best student of that program in the academic year 2008/2009. He spent three years working at KPMG Corporate Finance Portugal, in the Mergers and Acquisitions department. His main research interests are behavioural economics, water resource economics and behavioural finance.

Maureen L. Cropper is a Distinguished University Professor of Economics at the University of Maryland, a Senior Fellow at Resources for the Future, and a former Lead Economist at the World Bank. Her research focuses on valuing environmental programs using both stated and revealed preference approaches. She has served as chair of the EPA Science Advisory Board Environmental Economics Advisory Committee and as president of the Association of Environmental and Resource Economists. She is a member of the National Academy of Sciences, a Research Associate of the National Bureau of Economic Research, and a Fellow of the Association of Environmental and Resource Economists.

Partha Dasgupta is the Frank Ramsey Professor Emeritus of Economics at the University of Cambridge and Professorial Research Fellow at the Sustainable Consumption Institute, University of Manchester. His research publications have covered welfare and development economics, environmental and resource economics, intergenerational ethics, the theory of poverty traps, game theory, the economics of science and technology, the measurement of human well-being, and the idea of sustainable development. He is a Founding Member of the South Asian Network of Development and Environmental Economics (SANDEE), a Fellow of the British Academy and the Royal Society, Member of the Pontifical Academy of Social

Sciences, Foreign Associate of the US National Academy of Sciences, and author of *Economics: A Very Short Introduction* (OUP, 2007). In 2002 he was named Knight Bachelor by Her Majesty Queen Elizabeth II 'for services to economics'.

Paul Fletcher is an Honorary Consultant Psychiatrist and Wellcome Trust Senior Research Fellow in Clinical Science, and the Bernard Wolfe Professor of Health Neuroscience at the University of Cambridge. His research uses functional neuroimaging and psychopharmacological manipulations to explore disturbances in learning, inference, motivation, and decision-making. Early work focused on the role of frontal lobes to human learning and was followed by studies on dynamic brain responses during associative learning and psychosis. He has gone on to explore learning and motivational changes that characterize the health-harming behaviours of hyperphagia and obesity. He is a Fellow of the Academy of Medical Sciences and of the Royal College of Psychiatrists.

Ann Kinzig is a Professor in the School of Life Sciences and the Chief Research Strategist in the Global Institute of Sustainability at Arizona State University. Ann studies ecosystem services, conservation-development interactions, and the resilience of natural-resource systems. Current major research projects examine: the trade-offs between conservation and development goals in developing nations; the resilience of prehistoric landscapes in the American Southwest; and assessments of ecosystem services, their valuation, and mechanisms for ensuring their continued delivery. She is an Aldo Leopold Leadership Fellow and was selected as the first AAAS Roger Revelle Fellow in Global Stewardship in 1998.

Laura McGuire was a Research Assistant at the Sustainable Consumption Institute. She trained, and worked, as a professional actress before focussing on research on sustainability and she is currently considering new approaches to modifying implicit values to the environment using drama, theatre, and film at Edge Hill University.

Andrew J. Oswald is Professor of Economics at the University of Warwick. He serves on the board of editors of *Science*. His work lies mainly at the border between economics and behavioural science, and he is best known for his work on the economic and social determinants of happiness and mental health. His 1994 article (with Andrew Clark) 'Unhappiness and unemployment', in *Economic Journal* (104, pp. 648–59) is widely seen as seminal in the development of the economics of well-being. Andrew is an ISI Highly-Cited Researcher and has been a Professorial Fellow of the ESRC.

Charles Perrings is a Professor of Environmental Economics at Arizona State University, where he co-directs the Ecoservices Group with Ann Kinzig—a research (and research training) group that focuses on ecosystem services. He was the founding editor of the Cambridge University Press journal, *Environment and Development Economics*, and is Past President of the International Society for Ecological Economics. He has published 12 books and edited volumes and around 150 scientific papers in this field. He is a Fellow of the Beijer Institute of the Royal Swedish Academy of Sciences.

Drazen Prelec is a Professor in the Department of Economics, the Department of Brain and Cognitive Sciences and the Sloan School at the Massachusetts Institute of Technology. His research deals with the psychology and neuroscience of decision making (behavioural economics and neuroeconomics). He works both on the development of normative decision theory and the exploration of the empirical failures of that theory, using behavioural and fMRI methods. Recent research has sought to understand non-causal or diagnostic motivation and develop scoring systems for evaluating judgement in knowledge domains where no external truth criterion is available (such as long-range forecasts or legal interpretation). He has received a number of distinguished research awards, including the John Simon Guggenheim Fellowship.

Catarina Roseta-Palma is an Associate Professor in the Department of Economics of ISCTE Business School (Instituto Universitário de Lisboa). Her main research interests are environmental and natural resource economics, especially water management, behavioural models, uncertainty, and growth. She has worked with INAG (Portuguese Water Authority) on the implementation of the economic aspects of the Water Framework Directive in Portugal. She has also worked as a consultant for the Portuguese Environment Ministry, the European Commission and the River Basin Authorities of Alentejo and Algarve. Catarina is the vice-president of the European Association of Environmental and Resource Economists.

Gerry Stoker is Professor of Politics and Governance at the University of Southampton, UK, and Centenary Research Professor, Institute for Governance and Policy Analysis, University of Canberra, Australia. His 2006 Why Politics Matters won political book of the year award from the Political Studies Association of the UK. He is Director of Public Policy at Southampton. He was the founding chair of the think tank New Local Government Network and has advised governments in many countries on issues of democratic engagement, behaviour change, and public policy.

Dale Southerton is Professor of Sociology and Director of the Sustainable Consumption Institute at The University of Manchester, UK, and Director of the Sustainable Practices Research Group (funded by the ESRC, Defra, and the Scottish Government). His principal areas of research interest are consumption, sustainability, theories of practice and social change, innovation and material culture, time-use, and everyday life. He has published extensively in these fields, is the author of *Communities of Consumption: Place, Geographical Mobility and Identification* (VDM Verlag, 2009), editor of the *Encyclopedia of Consumer Culture* (Sage, 2011) and co-editor (with Alan Warde) of *The Habits of Consumption* (Open Access Book Series of the Helsinki Collegium of Advanced Studies, 2012), and (with H. Chappells and B. Van Vliet) *Sustainable Consumption: The Implications of Changing Infrastructures of Provision* (Edward Elgar, 2004).

Frank Trentmann is Professor of History at Birkbeck College, University of London. In 2012–13 he was a Professorial Research Fellow, Professor of History and Social Sciences at the Sustainable Consumption Institute, The University of Manchester, UK. He has been Fernand Braudel Senior Fellow at the European University Institute, as well as Visiting Professor at the British Academy, and at the École des hautes études en sciences sociales, Paris. Frank's research has covered the history and politics of consumption in the modern world. He is the editor of the *Oxford Handbook of the History of Consumption* (OUP, 2012). His *Free Trade Nation: Consumption, Civil Society and Commerce in Modern Britain* (OUP, 2008) was awarded the Whitfield Prize by the Royal Historical Society.

Alistair Ulph is Professorial Research Fellow of the Sustainable Consumption Institute and formerly Director of the Sustainable Consumption Institute, The University of Manchester, UK, where he was also Vice-President and Dean of Humanities (2004–10). His research interests are mainly in the field of environmental and resource economics, recently focussing on international aspects of environmental and trade policies, though he has also published in labour economics, industrial economics, and public economics. Over his career he has published eight books, including T*rade and the Environment, Selected Essays of Alistair Ulph* (Edward Elgar, 1999) and over 100 refereed papers. In 2000 he was elected Fellow of the Royal Society of Arts and President of European Association of Environmental and Resource Economists.

Alan Warde is Professor of Sociology and a Professorial Fellow of the Sustainable Consumption Institute, University of Manchester, UK. His research interests are wide but recently have centred on the sociology of consumption, especially issues of sustainability with special reference to food and eating. He is the editor of *Consumption* (Volumes I–IV) (Sage, 2010). He recently held for two years (2010–12) the Jane and Aatos Erkko Visiting Research Professorship in Studies on Contemporary Society, Helsinki Collegium for Advanced Studies, University of Helsinki, where he conducted the project 'Consumption and sustainability: towards a social scientific understanding'. The Professorship is awarded on the basis of an international competition for scholars in humanities and the social sciences.

Harold (Hal) Wilhite is a Professor and Research Director at the University of Oslo's Centre for Development and Environment (Norway) and Academic Director of a pan-University program entitled Environmental Change and Sustainable Energy (MILEN). His main research interests have been associated with theorizing consumption, energy use, and the transition to sustainable energy in developed and developing countries, including the United States, Japan, Norway, India, and Tanzania. He has also worked extensively on the policies of sustainable consumption and has been an advisor to IEA, OECD, and Norwegian efforts to develop a new framework for promoting sustainable energy consumption.

Richard R. Wilk is Provost Professor of Anthropology and Director of Food Studies at Indiana University. He has also worked as an applied anthropologist with UNICEF, USAID, Cultural Survival, and a variety of other development organizations. His early research on farming and family organization has been followed by work on consumer culture, globalization, television, beauty pageants, and food. His publications include more than 140 papers and book chapters, a textbook in *Economic Anthropology* (now translated into six languages), and several edited volumes. The most recent book is *Rice and Beans: A Unique Dish in a Hundred Places* edited with Livia Barbosa (Berg, 2012).

1

Introduction

Dale Southerton and Alistair Ulph

1.1 Rationale for this Book

In March 2012 the Sustainable Consumption Institute (SCI) at The University of Manchester in the UK held a two-day conference on the topic of *Sustainable Consumption: Multi-Dimensional Perspectives*, in honour of the distinguished economist Professor Sir Partha Dasgupta FRS FBA, our colleague in the SCI. The SCI was established in 2008 (with the help of a substantial donation from Tesco) with a key focus to research how to shift global patterns of consumption to make them more environmentally sustainable. The focus on *consumption* reflects the fact that, for example, in the context of climate change some 75 per cent of UK emissions of carbon are linked to household consumption. If the UK aimed to cut its carbon emissions by the extent needed to achieve a target of 4°C warming by 2100 (less demanding than the UK government's target of 2°C warming) this would require cutting UK emissions in 2050 by 60 per cent, relative to 1990 levels (Bows et al., 2012). To achieve such reductions it is vital that policy-makers understand how to bring about a major change in resource-intensive consumption.

The SCI's research draws on perspectives on consumption from a range of disciplines, in particular economics, psychology, sociology, and history; and it is clear that the understanding of what drives consumption differs widely across such disciplines. When Partha Dasgupta joined the SCI in 2008 he became engaged with our work on sustainable consumption, and as an environmental and resource economist who is used to drawing on perspectives from other disciplines (e.g. his work on nutrition) he became interested by the diversity of approaches to consumption outside of his 'home' discipline of economics. So when we proposed holding a conference in his honour, with the proceedings to be published, it was natural that the focus would be on the different perspectives on sustainable consumption from different disciplines.

As organizers of the conference and editors of this book, we sought contributors from neuroscience, ecology, psychology, economics, sociology, anthropology, and history; and we invited contributors who we knew valued working across disciplinary backgrounds. In our invitations we asked them to contribute papers which situated some of their recent research on aspects of sustainable consumption in the broader context of how their disciplines tackle the subject of consumption and how, in turn, their disciplinary perspectives relate to approaches presented by other disciplines. As an extension of this task, and when revising their contributions in light of discussions held at the workshop, authors were instructed to consider the prospects for developing understandings of consumption which explicitly attempt to integrate perspectives from different disciplines—in terms of theoretical approaches to consumption, empirical testing of such models, or policy implications. Organizing the workshop so that the discussant of a paper represented a discipline different from that of the author(s) facilitated such inter-disciplinary exchanges. We were encouraged by the lively discussions that took place at the workshop, very much in the spirit of its objectives.

In this Introduction we aim to capture that spirit of trying to develop a deeper understanding of consumption by drawing together insights from different disciplines. As an expository device, rather than simply summarizing each chapter in turn, we start by setting out a highly stylized model of one particular discipline's approach to consumption, and then summarize how each chapter relates to this model, seeking to extend or even abandon it. Since this book is in honour of Professor Sir Partha Dasgupta, we have chosen the approach used by economics. The model we present in section 1.2 is the simple version that students of economics first learn, and is probably consistent with how other disciplines view economists' thinking about consumption, with the key assumption being that consumers display individual rationality. Despite its simplicity we will note that, perhaps, this basic model is a bit richer than non-economists believe.

Subsequent sections of this Introduction preview the later chapters of the book, showing how this simple economists' model misses vital aspects of understanding consumption. In section 1.3 we preview four chapters which seek to elaborate on some aspect of the simple model presented in section 1.2 and point to its limitations. One important critique of the simple economists' model of consumption focuses on the assumption that individual consumer behaviour is driven by rationality, and in section 1.4 we preview the chapters which challenge that assumption. A second important critique of the simple economists' model focuses on the assumption that consumption is driven only by individual choices. In section 1.5 we preview the chapters which critique the methodological individualism of economists' models and the assumptions upon which they are based, instead emphasizing the significance of understanding the socio-cultural processes that shape trajectories of consumption. Finally in section 1.6 we summarize what we believe these chapters suggest about how we might develop more integrated theoretical models of sustainable consumption, what they suggest about the empirical techniques that might be employed to test such theories, and what they suggest about how policy-makers should design policies aimed to make consumption more environmentally sustainable.

1.2 The Simplest Economists' Model of Consumption

In this section we sketch the simplest economists' model of individual consumer behaviour (as first taught to economics students). The consumer is assumed to choose his/her most preferred path of consumption and leisure for the current and all future time periods (for simplicity assumed to be indefinite) subject to a budget (wealth) constraint that the present value of the cost of the chosen consumption path not exceed the present value of any initial (e.g. inherited) wealth plus the present value of all earnings the individual will make from working (for simplicity work is assumed to be the only source of income), and the constraint that in any time period the hours he/she spends working plus the time he/she desires for leisure cannot exceed the fixed number of hours available in that time period.

Formally the consumer's problem can be written as:

$$\max_{c_t, l_t}\{\sum_{t=0}^{t=\infty}\delta^t U_t(c_t, l_t)\} \quad s.t. \sum_{t=0}^{t=\infty} r^t(p_t c_t) \leq W_0 + \sum_{t=0}^{t=\infty} r^t(w_t h_t); \quad l_t + h_t \leq \bar{h} \quad (1)$$

c_t is a list of all goods the consumer wishes to consume in period t; l_t is the amount of leisure the consumer wishes to enjoy in period t; U_t is a utility function which captures the consumer's preferences for different consumption goods and leisure in time period t; δ, which is a number between 0 and 1, reflects the extent to which the consumer gives less weight to (discounts) utility in the next period relative to current utility. Later in this chapter we will discuss in more detail why a consumer might act this way, but briefly it reflects the rate at which the consumer is impatient for, say, enjoyment; r is the market rate of discount (or interest) at which the consumer can borrow or lend, W_0 is the consumer's initial (inherited) wealth, w_t is the wage the consumer expects to earn in different time periods, and h_t is the amount of work the consumer plans to do in period t.

We now elaborate on two key features of this simple model. It is assumed that the consumer has *rational* preferences, represented by the utility function U_t, for all the goods available in the economy. By *rational* economists mean that preferences are *complete* (they cover any possible set of choices he/she might make) and they are *transitive* (they are mutually consistent). These preferences might change as the consumer ages, but the consumer knows at the outset how they will change. Economists do not seek to explain how a consumer comes to have a particular set of preferences. As we have noted, the consumer's utility function is simply a device for representing his/her preferences—maximizing utility simply means making the most preferred choice from those that are available and affordable. In the light of later discussion it should be emphasized that rationality does not imply that the consumer's choices need be made consciously; if the solution to (1) yields stable patterns of consumption over time this is consistent with consumer behaviour becoming automatic or subconscious. There has been a long debate in economics about whether utility can be thought to capture anything which is measurable and comparable across different households—such as well-being, pleasure, or happiness. Later chapters (e.g. Chapter 3 by Andrew Oswald) discuss this question, but we shall assume that it is possible to think of utility as the consumer's assessment of his/her well-being, and this can be compared across consumers. For some purposes it is useful to assume that the utility function exhibits diminishing marginal utility (i.e. the additional well-being from an additional unit of consumption decreases the more one consumes). This is consistent with the notions of satiety, and that additional consumption of poor people is socially preferred to additional consumption of wealthy people.

A second key point is that the consumer faces a lifetime budget (wealth) constraint. The consumer may wish to spend more than his/her income in some periods (by borrowing—as when consumers take out mortgages) but, unless the consumer has significant inherited wealth, in other periods he/she will need to spend less than he/she earns (by saving). So a consumer cannot continuously increase consumption unless there is income to fund that consumption. In this very simple model, the only source of income comes from working. One of the starkest reminders of this wealth constraint is the pensions' crisis facing many advanced economies. A consumer's wish to enjoy a longer period of retirement (driven in part by increased longevity) without substantial reductions in post-retirement levels of consumption relative to pre-retirement levels of consumption has significant implications for the length of their working life and how much of the income earned while working is saved for retirement.

We now discuss four extensions to this simple model that relate to some of the issues raised in later chapters.

(1) Not all of the goods that affect the consumer's well-being are necessarily traded in markets, and this issue is pertinent for many environmental resources. There are two categories of goods for which this is relevant. The first is what economists call *public goods* (in contrast to the *private goods* consumers directly purchase). The characteristic of a public good is that the benefit any individual derives from its provision is unaffected by the benefit other individuals derive from it, unlike a private good, where one consumer's consumption of that good reduces the amount available for other consumers. An example of a pure public good is defence, or, in an environmental context, the global climate. The concern economists raise about public goods is that markets will undersupply such goods because a rational, self-interested individual will be unwilling to contribute what he/she truly benefits from the good, because he/she knows he/she can benefit from what other consumers contribute—there is *free riding*. It is for this reason that goods like national defence are usually provided by national governments financed by taxation. Of course a number of goods are neither purely public nor purely private; for example, education raises the employability skills of individuals (essentially a private benefit) but also raises the ability of individuals to engage in debates about public affairs (essentially a public benefit) and this is reflected in the complex mix of private and public funding for education (from nursery to college levels) seen in different countries.

A second reason why a number of goods, particularly many of the environmental services provided by nature, are not traded in markets is because there are no property rights to these goods (or if there are formal property rights they are expensive to enforce). Simple examples are clean air and many fish stocks or other species which affect biodiversity. The use of such resources by firms or households can have significant deleterious impacts but these are not reflected in the costs faced by firms or households—they are *external costs*. Economists argue that this provides another role for government intervention in the economy—through environmental taxes (e.g. a carbon tax) or by trying to create a set of tradeable property rights (e.g. carbon trading or tradable fishing permits) these external costs can be given explicit monetary values to be paid by those who generate such costs, and thereby provide an incentive for them to reduce such costs.

There is an obvious issue confronting governments in determining how much to invest in protecting biodiversity or what level of carbon tax to set, namely how to assess the value consumers place on environmental benefits. To see what might be involved we can extend the utility function in equation (1) to read:

$$U_t(c_t, l_t, E_t) \tag{2}$$

where, for simplicity, we think of c_t as a measure of total consumption by this consumer and E_t as the stock of some environmental resource. Suppose the government is contemplating policies which would increase the stock of this environmental resource by an amount denoted ΔE_t. This would make the consumer better off. To assess the extent of this benefit economists ask how much consumption would this consumer give up (denoted Δc_t) to leave him/her no worse off than before the increase in the stock of the environmental resource:

$$U_t(c_t - \Delta c_t, l_t, E_t + \Delta E_t) = U_t(c_t, l_t, E_t) \quad (3)$$

Δc_t is the value (or 'willingness-to-pay') this consumer attaches to this improvement in the environment, and similar values can be aggregated over all relevant consumers to assess the total value society places on this increase in the stock of the environmental resource. Note that given our assumption that the utility function is concave in consumption, then as an individual becomes richer he/she will be willing to give up more consumption for a given improvement in the environment. There is a large literature on economic valuation of environmental services which studies how such values might be calculated, using data on actual choices—such as the choice of where to live—or more usually hypothetical choices in answers to questionnaires. As Andrew Oswald notes (Chapter 3), the literature on happiness provides a similar way of assessing the value of improvements to the environment.

It's also perhaps worth noting that the normal assumptions economists make about preferences imply that the consumer will prefer a mix of different goods, which may produce what behavioural economists describe as 'moral licensing'—that if a consumer buys more of a good which is known to benefit the environment (or be environmentally benign) he/she may believe that provides a moral licence to buy more of another good which harms the environment (this interpretation of moral licensing has synergies with Wilk's account of moral balancing and compensatory ethics in Chapter 13).

(2) A consumer's preferences may not be directly for commodities per se, but for some 'higher' goals such as aesthetic experiences, or the chance to experience places in the world he/she has never visited, for which the purchase of say books or concert tickets in the first case or air flights to a different country in the second case are necessary inputs. This view is consistent with Lancaster's (1966) argument that what consumers value are certain *characteristics* of goods. Here utility is derived from these characteristics and the consumer fully understands the relationships (similar to what economists call production functions) linking any inputs of goods to outputs of characteristics. This view may be particularly relevant for environmental services—consumers may care about how their consumption decisions affect the environment. At a more straightforward level what consumers value may not be directly what

they purchase. For example, a consumer may ultimately value cooked food, and has choices between buying raw vegetables and meat and preparing these for a meal, buying pre-prepared food, or eating in a restaurant; to understand such choices one needs to understand the relationships between the different inputs to such processes, in particular the time such choices require. Such relationships again take the form of *household* production functions. As long as it is assumed that the consumer knows these production functions these extensions of the basic model are straightforward and do not really change the underlying economic explanation of consumption as noted by Partha Dasgupta in Chapter 2. There are also some similarities with sociological accounts that argue that consumption occurs as a consequence of performing practices—although such approaches regard practices as socially ordered and culturally reproduced, and therefore individuals' choices in purchasing are only one of many processes that shape patterns of consumption.

(3) We have focussed mainly on a consumer's consumption of goods, or the demand for goods, but a full account of an economy needs to include the supply of such goods, which, again in the simplest model, are assumed to be produced by firms, and the prices of the goods which enter the equation (1) are determined to ensure that the aggregate demand for goods just equals the aggregate supply of such goods. A related issue is that in equation (1) we have assumed that the only source of income to the consumer is the supply of labour, which implicitly assumes that labour is the only input to production. The consumer earns a wage for supplying labour, and this wage will reflect the consumer's ability, which will be partly innate but may also depend on investment in education and health (which we have already noted yield a mix of private and public benefits), and for this reason labour is also referred to as *human capital*. It is straightforward to introduce other key inputs to production, of which the most important are *physical capital* (machinery, buildings, infrastructure) and *natural capital* (environmental and natural resources such as fossil fuels, minerals, forests, agricultural land, water, biodiversity, etc.). These other inputs will also generate income for those who own the property rights to such resources (e.g. shareholders in firms or land owners); the term W_0 in equation (1) can be interpreted to include the value of all the income to be earned from such inputs.

As we have already noted, one problem with natural resources is that not all such resources have clearly defined property rights, which can lead to over-exploitation. But even if there are clear property rights and well-developed markets—for example, oil—the fact that the availability of such resources is ultimately constrained by what is available in the Earth's crust has long been seen by economists, dating back to Malthus and Ricardo, as placing an ultimate limit on what can be produced, and hence consumed, by mankind. There have been many predictions of such limits being imminent, but, so far, such predictions have proved wrong. Why? The reason is partly that estimates of natural resource availability have been proved pessimistic; but that cannot be an ultimate explanation because there is no gainsaying the finite nature of the world. The more important reason is that human ingenuity in devising new technologies (reflected in increased human capital), which allows more output to be produced with less inputs of natural resources or labour, has so far outstripped the pressures of diminishing natural resources and limited supplies of labour. Of course it is a moot question whether this will remain the case in the future (one of the best treatments of these issues can be found in Dasgupta and Heal's *Economic Theory and Exhaustible Resources*, 1979).

(4) Finally, in a number of the later chapters authors will refer to the concept of habitual behaviour by consumers. But the term 'habit' covers a range of rather different aspects of behaviour. Warde and Southerton (2012) provide a useful categorization of these different forms of habit, and we shall build on their categorization in this book. Thus we shall distinguish the following:

(a) *Acquired disposition*: this is where one's current consumption is affected by one's own past consumption. One possible reason why this may arise is that it is expensive (in time or money) to learn the characteristics of different commodities, and having learned that, say, a particular kind of car suits his/her tastes, that consumer continues to buy that kind of car.

(b) *Procedural automaticity*: this is where, as noted earlier, in a relatively stable environment (e.g. prices or incomes not changing significantly) frequent consumption becomes automatic and sub-conscious, rather than conscious; this will continue until there are significant shocks—large price rises with static or falling income.

(c) *Cultural procedures*: here it is not one's own past behaviour that shapes current behaviour but the cultural norms which shape the behaviour of neighbours, relatives, and work colleagues with whom one wishes to build social relationships. Examples might include dress codes, what is considered acceptable food, or the regulations of various clubs one might join.

(d) *Social learning*: just as acquired dispositions could be consistent with using one's own past experience to learn about the characteristics of goods one has not consumed before, so one can learn from interactions with others about the characteristics of goods they have consumed; the difference from cultural procedures is that the consumer is not trying to signal membership of any particular group, but to economize on the costs of learning about the characteristics of goods.

(e) *Sequences*: this is used to describe the effects of science or technology in shaping consumption behaviour, such as the development of out-of-town shopping malls affecting travel patterns of consumers, or domestic technologies that affect the sequencing of activities—as has been the case with laundry following widespread adoption of washing machines or food storage and preparation with freezer technologies.

The various conceptual variations of the term habit we have set out here suggest that the outcome of individual choices may be very different from what might have een selected if the consumer was acting rationally to seek his/her most preferred outcome. It is important to distinguish this from the situations we discussed in point (ii), where there are public goods or externalities, so that the outcome for an individual consumer depends not just on his/her choice but the choices of all consumers; in such situations, even if every individual acts rationally but independently (non-cooperatively) the outcome for all individuals may be much worse than if there was some mechanism for collective decision-making, such as a government. For example, each individual may care deeply about the damaging effects of climate change on their environment, but if one individual believes that his/her actions to reduce his/her individual carbon emissions have a (perhaps slight) personal cost, and will make a negligible difference to climate change if no-one else acts, then he/she may decide to take no action. This may look like people being stuck in their old habits, but the underlying explanation is quite different.

We have provided a very simplified account of the most basic economists' treatment of consumption. In considering other disciplines' perspectives on consumption we will consider their major challenges to the economists' analysis—the understanding of consumers' motivations; the various constraints on consumers' choices, such as the wealth constraint, are less controversial. We conclude this section by making a few methodological points. The model is undoubtedly parsimonious in its account of consumer behaviour, but parsimony can be a methodological virtue. First, the same basic model of individual behaviour underpins economists' accounts of not just consumption and environmental issues, but a wide range of other issues from very general accounts of the functioning of the economy (general equilibrium theory or game theory) to specific aspects such as international trade and trade policy. Having an account of consumer behaviour as it relates to the environment, which is orthogonal to accounts of individual behaviour needed to understand other aspects of the functioning of the economy would be of little value. Second, theories should lead to sharp predictions with a clear understanding of how they can be tested and falsified. Third, in social sciences it is also important that we move beyond just descriptions of the world to suggesting explanations and policies to improve the functioning of society. For that one needs both a clear account of how policies are formulated and how they might affect human actions, but also an ethical basis for recommending policies which relates to the explanations of those actions. We have noted that economists think of utility as a measure of individual well-being, and, in welfare economics, they provide accounts of how one might aggregate the measures of individual well-being into an overall measure of societal well-being with which to evaluate policies (these aggregate measures are *not* GDP, which is simply a measure of the value of aggregate output of those goods which are traded in markets). None of this gainsays the need for economists to take account of insights from other disciplines and how these might address the known weaknesses of economists' accounts of consumption (and of course, vice versa), and this is the purpose of this book. But, as Tirole (2002) notes, this should be done in a way that does not lose some of the virtues we've mentioned already—parsimony and a basis for welfare analysis. We return to this issue in section 1.6.

1.3 Extensions of the Simple Economists' Model of Consumption

In Chapter 2 Partha Dasgupta begins by emphasizing that because of various distortions in market economies, it is necessary to use *shadow* prices, not market prices, to properly value consumption and capital assets, distinguishing as we have done in section 1.2 between physical capital, human capital, and natural capital. Dasgupta adds a fourth important form of capital—social or institutional capital such as the legal system, which underpins entities such as households and firms and the property rights essential to the functioning of markets, and more informal structures, such as clubs and societies, and, vitally, trust. Shadow prices are particularly important for valuing natural capital, and there are three key elements to calculating shadow prices: the distribution of rights to natural resources between different households, the scarcity of natural resources to meet current and future needs, and the ease with which natural resources can be substituted for other resources, particularly physical capital. Where market prices differ from shadow prices, there is a role for government policy to use instruments such as environmental taxes to align market prices and shadow prices. This is particularly important for providing incentives for innovative technologies which can reduce the use of scarce natural resources—if they are underpriced the long-term trajectory of the economy is skewed. Provided all assets are correctly valued at their shadow prices, they can be aggregated to form an overall measure of wealth, and he notes a key result in assessing whether an economy is on a sustainable path: social well-being (defined in terms of the (weighted) average well-being of all individuals) increases if and only if wealth per capita increases.

Dasgupta then goes on to discuss three reasons why the conventional economists' treatment of consumer's preferences as outlined in equation (1) is inadequate for addressing sustainable consumption. The first is the existence of *habits*, in the sense of acquired disposition, which Dasgupta defines by the notion that a consumer's past consumption of a good may increase his/her preference to consume that good in the future. This is a kind of *intrapersonal externality*, but provided the consumer is far-sighted—that is, he/she fully realizes how today's consumption will affect his/her future preferences—he/she internalizes this form of externality, and there would be no need *on this count* for any policy to modify the consumer's behaviour (obviously if there are *interpersonal externalities* associated with environmental resources there will be a need for policy). We can think of this form of habits as being 'rational habits'.

The second respect in which the conventional economists view of consumer preferences is too simple, in that it omits the notion of 'competitive' or 'conspicuous consumption', dating back to Veblen (1899 [1924]), where some commodities act as status symbols (expensive cars, houses, clothing, jewellery, etc.), so that each consumer strives to distinguish him/herself from other consumers by buying more—or a more expensive version of such conspicuous commodities—generating a rat-race. This is a genuine *interpersonal externality* which leads to *overconsumption* of such goods. From an economist's perspective, notes Dasgupta, the policy recommendation would be for taxes on such luxury goods to correct for the external cost each individual's consumption of the conspicuous commodities imposes on other consumers.

The third aspect of consumer behaviour which deviates from the simple economists' model is social consumption, where consumption of some goods (called 'relational goods') signals that the consumer belongs to a particular social group; for example, by dressing or eating in a similar style. It is worth noting that sociological accounts of consumption regard processes of distinction and belonging as symmetrical and inter-related, hence clothing consumption can be a source both of classification and identification (e.g. Bourdieu, 1984). As Dasgupta notes, this differs from conspicuous consumption in an important respect—the consumer is not trying to consume *more* of the relevant goods, but in a *similar* way as other consumers (in a more extreme case, called 'solidarity goods', it is assumed that consumers wish to consume exactly the same amounts of these goods as other people). This leads to the possibility of multiple outcomes, distinguished by different levels of consumption of the relational goods, of which the outcome of a free market is the worst in terms of overall consumption of the relational goods in question. The problem here is one of *coordinating* individual behaviour: if it is possible to get agreement that everyone will cut consumption of such goods, and people trust others to comply, there may not be a need for intervention in the form of a consumption tax. (Of course some of the steps taken to ensure compliance can be severe; for example, in Amish communities, which have been able to coordinate on very restrained levels of consumption, significant deviation is punished by complete expulsion from the group—including from close family members.)

Dasgupta's chapter is an example of the methodological point made earlier, in that incorporating a few additional assumptions into the traditional economists' model allows one to capture a range of different consumer behaviours, but each with clear and different policy implications. Doing so, however, fails to account for why, and in what circumstances, might some consumer behaviour be attributed to mechanisms of competition and, for the same commodity, in other cases to conformity. This is a limitation of economic models to which we return in section 1.5.

Andrew Oswald, in Chapter 3, elaborates on three points raised by Dasgupta. First, Oswald has been a pioneer in persuading economists that surveys of happiness are an important new technique for trying to measure the well-being of individuals and society. In regular large-scale surveys individuals are first asked for information about their socio-economic characteristics and then answer questions about how they rate their overall happiness on a numerical scale, and how this compares to recent periods. Analysts then feed the answers to these questions into empirical analysis to measure how much various factors such as being employed, being married, enjoying good health, enjoying a clean environment, or having high income affects happiness. Oswald notes that a striking feature of this research is that the results are broadly consistent across different societies and different surveys.

Second, he argues that one of the striking findings that have emerged from this empirical work is that while at the individual level richer people are generally better off than poorer people, at the aggregate level happiness does not appear to increase as national income rises. This is interpreted as evidence that what matters to individuals is their *relative income* (i.e. their income relative to others) rather than their absolute level of income, as suggested by Easterlin (1974), and relates to the work of Veblen (1924) mentioned already on conspicuous consumption. Oswald notes (as demonstrated also by Dasgupta in section 2.1 of Chapter 2) that conspicuous consumption can generate an inefficient 'rat-race', in which households strive to purchase goods solely to 'keep up with the Joneses'. Such behaviour does not raise overall well-being, and this kind of inter-personal externality should be corrected with policies such as taxes on items of conspicuous consumption, similar to taxes on behaviour which imposes environmental externalities.

Finally, Oswald notes that because some of the variables that enter into the equations that explain measured happiness include individuals' experience of different aspects of the environment (such as different air pollutants), this allows analysts to consider how much income individuals might be willing to give up to obtain a cleaner environment. The results suggest that such 'willingness-to-pay' measures can be high—halving air pollution would raise happiness by as much as a 25 per cent increase in income. These happiness-based measures of willingness-to-pay can be used to complement the other techniques environmental economists have developed to calculate the monetary benefits of improving the environment—techniques such as hedonic pricing or contingent valuation methods.

In Chapter 4 Ann Kinzig and Charles Perrings consider more carefully how consumption impacts on ecosystems. The key point they make is that in thinking about sustainable consumption, attention should focus less on the effects of consumption on the carrying capacity of the environment and more on the effects of consumption on the stability and hence sustainability of ecosystems. They begin by noting that stability of an ecosystem depends on three key elements: (a) the overall diversity of species (increasing diversity generally, but not always, increases stability of an ecosystem); (b) the heterogeneity of the species within an ecosystem, in particular the degree to which different species react differently to shocks to the ecosystem, such as fire or disease (this is similar to arguments from finance theory that one wants to hold a portfolio of assets which respond differently to economic shocks—there is negative correlation between asset returns); (c) the degree of modularity, or connectedness between different ecosystems—for example, a river can provide a natural fire-break between ecosystems making them less vulnerable to propagation of fire.

Next, Kinzig and Perrings set out a simple dynamic system model which couples a model of human activity as reflected in an economy and a model of an ecosystem to study the extent to which such a coupled system can be operated sustainably. They show that this depends on two characteristics: the observability of the system—which is reflected in the prices of different assets in the system, and the controllability of the system and the extent to which human activity of consumption and investment affects all parts of the system. They show that if the system is completely observable and controllable then it can always be operated sustainably. However, in the more relevant circumstances where neither condition holds (for example, as noted by Dasgupta, many of the assets used in an economy are not traded through markets, so there is a need to construct 'shadow prices'), then such a system will only be sustainable if the parts of the ecosystem outside human control are themselves stable.

Finally, Kinzig and Perrings reflect on how consumption activities are affecting the stability of ecosystems. They note that of the 14 major ecosystems only two (tundra and boreal forests) have been relatively unaffected by humans, and six have been affected by between 50 per cent and 70 per cent of their landmass. The effects take three forms: (a) a significant loss of genetic diversity as humans have privileged certain species (e.g. 90 per cent of global food supplies depends on only 11 species) and sought to eradicate others (pests, competitors, etc.); (b) fragmentation of habitats making them more vulnerable; (c) greater homogenization of habitats with favoured species and their associated pathogens being introduced into habitats to which other species may have not developed immunity. They note that while a moderate amount of trade can add to species diversity, beyond such levels trade can destabilize systems. In summary, the study of sustainable consumption should focus on its effects on the stability of ecosystems.

Making consumption more sustainable may involve significant investments today with very long-term benefits, (e.g. investments in nuclear power or various forms of renewable energy to reduce emissions of carbon dioxide (CO_2), which will have benefits for reducing the risk of climate change only many decades into the future). Even if net benefits in each time period are correctly evaluated (using the shadow prices discussed by Dasgupta in Chapter 2) there is the further question of how society should value costs and benefits that occur in different time periods. The usual economic assumption is that a benefit in the future is worth less than the same benefit arising today; what economists call *discounting*. In Chapter 5 Maureen Cropper asks how future benefits should be discounted in the context of *project evaluation*, or cost–benefit analysis; that is, deciding whether or not to proceed with a *project* (which could be an investment project such as constructing a wind farm and selling the resulting electricity, or a policy project such as introducing a carbon trading scheme).[1] Cropper notes that the choice of discount rate has been a key focus of economic debate since the Stern Review (2006). Based on very similar assumptions about how the economy will be affected by climate change, Nordhaus (2007) used a discount rate of just under 5 per cent, to conclude that an appropriate current level of a carbon tax should be under $10 per ton of CO_2, while Stern used a discount rate of 1.4 per cent to conclude that a carbon tax should be over $100 per ton of CO_2. So the discount rate matters with respect to long-term policies such as calculating an appropriate level of carbon tax for achieving sustainable consumption.

Cropper begins by discussing the net present value approach to discounting, and the implications of uncertainty about the discount rate for project evaluation. Standard project evaluation uses a discount rate (often linked to rates in financial markets) that is assumed to stay constant for all future time periods when evaluating future costs and benefits. Weitzman (2001) showed that, if there is uncertainty about what the future constant discount rate will be, taking the expected net present value of future net benefits will yield a certainty-equivalent discount rate that, under reasonable assumptions,

[1] In equation (1) we assumed that the consumer discounts future *utility* at a constant rate δ, but project evaluation is concerned with how to discount future net benefits expressed in monetary units.

declines over time. Cropper presents examples, based on analyses of interest rates on US government bonds, which show that this can have a dramatic effect on how a net benefit in 150 years' time is valued.

But for the purposes of this book what is relevant is not how discount rates are set in a market but what an ethical basis is for setting discount rates. She presents the standard framework that underpins discounting in the social evaluation of projects:

$$\rho_t = \delta + \lambda g_t \tag{4}$$

where ρ_t is the social discount rate at time t, δ is the utility discount rate discussed in equation (1), λ expresses society's attitude to risk (or, in this simple framework, its attitude to intergenerational inequality), and g_t is the expected growth rate of consumption per head. Most economists argue that δ should be very small (it represents the risk that future generations may not exist) if not zero, so the key parameter is λ; the larger its value the less willing society should be to invest now in order to benefit future, wealthier, generations. Dasgupta (2008) has argued that Stern's choice of a value of $\lambda = 1$ is too low—it would imply that in a simple growth model society should save over 50 per cent of its income—and that $\lambda = 2$ is more plausible.

The final element is *expected* future growth rates, expected because there is considerable uncertainty about what future growth rates might be. Cropper shows that one needs rather strong assumptions about such uncertainty (e.g. shocks to growth are sustained for more than one period) to generate a declining discount rate and the decline is not as great as with market rates. Although economists largely agree on the theoretical basis for a declining discount rate, different models of what drives the future growth of the economy have markedly different implications for the pattern of decline, and so it has proved difficult to persuade policy-makers in the US to adopt a declining discount rate (unlike the UK and France).

Finally, Cropper notes that in discussion at the workshop the point was made that we should be as concerned with intra-generational variations in discount rates across different social groups or countries as with inter-generational variations in discount rates, though these intra-generational considerations should be reflected in the shadow prices proposed by Dasgupta in Chapter 2.

Some recent work by Dasgupta and Maskin (reported in Dasgupta, 2012) provides a rather different basis for declining discount rates. They distinguish between the discount rate used by an individual choosing to allocate his/her wealth over his/her finite but uncertain life-time (for whom the discount rate might be quite high, and is a private matter for the individual), and the discount rate used to weigh the (life-time) well-being of future generations relative to the current generation, which is an ethical matter for society and should have a lower discount rate. At any period of time, when society evaluates a project which lasts a long way in to the future, the interests of the current generation will become less salient in future years, and so the discount rate will decline.

The chapters summarized in this section represent extensions of the simple economists' model of consumption to consider richer accounts of the effect of other people's consumption decisions on an individual's own consumption, discounting, and environmental constraints, but without significantly challenging the assumptions of rationality and individualism. In section 1.4 we summarize the chapters that challenge the standard economists' model of individual rationality.

1.4 Challenging the Assumption that Individual Consumers always Behave Rationally

In this section we introduce a number of chapters which challenge the simple economists' assumption that consumption behaviour is driven by rational preferences. To introduce these chapters we make two general comments. First, these chapters draw on a large literature which has come to be known as behavioural economics. Drawing on findings from neuroscience and psychology that seem to conflict with the implications of rational preferences, researchers seek to build a richer theory of individual behaviour and test the implications in laboratory or field experiments. Some of the work in behavioural economics does not challenge the general economists' statement of rationality, but rather some of the simplifying assumptions economists have used to get tractable models with testable implications (such as the assumptions in equation (1) of a constant utility discount rate and in equation (4) of a constant rate of risk aversion). But other research seeks to explain behaviour inconsistent with the simple rationality assumption (e.g. the sunk cost fallacy, prospect theory and the asymmetric value of gains or losses from some reference level of utility, concern for what others do through conspicuous or social consumption, as noted by Dasgupta, or concern for fairness, self-esteem, and the endogenous development of 'biased' rather than 'truthful' memories). Excellent summaries of some of the key findings in behavioural economics can be found in Tirole (2002), Camerer, Loewenstein, and Rabin (2004), Bernheim and Rangel (2007), and for some more critical assessments Harrison (2005), Pesendorfer (2006), and Rubinstein (2006).

Second, some of the chapters in this section draw on research concerning the complex structures of the brain, which, for simplicity, we can define as the 'conscious' and 'subconscious', with the majority of brain activity being subconscious. The conscious element is relatively slow and energy-intensive, and so deployed mainly for coping with unusual or threatening circumstances or learning new skills; in stable external environments or once new skills have been learned behaviour becomes subconscious, which not only economizes on energy but allows faster response times (e.g. learning to drive a car or hit a tennis ball). Much human behaviour, in these terms, can be seen as 'instinctive' or 'habitual' (in the sense of procedural automaticity) with the conscious brain re-engaging in unfamiliar circumstances (e.g. driving in a strange city or unusual weather conditions). While the economists' model of rational behaviour only requires the consumer to have rational preferences—it does not imply that all consumption decisions have to be made consciously (so there could be 'rational habits')—it does not follow that all procedurally automatic behaviour is necessarily rational. It is an important empirical question whether all procedurally automatic behaviour remains rational.

In Chapter 6 Paul Fletcher summarizes neuroscience research on what drives consumption of food. He starts by outlining a simple homeostatic model which seeks to balance the input of food with the body's expenditure of energy, so the reward value of additional food is inversely related to the level of hunger. A key hormone for monitoring satiety is leptin, and absence of this hormone leads to severe obesity. In leptin-deficient individuals, images of food triggered large responses even when they had just eaten, and even if the images were of unappetising food. These individuals eat when they are not hungry, and this is a great concern for obesity levels.

To understand this problem Fletcher introduces the concepts of *appetitive behaviours* and *consummatory behaviours*, the former being what governs the processes of obtaining and preparing food, the latter the process of consuming the food (this distinction is perhaps similar to the one Lancaster made between ultimate goals and the household processes needed to meet these goals, or the distinction in practices discussed later by Alan Warde). The former are the interesting behaviours. In this context the brain is viewed as seeking to maximize rewards, and this involves learning, through a prediction-error model, what actions lead to rewards. The brain seeks to make such interactions with the external world more efficient; for example, if a stimulus becomes a reliable predictor of a reward the brain reacts to the stimulus as if it was the reward (dissociation). Fletcher describes interesting experiments in which this reaction happens even if the stimulus is received subconsciously.

Neuroscientists define *habits* as actions which are driven by a stimulus rather than being goal-directed. Such habits can be efficient. The danger, he notes, is that habits persist, even if the reward is no longer desired. Experiments have shown that if an animal learns that a particular action (pressing a lever) delivers food, it will continue with that action even when it is sated, or no food is delivered, or the food triggers nausea. Moreover, when faced with complex, conflicting problems animals and humans can abandon goal-directed behaviour and engage in habitual behaviour. Habits also persist despite long periods of abstinence—alcoholics or drug-addicts may relapse after encountering people, places, or objects associated with previous experience.

Fletcher briefly reviews work on how people learn from others, and though the brain responses are similar to those when they learn from their own past experience, they are not identical, in part because individuals need to assess the reliability of the person they are observing. Finally he notes some policy implications; obviously habituation makes behaviour less responsive to standard policy levers, and successful therapeutic strategies have involved re-learning the significance of cues to extinguish their significance, and he suggests this may have implications for policies towards advertising and logos.

Drazen Prelec also focuses on the issue of why humans might fail to make rational decisions. In Chapter 7, he draws on interesting experimental psychological approaches to understanding human behaviour, grounded originally in the work of B. F. Skinner and later Richard Herrenstein in the Harvard pigeon labs. Prelec is concerned with the issue of how individuals tackle a sequence of decisions, with the potential for what he calls 'internalities'—individuals may be focussed on the immediate gains from a decision they make and fail to take account of the effect this may have on subsequent well-being, analogous to the economists' notion of 'externalities' where an individual ignores the effect of his/her decisions on the well-being of other individuals. Based on observations of pigeons' feeding habits, Herrenstein had postulated that individuals would seek to equalize the *average* return to different activities (which was defined as *melioration*), whereas economists postulate that individuals trying to maximize well-being would seek to equalize the *marginal* return over different activities. But when individuals are faced with complex sequences of choices, they may find it very difficult to work out what choices would maximize their well-being. Prelec illustrates this with the famous 'Harvard game'. An individual has to press one of two buttons, red or blue, and, to maximize payoff, the individual has to press a button as frequently as possible. Pressing a red button leads to an immediate delay 2 seconds shorter than pressing a blue button, but increases the delay in the subsequent ten choices by 0.4 seconds each, irrespective of what the subsequent choices are. Hence pressing red has an overall cost of 2 seconds. The strategy that maximizes long-term payoff is to always press the blue button. Subjects are not told what the structure of delays is, and empirical tests show that individuals typically increase the frequency of pressing the red button, and get close to *minimizing* their long-term payoffs.

Now while this decision problem may appear simple when you are told the rule, individuals have to work this rule out from their observations, and, a priori, there are an infinite number of possible history-dependent structures to such choices. Even powerful computers may take thousands of choices to learn the correct strategy. Prelec discusses what such experiments might tell us about behaviour outside the laboratory; on the one hand, laboratory participants can focus more on trying to understand what is driving the results of their choices, and, in a short period of time are not prone to hyperbolic discounting; on the other hand, the stakes in laboratory experiments are small, and individuals do not have the opportunity to learn from others.

Prelec discusses the implications of the results of the 'Harvard game' for actual consumption. He notes first that the payoffs in the 'Harvard game' are similar to some forms of soft addiction—for example, to sleeping tablets—so this could complement the analysis of Fletcher. He then builds a simple model to derive a new result which explains why 'melioration' (equalizing average returns) would lead individuals to over-consume relatively cheap, low quality commodities (e.g. junk food) rather than more expensive, higher quality goods compared to optimizing behaviour (equalizing marginal returns). Finally, he notes that while much of his focus has been on situations where it is difficult for individuals to monitor the long-term consequences of their decisions, problems can arise even when the long-term implications are easily monitored. The example he uses is building a wine cellar, where an individual gains pleasure from both drinking wine and having a stock of wine. But if the outcome depends on a sequence of one-off choices of whether to drink an expensive bottle, then he argues that there can be a positive feedback effect in which an individual with an initially large cellar abstains from drinking the bottle now, adding to the cellar, while an individual with identical preferences but an initially small cellar drinks the bottle now, keeping the cellar small.

Prelec's overall conclusion is that if an individual's consumption is the consequence of long sequences of decisions, then results from experimental psychology may challenge the economists' presumption that such decisions correctly reveal the individual's preferences. Moreover, while economists have policy recommendations on how to deal with externalities, it is not clear what policies could tackle internalities.

Geoff Beattie and Laura McGuire focus on a different strand of psychological research—the question of why many social surveys show that around 80 per cent of people say they are willing to change their behaviour to help mitigate climate change, yet in practice they do not (what is called the value–action gap). In Chapter 8 they begin by offering some explanations for why this might occur through exploration of the differences between peoples' *explicit attitudes*, governed by the 'conscious', slow, part of the brain, and their *implicit attitudes*, governed by the 'subconscious' or fast part of the brain. These attitudes might differ because explicit attitudes reflect peoples' wish to appear in a certain light to others (more caring about the environment) or because when individuals are under time pressure their choices are more likely to be governed by their subconscious brains, and hence by their implicit attitudes.

There are now well developed methods for testing for implicit attitudes, and work by Beattie and McGuire's research team has shown that indeed there are significant differences between individuals' implicit and explicit attitudes towards the environment. These differences can be represented by a four-fold classification: 'true greens', whose implicit and explicit pro-environmental attitudes are the same; 'hidden greens', whose implicit attitudes are more pro-environmental than their explicit attitudes; 'surface greens', whose explicit attitudes are more pro-environmental than their implicit attitudes; and 'non-greens', whose implicit and explicit attitudes are not pro-environmental. More significantly they show that when confronted with information about the environment, such as the carbon content of products displayed in carbon labels, it is peoples' implicit attitudes that explain how much attention people pay to that information, rather than their explicit attitudes. This experimental work is based on samples of students and it would be important to repeat such tests on a broader sample of consumers to understand how useful or feasible it may be for policy-makers to target behavioural change policies to the four different groups of individuals set out here.

In Chapter 9 Ricardo Correia and Catarina Roseta-Palma argue that economists' analysis of household water demand and policies to control such demand would benefit from taking on board some of the insights from behavioural economics. They survey the recent literature on residential water demand and note the general finding of low price and income elasticities, suggesting that conventional economic approaches to restricting water demand through prices may be limited, and also the rather sparse literature on the application of behavioural economics to water demand. They suggest a number of reasons why there has been very limited uptake of behavioural economics in this field, the most significant being inadequate data to test such approaches (including their own frustrations at trying to collect such data from Portuguese water companies).

The main part of this chapter outlines four applications of behavioural economics. The first application is to understand the structure of prices for water. Conventional economic arguments would suggest that economies of scale in supplying water should lead to declining prices as consumption increases, yet most companies use increasing prices. They consider some standard economic explanations for this observation, but believe that a promising explanation is the use of prospect theory and loss aversion (Kahneman and Tversky, 1979) in which the initial block price is the reference price and an increasing block price would be viewed by consumers as a loss, reinforcing the incentive to limit consumption. The second, closely related, application is that an implication of prospect theory is that price and income elasticities of demand will be asymmetric around the reference price, with higher prices having a higher elasticity than lower prices, and this has implications for both the empirical testing of water demand and pricing policy. The third application of behavioural economics is the social aspect of water demand, in particular that the concept of fairness (Kahneman, Knetsch, and Thaler, 1986) would suggest that if water consumers consider water companies' prices to be fair, they will accept that companies should make a reasonable positive profit. However, Correia and Roseta-Palma note that most water companies actually make a loss, and discuss how the concept of fairness might be extended to explain this. Finally, based on work by Festinger (1954), they state that providing water consumers with information about the water consumption of other households could be another way of setting the consumer's reference level of consumption, and note some related studies in energy economics.

The findings from behavioural economics, recently popularized by Thaler and Sunstein (2008) as 'nudging' individuals to change their behaviour, have attracted interest from politicians looking for policies to shift consumption to more sustainable patterns in addition to, or as a substitute for, fiscal or regulatory approaches. In Chapter 10 Gerry Stoker summarizes how UK policymakers are taking seriously some of the lessons from behavioural economics and notes some political implications of such approaches. After summarizing some of the key findings from behavioural economics relevant for sustainable consumption, Stoker notes some concerns raised, particularly those expressed in a recent report on behavioural change produced by the Science and Technology Committee, House of Lords (2011). First, there is an over-emphasis on subconscious behaviour at the expense of conscious behaviour whereas for long-term change both are likely to be involved. Second, there are still some key aspects that need more research, such as the role of emotions or how genes interact with environmental factors to drive behaviour. Third, the extent to which findings from specific studies can be generalized to population level (e.g. transferability of behavioural change interventions across different cultures)—though he notes that the government has been careful to run some trials of interventions precisely to get better evidence on some of these issues.

While noting the importance of results from behavioural economics, Stoker raises five issues about the political aspects of introducing such approaches into policy. First, there is a question of whether 'soft' policies coming from nudges are viewed as a substitute for 'hard' policies such as taxes or regulation (which could be linked to the concept of smaller government), or as a complement to them; the UK Coalition government has shifted its position on this somewhat. Second, while nudges may be a soft form of intervention, they are still an intervention, and whereas taxes or regulations are explicit and in principle applicable to all individuals, nudges are less explicit, in particular about the moral basis for their implementation. Third, if nudges are implemented in a top-down way there is an issue that for nudges to work there needs to be a degree of trust in who is providing advice, and that trust may be lacking. Fourth, it may be better for nudges to operate at a community level (similar to the work of Nobel laureate Elinor Ostrom, who has shown that some small communities may manage common environmental resources efficiently without the need for significant government intervention). This also has the benefit of learning from different local experiments. However, there is a question as to whether there are adequate resources at a local government level to design such experiments, and while a local approach may be desirable for local environmental problems it may be less relevant for major national and international environmental problems, such as climate change. Finally, he notes that 'nudging' may fail in the highly competitive atmosphere of inter-departmental politics unless there is a strong central champion.

Having summarized the chapters that challenge the economists' assumption that individuals act rationally, section 1.5 summarizes the chapters that challenge the economists' individualistic stance and focus on broader socio-cultural factors that shape consumption activities, patterns, and trajectories.

1.5 Looking beyond the Individual Consumer: Socio-cultural Explanations of Consumption

As we have seen, in the simplest economists' model economic agents (econs for short) choose optimally. With respect to consumption, econs make choices, usually in the context of markets, based on their preferences. Analytically what matters is the outcome of those choices: the volume and form of goods and services consumed (or, more accurately, purchased and acquired) that results from the aggregate choices of econs. These outcomes are then correlated with other variables to estimate, for example, the degree to which current and projected levels of consumption produce well-being (or welfare). Missing from such approaches are consideration of the socio-cultural factors that shape why particular patterns of consumption emerge and take a particular form or which adequately explain how and why preferences vary across social groups and cultural contexts. For example, explaining the rapid diffusion of the freezer across UK households cannot simply be explained in terms of its utility, especially as its utility has changed during the period of its diffusion (Shove and Southerton, 2000). The key question is why did the freezer become so useful; what other forms of consumption and socio-cultural change happened to make it such a necessary device; and, what can we learn from such processes in order to address the emergence of similarly resource-intensive forms of consumption in the future. If we wish to explain the kinds of generic factors identified by those that challenge or extend the simplest economists' model (e.g. Dasgupta's account of habitual, competitive, and conformist consumption, Chapter 2) then a deeper understanding of the, often context-dependent, socio-cultural processes that underpin those factors is necessary.

Sociological, historical, and anthropological accounts of consumption (not to mention those found in philosophy, human geography, and innovation studies) seek to explain the critical processes that produce current patterns and trajectories of consumption and, more broadly, understand how 'normal' ways of life are formed, reproduced, and change. Consumption itself is understood less in terms of the acquisition of goods and services (i.e. principally purchasing), although of course this matters immensely, and more with respect to the symbolic, communicative, and practicable application of goods and services in ways that deliver socially sanctioned and culturally acceptable ways of living (Warde, 2010). This requires a focus on socio-cultural variations in patterns of consumption across social groups, across space and over time. Such a framing means these disciplines ask different kinds of questions than do economists, such as:

- What are the (multiple) trajectories of change over time and across space in what and the way people consume?
- How are these trajectories patterned and related to one another?
- What role does consumption play in communicating meanings, values, aspirations, and social differences?
- How are social norms, cultural conventions, and expectations of acceptable ways of life formed, and how do particular ways of consuming become embedded in those ways of life as 'normal'?

While the first two types of questions are recognized in the micro-level analyses of consumption used by economists, as noted already, this is often without providing a fully articulated account of how such variables might be expected to influence consumption.

Sociological, historical, and anthropological disciplines start from a position that there is nothing inevitable or necessarily rational about the particular forms of consumption that occur in the course of people conducting their day-to-day lives. Often historically specific and contingent processes underpin widespread and taken-for-granted 'normalities' of daily life. That, at any particular moment in time, we see shifts towards self-servicing as with the proliferation of domestic appliances in the 1960s and 1970s (Gershuny, 1978), a rise of eating out relative to eating at home (Cheng et al., 2007) or supermarket shopping (Humphrey, 1998) cannot be adequately explained as a matter of millions of individual choices and preferences. These major shifts in the way that people organize and conduct their lives, facilitated by particular forms of consumption, are the consequence of inter-related processes related to, for example, labour markets; domestic divisions of labour; the design, use, and cultural conventions associated with the home; working practices and time-use pressures; technological and social innovations; as well as matters of social distinction and symbolic status. While economists' explanation of consumption might take account of some processes at the micro level, it is understanding how these processes interact with each other and vary in their effects on different forms of consumption, and different social groups, that generates the critical insights necessary for explaining the centrality of resource-intensive modes of consumption and how they might be re-directed in ways that render ways of life more sustainable.

The remaining chapters of this book are each informed by what has come to be known as the 'practice turn' in contemporary social theory (Schatzki et al., 2001). The critical premise is that 'consumption occurs as items are appropriated in the course of engaging in particular practices' (Warde, 2005, p. 131). Primarily, practices drive and shape consumption—to understand consumption we need to focus on what people do rather than primarily on what they acquire (purchase) and possess (an approach that has some early reflections in the work of Lancaster (1966), which we have already noted). Epistemologically, this observation follows 'practice theories' in arguing that empirical analysis should start with practices as the unit of analysis, as opposed to the methodological individualism associated with theories that focus on the deliberations or actions of atomized individuals (or 'portfolio models of action'—see Warde, Chapter 12). The philosophical basis of this position can be found in the observation that many human activities are performed through forms of practical understandings and non-propositional tacit knowledge (knowledge whose content cannot be linguistically formulated by its agents) and, consequently, such actions are prior to individual cognition. As Warde (2005, p. 137) puts it, in the context of consumption, 'activity generates wants, rather than vice versa'. Such approaches challenge theories that place mental phenomena such as reason, will, consciousness and goals as the fundamental bases of human action. Indeed, some even suggest that it is only through performing practices that mental phenomena can be understood and articulated; it is only through the doing of activity that those activities become intelligible and attitudes, choices, and preferences can be formed.

The chapters presented in the third part of this collection are each informed by perspectives that seek to examine the detailed socio-cultural processes that shape the way that social practices are organized, performed, and experienced. They each look beyond the individual consumer as the unit of analysis to identify critical trajectories of how social lives change and what role (resource-intensive) consumption plays in those processes. In doing so, these contributors extend and raise cautionary insights about the fundamental assumptions that underpin the foundational principles of economists' models.

Frank Trentmann (Chapter 11) sets out a first cautionary account in his commentary on historical analyses of consumption. Historical approaches, he argues, have been dominated by two concerns. First, the rise of a consumer culture characterized by the commercialization of exchange and an emergent sovereign consumer whose individual choices and lifestyle (i.e. style of consumption) have superseded class cultures and reciprocity as mechanisms mediating social lives. While such accounts tend to present the 'consumer' as a triumph of greater individual freedoms, self-interested materialism is considered to be the corresponding price paid. The second concern is with identifying the major drivers of commercial consumer cultures. Emphasis has been focused on processes such as urbanization, globalization, and commercialization, with analysis centred on commodity chains and flows of goods and people around the globe or regions of it. Through these foci, conventional historical accounts have presented consumption as being on the rise, driven by individual desires and distributed, often unevenly, across the globe and social groups through dominant and long-term historical processes.

Trentmann advances three critiques of these popular historical representations of consumption, and in doing so also raises critical questions of economists' models. The first addresses the emphasis within historical studies that consumption is driven by individual desires for consumption, particularly in relation to the pursuit of luxuries and social status. By changing the lens for analysing consumption away from the conspicuous towards more ordinary forms of consumption, Trentmann uses the example of water consumption to show different explanations for its increase. While much historical research has focused on the marketing of ideals around personal and domestic cleanliness, he charts the forms of resistance to having infrastructures for running water installed in buildings first in mid-nineteenth-century London and later in the rural English communities of the 1920s and 1930s. Citizens feared that installation of such water infrastructures would 'multiply their tax bills'. The impetus for water infrastructures was not derived by the desires of citizens, but by the private monopoly of water companies supported by landlords and local governments who recognized the significant opportunities for improving public health and relieving space pressures in urban locations by removing public cisterns. In the case of water, it was less a matter of consumer demand that was the motor for changing consumption and more issues related to politics and power, which had the longer term effect of changing norms and conventions around social standards and cultural expectations of the practices that are facilitated by having domestic running water (e.g. washing clothes and bodies, and cleaning homes).

Trentmann's second critique concerns the historical premise of the much vaunted concept of conspicuous consumption; a concept that, as we have seen, underpins the elaborated economists' model of status competition as a possible effect on consumer preferences. Building on earlier concerns about 'luxury fever', Veblen's classic account of the 'Leisure Class' presented a late nineteenth-century USA with a burgeoning new rich who displayed their wealth and status through conspicuous consumption. While the idea of consumption as emulative and status driven pervades contemporary theory, Trentmann warns of the historical contingency of this idea. He shows that the conspicuous consumer was only one type, and that there were very different and equally numerous kinds of non-conspicuous consumers at that time in the USA. And, of course, those less conspicuous Americans, who spent their money on politics, the military and philanthropy, were by definition less visible to social commentators. Indeed, it is argued that it is only in the context of the USA, a country without traditional nobility, that conspicuous consumption in the form identified by Veblen can adequately be applied to explain even a small part of the consumption that occurred in that society. Drawing on the work of Jean-Pascal Daloz, Trentmann outlines the diverse strategies of distinction employed by elite groups and the many alternative, yet equally as plausible, explanations for the pursuit of luxury and social status that included cultural cultivation of tastes and expertise. That economic models place such emphasis on a historically, socially, and culturally contingent and contested concept to explain key aspects of consumption is deeply problematic and risks distorting analyses.

Finally, Trentmann critiques the emphasis placed on individual consumption in contemporary theory. In tones reminiscent of conventional sociological accounts of welfare provision, he argues that a lot of consumption is 'collective' rather than individual. Much of what people consume, both in historical and contemporary terms, are provided by the state and through firms. States and firms provision a wide range of everyday forms of consumption, whether in the form of education or health services, housing, the supply of food or transport, or even childcare and domestic services (note, this distinction is not quite the same as that of public and private goods, with states providing many private as well as public goods). And, of course, much consumption occurs between businesses. These 'collective forms' of consumption are important mechanisms that profoundly affect personal and household consumption. In the final analysis, Trentmann urges historical studies to step out of the shadows of the methodological individualism of economic theories to pay full attention to the varieties of historical and socio-cultural processes that come to shape contemporary patterns of consumption, and to bring collective consumption back into the analytical frame as a mechanism that shapes the longer-term trajectories of these patterns.

Reflecting on sociological approaches, Alan Warde (Chapter 12) also begins by arguing that the fundamental models of human action underpinning dominant accounts of consumption are flawed. This model, characterized as the 'portfolio model of action' by its critics, holds as its principal that action is voluntaristic, conducted by active, reflexive, and self-interested agents who steer their (consumption) behaviour in particular directions. There are, of course, many variations of application, but the portfolio model of action holds the individual (and their aggregate actions) as, ultimately, the key unit of change in patterns of consumption and, therefore, the unit to which all analysis should be directed. The challenge of sustainability lays bare the flaws to this model: the 'value–action' gap presenting a simple but stark example of the incapacity of individual preferences to explain the dynamics of consumption. Put simply, Warde's argument is that the dominant theoretical, conceptual, and methodological tools of the social and economic sciences, when applied to the study of consumption, are inadequate for addressing sustainable consumption.

In setting out this position, Warde schematically identifies three core foci of intellectual attention, each broadly corresponding to over-lapping phases in the development of social scientific approaches to consumption. These are: acquisition, usually through forms of exchange (whether through markets or other mechanisms such as reciprocity) of goods and services; appreciation which covers the symbolic, aesthetic, and communicative aspects of consumption; and appropriation, with attention focused on the use of goods and services for personal and social purposes. It is the first two that have received disproportionate attention, and consumption has come to be framed primarily as a code or language of cultural communication of identity and social status, while the last with its emphasis on the use of goods and services for practicable accomplishment of everyday activities has been underplayed (again the Lancaster model has some links to this view in that consumption of goods are inputs to household activities). This model of the individual who employs consumption (or their 'lifestyle choices') to express who they are, who they associate themselves with, and who they want to be is, for Warde, based on a weak definition of consumption: one which reduces it to the act of purchase and display, usually in the context of consumer sovereignty whereby 'freedom of choice' comes to take on a privileged, yet entirely inappropriate, conceptual significance.

This skewing of social and economic analysis has not only bracketed processes of appropriation out of the frame of analysis but, more significantly, less agentic, semi-conscious, non-deliberative, and un-calculating dimensions of human action. Captured by the more generic terms of habits and routines, these forms of action have come increasingly under the spotlight due to the flaws exposed by the challenge of sustainability to orthodox models of consumption and human action. Warde summarizes three sets of accounts that seek to address this intellectual gap, each taking conceptual analysis further away from the dominant portfolio model of action. First are accounts that Warde characterizes as addressing 'mindlessness', which include behavioural economics accounts of automaticity and 'nudges'. Second are accounts from neuro- and cognitive psychology and cultural sociology, which place emphasis on environmental cues that provide stimuli for action. In these accounts, the brain does not cause behaviour but is merely a conduit for carrying out actions stimulated by external environments. For most actions, little if any thought and deliberation are required (a point illustrated by Fletcher in Chapter 6). Ideas of 'distributed agency' underpin both approaches: culture, the environment, objects, and institutions shape human action as much as do human minds.

The third approach goes one step further to argue that habitual and routine forms of actions are learned, socially structured, and collectively derived. Drawing on the works of Marcel Mauss and Pierre Bourdieu, Warde discusses the concept of 'habitus, systems of durable, transposable dispositions, structured structures predisposed to function as structuring structures' (Bourdieu, 1990, p. 53). The habitus captures three senses of 'habit' discussed earlier in this chapter—acquired dispositions, cultural procedures, and social learning. The emphasis, however, is that the habitus is a socially shared set of dispositions that underpin the performance of practices; individuals 'acquire dispositions' only in the context of the shared performance of practices where they 'learn' competent forms of conduct. Critically, these processes that produce shared dispositions towards consumption are structured through social relations—through processes of identifying with those who share dispositions and differentiating from those who do not. These are not simply subjective judgments—through processes of identification and differentiation the habitus acts to bind social groups based on the volumes of economic (wealth), cultural (knowledge and skill), and social (networks) resources possessed by group members. Habitus is not merely the property of individuals but of social groups, and it is formed and reproduced from the relations between those groups (Bourdieu, 1984).

In conclusion, Warde calls for different conceptual and methodological tools in order to explore the social patterning of habits and routines. This, he argues, is necessary if the agreed focus is to shift ways of life in advanced capitalist societies in directions that will render every-day, ordinary forms of consumption less resource-intensive and more sustainable. Conceptually, further development of practice theoretical ideas are needed in order to move beyond the methodological individualism of portfolio models of action. Warde suggests the greatest conceptual insights can be found through attention to: the temporal rhythms, sequencing, and coordination of everyday practices; the reproduction of practices through cultural procedure; and formation of group-based dispositions. To facilitate such insights methodological developments are required, and for this task Warde champions the potential of Qualitative Comparative Analysis to reveal mutual and relational processes that shape consumption (as opposed to linear models), and time diary data for revealing the shared, coordinated, and institutionalized patterning of what people (consumers) do.

By drawing on anthropological understandings of consumption, Hal Wilhite (Chapter 13) extends the critique that economic models extract mechanisms but in doing so bracket out of analysis the critical contexts in which processes of social change occur. He points to the recent interest in 'bodies' as sites of socio-cultural change, which Wilhite presents as a corrective to the modern focus of human actions as being derivative of mental states, meanings, cognition, and deliberative choice. Commensurate in many ways with the account of Fletcher, which emphasizes the neurological impetus of bodily actions, Wilhite's focus is on how the physicality of bodies affects trajectories of consumption patterns.

Focusing on research conducted in the Indian state of Kerala, Wilhite argues that bodily practices (such as the spaces and places in which bodies can be located, the use of the senses with respect to what can be touched, bodily cleanliness, and bodily adornment), shape and are shaped by patterns of consumption. Examples including food preparation and cleanliness are used to demonstrate how patterns of consumption develop in tandem with bodily practices. This is, perhaps, most clearly demonstrated with the discussion of domestic technologies and particularly the use and spread of refrigerators in Kerala. The utility of a refrigerator in a hot and humid climate is self-evident. However, the cultural history of bodily practices in India, in which prepared food should be eaten immediately rather than stored and cold food and drinks were regarded as bad for the body, meant that this latent demand for cold food storage was not met. That is until changes in the working practices of women together with cultural conventions surrounding the importance of cooking meals from scratch precipitated the relaxing of bodily and cultural resistance to the advantages of refrigerated storage.

The point of examples such as the refrigerator is not simply to identify that culturally entrenched bodily practice is resistant to change (or that utility maximization wins over in the end). Rather, the example shows the critical interactions between: culture (i.e. conventions surrounding eating food immediately after preparation); bodily practices (i.e. the preparation and ingestion of hot food); material objects (e.g. the refrigerator which 'scripts' the kinds of foods that people store and prepare, and how they eat); and social change (in this case the growth of women in paid employment). Removing the contextual detail of bodily practices and cultural conventions from the analysis of trends such as the apparently delayed consumption of refrigerators is to remove explanation as to how and why 'preferences' for consumer goods change and why they do so at particular moments of time.

Like other contributions to this volume, our final chapter (Chapter 14) by Rick Wilk begins by problematizing the veracity of fundamental assumptions about contemporary consumption. The first is its association with modern western cultures and their 'unique' capacities for rationality, economic and technological advancements, and civilized manners. Consumption has been regarded in much of the social and economic sciences as a critical feature of modernity, and the consumption associated with non-western and past societies explained through a language of ritual, feasting, and ceremony. It is these assumed characteristics of contemporary cultures of consumption that underpin accounts which, straightforwardly, posit that insatiable needs, wants, and desires are both driven by and achieved through the consumption of more and more goods and services. Instead, Wilk demonstrates, if there is any universal characteristic of the human condition that underpins consumer culture it is the desire for the moral balancing of virtue and excess. Using the metaphors of grasshoppers (who live for the moment in perpetual instant gratification) and ants (who save for the future and defer gratification), Wilk shows moral economies of indulgence and frugality, and of spending and saving.

This moral tension captured in various literatures as hedonism and pleasure versus discipline and thrift, excess and binge versus abstinence and sobriety, are illustrated through a number of empirical studies. Perhaps most pertinent are studies that show the recursive relationship between dieting and binging—dieters tend to put on weight precisely because the virtue of controlled eating provides the moral license (elsewhere described as 'moral balancing' or 'compensatory ethics') for excessive eating. These moral balancing acts expressed through consumption are neither a personal deficiency nor contemporary phenomena—but happen across the range of human actions in daily life and can be identified in a wide range of cultures across space and over time. Far removed from 'econs', this understanding of consumption reveals that key variables (such as social competition and conformity) are recursive—they exist and operate together in constant tension with each other.

The implications for trying to achieve 'sustainable' consumption that result from this analysis are stark. In promoting or encouraging 'consumers' to make greener choices the outcome may well be more total consumption, since the cultural understanding of consuming some 'greener' goods and services legitimates the continued consumption of less green goods and services. Imploring consumers to make moral judgements about how and what they consume, in the context of moral balancing, will not tackle the problem of sustainability unless that consumption is about less, not green, consumption. For Wilk, re-instituting contemporary sumptuary laws and maximum wages would be one set of mechanisms that could recognize the 'limits of wealth' (and there are economic models which predict 'limits of wealth', including that presented by Dasgupta in his contribution to this book). But, for such ideas to gain traction in political-economic discourse requires understandings of consumption to move beyond economic individualism, ideas of infinite economic growth, and the precept that consumers choose optimally, and toward understandings of the moral balancing between self-expression (and social competition) and conformity (or the desire to belong), indulgence and frugality, and spending and saving.

1.6 Towards a More Integrated Understanding of Sustainable Consumption

When disciplines are lined up against one another around a particular topic of enquiry the tendency is to draw out and highlight the intellectual tensions. In this introduction we have set up economic models of consumption as our entry point for discussion, and then summarized how the other disciplinary contributions to this book address the topic of consumption and the challenge of sustainability. There are many intellectual tensions that are played out in the chapters of this book, ranging from epistemological differences between methodological individualism and portfolio models of action to the emphasis on practices and context-dependent socio-cultural processes; and including the significance and application of some key concepts such as habits or conspicuous consumption. For all the theoretical, conceptual, and methodological tensions we maintain that it is more instructive to focus on the synergies—for they are also plentiful. In this section we summarize some of these synergies in terms of theoretical understandings of consumption, empirical studies of consumption, and policy implications. We shall not only look at existing synergies but also note where we think there is scope for future synergistic research.

1.6.1 *Conceptual Synergies*

There are three main areas of such synergies with important implications for areas of future research.

(A) INDIVIDUAL DELIBERATIVE ACTIONS

As we noted in section 3, one area that has attempted to build links between disciplines is the sub-discipline of behavioural economics, which has sought to combine insights from psychological and economic understandings of individual behaviour, as exemplified in Chapter 9 by Correia and Roseta-Palma. As Croson (2013) notes, this can be thought of as taking the economists' very parsimonious model of consumer behaviour and adding in additional factors drawn from psychology—such as the importance of the status quo (gains and losses are not viewed symmetrically), prospect theory (individuals are 'risk averse' about gains but 'risk loving' about losses), the excessive weight attached to low probability events, and various biases, such as the importance of default options. These extensions make models less parsimonious, so there are more parameters to help explain observed behaviour. On the other hand a weakness of the sub-discipline is that it consists of a set of possible biases rather than a systematic account of behavioural economics which might allow social scientists to say when such biases might be applicable. One particular limitation is that while behavioural economics has made some attempt to explain inter-temporal decisions such as savings behaviour, there is less work on inter-generational decision-making (as discussed by Cropper in Chapter 5).

An important area for further work is to build stronger links between behavioural economics and insights from sociology and anthropology. There is some acknowledgement in behavioural economics of the social context within which consumption decisions are made, such as giving people information about how much energy their neighbours use, but there is a need to build a deeper understanding of what constitutes a sense of individual and collective identity, whether these are consistent and how they are shaped. Two specific areas where more integration would be helpful were those noted by Dasgupta (Chapter 2), Oswald (Chapter 3), and Wilhite (Chapter 12)—understanding competitive consumption decisions (the Veblen effect) and understanding consumption decisions driven by a desire for conformity, as exemplified in social norms. As with the concern we noted about behavioural economics, what is needed is not just separate accounts of these two phenomena but recognition (as highlighted by Wilk in Chapter 14) that individuals display both features. An integrated account that fully recognizes the relationships between individual and collective identities is required, and the development of Bourdieu's concept of habitus (an elaboration of Dasgupta's observations about consumption as competition and conformity in Chapter 2, and a position outlined by Warde in Chapter 12) provides one potential entry point for just such an account.

Finally, as stated in section 2, and Dasgupta notes in Chapter 2, economists' standard account of individual behaviour informs not just positive accounts of consumption decisions but normative accounts of what constitutes better allocations of resources. As we build richer models of individual consumption behaviour it will be important to consider what this implies for understandings of welfare; for example, the axiom of revealed preference may no longer hold.

(B) HABITUAL ACTIONS

We noted in section 2 that a number of disciplines stress the importance of habitual actions, though the concept is used differently in different disciplines and, drawing on work by Warde and Southerton (2012), we set out a schema identifying different ways habits are conceived. Moving beyond conceptual clarification there are three areas of synergy identified in the chapters of this book.

The first relates to automated responses to external stimuli (as discussed by Fletcher, but also by Warde and implicated in the chapter by Beattie and McGuire), sequences of decisions (Prelec), and actions embedded in cultural procedures (Warde). A better understanding of neurological, psychological, and cultural factors that affect and produce habituated action is, as we have seen, critical if we are to advance understandings about those forms of behaviour that cannot easily be explained by the Portfolio model of the deliberative individual actor.

Second is the importance of recognizing that many apparently habitual and routine forms of action need to be analysed in relation to the practices that shape patterns of consumption. For example, the consumption of water or electricity is often a consequence of performing particular practices—the good (water) provides a service (say, e.g. a shower) and it is the practice (of showering) that matters to the consumer. Of course, pricing the good such that the service becomes unattainable to achieve with its current frequency for many consumers is one way of changing the practice, but nevertheless it is the practice that needs to change. It may not be politically or ethically possible, or desirable, to seek to restrict access to goods and services in all cases, and therefore understanding the significance and organization of practices in everyday life is necessary to identify how those practices can be encouraged in particular directions.

Finally, a number of contributors emphasize the significance of cultural conventions and customs in shaping habitual forms of consumption. Whether related to neurological or sensory reactions to particular foods, cultural understandings of health, cleanliness, personal comfort, or socially acceptable behaviour, it is clear that apparently habitual actions are embedded in long-term cultural trajectories that significantly vary across social groups and contexts (as demonstrated most clearly in the chapters by Wilk and Wilhite). While we may be able to identify generic processes and factors that affect consumption patterns (e.g. the discussions provided by Dasgupta, Oswald, Prelec, and Warde), those processes and factors play out differently across socio-cultural contexts (as demonstrated by Trentmann).

(C) BEYOND PERSONAL AND HOUSEHOLD CONSUMPTION

A number of contributions to this book look beyond the usual frame of analysis that centres on individual consumers. Kinzig and Perrings, for example, sketch out the relationships between ecosystems and consumption—each framing and affecting the other. In a different sense, Trentmann points out that much consumption is done by businesses, states, and other organizations and, as such, it is important not to disproportionately focus analysis on the consumption activities of private citizens or households. To this he adds that much consumption is provisioned outside of market mechanisms.

Warde's (1990) account of modes of provision is, perhaps, worth re-stating in this context because it provides a framework that could generate interdisciplinary thinking beyond personal consumption. Table.1.1 outlines an ideal-type model of modes of provision. The key point is that the way in which consumption is provisioned affects how people or organizations access those goods and services, the manner in which those goods are delivered, and the experience of consumption. It is not only individuals or households who engage in consumption—business consumes goods and services, some of which might be provisioned through markets and others through states. In advanced economies, such modes of provision are complex—often a mix of market and household provision (e.g. market provision of ingredients but household or communal provision of the assembled meal) or state and market provision (such as health care in the UK). Modes of provision are governed and regulated by a range of institutions, and often dependent on shared infrastructures. It is the relationships between such modes of provisioning that configure the patterns of consumption that are formed from the activities of private individuals, households, and a whole host of organizations from commercial businesses to governmental organizations and NGOs.

Recognizing that an understanding of consumption requires analysis beyond the activities of individuals and households is also to acknowledge that it takes place within institutional frameworks. Three kinds of institutional settings can be identified: (i) what is consumed depends on both what individuals, businesses, and states consume (demand) and what it is economic to produce (supply), so the key institutions here are firms; (ii) in advanced economies much consumption is of a quasi-collective nature—for example, health, education, sanitation—so the key institutions are government

Table 1.1. Modes of provision: from production to consumption

Mode of provision	Mode of access/social relations	Manner of delivery	Consumption experienced as
Market	Price/exchange	Managerial	Consumer/customer
State	Need/right	Professional	Citizen/client
Household	Family/obligation	Family	Private self/family member
Community	Social network/reciprocity	Volunteer	Friend/neighbour/affine

agencies, firms, and third sector organizations such as charities; (iii) the nature of the infrastructure (e.g. transportation, internet) that affects what sources of consumption individuals, households, or organizations can access, for which the key institutions are government agencies. As with individual behaviour, different disciplines give different accounts of how such institutional factors are determined. As Trentmann (Chapter 10) shows, there has been considerable variation over time and space in the mix of institutional provision of sanitation just within the UK, so it is unrealistic to expect any single overarching explanation of such institutional behaviour; nevertheless it is worth considering possible synergies.

In sketching out existing and possible future synergies between disciplines in understanding sustainable consumption, we are not suggesting that it will be possible or even necessarily desirable to try to build some grand unified theory of consumer behaviour. Equally that should not stop us exploring areas where some attempted synergies will prove fruitful.

1.6.2 *Empirical Testing of Consumer Behaviour*

As would be expected, the different conceptual understandings of sustainable consumption across disciplines have resulted in a wide range of empirical approaches for testing these theoretical predictions. The choice of empirical approach should always be driven by what one is trying to explain, and these can differ from lab-based experiments in neuroscience and psychology, cross-section and time-series studies of demand in economics and sociology, qualitative studies of consumer behaviour using questionnaires, interviews, and so on, historical studies based on archive material, and anthropological studies based on close observation of specific communities.

An important reason why these empirical approaches differ is the scale of empirical analysis of consumption, from lab-based micro-analysis of individual thoughts and actions in neuroscience and psychology (as in the chapters by Fletcher, Prelec, and Beattie and McGuire) and cross-section economic studies (e.g. the studies of happiness and consumption in the chapter by Oswald), meso-level studies of processes (as in Wilhite's account of bodies in his chapter), models that take some account of social context (as in some cross-section econometric studies that take account of individuals' class, occupation, age, and education, etc.), richer models that handle socio-cultural and contextually specific processes that affect consumption (as in the studies mentioned in the chapter by Warde) to aggregate studies of consumption as in macro-level econometric studies mentioned by Dasgupta in his chapter. An obvious way to enrich empirical analysis is for researchers to compare empirical findings across these different scales, and to develop approaches which are 'scalable'—capable of being used at these different levels.

It will be important to consider how the greater cross-disciplinary theoretical work we outlined above in section 1.6.1 will affect empirical work. We suggest three ways in which empirical work might be developed further. First, it will be useful to extend existing methodologies. An obvious way would be to use richer data sets to allow more socio-contextual variables to be employed in cross-section econometric models. As another example, some of the psychological work using eye-tracking studies reported by Beattie and McGuire in Chapter 8 could be used in stores to monitor actual consumer behaviour, rather than using lab-based studies. More interesting are empirical developments monitoring patterns of consumption that result from the way different social groups perform practices—that is methods which capture what people do and not only what they buy. Time diary methodologies provide detailed accounts of human activity, while Qualitative Comparative Analysis provides a systematic methodology for explaining the socially patterned meanings and cultural dispositions that underpin how and why groups perform activities in particular ways. Finally, it will be important to develop methodologies capable of analysing the two-way inter-related processes of how consumption shapes ecosystems and cultures, and how ecosystems and culture shape consumption. Comparative methodologies are needed.

With respect to data, as already noted, the greater availability of rich data sets (e.g. linked across different countries to get greater cross-sectional variability) and the increased power of modern statistical and computing techniques will allow empirical studies of consumption to take account of a much wider range of explanatory variables. There seems huge scope to analyse time diary (what people do, patterning of behaviours/practices/actions, and institutional forms) and transactions (what people actually acquire—and, if possible, data that captures other forms of acquisition—e.g. gifts) data. Such data can reveal the socio-cultural and economic patterning of deliberative and habitual actions, and the 'supra-individual' conditioning of collective consumption (e.g. how acts of consumption are coordinated). We now have such data stretching back over 20–30 year periods, making explorations of longer term processes possible to recover.

Transactions and expenditure data also fit our 'scalable criteria'—capable of micro analysis of what people buy, when they buy it, meso-level analysis revealing how people coordinate and service practices, and macro-level analysis of consumption patterns.

1.6.3 *Policy implications*

The richer views of consumption set out in the chapters of this book have important implications for how policies to make consumption more sustainable might be developed and implemented. As we noted in section 1.2 the conventional economists' approach is to argue that the environmental cost of consumption should be reflected in the prices consumers face for different goods, through the introduction of appropriate environmental taxes or the use of tradable emission quotas. While there has been some success in the use of such policies (Hahn, 1989), policy-makers are looking at a wider range of possible policy measures.

The work in behavioural economics noted earlier has encouraged a number of governments (e.g. UK, France, Netherlands, and USA) to consider the implications of this work for policy, particularly in the areas of energy and water demand. A few examples noted by Croson (2013) are: (i) giving people information about how their monthly electricity consumption compares with neighbours has been shown to have an effect in reducing such consumption, but only if this is implemented over a reasonably long period (18–24 months); (ii) telling people where rubbish is disposed makes them more likely to recycle or dispose of rubbish more carefully. As Croson notes, policy-makers are clear that such approaches complement, rather than replace, conventional economic policies. Moreover, as Stoker notes in Chapter 10, there are important political issues about the limits to which such interventions in individual behaviour are deemed to be legitimate, a concern shared by Croson (2013) who notes the importance of gaining consumers' trust for such 'nudges' to be effective, and this favours policy interventions which are felt to widen choices rather than narrow them.

As we noted in section 1.6.1 one limitation of the behavioural economics approach which underlies nudges is that there is not yet a clear basis for determining which policies might work for particular groups of people so that policies could be better targeted (compare the suggestion from Beattie and McGuire in Chapter 8 of a need to distinguish types of consumer by a mix of implicit and explicit attitudes). Furthermore, significant doubts remain about the scope of nudge approaches for tackling sustainable consumption given the scale of the challenge. While nudges have a role in the policy mix they can, at best, represent only a relatively limited set of policy responses to affect more sustainable consumption.

As noted, environmental economists tend to argue for the use of price-based environmental policies, such as taxes and tradable emission quotas, rather than more regulatory approaches, on the grounds that price-based policies are more efficient. One obvious reason for a difference in policy approach is that not all countries would have the necessary administrative infrastructure to impose effective environmental taxes. However, putting that aside, a number of the chapters in this book question economists' preference for price-based instruments. For example, strong habitual effects (Fletcher, Chapter 6 and Prelec, Chapter 7) make consumption less responsive to price changes, certainly in the short-term, so to work quickly any required price change would have to be large, and perhaps politically infeasible. In the extreme cases of addiction to alcohol or drugs there are clear divisions of policy response in many advanced countries, with the use of high taxes or minimum prices for trying to restrict alcohol consumption while criminalizing trade in drugs like cocaine or heroin.

In the case of strong competitive or conspicuous consumption effects, while many economists would follow Dasgupta's argument (in Chapter 2) about the need to tax the relevant goods, Wilk calls for the use of sumptuary laws to limit individual consumption. In the case of social norms, Dasgupta noted the issue of multiple possible equilibria and hence a coordination problem. However, more recent analysis reported in Dasgupta, Southerton, Ulph, and Ulph (2014) suggests that social norms may make consumption of the relevant goods unresponsive to changes in prices, so if there was a need to reduce consumption of such goods for environmental reasons then that would require a regulatory approach as argued by Wilk.

As we have noted, an important limitation of economists' analysis is that they do not seek to explain what drives individual consumer preferences, and hence what forces might cause consumption to change. A deeper understanding of the drivers of consumption patterns, and particularly what causes them to change over time, would help us devise appropriate policies to help steer such changes in consumption in a more sustainable direction.

In summary, in terms of theoretical, empirical, and policy-related analyses there is much fruitful work to be done in the future from learning across disciplinary boundaries.

References

Bernheim, D. and Rangel, A. (2007) 'Towards Choice-Theoretic Foundations for Behavioral Welfare Economics', *American Economic Review*, 97(2): 464–70.

Bourdieu, P. (1984) *Distinction: A Sociological Critique of the Judgement of Taste*. London: Routledge and Kegan Paul.

Bourdieu, P. (1990) *The Logic of Practice*. Cambridge: Polity Press.

Bows A. et al. (2012) *What's Cooking? Adaptation and Mitigation in the UK Food System*. Manchester: Sustainable Consumption Institute Report, University of Manchester.

Camerer, C. Loewenstein, G., and Rabin, M. (2004) *Behavioral Economics*. Princeton, NJ: Princeton University Press.

Cheng, S-L., Olsen, W., Southerton, D., and Warde, A. (2007) 'The Changing Practice of Eating: Evidence from UK Time Diaries, 1975 and 2000', *British Journal of Sociology*, 58(1): 39–61.

Croson, R. (2013) 'Using Behavioral Economics to Influence Environmental Decisions', Paper Presented to European Association of Environmental and Resource Economists Conference, Toulouse.

Dasgupta, P. (2008) 'Discounting Climate Change', *Journal of Risk and Uncertainty*, 37: 141–65.

Dasgupta, P. (2012) 'Time and the Generations' in R. Hahn and A. Ulph (eds) *Climate Change and Common Sense: Essays in Honour of Tom Schelling*, Oxford: Oxford University Press.

Dasgupta, P. and Heal, G. (1979) *Economic Theory and Exhaustible Resources*. Cambridge: Cambridge University Press.

Dasgupta, P., Southerton, D., Ulph, A., and Ulph, D. (2013) 'Consumer Behaviour in a Social Context: Implications for Environmental Policy', *mimeo*, Sustainable Consumption Institute, University of Manchester.

Easterlin, R. (1974) 'Does Economic Growth Improve the Human Lot? Some Empirical Evidence' in P. David and M. Reder (eds) *Nations and Households in Economic Growth: Essays in Honor of Moses Abramowitz*. New York: Academic Press.

Festinger, L. (1954) 'A Theory of Social Comparison Processes', *Human Relations*, 7: 117–40.

Gershuny, J. (1978) *After Industrial Society? The Emerging Self-Service Economy*. London: Macmillan.

Hahn, R. (1989) 'Economic Prescriptions for Environmental Problems: How the Patient Followed the Doctor's Orders', *Journal of Economic Perspectives*, 3(2): 95–114.

Harrison, G. (2005) 'Book Review: Advances in Behavioral Economics', *Journal of Economic Psychology*, 25: 793–5.

House of Lords (2011) *Behavioural Change*, Science and Technology Committee *(Second Report)* London: HMSO.

Humphrey, K. (1998) *Shelf Life: Supermarkets and the Changing Culture of Consumption*. Cambridge: Cambridge University Press.

Kahneman, D., Knetsch, J., and Thaler, R. (1986) 'Fairness as a Constraint on Profit Seeking: Entitlements in the Market', *American Economic Review*, 76(4): 728–41.

Kahneman, D. and Tversky, A. (1979) 'Prospect Theory: An Analysis of Decisions under Risk', *Econometrica*, 47(2): 263–92.

Lancaster, K. J. (1966) 'A New Approach to Consumer Theory', *Journal of Political Economy* 74: 132–57.

Nordhaus, W. (2007) 'A Review of the *Stern Review of the Economics of Climate Change*' *Journal of Economic Literature*, 45: 686–702.

Pesendorfer, W. (2006) 'Behavioral Economics Comes of Age: A Review of *Advances in Behavioral Economics*', *Journal of Economic Literature*, 44(3): 712–21.

Rubinstein, A. (2006) 'Discussion of Behavioral Economics' <http://arielrubinstein.tau.ac.il/papers/behavioral-economics.pdf>.

Schatzki, T. R. et al. (2001) *The Practice Turn in Contemporary Theory*. London: Routledge.

Shove, E. and Southerton, D. (2000) 'Defrosting the Freezer: From Novelty to Convenience—A Narrative of Normalisation', *Journal of Material Culture*, 5(3): 301–19.

Stern, N. (2006) *The Economics of Climate Change: The Stern Report*. Cambridge: Cambridge University Press.

Thaler, R. and Sunstein, C. (2008) *Nudge: Improving Decisions about Health, Wealth and Happiness*. New Haven: Yale University Press.

Tirole, J. (2002) 'Rational Irrationality: Some Economics of Self Management', *European Economic Review*, 46: 633–55.
Veblen, T. (1899 [1924]) *The Theory of the Leisure Class: An Economic Study of Institutions*. London: George, Allen and Unwin.
Warde, A. (2005) 'Consumption and Theories of Practices', *Journal of Consumer Culture*, 5(2): 131–53.
Warde, A. (ed.) (2010) *Consumption, Vols I-III*. London: Sage.
Warde, A. and Southerton, D. (2012) 'Social Sciences and Sustainability', in A. Warde and D, Southerton (eds) *The Habits of Consumption*. Helsinki: Open Access Book Series of the Helsinki Collegium of Advanced Studies.
Weitzman, M. (2001) 'Gamma Discounting', *American Economic Review*, 91: 260–71.

Part I

Extensions of the Simple Economists' Model of Consumption

2

Sustainability and the Determinants of Personal Consumption

Partha Dasgupta[1]

2.1 Introduction

There is now a substantial literature exploring humanity's interchanges with nature. It ranges from scientific studies of specific resources (fisheries, wetlands, the atmosphere as a carbon sink), via such overarching reviews as the Millennium Ecosystem Assessment (MEA) (MEA, 2005a–d), to popular accounts that summarize those findings and conclude that unless we act urgently, humanity is most likely to go down the proverbial tube (Myers and Kent, 2000). On the other hand, there is a prominent literature (Ridley, 2010) that studies episodes from history and contemporary economic growth only to conclude that the worries expressed are misconceived, because technology can be relied upon to save the situation.

Neither set of studies offers an analysis of the processes that characterize humanity's interchanges with nature. The former literature doesn't offer reasons why the human–nature system *isn't* self-correcting, while the latter literature doesn't provide reasons why it *is* self-correcting. Recently the Royal Society (2012) studied human–nature interchanges by focusing on the interface of population, consumption, and the natural environment. As the

[1] This chapter is based on lectures delivered at the *Sustainable Consumption: A Multifaceted Approach* conference, hosted by the Sustainable Consumption Institute, University of Manchester, 8–9 March 2012 and at the School of International and Public Affairs, Columbia University, 2 April 2012, and the Inaugural Humanitas Visiting Professor Lecture on Economic Thought at the University of Oxford on 9 May 2012. I have benefitted from the comments of Vincent Crawford, Robert Solow, Joseph Stiglitz, and most especially discussions with Dale Southerton and Alistair Ulph.

document is a state-of-the-world report, it too doesn't attempt to identify in any detail the processes at work at the population-consumption-environment nexus.

In this chapter I attempt a partial study of those processes. For tractability I limit myself to the consumption–environment interface, ignoring demographic matters. To strive for generality, however, I do not specify the scale at which human–nature interchanges are assumed to take place. The economy under study could be a household or a village, a district or a state, or a country or the world as a whole. Scale matters, of course, but I track those features that would appear to be common across scales.

Two features are given prominence in what follows. The first consists of *externalities*, a class of phenomena that are ubiquitous in the world we know, because for many commodities markets either do not exist (e.g. because property rights to them are weak) or are not competitive when they do exist. Externalities are the unacknowledged or unrecorded consequences for others (including future generations) of actions taken by one or more persons. Environmental externalities have, of course, been much studied (Meade, 1973; and an enormous literature in environmental and resource economics). To that well-known literature I add three types of externalities that arise directly from humanity's preferences for the consumption of goods and services. They have been far less studied in contemporary economics.

The second feature consists of *non-linearities* with positive feedback, which are a pervasive characteristic of natural systems. That nature's processes are all too frequently non-linear is well known (Steffen et al., 2004). The point of importance for us here is that the adverse consequences of consumption and environmental externalities are accentuated in the presence of those non-linearities.

By adverse consequences I mean losses in human well-being. I argue that the ubiquity of externalities means (i) that the human–nature system is not self-correcting (markets on their own do not suffice either for economic efficiency or equity); (ii) that depending on the character and scope of the externalities, the necessary correctives require collective action at various levels of society; and (iii) that there is urgency in eliminating the externalities that are subject to non-linearities.

Estimating externalities is one of the tasks in economic evaluation. Section 2.2 contains an overview of the reasons we as citizens evaluate economies. Two motivations are identified, involving respectively the need to assess the performance of economies and to identify good policies. The former involves sustainability analysis, while the latter defines policy analysis. It is shown that the criterion function appropriate for both types of evaluation is an inclusive notion of wealth, which is a weighted sum of the economy's stocks of capital assets. A formal proof is presented in Appendix 1.[2]

Traditional models of growth and development were built round the accumulation of an economy's 'productive base', which included reproducible capital (roads, buildings, ports, machinery, and equipment) and human capital (population, knowledge, skills, and health). That can be shown to have been far too narrow. Natural capital, among other factors of production and consumption, is typically missing from the models. Moreover, the idea of a productive base is broader than capital assets. Section 2.3 explains why.

The presence of externalities is a reason why the weights that should be awarded to capital assets are not their market prices but shadow prices. In section 2.4 I review the idea of shadow prices and in Appendix 2 I construct a model economy to illustrate how they relate to one another.

Prevailing methods for estimating shadow prices are based on the assumption that, barring public goods, there are no consumption externalities. Put another way, people are seen as egotists (section 2.5). This is bad practice. So, in sections 2.5–2.7, I study ways to enlarge the prevailing model of human motivation. The approach I adopt is by way of a study of consumption externalities. Three potentially important types of externalities are examined: the acquisition of taste, competitive preferences, and social preferences. They differ greatly in the way their presence influences the allocation of resources. I show that the externalities arising from our consumption of goods and services (which are flows) should be embodied in the shadow prices of capital assets (which are stocks). To pretend consumption externalities don't exist in a world where they are rampant results in misleading estimates of shadow prices. The chapter concludes (section 2.8) with remarks on the influence of non-linearities and externalities on the dynamics of human–nature systems.

2.2 Economic Evaluation

Economic evaluation is an essential activity. We evaluate our own household's economic circumstances, we worry that green is a vanishing colour in our towns, we are puzzled by the growing inequality in living standards in much of the world, we are concerned about the character of economic development in our own country and we despair that sustained economic development remains a distant goal in Africa. And we have views on the role incentives and governance play in economic life.

Economic evaluation is also a compulsive activity. We commonly discuss the economic performance of nations with our friends and neighbours, read

[2] The account is based on Dasgupta and Maler (2000).

reports and commentaries in newspapers and magazines, listen to the views of experts on radio and television, and occasionally take our concerns to our political representatives. We evaluate economies so as to assess and prescribe, and do so because we are curious to know the answer to five questions:

(A) How is the economy doing?
(B) How has it been doing in recent years?
(C) What should our forecast of the economy's performance be under 'business as usual'?
(D) How is the economy likely to perform under alternative policies?
(E) Which policies should we recommend?

Questions A and B direct us to *assess* the performance of economies; questions D and E on the other hand are prompted by the need to *prescribe* policy. Because any change in policy is a perturbation to 'business as usual', answering question C is essential if we are to respond to questions D and E.

Assessment should precede prescription. It could be foolish to look for improvements if an economy is doing well: the world is littered with failed policies. If on the other hand the economy has been doing badly, we should certainly search for policies that would improve matters. The problem lies in knowing what to look for in order to evaluate the economy's performance. National economic accounts are relevant at this point. They are needed if we are to address any of the five questions. Being 'descriptors', they provide the raw material for economic evaluation. Unfortunately the framework for national accounts currently in use suffers from narrowness in their coverage. Vast quantities of information relevant for economic evaluation do not appear in the accounts. Some don't because the appropriate data are hard, even impossible, to collect; others do not only because until recently the theory of economic evaluation didn't ask for them. The demand for *green national accounts* has arisen because it was noticed that humanity's dependence on nature remains in large measure unrecorded. Contemporary national accounts are in many ways an unsatisfactory basis for economic evaluation.

I refer to the person doing the evaluation as the 'social evaluator'. The social evaluator could be a citizen, thinking about things before casting his/her vote on political candidates; an ethicist hired to offer guidance to the government; a government official; and so on. Being a *social* evaluator, the person takes into account the interests and desires of others, not just those of his/her own self.

2.2.1 *Consumption and Well-Being*

I assume that the currency in which evaluation is done is human well-being. Because future generations matter, human well-being means *inter-generational well-being*, which for brevity I will call *social well-being*. There are broader ethical viewpoints that include the welfare of all sentient beings or the dictates of a Higher Authority. But as I have nothing of substance to say about those considerations, they are ignored here. Conceptually, nothing will be lost by that neglect.

It is customary to regard consumption goods and services as the direct sources of human well-being. Social well-being is then taken to be a function of the distribution of *consumption* across contemporaries and the generations. But there are thinkers who have argued that the real source of a person's well-being lies in those activities and engagements that are consonant with the person's reasoned projects and purposes. Friendships, associational activities, meaningful work, and the contemplation of objects and ideas of beauty are the basis of living, or so it has been argued.[3] Customary thinking can accommodate that viewpoint. Goods and services are necessary inputs in anything we do or in the development of the kind of person we wish to be. In reduced form, human well-being is therefore dependent on the consumption of goods and services.

We will see presently that the distinction between consumption goods and services and the commodities that are inputs in the production of consumption goods and services is often blurred. There are commodities that serve as both consumption and capital goods. And there are goods that are both producer goods and aspects of well-being itself. Health and education are obvious examples. Good health is an aspect of well-being; it also enables a person to be productive.

2.2.2 *Policy Analysis and Sustainability Analysis*

Policy analysis, including *project evaluation* (or *cost–benefit analysis*), addresses questions D and E. The idea is to evaluate an economy *at a point in time*, before and after a hypothetical change (the policy change) has been made to it, so as to judge whether the change is desirable. Say a government official has been asked to determine whether a wetland should be drained in order to build a shopping mall. The official's task would be to assess the economy with and without the wetland conversion and compare the two situations normatively (question D). In principle, policy analysis can be used iteratively to identify 'optimum' development, which is a development path a society would ideally wish to follow (question E).

In contrast to policy evaluation, the notion of *sustainable development* is prompted by questions B and C. The idea is to evaluate economic change when the change is brought about *by the passage of time itself*.

[3] Moore (1903) is probably the most recognizable exponent of the view in recent centuries. He came very close to reducing ethics to aesthetics.

2.2.3 *The Idea of Sustainable Development*

Policy analysis is a clear enough notion; it involves evaluating policy changes by studying their potential impact on social well-being. But what is sustainability analysis?

The requirement that an object should be sustained over a period of time means it shouldn't diminish over the period. In their classic Report, the Brundtland Commission (World Commission on Environment and Development, 1987) re-cast questions B and C by interpreting the object of interest as *human needs*. The Report defined sustainable development as 'development that meets the needs of the present without compromising the ability of future generations to meet their own needs'.

Say an economy has been enjoying economic growth by investing in buildings, factories, agriculture, mines, and transport. If those investments have been accompanied by a depletion of the economy's forests, wetlands, and aquifers, the social evaluator should ask whether economic growth there is sustainable or whether future needs will be compromised. The widespread acknowledgement today that national accounts should include the use and depletion of 'natural capital' can be traced to that Report.

Notice that the quoted line from the Brundtland Commission Report mentions 'human needs', not 'human well-being'. In the Commission's view, sustainable development requires that future generations will have no less of the *means* to meet their needs than we do currently; the Report doesn't ask for more. As needs are the austere component of well-being, a country's economic development could be sustainable in the Commission's sense without it having to promote social well-being.

Notice also that the Commission's definition is directed at sustaining the factors required to satisfy human needs (food, clothing, shelter, personal relationships, leisure activities). But those factors would be available only if the society in question had access to adequate quantities of capital assets to produce them. Sustainable development in the Commission's judgement requires that relative to their populations, each generation should bequeath to its successor access to at least as large a quantity of what may be called a society's *productive base* as it had itself inherited from its predecessor. The stress is on 'access', not 'possession', because trade with others enables an economy to rely on assets it does not itself possess. In the world economy, however, access means possession. For simplicity of exposition, I use the term 'possession' in what follows.

The term 'productive base' suggests a full array of capital stocks. Here we will see that it includes a lot more. But the Commission's wording suggests that in its view sustainability analysis should track movements in an economy's portfolio of capital assets over time. Here we take social well-being to be the object of primary interest in economic evaluation. So, by 'sustainable development' we will mean a development path along which social well-being doesn't decline. Formally, we have

Definition 1: economic development is sustained over a period of time if social well-being does not decline over the period.

Propositions 1 and 3 (section 2.2.4) identify a close connection between social well-being and the social worth of the economy's productive base. The Propositions also imply as corollaries that neither gross domestic product (GDP) nor the United Nations' Human Development Index (HDI) is a suitable index for use in economic evaluation.

2.2.4 *Wealth*

Sustainability analysis can be applied as well to the past. We frequently ask whether an economy in which we are interested has been developing in a sustainable way. As policies apply only to the future, it is reasonable to ask whether the policies under review are likely to lead to sustained economic development.

An economy's productive base includes stocks of capital assets it has inherited from the past. Imagine that we are successful in finding a scalar index of those stocks with the property that its movement over time faithfully tracks movements in social well-being. The index could then be used in sustainability analysis. If it also emerged that the index is a *weighted sum* of the capital stocks, the social evaluator could be given the weights and be required only to estimate changes in the stocks over the period under review. It transpires that the required index in sustainability analysis *is* linear, provided the weights are chosen to reflect the scarcity values of assets. The finding is proved in Appendix 1.

An asset's scarcity value is called its *shadow price*. Formally, we have

Definition 2: an asset's shadow price is the contribution a further unit of it would make to social well-being, other things being equal.[4]

It helps to formalize. Let t be the date at which the economic evaluation is undertaken and let the unit of account be social well-being. Assume there are N capital assets. Let $P_i(t)$ be the shadow price of asset i at time t, and $K_i(t)$ the stock of asset i at t ($i = 1,2,\ldots, N$). Write $\boldsymbol{K}(t)$ as the vector of assets at t: $\{K_1(t),\ldots, K_i(t),\ldots, K_N(t)\}$. In sections 2.2, 2.4, and Appendices 1 and 2 we confirm that the shadow price of asset i at time t is a function of $\boldsymbol{K}(t)$ and possibly of t also. So we write that shadow price as $P_i\ (\boldsymbol{K}(t),t)$.

[4] A pollutant's shadow price would be negative.

Capital assets are the means by which consumption goods can be produced and distributed. An asset's shadow price is therefore a derived value. In common parlance, a person would be said to have invested in an asset if his/her portfolio now contains more of it. By the same token, the person would be said to have disinvested in an asset if his/her portfolio now contains less of it. That suggests an economy's development path can be described in terms of movements in the portfolio of assets. The suggestion turns out to be true.

Define the economy's *wealth* at *t* as

$$W(t) = {}_i\sum[P_i(\boldsymbol{K}(t), t)K_i(t)]. \tag{1}$$

The fundamental result in sustainability analysis is

> Proposition 1: wealth and social well-being mutually track one another—during any period of time wealth increases if and only if social well-being increases.

Let $V(t)$ denote a scalar index of social well-being at t. If we confine ourselves to sustainability analysis that covers only a brief period, Proposition 1 can then be expressed formally as

> Proposition 2: $dV(t)/dt \geq 0$ if and only if ${}_i\sum[P_i(\boldsymbol{K}(t),t)dK_i(t)/dt] \geq 0$.[5] (2)

Proposition 2 is an equivalence relationship. On its own it cannot tell the social evaluator whether an economy is following (or has followed) a sustainable development path. It only offers a criterion function for use in sustainability analysis. That function is wealth.

Proposition 2 also comes tantalizingly close to saying that wealth can serve as the criterion function in policy analysis as well. In fact it can.

> Proposition 3: wealth is the appropriate criterion function for both sustainability and policy analyses.

Wealth is different from income. Wealth is a stock, whereas income is a flow. Wealth is the dynamic counterpart of income. Income and wealth would move in the same way over time if the economy under study is in a steady state. That's because in a steady state the composition of the economy remains the same over time, which in turn implies that relative shadow prices remain constant over time. Outside steady states, though, wealth and income can point at different directions and a choice has to be made between them. Proposition 2 says that it is wealth, not income, that should be used in economic evaluation.

Capital accounts are the basis for economic evaluation. Income and expenditure accounts are a necessary input in the construction of capital accounts

[5] Proposition 2 can be extended to cover any period of time, no matter how lengthy, by integrating the time derivatives. See Dasgupta and Maler (2000).

(Proposition 5), but it is the latter that gives the social evaluator information about the economy's portfolio of assets. Economic evaluation involves the study of how an economy's assets are managed and how they ought to be managed.

2.3 Unravelling the Productive Base

An economy's wealth is a scalar measure of its productive base. The productive base of an economy consists in turn of an array of capital assets. What are they? The question is in fact a lot more complex than would appear at first blush. Nevertheless, a formal analysis enables us to answer it (Appendix 2). Here we construct a classification based on that analysis.

2.3.1 *Classification of Assets*

(1) *Reproducible capital* (roads, buildings, ports, machinery, equipment). Reproducible capital is frequently called 'manufactured capital'. Contemporary national accounts divide an economy's investment in reproducible capital into sectoral investments (manufactures, mining, forestry, agriculture, etc.). Other things being equal, raising the rate of investment in reproducible capital increases the size of an economy's future productive base. Market prices are typically used to measure investments in reproducible capital.

(2) *Human capital* (knowledge, skills, health). When economists write about human capital, they usually mean 'knowledge and skills'. But health is another aspect of human capital. As both education and health are embodied in people, they together make for human capital. We consider them in turn.

(a) *Education.* The kind of knowledge included in human capital is in many ways tacit, something a person acquires and is private to him/her. But as teachers are painfully aware, knowledge isn't costlessly transferable from one person to another; so, education involves costs and should be seen as investment in people.

Knowledge and skills are both ends and means. Reading is a pleasurable activity and thus a form of consumption. The direct benefits of literacy are then reflected in the social value of consumption (consumption's shadow price). But being able to read is also of indirect value: literacy enhances a person's productivity, implying higher earnings and greater access to consumption goods. Education therefore offers joint benefits. There are now well-known techniques for estimating the value of human capital in a society in terms of earnings. Klenow and Rodriguez-Clare (1997), using methods developed by Mincer (1974), offer illustrations of ways to measure human capital in the form of education attainment.

So far I have stressed the benefits someone enjoys from education. They are private benefits. But when someone learns to read and write and becomes numerate, not only does he/she enjoy a benefit, others do too because they can now communicate with that person. The acquisition of education thereby confers 'externalities', a notion that is developed in detail in section 2.6.1. Total benefits of education are the sum of private and external benefits.

(b) *Health*. Health brings both direct and indirect benefits: an absence of pain is one of the defining characteristics of well-being; and other things being equal healthier people are also more productive. Disability lowers productivity, which can be measured in principle and often in practice. At an extreme, malnourished people lack energy and stamina and are at the bottom of the earnings schedule. Improvements in health over time can thus be measured in terms of increased productivity.

Investments over time in a person's health are complementary, in that damage to one's health at an early stage of life cannot easily be compensated for in later years. Although the ability to use knowledge for one's ends is often thought to be 'innate' ('in the genes', as the saying goes today), recent work in developmental biology has found that what goes by the name 'innate ability' is in part acquired and can be traced to a person's early nutritional and disease history. The epidemiological environment of an infant influences the development of her innate ability as she grows into an adult.[6]

Health is a means to a good life. But good health also brings direct benefits. By bringing relief from pain, medication improves the quality of consumption (meals taste better in the absence of a headache!) and thereby an improvement in the quality of life. Medication would thus appear to be a form of consumption.

It is an intriguing and fortunate fact that expenditures that bring relief from pain, or avoid disability, or immunize someone against infectious diseases also help to extend their life. Medication, immunization, and medical treatment thus give rise to joint products: relief from pain and discomfort, greater productivity, and a longer life. In their work on the measurement of wealth, Arrow et al. (2012) estimated the value of enhanced life expectancy in a number of countries during the period 2000–5. Following a review in section 2.4.3 of the steps needed to estimate shadow prices, their methods are reproduced in Appendix 1.

[6] For a recent overview of the subject, see Dasgupta (2012b).

I have so far classified the benefits an individual enjoys from an improvement in his/her health. But when someone is immunized against an infectious disease, not only does that person enjoy the benefits, others do too, because they are now less likely to catch the disease. So, immunization confers 'externalities', a phenomenon studied in section 2.6.1. Those 'external' benefits should be added to private benefits if we are to estimate the total benefits of health improvements.

(3) *Natural capital* (local ecosystems, biomes, sub-soil resources). Natural capital is of direct use in consumption (fisheries), of indirect use as inputs in production (oil and natural gas; the wide array of ecosystem services), and of use in both (air and water). The value of a resource may be *utilitarian* (as a source of food, or as a keystone species)—many people call this its *use-value*; it may be *aesthetic* (places of scenic beauty), or it may be *intrinsic* (primates). It may be all these things (biodiversity). Their worth to us could be from extraction (timber, gum, honey, leaves, and barks) or from their presence as a stock (forest cover), or from both (watershed). The stock could be an index of quality (air quality) or quantity. Quantity is sometimes expressed as a pure number (population size); in various other cases it is, respectively, (bio)mass, area, volume, depth. But even quality indices are often based on quantity indices, as in 'parts per cubic centimetres' for measuring atmospheric haze.

Ecosystems are one large aspect of natural capital. They provide innumerable services to us. Among the visible products are food, fibres, fuel, and fresh water, but many remain hidden from view. Among other things, ecosystems maintain a genetic library, preserve and regenerate soil, fix nitrogen and carbon, recycle nutrients, control floods, mitigate droughts, filter pollutants, assimilate waste, pollinate crops, operate the hydrological cycle, and maintain the gaseous composition of the atmosphere. As those services are not visible, it is easy to overlook them. However, with some ingenuity it is possible to estimate the benefits we enjoy from them. In this section I report some of those findings.

Ecosystems offer joint products: wetlands recycle nutrients and produce purified water; mangrove forests protect coastal land from storms and are spawning grounds for fish; and so on. Unhappily, social tensions arise in those many cases where an ecosystem has competing uses (farms versus forests versus urban development; forests versus agro-ecosystems; coastal fisheries versus aquaculture). As natural capital is a mesh of resources, what one means by an ecosystem is usually influenced by the scope of the problem being studied. A number of ecosystems have a near global reach ('biomes', such as the Savannah), some cover entire regions (river basins), many involve clusters of villages (micro-watersheds), while others are confined to the level of a single village (the village pond). The tropics harbour some of the most fragile environments. Hassan et al. (2005) and Reid et al. (2005) contain a classification of ecosystems. They also provide an account of the stresses that are being experienced by both global and local ecosystems.

Environmental pollutants are the reverse of natural resources. In some cases the emission of pollutants amounts directly to the depreciation of reproducible capital (corrosion of material infrastructure). In others it means a degradation of ecosystems (eutrophication of lakes). Roughly speaking 'resources' are 'goods', many being sinks into which pollutants are discharged (rivers, the atmosphere, and the oceans are among the sinks); while 'pollutants' (the degrader of resources) are 'bads'. Pollution is the other side of conservation.[7]

In a far reaching publication, the MEA (MEA, 2003) studied the state of the world's *ecosystems*. The authors created a four-way classification of ecosystem services: (i) *provisioning* services (food, fibre, fuel, fresh water); (ii) *regulating* services (protection against natural hazards such as storms; the climate system); (iii) *supporting* services (nutrient cycling, soil production); and (iv) *cultural* services (recreation, cultural landscapes, aesthetic or spiritual experiences). Provisioning and cultural services and a variety of regulating services (such as disease regulation) contribute directly to human well-being, whereas supporting services (soil production) contribute indirectly (by providing the means of growing food crops). As these services are frequently in competition with one another, choices have to be made. The long history of agriculture is one where ecosystems were transformed from supplying regulating and supporting services to supplying provisioning services. More familiar is the large scale process by which ecosystems are being destroyed for industrialization and urbanization.

(4) *Population* (size and demographic profile). Conceptually, this category raises the deepest problems, because people are both the reason well-being should occupy the ethical core of sustainability and policy analyses and the means to the realization of well-being. Arrow et al. (2003) showed that estimating shadow prices of populations poses especial problems. However, population in economic models is frequently assumed to be an exogenous function of time. Under that assumption it is possible to show that population can be included in economic evaluation by replacing wealth by wealth per capita (Dasgupta, 2001 [2004]; Arrow et al., 2012). That is the route we adopt here. Proposition 1 can then be restated as

> Proposition 4: wealth per capita and social well-being mutually track one another: per capita wealth increases if and only if social well-being increases.

It is as well to illustrate Proposition 4's significance.

[7] This classification was explored in Dasgupta (1982).

Imagine a closed economy with constant population. In a given year, it invests $5 billion in reproducible capital and human capital. However, natural capital is depleted and degraded by $6 billion (all expressed in shadow prices of course!). Owing to the disinvestment, the economy's wealth will have declined over the year by $1 billion. Proposition 1 says development was unsustainable that year. The example also shows that GDP is unsuitable to serve as a criterion by which to judge sustainability. It also shows why HDI is unsuitable. Neither records the depreciation of capital (Appendix 3). Crude estimates suggest that during 1970–2000 wealth per capita in a number of countries in sub-Saharan Africa and South Asia declined even though GDP per capita rose and HDI improved (Dasgupta, 2001 [2004]).

There are three further categories of goods that are components of an economy's productive base but which, for reasons that will be shown, should *not* be included on our list of capital assets in Propositions 1–4.

2.3.2 *Knowledge*

Science and technology, and the arts and humanities are commonly regarded as capital assets. The category includes such objects as nature's laws, abstract theorems, formulae, algorithms, and historical and cultural narratives. They are durable, intangible public goods (once discovered, they are in principle there for all to use, repeatedly).

Many people regard knowledge to be the most significant feature of our productive base. Note though that for someone to make use of a piece of knowledge, three conditions must be met: (i) a recognition by the person that the knowledge exists; (ii) the person should have the relevant skills (human capital!); and (iii) there should be no legal or social barrier to applying the knowledge. Research and development involves investments that advance codified knowledge. Frequently though, knowledge can be obtained freely from external sources (for example, once patents have expired). These aspects of knowledge suggest that its instrumental role lies in conferring value to other forms of assets. Before the advent of the iron-age, for example, iron ore was of little value. But once the art of extracting the ore and converting it into useable iron was discovered, the ore acquired value. Its shadow price rose.

Knowledge is not an asset that directly enters the formula for wealth in equation (1); instead, it enters the formula via the shadow prices of those assets that do enter the formula, namely, reproducible, human, and natural capital. The models in Appendices 1 and 2 explain how. Arrow et al. (2012) demonstrate a practical way to incorporate gains in knowledge in the structure of shadow prices.

Some kinds of knowledge are also consumption goods. Contemplating a beautiful idea enhances well-being directly, as does reading literature. Such knowledge has direct value.

2.3.3 *Time*

A society's productive base can change, for the better or worse, simply because of the passage of time. Consider a small oil exporting country. Being small, the country has no control over international oil prices. Meanwhile, or so let us imagine, an oil cartel, of which our country is not a member, raises the price of oil on a continual basis. Our country therefore enjoys capital gains on its reserves without having to engage in any form of capital accumulation. Its productive base expands.[8] Similarly, it could be that the country enjoys an expansion of its knowledge base by deploying scientific advances elsewhere without paying for that privilege. In both circumstances our country enjoys an expansion of its productive base simply by waiting. Its wealth increases correspondingly. Recall that in equation (1), the shadow price of an asset was regarded in principle to be a function of time. Like increases in knowledge, the passage of time in itself can influence the structure of shadow prices.

2.3.4 *Institutions*

What about institutions? When scholars try to understand the progress or regress of societies, it is not uncommon today to refer to 'religious capital', 'social capital', 'cultural capital', and more broadly 'institutional capital'. Nevertheless, as in the case of knowledge and time, institutions should not be regarded as a form of asset in sustainability and policy analyses. Let us see why.

Institutions are the myriad of formal and informal arrangements among people influencing the allocation of resources, both at a moment in time and through time. Households, firms, communities, and the state are obvious examples of institutions. But institutions also include a broader kind of 'enabling' assets, such as the rule of law, social norms of behaviour, and habitual social practices.

How do institutions enter sustainability and policy analyses? They do so by influencing the value of other capital assets. Suppose the state apparatus in a country is corrupt, in particular the judicial system is unreliable. Because people find it difficult to protect their property rights, the value of the assets

[8] The same logic says that, other things being equal, an oil importing country would find its productive base shrinking as the international price of oil rose over time.

they own is small, other things being equal. Corruption reduces the social worth of assets.[9]

Institutions influence the composition of consumption and saving and the character of future institutions. There are institutions that foster progress by having in place a structure of incentives that encourage people to allocate goods and services in their most productive uses. But institutions aren't enough. If societies are to progress, people must trust one another and have confidence in their institutions. Well developed competitive markets, tight social norms, and codes of conduct, and good governance together can combine to help create and maintain trust and confidence. But mutual trust and the cooperation that can result from it can't be guaranteed even under sound institutions. Opportunistic behaviour can beget opportunistic behaviour. Institutions can founder under a cascade of opportunism unless there are checks and balances in place by virtue of the presence of a mesh of countervailing institutions.[10]

Institutions aren't static. Just as they influence the allocation of resources, the allocation of resources influences the evolution of institutions. Lipset (1959), for example, has argued that economic development fosters democracy. A good theory of political economy would include an account of the mutual influence of institutions, preferences, human motivations, and the productive base of an economy.

A prime example of the mutual influence of institutions and economic development is provided by financial institutions. Expansion of financial institutions helped initiate economic development in late medieval Europe. By the same token, the technological changes that have accompanied economic growth over the centuries have encouraged the creation of new financial institutions; but not necessarily for the better. Ideal financial markets would not suffer the way countries have suffered recently; in practice, however, financial markets create externalities (discussed further). Currently they have given rise to severely detrimental externalities.

Financial institutions create and legitimize financial capital. However, the latter should not be regarded as a separate category of assets. Financial capital consists of claims to capital assets, nothing more. Someone who owns shares in a firm has claim to a share of the market value of the firm. That person's shares reflect the market value of the assets to which he/she has claim. The same holds for currency and bonds. They are claims to whatever bundle of goods and services the shareholder wishes to have, subject only to the market value of the bundle not exceeding the value of the currency and bonds he

[9] No doubt the purpose of corrupt practice is to enhance the market worth of assets owned by the practitioner. In the text we are referring to the *social* worth of assets.

[10] On the role of trust in sustainable development, see Dasgupta (2011).

holds. To include financial capital in the wealth of nations would be to overcount hopelessly.

2.4 Shadow Prices

Propositions 1–4 tell us that social well-being and an economy's stock of capital assets are linked by shadow prices (Definition 2). Shadow prices have been widely discussed in policy analyses. The theory of social cost benefit analysis contained techniques for estimating shadow prices of consumption and investment flows (Little and Mirrlees, 1968, 1974; and a series of applied studies based on them). Propositions 1 and 2 say that shadow prices are useful in sustainability analysis as well.

2.4.1 *Externalities*

How are shadow prices related to market prices? In idealized circumstances, an asset's shadow price equals its market price. In normal circumstances, however, the two sets of prices differ. By 'normal circumstances' I mean circumstances in which individual actions give rise to externalities, a class of phenomena that are ubiquitous in the economies we have come to know, because markets for many commodities either do not exist (say, because property rights to them are weak) or are not competitive when they do exist. *Externalities are the differences between shadow prices and market prices* (equation (2)).

Externalities are rampant when we put environmental resources to use because property rights to prominent classes of environmental resources are difficult to enforce, often impossible even to define. By 'property rights' we should mean not only private property rights, but also communitarian rights, even national rights. One reason property rights to various types of environmental resources are weak is their mobility. The wind blows, rivers flow, fish swim, deer flee, birds and insects fly, and even earthworms are known to move. Property rights to an object are difficult to enforce if you cannot harness it.

To illustrate, consider that the oceans beyond national jurisdiction are open to all. The absence of property rights to the fisheries there means that firms are not required to pay a fee for the fish they harvest. But the fisheries harbour finite stocks and have a positive value. So there is overfishing in the open seas. That in turn implies that the price of fish in the market is less than its shadow price.

Carbon in the atmosphere raises the reverse problem. People currently don't have to pay anything for the right to emit the carbon they generate at home. However, worldwide further additions to the stock of carbon in the atmosphere would have a negative value. The market price of carbon in the atmosphere is zero, even though its shadow price is negative. We can therefore be confident that carbon emissions are excessive, from which it follows that consumption goods with embedded carbon are priced lower than they should be.

2.4.2 *Scarcity and Time*

Capital assets are the source of the consumption services we enjoy. Because social well-being depends on the distribution of well-being among contemporaries and among the generations, shadow prices reflect distributional considerations too. The shadow price of an asset in the hands of someone needy would be higher than the shadow price of that same asset if it were in the hands of someone well-off, other things being equal.

Economic forecasts include future scarcities of goods and services. Those scarcities are reflected in shadow prices. Moreover, the greater is the weight placed on future well-being in the conception of social well-being, the larger would be the influence of future scarcities on today's shadow prices. It follows that the shadow price of, say, an environmental resource depends on the degree to which other capital assets can substitute for it in production, not only today, but in the future as well. Other things being equal, the smaller are those substitution possibilities; the larger is the shadow price of the resource.

2.4.3 *Estimating Shadow Prices*

Three pieces of information are required for estimating shadow prices:

(1) A descriptive model of the economy moving through time, including not only technological possibilities and ecological processes, but also preferences, tastes, personal and social values, and policies.
(2) The size and distribution of the economy's capital assets at the date at which the economic evaluation is undertaken.
(3) A conception of social well-being.

Forecasts are not mere guesses. If they are to carry conviction, forecasts should be based on a defendable theory of the social and natural processes that shape a society's future. A good forecast would be based on requirements (1) and (2) above. Information on (2) can be used in (1) to track the economy into and over the future. Recall Definition 2. It says shadow prices are based on counter-factuals: they are determined not only by the forecast of the shape of things to come, but also by forecasts of future development were the current portfolio of capital assets to have been otherwise. If they are to carry conviction, economic forecasts need to be based on a defendable theory of the evolving political economy shaping the society under study. The formal model in Appendix 2 shows how requirements (1)–(3) can be met by the social evaluator.

As noted previously, externalities create gaps between shadow prices and market prices. If $R_i(t)$ is the market price of asset i at t, $E_i(t)$ is the social value of the externalities generated by i's use at t, and $P_i(t)$ is the market price of i at t, then

$$P_i(t) = R_i(t) + E_i(t). \tag{3}$$

$E_i(t)$ embodies the externalities generated by i at t over the future. To cite an example of much current interest, consider that a further addition to the stock of carbon in the atmosphere today will have effects (the externalities) lasting many years. If asset $K_i(t)$ denotes the stock of carbon in the atmosphere at time t, $E_i(t)$ would reflect those effects. If increased concentration of carbon in the atmosphere is predicted to be bad for the economy in question, $E_i(t) < 0$. If carbon emissions are not taxed, $R_i(t) = 0$. In that case $P_i(t) = E_i(t) < 0$.

In estimating shadow prices there should be no presumption that the economy is on an optimum trajectory (Dasgupta, Marglin, and Sen, 1972). The prices ought to be estimated on the basis of the social evaluator's economic forecast (his/her response to question C). To illustrate, consider woodland. Among other things, woodland is the habitat for insects and birds. Agriculture benefits from pollination. If an economy's development path is forecast to be rapacious of its woodlands, there will be acute scarcity of woodlands in the future. The woodland's shadow price today would be high, other things being equal. Shadow prices contain a great deal of information about the economy's prospects.

2.4.4 *Common Misconception*

Wealth is a weighted sum of an economy's stock of capital assets (equation (1)). Shadow prices are the weights. They are the rates at which assets substitute for one another in the measure of wealth. There are scholars (Daly et al., 2007) who worry that the linear form of wealth hides an awkward assumption, that reproducible and human capital are always able to substitute for natural capital.

The worry is based on a misconception. Proposition 1 has no empirical content, it is an equivalence relationship. The Proposition offers a tool for sustainability analysis. It says that if the social evaluator seeks to know whether an economy is on a path of sustainable development, he/she should keep track of the economy's wealth, it says nothing more. Proposition 1 doesn't presume that capital assets can substitute for one another in production or consumption, nor does it insist they are complements. The presence or absence of substitution possibilities in production and consumption among various categories of capital assets enter sustainability analysis via shadow prices. Imagine, for example, that asset h is a form of natural capital that is now close to a dangerously low level, crossing which would prove catastrophic to the economy. Suppose too that the exact point at which the threshold would be crossed is unknown. In such a case, if $h+1$ is a run-of-the-mill asset, $P_h(t)/P_{h+1}(t)$ would be a gigantic number; so large, perhaps, that it wouldn't be possible to accumulate sufficient quantities of $h+1$ as compensation for any further decline in the stock of h.[11]

2.4.5 *Net Domestic Product and the Bounds of Consumption*

The reason GDP is unsuitable for either sustainability or policy analysis is that it doesn't record the depreciation of capital. But what about *net domestic product* (NDP)?

NDP is GDP minus capital depreciation; or to put it equivalently, NDP is consumption plus *net* investment. The word 'investment' could be thought to embody a sense of robust activism, but that's only because national income statisticians have traditionally limited the term's use to the accumulation of reproducible capital. We have found it necessary to extend the notion of capital beyond reproducible assets to include human capital and natural capital. So we are obliged to stretch our intuitive notion of 'investment' to include the growth of natural capital; which means, for example, that to leave a forest unmolested is to invest in the forest. By 'net investment' in asset i we simply mean the value of the net change in the stock of i at t: $P_i(\mathbf{K}(t),t)\mathrm{d}K_i(t)/\mathrm{d}t$.

As previously, let social well-being be *numeraire*. If $C(t)$ is aggregate consumption and $Q(t)$ is the shadow price of consumption,

$$(NDP)_t = Q(t)C(t) + {}_i\sum P_i(\mathbf{K}(t), t)\mathrm{d}K_i/\mathrm{d}t. \tag{4}$$

If population changes at a constant rate, we interpret $C(t)$ as per capita consumption and net investment as the value of net changes in per capita capital assets. Now recall Proposition 2. Equation (4) allows us to recast it as

Proposition 5: $\mathrm{d}V(t)/\mathrm{d}t \geq 0$ if and only if $C(t) \leq (NDP)_t/Q(t)$.

Proposition 5 contains the ethical significance of net domestic product. It says that *NDP is the upper bound for aggregate consumption if development is to be sustainable.*[12] Propositions 2 and 5 display the connection between a nation's income accounts and its capital accounts.

[11] The remarks here have been adapted from Arrow et al. (2007), which was a reply to Daly et al. (2007).

[12] An early version of the Proposition was proved by Solow (1974) and Hartwick (1977).

2.5 Eliciting Well-Being

Two fundamental questions have been embedded in our account of sustainability analysis:

(1) What are the determinants of human well-being?
(2) How can social well-being be retrieved from available data?

2.5.1 *Direct and Indirect Methods*

Scholars have studied the determinants by asking variously

(i) What is the human good?
(ii) What do people care about?
(iii) What do people say when asked how they are, or how they feel?
(iv) What considerations do people take into account when choosing?
(v) What do they choose?

It is tempting to assume that one can move seamlessly from (i) to (v). But (i) is a deep question in ethics, while (ii) is prompted by the need to understand human desires and aspirations, whereas (iii) is about the responses people make to questionnaires, and (iv) and (v) involve the psychology and sociology of behaviour. There are potential bottlenecks at each link in the chain leading from (i) to (v), although much of the economics literature moves between them without much pause. The theory of 'revealed preference', for example, tells the investigator to postulate the form of an answer to question (ii), study data on (v), and draw conclusions about the structure of the postulated answer to question (ii). Applications of revealed preference theory are rather like reverse engineering. But with a difference: the econometric methods that are almost always deployed for drawing conclusions about the structure of the postulated answer to (ii) are such that it isn't possible to judge whether the postulate was correct to begin with. This is a matter to which I return.

Even so, why waste time measuring well-being indirectly via the factors that influence it, why not measure the thing itself?

2.5.2 *Happiness Surveys*

The reason is that measuring well-being directly, say, through questionnaires, is limiting. Large scale surveys, such as the World Values Survey, the Euro-Barometer, and Gallup, which publish responses people give to questions regarding their sense of well-being (e.g. how happy or secure they feel or how trustworthy they regard others to be) provide useful information, but are too coarse-grained for use in economic evaluation. Thousands of

Americans, for example, have been asked every year or two since 1972 the question 'Taken all together, how would you say things are these days—would you say that you are very happy, pretty happy, or not too happy?' In the Gallup World Poll, which was conducted during 2005–9, randomly chosen subjects in 155 countries were asked to reflect on their overall satisfaction with life on a score of one to ten. Those who responded with a high score were classified as 'thriving'. Respondents were also asked to recall how they had felt the previous day—whether they had felt well respected, free from pain, intellectually engaged, well rested, and so forth. Answers to those questions enabled researchers to score the subjects' daily experiences. The percentage of people who were found to be thriving on a combined index based on those scores was then used to rank countries in terms of what has been called Gallup's 'happiness index'. Happiness indices aggregate personal well-beings and equate personal well-being with reported expressions of happiness.

In view of the scope of the questions posed in the surveys, there should be little surprise that the findings are not entirely consistent with one another, nor that they haven't revealed fine-grained features of the human experience. On large-scale matters, though, the surveys have proved illuminating. They have shown that a person's income influences his/her state of mind (the poor are less happy than the rich), that personal security and political participation matter, that being unemployed or suffering from chronic pain are sources of much unhappiness, and that societies are happier where people are more involved in civic activities. Surprisingly, the surveys have found that affluent societies haven't become much happier even though over the decades their incomes have grown.[13]

The findings offer guidance to governments. They tell us, for example, that people care about their place in the distribution of income (perhaps we equate income with status), that unconditional growth in GDP should not be a social goal, that protection against physical and mental insults raises happiness, and that civic life is a good thing. But they don't say how governments are to identify good forestry policies or how to decide whether permission should be granted for converting mangroves into shrimp farms. As always, the Devil is in the details; and as economic evaluation is in great measure a study of details, happiness surveys are of little use there.

Whether happiness should be included in discourses on human well-being depends on the purpose of the exercise. There are democratic theories that don't see the state's business as being concerned with citizens' happiness; they see it rather as ensuring that citizens' material needs and freedoms are met.

[13] Layard (2005), Clark et al. (2008), Bok (2009), and Graham (2009) contain accounts of the various surveys on happiness.

Devising personal projects and advancing one's purposes is the individual's business, not the state's; or so the argument goes.[14]

That said, ethical theories that ignore experiential states are of limited value. It would be distinctly odd if we were to value the formation of the capacity to prepare life plans but were indifferent to its realization and the experiential states that go with its realization. Seeking happiness would seem to be a deep-felt need among humans. But that only means questions (iv) and (v) on the list in section 2.5.1 are pertinent in economic evaluation. Observing what people choose and do under different circumstances is one route to addressing question (ii).

2.5.3 *Stated and Revealed Preferences*

People's responses to questions regarding their 'willingness-to-pay' for specific non-market goods can reveal information of direct use to the social evaluator. In democratic societies local governments are obliged to determine the extent to which citizens care about local public goods such as libraries, parks, and street lights. Usually 'willingness-to-pay' is expressed in monetary units (i.e. in terms of specific bundles of marketed goods and services). Survey methods and statistical techniques such as Contingent Valuation Methods (CVMs) have been developed by environmental economists to elicit citizens' willingness-to-pay for the conservation of natural habitats—wetlands, lakes, woodlands, and so forth. Economists have also used prices of real estate to estimate the additional price residents have revealed as being willing to pay for residing in locations with more agreeable surroundings (this is the 'hedonic price' method of eliciting preferences over the quality of residential location). Non-governmental organizations use such information as weapons against moves to transform natural habitats into industrial parks.

But there are caveats. The new behavioural economics has recorded that people are frequently inconsistent in their choices, make simple computational errors, and are bad at probabilistic judgments. Survey methods such as CVMs have come under heavy criticism for their ambiguity (Hausman, 2012). However, surveys have also revealed unexpected features in our values that should inform social ethics, they should not be regarded as ambiguities. People appear to have a more refined notion of what is meant by a commodity than is suggested in economics textbooks. For example, the willingness to pay (for preservation of an object of desire) has been found in surveys to differ substantially from the willingness to receive (in compensation for destruction of that same object). There is evidence too that we value objects especially if

[14] Rawls (1972).

we possess them: we demand more in compensation for parting with an object than we are willing to pay for obtaining that same object, a fact that should influence our notions of distributive justice.

The distinction between the constituents of well-being and the factors that determine well-being is blurred in the case of some items. Is education a constituent of well-being or is it a factor influencing well-being? One can argue it is both. The acquisition of education is partly an end in itself and partly a means to increasing future incomes by improving skills. Aristotelian ethics emphasizes the former, while the economics of 'human capital' lays stress on the latter. That education has both flavours doesn't pose a problem so long as we are able to track the two and their contributions to well-being. Double-counting is a virtue when a 'commodity' offers joint benefits. Education ought to be counted twice. The same can be said of health.

2.5.4 *Human Traits*

By far the most common stance among economists in the search for what people care about ((ii) in the list in section 2.5.1) is to begin by postulating the character of human motivation. The move from there is to derive testable implications of the postulate in well-defined environments (e.g. in market democracies) and study behavioural data (e.g. market data and voting records) for support and for determining the relative weights people award to the various objects of choice.

In contemporary economics far and away the most common postulate regarding human traits is that people are egotists.[15] By an egotist I mean someone whose well-being depends only on his or her consumption of goods and services. If the person's choices are guided solely by his/her sense of personal well-being, his/her demand for goods and services would be a function of market prices and that person's wealth, nothing else.[16]

The problem with the assumption is that vast quantities of evidence in anthropology, psychology, and sociology run counter to it. That may explain why critics have characterized the individual in contemporary economics as 'deracinated, alienated, atomized—a balloon tethered to nothing'. A possible claim that the motivations of the egotist reflect his/her 'rational self-interest' has been dismissed by many scholars on grounds that they can't reflect the

[15] The most up-to-date account of the vast empirical literature on the consumption and saving behaviour of egotists is in Attanasio and Weber (2010). A special session at the 2011 annual conference of the Royal Economic Society was devoted to revealed preference theory as applied to egotists. See Vermeulen (2012).

[16] The unit under study in the standard model is not so much a person as a household, because consumption data are usually obtained at the level of households. The standard model sees households as being entirely asocial.

egotist's rational self-interest, as there is no adequate 'self' for such a person to be. There was enormous insight in the late Mary Douglas' observation that poverty is when you cannot afford to invite your neighbour to tea.[17]

In section 2.6 I begin by sketching the egotist's motivations (see also the Introduction by the editors). I then study the way the acquisition of taste for certain goods can be modelled formally. In section 2.7 I study two sorts of social traits in the human person, namely, the competitive urge (e.g. the desire for status) and the need to 'belong' (e.g. conformism). It is shown that they have very different policy implications.

It helps to imagine a timeless economy. For expositional ease that is what I do here. But in each case I embed the timeless model in an inter-temporal setting to show when and how *consumption history* matters in the long run.

2.6 Consumer Motivation, 1: Autonomous Effects

Economic textbooks concentrate on the doings of the egotist. For completeness I provide an outline of the model before developing extensions.

2.6.1 *The Egotist*

We suppose there are M consumption goods and services (labelled $m = 1,2,\ldots,M$) and confine ourselves to a representative person in the economy. Let $\boldsymbol{C}$ denote that person's consumption bundle $\{C_1,\ldots,C_m,\ldots,C_M\}$. His/her well-being, U, is understood to be an increasing function of every component of $\boldsymbol{C}$. If $\boldsymbol{Q}$ is the vector of market prices and I is the person's income (in an inter-temporal model, this would be his/her wealth), that individual's demand for goods and services can be obtained from the solution to the following:

Choose $\boldsymbol{C}$ so as to maximize $U(\boldsymbol{C})$, subject to ${}_m\sum Q_mC_m \le I$. (5)

Problem (5) yields the optimality conditions

$$\partial U/\partial C_m = \mu Q_m,\ \text{for}\ m = 1,\ldots,M;\ \mu > 0,$$

$${}_m\sum Q_mC_m = I. \tag{6}$$

Equations (5) and (6) are $M+1$ in number and there are $M+1$ unknowns, $\{Q_1,\ldots,Q_M\}$ and μ. Assuming it is unique, the solution yields the individual's

[17] Bourdieu (1984) is the modern classic on humans as social creatures. For a remarkable body of applied work in which human motivation is read to be otherwise than that of the egotist, see Douglas and Isherwood (1996), Warde (1997), Warde and Marten (2000), Warde and Southerton (2012), and Southerton, Olsen, and Warde (2012). The authors study data on food, clothing, and reading habits, respectively. The editors describe that literature in their Introduction.

demand functions $C_m(Q,I)$, one for each commodity. That's person's consumption of m is then predicted to be $C_m(Q,I)$. The idea is to estimate $C_m(Q,I)$ for each m on the basis of consumption behaviour observed in the market, and then infer the U-function. That's the reverse engineering I mentioned earlier.

In what follows I consider three extensions of the standard model.

2.6.2 *Unidirectional Externalities in the Acquisition of Taste*

One extension incorporates 'learning', a notion that has a number of interpretations.[18] What is common among them all is that a person's past selves influence his/her current self's demand for goods and services. Of particular interest is the case where the person acquires a taste for a commodity.

Consider someone who is aware that by consuming commodity 1 he/she would acquire a taste for it. Let Z_1 be an index of that person's past consumption of the good (say a weighted sum of his/her past consumption levels). We are now to imagine that the person's well-being over goods at a point in time is given by the function $U(C,Z_1)$. As previously, I assume that the person's consumption preferences are consonant with his/her sense of well-being. U is taken to be an increasing function of each of the components of C. To make the consumption of commodity 1 have 'bite', we assume that U satisfies

$$\partial U(C, Z_1)/\partial C_1 + \partial U(C, Z_1)/\partial Z_1 > 0, \qquad (7)$$

which means that if the person were to have enjoyed a higher uniformly maintained level of consumption of good 1, his/her current U would have been higher.

Condition (7) says that consumption of good 1 creates an externality on the person's future selves. Of course, if the person is far sighted, he/she would choose the kind of influence he/she would want to have on his/her future selves. In as much as a person's past selves influence his/her future selves (but not vice versa!), the externalities are unidirectional. There would, however, be no resource allocation failure if the person were far sighted. The person will have internalized those inter-temporal externalities.[19]

Ryder and Heal (1973) embedded the aforementioned model in an intertemporal setting and studied optimum consumption pattern for an immortal person whose instantaneous utility (or well-being) function satisfies condition (7). The authors identified a wide range of cases where the long-run

[18] See Warde and Southerton (2012) and Southerton (2012).

[19] Dependence of one's utility today on past consumption is the basis for 'addiction'. Drazen Prelec (Chapter 7) notes that people differ in their ability to free themselves from the scourge and that people are prone to overestimating their ability to do so.

consumption pattern of the person is a function of his/her consumption history. In cases where long-run consumption patterns are steady states, the dynamical system describing the individual's optimum consumption pattern was found to harbour multiple steady states. It means a pair of consumption histories on different sides of a separatrix can be expected to lead to widely different consumption futures. That is the sense in which history matters.

The Ryder-Heal model is lean and stark. The development of taste is no doubt influenced by the availability of time, a matter that was eschewed by the authors. Differences in the ecological and technological landscape of societies shape differences in culture. The Ryder-Heal model shows, however, that socio-cultural differences can emerge even when there are no differences in the underlying landscapes.

Important forms of resource allocation failure arise when the assets that are important in the production of goods that are subject to the acquisition of taste are underpriced (say, because of a lack of property rights to the assets). Developing a taste for goods that are energy intensive in production and use is salient here. In such cases past consumption of the good reinforces environmental externalities. It is a point to which I return in section 2.8.

2.7 Consumer Motivation, 2: Social Externalities

Far more problematic for the applied economist studying consumption behaviour are reciprocal externalities. We humans are both competitive and social. We want to attain status in our community in certain ways and simultaneously desire to be like others in other ways. These considerations suggest two types of reciprocal consumption externalities. The two are often bracketed in the econometric literature under the heading, 'peer-group effect' (Maurer and Meier, 2008; Kuhn et al., 2011); but they are very different. Let us see why and how.

2.7.1 *Competitive Consumption*

In his classic work on the Gilded Age, Veblen ([1899] 1925) spoke of 'conspicuous consumption' so as to draw attention to consumption as a status symbol (flashy cars, fineries, mansions). If a commodity is to serve as a status symbol, its consumption must be observable by others—hence the double-edged title of Veblen's classic.

Veblen's notion of status has been extended greatly to cover the more general tendency of people to try to out-do the 'Joneses'.[20] To formalize,

[20] See Duesenberry (1949), Leibenstein (1950), Hirsch (1977), Alessie and Kapteyn (1991), Kapteyn et al. (1997), Oswald (1997), Maurer and Meier (2008), and Layard (2005), among many

consider a world with two consumption goods (labelled 1 and 2), of which commodity 1 is 'conspicuous'. We may think of commodity 1 as a 'positional good' (Hirsch, 1977). Commodity 2 is assumed to be 'inconspicuous'. Q_1 and Q_2 are their market prices (in units of well-being). Let C_1* denote the average consumption of good 1 in the economy.

To draw out the implications of competitive consumption in a simple way, assume that the economy consists of a large number, N, of identical people. Write $Y_1 = C_1/C_1^*$. An individual's preferences for consumption goods are represented by

$U(C_1,Y_1,C_2)$, where U is a concave, increasing function of C_1, Y_1, C_2. (8)

The dependence of U on Y_1 (= C_1/C_1^*) reflects the person's competitive motivation. If that indovidual's wealth is W, the problem he/she solves is:

Choose C_1 and C_2 so as to maximise $U(C_1,C_1/C_1^*,C_2)$ subject to the budget constraint $Q_1C_1 + Q_2C_2 \leq W$. (9)

The externality is reciprocal: each person's consumption of commodity 1 affects all other people directly. To be sure, because N is large no one can on their own influence C_1*; but the sum of the infinitesimal influences sums a finite amount, which is why market equilibrium would be inefficient.

Because no one can on their own influence C_1* in a large economy, the representative individual regards it as a parameter. The person's optimum purchases would be characterized by the conditions

$$\partial U/\partial C_1 + (\partial U/\partial Y_1)/C_1^* = \mu Q_1, \mu > 0, \quad (10a)$$

$$\partial U/\partial C_2 = \mu Q_2, \quad (10b)$$

$$Q_1C_1 + Q_2C_2 = W. \quad (10c)$$

The second term on the left hand side of equation (10a), which is positive, represents the externality.

Equations (10a–c) contain three unknowns, C_1, C_2, and μ. Under our assumptions the solution to equations (10a–c) is unique. The person's demand functions are therefore $C_1(Q_1,Q_2,W,C_1^*)$ and $C_2(Q_1,Q_2,W,C_1^*)$. In market equilibrium, $C_1 = C_1^*$ (people are identical, remember).

Now consider the socially ideal allocation. In order to achieve it, each person would be made to take into account his/her (infinitesimal) impact on the average consumption level when purchasing good 1. As noted previously,

others. There is no reason to believe that 'conspicuous consumption' isn't observed among the poor in poor countries Moav and Neeman (2012) contains a nice account.

the sum of the impacts would not be negligible. By regarding N–1 to equal N, we note that the social optimum is given by the conditions

$$\partial U/\partial C_1 + [(\partial U/\partial Y_1)/C_1{}^*](1 - Y_1) = \mu Q_1, \mu > 0, \tag{11a}$$

$$\partial U/\partial C_2 = \mu Q_2, \tag{11b}$$

$$Q_1 C_1 + Q_2 C_2 = W. \tag{11c}$$

In a social optimum $Y_1 = 1$. That means equations (10a) and (11a) differ. In equations (11a–c) the reciprocal externalities are absent because the effect of each individual's consumption on all others has been taken into account.

Comparison of equations (10a–c) and (11a–c) shows there is excessive consumption of commodity 1 in market equilibrium.[21] To put it figuratively, consumers in the market economy are engaged in a 'rat race'. Each person tries to consume more of commodity 1 than the others. Of course, in equilibrium no one is successful in beating the others: as people are identical, all consuming the same quantity. The process creates a 'problem of the commons', albeit in a different sphere from common property resources. Structurally, however, they are the same. They both reflect aspects of the well-known Prisoners' Dilemma in game theory.

How could people be made to take the externalities they impose on others into account when deciding how much to consume? It is a familiar notion in public economics that the way to do that is for the government to impose a consumption tax on commodity 1. Denote the tax by T_1 per unit consumed. The price consumers would have to pay for good 1 would be Q_1+T_1. The trick is to choose T_1 so that equations (10a–c) become identical to equations (11a–c). Public policies are to be chosen in such a way that individual incentives are in line with the realization of the social optimum.

2.7.2 Social Consumption, 1: Fads, Fashions, and Relational Goods

People also adopt patterns of consumption that reflect a desire for conformity. Fads are brief occurrences of such patterns, but conformism can persist if it serves the need for social belonging. We will study how.[22]

Social preferences aren't confined to cases where people merely desire to conform to the group norm. It can be that people want to engage in communal activities and identify certain commodities that serve as focal points. Commodities whose demand is in part subject to social preferences have

[21] A formal proof in a dynamic economy was constructed by Arrow and Dasgupta (2009).

[22] The most thorough econometric investigation into the structure of such preferences is Blume et al. (2011).

been called 'relational goods' (Donati, 2011). Religious expenditures, for example, are built around relational goods. Club goods are other examples. Food and clothing and reading habits would appear to be driven at least in part by social preferences. Conformism plays a role in reproductive behaviour as well (Dasgupta, 1993; Bongaarts and Watkins, 1996; Jensen and Oster, 2009).

To see how social preferences work, consider again a two-good economy. We imagine that social preferences revolve round commodity 2. Let C_2* be its average level of consumption. (More generally, C_2* would be the average consumption of commodity 2 in the group with which the individual we are studying identifies.) Adopting the same notation as previously, we assume that an individual's well-being can be represented by the function U:

$$U(C_1, C_2, C_2^*) = R(C_1, C_2, C_2^*) - \alpha(C_2 - C_2^*)^2, \text{where}$$
$$R \text{ is a concave, increasing function of } C_1, C_2, C_2^*, \text{and } \alpha > 0.\text{[23]} \quad (12)$$

Notice that in equation (12) C_2* appears in the domain of R. That says the economy-wide consumption of commodity 2 is an aspect of the social environment individuals care about. The average level of consumption of commodity 2 is a local public good. The situation being modelled is rather like people wanting to live in a community where dinner parties among neighbours are a social norm, but where no one wants to outshine others in the quality of the food and wine they serve. Common courtesies have to be maintained and standards kept. Put another way, there is not only a desire to join in the communal activity, but also a desire for communal activities, period.

We suppose people choose consumption bundles to further their personal well-being. Population size (N) is large and people are identical. As no one on his/her own can affect C_2*, it is a parameter for the representative person. If W is the person's wealth, and Q_1 and Q_2 are the market prices, his/her optimum choice of C_1 and C_2 satisfy the conditions

$$\partial R/\partial C_1 = \mu Q_1, \mu > 0, \quad (13a)$$

$$\partial R/\partial C_2 - 2\alpha(C_2 - C_2^*) = \mu Q_2, \quad (13b)$$

$$Q_1 C_1 + Q_2 C_2 = W.\text{[24]} \quad (13c)$$

Equations (13a–c) are three in number, and there are three unknowns, C_1, C_2, and μ (the marginal utility of wealth). Under our assumptions the solution is unique.

In market equilibrium, $C_2 = C_2$*. That means equations (13a–c) become

[23] The quadratic loss function, which is what drives people to choose conform over the purchase of commodity 1, has been studied for its usefulness in empirical work by Blume et al. (2011).

[24] I am assuming that the individual chooses to consume both commodities.

$$\partial R/\partial C_1 = \mu Q_1, \mu > 0, \tag{14a}$$

$$\partial R/\partial C_2 = \mu Q_2, \tag{14b}$$

$$Q_1 C_1 + Q_2 C_2 = W.^{25} \tag{14c}$$

The model admits to two kinds of externalities. First, people value $C_2{}^*$ per se, which means market equilibria suffer from a 'public goods' problem. Secondly, as individuals want to relate to others via their consumption of commodity 2, there is a pure consumption externality. The market doesn't register either form of externality. As the population is assumed to be large, the effect of an individual's choice of C_2 on $C_2{}^*$ (the externality) is no doubt small, but the sum of the externalities is non-negligible. Moreover, if α is not too small, there are multiple solutions for equations (14a–c). Furthermore, the equilibria can be ranked in terms of individual well-being. The system here resembles a 'coordination game' in game theory (Dasgupta, 1993; Durlauf and Young, 2004). Owing to the externalities, none of the market equilibria, however, corresponds to the social optimum.[26]

2.7.3 *Social Consumption, 2: Solidarity Goods*

To confirm the above claims in the simplest possible manner, consider a version of equation (12), which reflects in an extreme form the motivation to consume commodities that have been called 'solidarity goods' (Sunstein and Ullmann-Margalit, 2001):

$$U(C_1, C_2, C_2{}^*) = V(C_1), \text{subject to } C_2 = C_2{}^*;$$

V is a (strictly) concave and increasing function of C_1. (15)

The idea underlying U in equation (15) is that some consumption choices (over C_2 in this instance) reflect preferences for consuming as others do and for a society where people enjoy solidarity but not for any particular preference for personal consumption.[27]

If W is an individual's wealth and Q_1 and Q_2 are the market prices, the individual's optimum choice of C_1 and C_2 satisfy the conditions

$$\partial V/\partial C_1 = \mu Q_1, \mu > 0, \tag{16a}$$

$$\rho = \mu Q_2, \rho > 0, \tag{16b}$$

[25] I am assuming that the individual chooses to consume both commodities.

[26] Social optimum is unique because individuals are identical.

[27] The equality constraint in the definition of U in equation (15) is the limiting case of the quadratic loss function in equation (12) when α is infinity.

$$Q_1C_1 + Q_2C_2 = W \tag{16c}$$

$$\rho(C_2 - C_2{}^*) = 0. \tag{16d}$$

Equations (16a–d) are four in number, and there are four unknowns: C_1, C_2, μ (the marginal utility of wealth), and ρ (the shadow price of breaking the constraint $C_2 = C_2{}^*$). Under our assumptions, the solution to the individual's optimization problem is unique.

That the structure of preferences in equation (15) supports multiple, rankable market equilibria is intuitively obvious. If everyone else consumes commodity 1 only, each person would consume only commodity 1; but if everyone else spends some of their wealth on commodity 2, each person would consume that same quantity of commodity 2. There is in fact a continuum of equilibria. It is obvious, too, that equilibria can be ranked in terms of personal preferences. Among them the best has $C_2{}^* = 0$: no one consumes commodity 2.

Providing an incentive to everyone so as to implement the best of all market equilibria would not (at least not in principle) require external enforcement. If people trust one another, a mere agreement would suffice. The problem is one of co-ordination. One way to achieve that assurance would involve 'nudging' one another to opt for a targeted alternative.

2.7.4 *Social Consumption, 3: Social Identity*

The personal need to belong to a community extends to cases where more than one commodity can serve as relational goods. The desire to belong to one's community leads to consumption clusters across communities. Let us see how.

Consider a three-good economy, where the structure of preferences in a world with identical consumers is given by

$$U(C_1, C_2, C_3) = R(C_1, C_2, C_3) - \alpha(C_2 - C_2{}^*)^2 - \beta(C_3 - C_3{}^*)^2,$$

R is a concave, increasing function of C_1, C_2, and C_3; α, $\beta > 0$. (17)

In equation (17) either (or both) of the pair of commodities 2 and 3 can serve as the object of conformism. We may now retrace the reasoning in section 2.7.2 to show that if the coefficients α and β are large, there is a double-multiplicity of market equilibria. In one class of equilibria people co-ordinate mainly on commodity 2, whereas in the other class they co-ordinate on commodity 3. Consider two communities that have co-ordinated at commodities 1 and 2, respectively. Suppose the two commodities differ significantly in their material composition. An external observer would conclude that the economies harbour widely different cultures. But the emergence of the two cultures could have been due to accidents of history, nothing else. We should conclude that it is futile to seek a rationale for all social practices. Some will have no explanation for their presence.

2.7.5 *Implications for Sustainability*

The general point relating our analysis here to the discussion on sustainable development is this: under social preferences the economy could find itself in one of possibly many equilibria. Some equilibria would be more intensive in their use of natural capital than others (frequent air travel for leisure as against joining book clubs). And when we embed the model in a dynamic setting, the figure of history rears itself again here. As in the case of competitive consumption, it is possible that in the past the under-pricing of natural capital served as a focal point for determining which consumption practice got established. Pure analysis cannot tell which consumption pattern once served as a focal point. Chance factor may have played a role. Economies that in the distant past were identical in their fundamentals can look very different today.

Of course, if current consumption influences future preferences, a taste for the relational good would be expected to develop. Even if others were to switch their consumption pattern to an environmentally friendly one, a person's own consumption history would reduce his/her psychological ability to make that same switch. We economists should not expect economic convergence among nations as readily as we do when studying economic development.

2.8 Non-linearities and Externalities[28]

The deleterious effects of environmental and consumption externalities are made urgent by the presence of non-linearities in the processes at work at the consumption–environment nexus. As so many of the non-linearities involve positive feedback (Lenton et al., 2008) environmental stresses are amplified.

That non-linearities are ubiquitous in the processes governing the Earth system is a central message of the environmental sciences (Steffen et al., 2004). That they are inevitable in social systems suffering from harmful environmental externalities is a finding in modern economics (Starrett, 1972). The latter implies that creating competitive markets for externalities as a way of preventing those unintended consequences from occurring is not an option. Taxes

[28] This section is based on Dasgupta and Ehrlich (2012).

and quantity restrictions are a necessary complement to market prices. But instituting taxes and quantity controls requires collective action among affected parties. For that to come about, the parties need to be aware of the character of those externalities. That is beginning to happen in the case of some global commons, especially the atmosphere as a sink for carbon emissions (World Bank, 2010), but to date there have been few studies that estimate the magnitude of consumption externalities and the environmental externalities associated with humanity's use of such biomes as the oceans and tropical forests. What we do have are not much more than guesses.

At local levels non-linearities have played havoc throughout history. Sharp reductions in the productivity of the local natural resource base caused populations to migrate to unfamiliar and risky terrains. However, in days when human population was thin and consumption was low relative to Earth's then capacity, the non-linearities in coupled human–nature systems were globally less pronounced than they are now. Matters are different today, as we push against strong non-linearities operating at the global level. Moreover, non-linearities in human–nature systems are increasingly coupled with one another across space and time through trade in goods and services. That has aggravated problems by making individual risks overly correlated with one another. Because non-linear systems can undergo regime shifts, lead times from recognition by a society that part of their system is near a tipping point to it tipping into an unpalatable state are increasingly short. Currently, over 45 per cent of the 45–60 billion metric tons of carbon that are harnessed annually by terrestrial photosynthesis is being appropriated for human use (Vitousek et al., 1986, 1997). Fifteen of the 24 major ecosystem services examined in the MEA were found to be either degraded or currently subject to unsustainable use (MEA, 2003). Globally, sustainable development is very unlikely to be achievable without measures that correct for the environmental and consumption externalities that have been studied here.

It is often suggested that technology can be relied upon to come to humanity's aid (Ridley, 2010). But new technologies do not appear out of thin air. Innovators respond to incentives; institutions matter. The under-pricing of natural capital is salient here, because it influences the direction of research and development. The latter in turn influences the character of technological change. Because nature's services are under-priced in the market, innovators have little reason to economize on their use. We should not be surprised when new technologies are rapacious in the use of natural capital. The cumulative adoption of such technologies and practices over the centuries has locked us into an infrastructure that will prove very hard to dislodge. The fixity of accumulated capital locks us in. Spill-over in research and development is yet another kind of externality. The need for subsidies for research and development in 'clean' technologies is a necessary corollary.

In any event, we should be sceptical of any theory of economic progress that places an overwhelming burden on an experience not much more than 250 years old. Extrapolation into the past is a sobering exercise: over the long haul of history (a 5000 years stretch, say, up to about 250 years ago), economic growth even in the currently-rich regions was for most of the time not much above zero. Until 1500 CE most people lived under the proverbial $2 a day and world population remained well under a billion. We live in a very different world now.

Appendix 1: Wealth as Criterion Function in Economic Evaluation

The evaluation exercise is assumed to take place at date t (≥ 0), where t is taken to be continuous. Both sustainability and policy analyses require the social evaluator to consider the inter-generational distribution of well-being. In order to simplify the exposition, I assume there is a single consumption good, C. There are J people in the economy ($j = 1,2,\ldots,J$). The distribution of consumption at date t is $\mathbf{C} = \{C_1,\ldots,C_j,\ldots,C_J\}$. We will keep the model very general by simply assuming that the flow of societal well-being at date s ($\geq t$) is $U(\mathbf{C}(s))$. The formulation accommodates in turn egotistical, competitive, and social preferences.

There are N capital assets. Let $K_i(t)$ denote the quantity of the ith asset ($i = 1,2,\ldots,N$). As in the text, we write the vector of capital assets as $\mathbf{K}(t)$. An economic forecast at t is a pair of functions $\{\mathbf{C}(s), \mathbf{K}(s)\}$, $s \geq t$. Recall the discussion in sections 2.2–2.4. At t the economy inherits $\mathbf{K}(t)$. The basis of an economic forecast at t is a (one–one) mapping from possible $\mathbf{K}(t)$s to the set of possible sequences $\{\mathbf{K}(s)\}$ for $s \geq t$.[29] Actual forecasts require that forecaster to considered counter-factuals (what would my forecast be if the vector of assets at t was otherwise?). I demonstrate that in Appendix 2 with the help of a simple model.

Let $V(t)$ denote social well-being at t. For the purposes of illustration we take $V(t)$ to be of the 'utilitarian' form

$$V(t) = \int_t^\infty [U(\mathbf{C}(s))e^{-\delta(s-t)}]ds, \delta > 0. \qquad \text{(A1.1)}$$

Assume that the integral exists. Equation (A1.1) reflects the ethical calculus with which we address the questions with which we started (section 2.2: questions (A)–(E)).

Including as it does both current and future flows of well-being, $V(t)$ is a stock. As the future is uncertain, the social evaluator's interpretation and attitude toward that uncertainty is assumed to have been incorporated in $V(t)$, via the Us.

For simplicity of exposition I assume the socio-ecological system under study is time-autonomous. It follows that social well-being at t can be expressed as $V(\mathbf{K}(t))$.[30] In order to maintain symmetry among the various goods and services, we will measure all

[29] Dasgupta and Maler (2000) called that mapping 'resource allocation mechanism'.
[30] For an account of systems that are non-autonomous, see Arrow et al. (2012).

shadow prices in terms of social well-being V. Let $Q_j(t)$ denote the shadow price of person j's consumption at t. From equation (A1.1) it follows that

$$Q_j(t) = \partial U(\mathbf{C}(t))/\partial C_j(t), \tag{A1.2}$$

Let Δ denote a small perturbation. Assuming V is differentiable, we have

$$\Delta V(\boldsymbol{K}(t)) =_i\sum[\partial V/\partial K_i(t)]\Delta K_i(t).^{31} \tag{A1.3}$$

Define $P_i(\boldsymbol{K}(t))$ as

$$P_i(\boldsymbol{K}(t)) = \partial V/\partial K_i(t). \tag{A1.4}$$

$P_i(\boldsymbol{K}(t))$ is the shadow price of asset i.

It proves instructive to study the relationship between $Q(s)$ for all $s \geq t$ and $P_i(\boldsymbol{K}(t))$. Imagine the economy receives $\Delta K_i(t)$ units of asset i at t free of charge. The gift perturbs the economy over time. To calculate the perturbation, use equation (A1.1) to obtain

$$[\partial V/\partial K_i(t)]\Delta K_i(t) = \int_t^{\infty}\{[_j\sum \Delta U/\Delta C_j(s)]\Delta C_j(s)\}e^{-\delta(s-t)}ds. \tag{A1.5}$$

Using equations (A1.2) and (A1.4), equation (A1.5) can be re-expressed as

$$P_i(\boldsymbol{K}(t))\Delta K_i(t) = \int_t^{\infty}[_j\sum Q_j(s)\Delta C_j(s)]e^{-\delta(s-t)}ds. \tag{A1.6}$$

Equation (A1.6) is a fundamental relationship. It shows the basis on which shadow prices of capital assets are to be estimated. It says that the worth of a marginal unit of a capital asset is the contribution it makes to future consumption. Notice that we have not assumed the economy to be following an optimum path. Shadow prices should be based on forecasts, not mythology.

Rewrite the expression for wealth (W) in equation (1) in the text:

$$W(t) =_i\sum[P_i(\boldsymbol{K}(t))K_i(t)]. \tag{A1.7}$$

Now use equations (A1.3) and (A1.4) to obtain

$$\Delta V(\boldsymbol{K}(t)) =_i\sum P_i(t)\Delta K_i(t). \tag{A1.8}$$

In sustainability analysis,

$$\Delta V(\boldsymbol{K}(t)) = [dV/dt]\Delta t. \tag{A1.9}$$

Taken together, equations (A1.7)–(A1.9) represent Proposition 1.

The standard technique for policy evaluation is social cost–benefit analysis. The idea is to evaluate a perturbation (the policy change) by calculating the present discounted value (PDV) of net social benefits. Equation (A1.5) says that the PDV of net social benefits measures the change in wealth that is occasioned by the perturbation. That establishes Proposition 2.

[31] For a justification of the differentiability of V even when tipping points lie in an uncertain future, see Dasgupta (2001 [2004]).

Appendix 2: The Basis of Economic Forecasts

It was noted in the text that three pieces of information are required for estimating shadow prices:

(1) A descriptive model of the economy moving through time, including not only technological possibilities and ecological processes, but also preferences, tastes, values, and policies.
(2) The size and distribution of the economy's capital assets at the date at which the economic evaluation is undertaken.
(3) A conception of social well-being.

It will pay to construct a formal model to illustrate.

A2.1 Human–Nature Systems

There is a single reproducible commodity that can be consumed or saved. Output Y of the commodity is produced by means of three capital assets: itself (i.e. reproducible capital, K), human capital (H), and services extracted from ecological capital (B). For vividness we will imagine that extraction amounts to depleting the ecosystem's biomass. For simplicity of exposition it is assumed that population is constant and the economy is deterministic. Aggregate consumption is denoted by C.

The economy is imperfect. Human behaviour is described by three parameters: a constant proportion, a_C, of Y is consumed; a constant proportion, a_H, of Y is invested in the accumulation of human capital; and a constant proportion, a_B, of the ecosystem is extracted for use in production. The unit cost, e_B, of extracting ecosystem services, measured in units of output, is assumed to be independent of the rate of extraction.

Time is denoted by s, t ($s \geq t \geq 0$). The evaluation is conducted at t. The fundamental income–expenditure identity at any date s is then

$$dK(s)/ds = (1 - a_K - a_H - a_C)Y(s) - e_B a_B B(s) > 0. \qquad \text{(A2.1)}$$

Let the flow of ecosystem services in production be E. It follows that

$$E(s) = a_B B(s). \qquad \text{(A2.2)}$$

Production of the reproducible commodity is given by the aggregate production function

$$Y(s) = A(s)F(K(s), H(s), E(s)). \qquad \text{(A2.3)}$$

Y is gross domestic product. In equation (A2.3), A denotes total factor productivity. Marginal products of the three factors of production are assumed to be positive. For conceptual ease we imagine that F is a textbook, concave function. $K(t)$, $H(t)$, $B(t)$, and $A(t)$ are given as 'initial' condition.

As B is an ecosystem, it is self-regenerative, but only if biomass doesn't fall below a threshold. The simplest system with those properties involves the familiar quadratic growth function. So we write the net-regenerative rate as

$$dB(s)/ds = -\alpha + rB(s)[1 - B(s)/\beta] - E(s), \text{for } B > 0$$
$$= 0 \text{ for } B = 0,$$
$$\alpha, r, \beta > 0. \quad \text{(A2.4)}$$

Let us assume the ecosystem is alive at $t = 0$. That means $rB(0)[1-B(0)/\beta] > \alpha$. The existence of a *threshold* ($\alpha > 0$) means the human–nature system is non-linear. If B falls below the level given by the equation $rB[1-B/\beta] = \alpha$, the ecosystem is doomed.[32]

Growth in human capital is assumed to be proportional to expenditure on it. Hence

$$dH(s)/ds = a_H Y(s). \quad \text{(A2.5)}$$

In order to demonstrate how exogenous changes to the economy are accommodated in economic evaluation, we assume that knowledge, which we identify with total factor productivity, A, grows at a constant exogenous rate, ρ (> 0). That means

$$dA(s)/ds = \rho A(s). \quad \text{(A2.6)}$$

And finally,

$$C(s) = a_C Y(s). \quad \text{(A2.7)}$$

One may regard the system as consisting of four state variables: K, H, B, and A. But that's only to pretend the system is time-autonomous. Because A grows exogenously, it is a mere transform of t. The system is in truth non-autonomous. Nevertheless, for simplicity of exposition we shall regard A to be a state variable. The description of the dynamics of the human–nature system is now complete. It is given by equations (A2.1)–(A2.7).

For any initial condition $\{K(t), H(t), B(t), A(t)\}$ equations (A2.1)–(A2.7) can be used to track the economy's future trajectory. In particular, for any $\{K(t), H(t), B(t), A(t)\}$ the social evaluator would be able to forecast $C(s)$ for all $s > t$. We may then write $C(s) = C(K(t), H(t), B(t), A(t))$, or equivalently $C(s) = C(K(t), H(t), B(t), A(t))$.

What remains is a conception of social well-being (item (i3) in the earlier list). As in the text, let $U(s)$ denote the flow of well-being at t. For illustrative purposes I assume that aggregate consumption is the sole factor determining U. So, $U(s) = U(C(s))$. Let $V(t)$ denote social well-being at t. As in Appendix 1 we take $V(t)$ to be of the 'utilitarian' form

$$V(t) = \int_t^{\infty} [U(C(s))e^{-\delta(s-t)}]ds, \delta > 0.^{33} \quad \text{(A2.8)}$$

Assume $dU(C)/dC > 0$. A concern for inter-generational equity requires that $d^2U(C)/dC^2 < 0$. δ is the rate of pure time preference. Expression (A2.8) reflects an ethical basis for economic evaluation (section 2.2, questions (A)–(E)).[34]

We have confirmed that consumption at every future s can be written as a function of the state variables at t. That means social well-being at t (equation (A2.8)) is a function of $\{K(t), H(t), B(t), A(t)\}$. So we may write $V(t) = V(\{K(t), H(t), B(t), A(t)\})$. It

[32] The specification in equation (A2.4) is taken from Dasgupta (1982).
[33] Assume that the integral exists.
[34] See Dasgupta (2012) for various ways in which the use of (A2.8) can be justified.

follows that the shadow price of each of the three capital assets at t are functions of $\{K(t), H(t), B(t), A(t)\}$.

A2.2 NDP, Shadow Prices, Thresholds, and Substitutability

Equation (A1.4) of Appendix 1 noted that if an economy experiences exogenous changes, shadow prices are explicit functions of time. In the absence of a detailed model, however, it is not possible to determine the way the exogenous changes should be attributable to the various assets. As in Appendix 1 we take the convenient route of allocating the influence of time neutrally across the three assets. So, using equation (A1.4) in Appendix 1, define

$$P_K(t) = \partial V(t)/\partial K(t), \quad \text{(A2.9a)}$$

$$P_H(t) = \partial V(t)/\partial H(t), \quad \text{(A2.9b)}$$

$$\text{and } P_B(t) = \partial V(t)/\partial B(t), \quad \text{(A2.9c)}$$

$$P_A(t) = \partial V(t)/\partial A(t). \quad \text{(A2.9d)}$$

Gross domestic product (GDP) at date t is $Y(t)$. On using equation (A2.3) and writing GDP at time t as $(GDP)_t$, we have

$$(GDP)_t = A(t)F(K(t), H(t), E(t)). \quad \text{(A2.10)}$$

Alternatively, as is done when preparing national accounts, GDP can be expressed as aggregate consumption plus gross capital investment.

In contrast, net domestic product (NDP) is GDP minus depreciation of capital assets. Therefore, NDP can be expressed as aggregate consumption plus *net* investment. The shadow price of C in well-being *numeraire* is $dU(C)/dC$. So we have

$$\begin{aligned}(NDP)_t = {} & [dU(C(t))/dt]C(t) + P_K(t)dK(t)/dt + P_H(t)dH(t)/dt \\ & + P_B(t)dB(t)/dt + P_A(t)dA(t)/dt.\end{aligned} \quad \text{(A2.11)}$$

Data on the variables on the right hand side of equations (A2.1), (A2.4), and (A2.5) and figures for the shadow prices of the three assets (equation (A2.9a–d) enable the national income statistician to estimate $(NDP)_t$.

Two further points deserve mention:

(1) Future scarcities are reflected in shadow prices via the economic forecast. For example, the $P_B(t)$ depends on the degree to which K and H can substitute for it in production today and in the future and how far technological innovations (A) can override ecological scarcities. The extent to which those substitution possibilities exist can be read from the production function $AF(K,H,E)$ in equation (A2.3). It is customary to say that an asset is *essential* if substitution possibilities between it and other assets in either consumption or production are very limited (technically, less than 1). If B in the present example is essential, α in equation (A2.4) would play a pivotal role in public policy. P_B would rise sharply if B were to come near to its threshold.

(2) If δ is large (low), the influence on today's shadow prices of future scarcities would be attenuated (large). δ reflects the social concern over the inter-generational distribution of well-being. Assets' current shadow prices reflect not just current scarcities, but future scarcities too. If δ is tiny and B is expected to remain an essential asset, P_B would be large today even if the forecast says B will not hit its threshold until quite some time in the future.

Appendix 3

Currently the most popular pair of indices of societal well-being is gross domestic product (GDP) per capita and the distribution of GDP. In the text it was shown that GDP is not an index of inter-generational well-being. That should come as no surprise. The construction of GDP wasn't meant to serve the purposes of economic evaluation over the long run. GDP is a measure of market activity and was designed for use in a world where a significant proportion of people were unemployed and resources lay idle. The gap between potential and actual outputs can be estimated as well from GDP. Time series of GDP enable macroeconomists to study household and corporate behaviour. Moreover, as national income is the source of government taxation, finance ministers are naturally drawn to GDP forecasts. And finally, estimating depreciation and obsolescence introduces errors. As a criterion for evaluating short run economic policy, GDP has served admirably. In this chapter I have argued though that the practice of ignoring depreciation of reproducible and human capital and degradation of natural capital is indefensible practice in economic evaluation concerning the long run.

Nevertheless, GDP is so attractive that without international cooperation it would be hard for any government to abandon it as an index of progress. Why?[35]

A3.1 Inadequacy of GDP

GDP is the total value of the final goods and services an economy produces. So the rogue word in GDP is 'gross'. GDP doesn't deduct the depreciation of capital that accompanies production. In particular, it doesn't deduct the depreciation of natural capital.

In the quantitative models that appear in leading economics journals and textbooks, nature is taken to be a fixed, indestructible factor of production. The assumption is wrong. Agricultural land, forests, watersheds, fisheries, fresh water sources, river estuaries, and the atmosphere are capital assets that are self-regenerative but suffer from depletion or deterioration when they are over-used. (I am excluding oil and natural gas, which are at the limiting end of self-regenerative resources.) To assume away the physical depreciation of capital assets is to draw a wrong picture of future production and consumption possibilities that are open to a society.

[35] I gloss over differences between GDP and GNP (gross national product) because nothing is lost by doing so.

Here is an illustration of what goes wrong when depreciation is ignored. Repetto et al. (1989) and Vincent et al. (1997) estimated the decline in forest cover in Indonesia and Malaysia, respectively. They found that when depreciation is included, national accounts look quite different: net domestic saving rates are some 20–30 per cent lower than recorded saving rates. In their work on the depreciation of natural resources in Costa Rica, Solorzano et al. (1991) found that the depreciation of three resources—forests, soil, and fisheries—amounted to about 10 per cent of GDP and over a third of domestic saving.

A3.2 Inadequacy of the Human Development Index (HDI)

Many among those who have been troubled by the deficiencies of GDP as a measure of long-run well-being have advocated the use of the United Nations' Human Development Index (HDI). HDI is a linear index of GDP per capita, life expectancy at birth, and literacy. The former is a measure of economic activity, while the latter two measure reflect aspects of 'human capital' (health and education, respectively). HDI is a pure number, lying between 0 and 1. Since 1990, the United Nations' Development Programme (UNDP) has used HDI each year to rank countries. But users of the index (including UNDP) have gone further and tracked the HDI of countries over time, to judge whether a country has improved its performance or fallen behind. And there lies one of its problems. It will be shown here how and why.

To describe HDI formally, let j ($j = 1, 2, 3$) denote a desirable attribute: 1 for GDP per head; 2 for life expectancy at birth; 3 for literacy. Suppose the number of countries being compared is N ($k = 1,2,\ldots,N$). Let $X_{jk}(t)$ be the numerical index of attribute j in country k. Write $\max\{X_j\}$ as the highest figure attribute j can possibly attain (100 per cent for literacy; 80 years (say) for life expectancy; 50,000 international dollars (say) for GNP per head). And write $\min\{X_j\}$ as the minimum figure j can possibly attain (e.g. 0 per cent for literacy). UNDP defines country k's 'performance gap' in attribute j in year t to be

$$I_{jk} = [\max\{X_j\} - X_{jk}(t)]/[\max\{X_j\} - \min\{X_j\}]. \tag{A3.1}$$

In words, the numerator in equation (A3.1) is the *gap* between the maximum value j can attain and the value attained by country k; while the denominator is the gap between the highest possible value of j and the lowest possible value. Clearly, I_{jk} is a number lying between 0 and 1, depending on the performance of the country.

Now use equation (A3.1) to construct the *average performance gap* for country j as

$$I_k(t) = {}_j\sum[I_{jk}(t)]/3.$$

$I_k(t)$ is a number lying between 0 and 1.

HDI for country k in year t is then defined as,

$$[HDI(t)]_k = (1 - I_k(t)). \tag{A3.2}$$

Equation (A3.2) says that $[HDI(t)]_k$ is a number lying between 0 and 1; the higher is $[HDI(t)]_k$, the better is country k's achievements in terms of the three attributes.

HDI has been much advertised by the UNDP for over two decades in its annual *Human Development Report*. And because it is a simple index, HDI now has many adherents. But as a quality-of-life measure at a moment in time, it cannot be taken seriously. First, formula (A3.2) is entirely ad hoc. There are an infinite number of indices that could be created to reflect the idea that GDP per capita, life expectancy at birth, and literacy matter. Take some other index based on those same attributes, and we would obtain a different ranking of contemporary countries. The tradeoffs between the three attributes are not justified; they are postulated and taken as desirable. When the classical utilitarians proposed the *sum* of individual utilities as the desired social objective, they offered a moral conception to justify the move. UNDP by-passed any thought of producing a justification.

UNDP (2010) has introduced greater substitution possibilities among its three constituent indices than the linear form of equation (A3.2). But the authors have provided no justification for the functional form. And it reveals absurd tradeoffs. Ravallion (2012) has shown, under the new HDI, the value of longevity in Zimbabwe is a miserable US 51 cents per year. That means if Zimbabwe's authorities were to make a policy change that increases national income by a mere US 52 cents per person per year, the country will have promoted human development!

The second thing to note about HDI is the absence of natural capital. That alone should tell us that HDI is incapable of serving effectively in sustainability analysis. In view of Proposition 3, HDI is incapable of serving effectively in policy evaluation as well.

In either count, HDI is unsuitable for judging the performance of economies over time. Both theory and empirics show that a society's HDI could increase over a period of time even as its productive base (i.e. wealth per capita) declines (Dasgupta, 2001 [2004]). As an index of social well-being HDI has to be rejected.

References

Alessie, R. J. M. and Kapteyn, A. (1991) 'Habit Formation, Interdependent Preferences, and Demographic Effects in an Almost Ideal Demand System', *Economic Journal*, 100(3): 404–19.

Arrow, K. J. and Dasgupta, P. S. (2009) 'Conspicuous Consumption, Inconspicuous Leisure', *Economic Journal*, 119 (541): F497–F516.

Arrow, K. J., Dasgupta, P., Goulder, L., Daily, G., Ehrlich, P. R., Heal, G. M., Levin, S., Mäler, K.-G., Schneider, S., Starrett, D. A., and Walker, B. (2007) 'Consumption, Investment, and Future Well-Being: Reply to Daly et al.', *Conservation Biology*, 21(5): 1363–5.

Arrow, K. J., Dasgupta, P., Goulder, L. H., Mumford, K., and Oleson K. (2012) 'Sustainable Development and the Measurement of Wealth', *Environment and Development Economics*, 17(03): 317–35.

Arrow, K. J., Dasgupta, P., and Mäler, K.-G (2003) 'The Genuine Savings Criterion and the Value of Population', *Economic Theory*, 21(2): 217–25.

Attanasio, O. P. and Weber, G. (2010) 'Consumption and Saving: Models of Intertemporal Allocation and Their Implications for Public Policy', *Journal of Economic Literature*, 48(3): 693–751.

Blume, L. E., Brock, W. A., Durlauf, S. N., and Ioannides, Y. M. (2011) 'Identification of Social Interactions', in J. Benhabib, M. O. Jackson, and A. Basin (eds) *Handbook of Social Economics*, Amsterdam: North Holland.

Bok, D. (2009) *The Politics of Happiness: What Government Can Learn from the New Research on Well-Being*, Princeton N.J.: Princeton University Press.

Bongaarts, J. and Watkins, S. C. (1996) 'Social Interactions and Contemporary Transitions', *Population and Development Review*, 22(4): 639–82.

Bourdieu, P. (1984) *Distinction: A Social Critique of the Judgment of Taste*, London: Routledge and Kegan Paul.

Clark, A. E., Frijters, P., and Shields, M. A. (2008) 'Relative Income, Happiness, and Utility: An Explanation for the Easterlin Paradox and Other Puzzles', *Journal of Economic Literature*, 46(1): 95–144.

Daly, H. E., Czech, B., Tranger, D. L., Rees, W. E., Grover, M., Dobson, T., and Trombulak, S. C. (2007) 'Are We Consuming Too Much - for What?', *Conservation Biology*, 21(5): 1369–82.

Dasgupta, P. (2011) 'A Matter of Trust: Social Capital and Economic Development', in J. Lin and B. Plescovik (eds) *Annual World Bank Conference on Development Economics, Global 2010: Lessons from East Asia and the Global Financial Crisis*, New York: World Bank.

Dasgupta, P. (1993) *An Inquiry into Well-Being and Destitution*, Oxford: Clarendon Press.

Dasgupta, P. (1982) *The Control of Resources*, Cambridge, Mass.: Harvard University Press.

Dasgupta, P. (2001 [2004]) *Human Well-Being and the Natural Environment*, 2nd edn. (2004). Oxford: Oxford University Press.

Dasgupta, P. (2012a) 'Time and the Generations', in R. W. Hahn and A. Ulph (eds) *Climate Change and Common Sense: Essays in Honour of Thomas Schelling*, Oxford: Oxford University Press.

Dasgupta, P. and Ehrlich, P. (2012b) 'Hidden Features in the Population-Consumption-Environment Nexus', Discussion Paper, Center for Conservation Biology, Stanford University.

Dasgupta, P. and Mäler, K.-G. (2000) 'Net National Product, Wealth, and Social Well-Being', *Environment and Development Economics*, 5(1): 69–93.

Dasgupta, P., Marglin, S., and Sen A. (1972) *Guidelines for Project Evaluation*, New York: United Nations.

Donati, P. (2011) *Relational Sociology: A New Paradigm for the Social Sciences*, London: Routledge.

Douglas, M. and Isherwood, B. (1996) *The World of Goods: towards an anthropology of consumption.*, London: Routledge.

Duesenberry, J. S. (1949) *Income, Saving and the Theory of Consumer Behavior*, Cambridge, Mass.: Harvard University Press.

Durlauf, S. and Peyton Young, H. (eds) (2004) *Social Dynamics*, Cambridge, Mass.: MIT Press.

Graham, C. (2009) *Happiness Around the World: The Paradox of Happy Peasants and Miserable Millionaires*, Oxford; Oxford University Press.

Hartwick, J. M. (1977) 'Intergenerational Equity and the Investing of Rents from Exhaustible Resources', *American Economic Review*, 66(5): 972–4.

Hassan, R., Scholes, R., and Ash, N. (eds) (2005) *Ecosystems and Human Well-Being: Current State and Trends, Volume 1—Millennium Ecosystem Assessments*, Washington D.C.: Island Press.

Hausman, J. (2012) 'Contingent Valuation: From Dubious to Hopeless', *Journal of Economic Perspectives*, 26(4): 43–56.

Hirsch, F. (1977) *Social Limits to Growth*, London: Routledge.

Jensen, R. and Oster, E. (2009) 'The Power of TV: Cable Television and Women's Status in India', *Quarterly Journal of Economics*, 124(3): 1057–94.

Kapteyn, A., van de Geer, S. A., van de Stadt, H., and Wansbeek, T. J. (1997) 'Interdependent Preferences: An Econometric Analysis,' *Journal of Econometrics*, 10(3): 665–86.

Klenow, P. J. and Rodriguez-Clare, A. (1997) 'The Neoclasical Revival in Growth Economics: Has It Gone Too Far?', in B. Bernanke and J. Rotenberg (eds) *NBER Macroeconomics Annual 1997*, Cambridge, Mass.: MIT Press.

Kuhn, P., Kooreman, P., Soetevent, A., and Kapteyn, A. (2011) 'The Effect of Lottery Prizes on Winners and Their Neighbors: Evidence from the Dutch Postcode Lottery', *American Economic Review*, 101(5): 2226–47.

Layard, R. (2005) *Happiness: Lessons from a New Science*, New York: Penguin.

Leibenstein, H. (1950) 'Bandwagon, snob, and Veblen Effects in the Theory of Consumers' Demand', *Quarterly Journal of Economics*, 64(2): 183–207.

Lenton, T. M., Held, H., Kriegler, E., Hall, J. W., Lucht, W., Rahnstorf, S., and Schellnhuber, H. J. (2008) 'Tipping Elements in the Earth's Climate System', *Proceedings of the National Academy of Sciences*, 105(6): 1786–93.

Lipset, S. M. (1959) 'Some Social Requisites of Democracy: Economic Development and Political Legitimacy', *American Political Science Review*, 53: 69–105.

Little, I. M. D. and Mirrlees, J. A. (1968) *Manual of Industrial Project Analysis in Developing Countries: Social Cost Benefit Analysis*, Paris: OECD.

Little, I. M. D. and Mirrlees, J. A. (1974) *Project Appraisal and Planning for Developing Countries*, London: Heinemann.

Maurer, J. and Meier, A. (2008) 'Smooth it Like the "Joneses"? Estimating Peer-Group Effects in Intertemporal Chice', *Economic Journal*, 118(527): 454–76.

MEA (Millennium Ecosystem Assessment) (2003) *Ecosystems and Human Well-Being: A Framework for Assessment*, Washington, D.C.: Island Press.

MEA (Millennium Ecosystem Assessment) (2005a) Hassan, R. Scholes, R., and Ash, N. (eds) *Ecosystems and Human Well-Being, I: Current State and Trends*, Washington, D.C.: Island Press.

MEA (Millennium Ecosystem Assessment) (2005b) Carpenter, S. R., Pingali, P. L., Bennet, E. M., and Zurek, M. B. (eds) *Ecosystems and Human Well-Being, II: Scenarios*, Washington, D.C.: Island Press.

MEA (Millennium Ecosystem Assessment) (2005c) Chopra, K., Leemans, R, Kumar, P., and Simmons, H. (eds) *Ecosystems and Human Well-Being, III: Policy Responses*, Washington, D.C.: Island Press.

MEA (Millennium Ecosystem Assessment) (2005d) Capistrano, D., Samper, C., Lee, M. J., and Randsepp-Hearne, C. (eds) *Ecosystems and Human Well-Being, IV: Multiscale Assessments*, Washington, D.C.: Island Press.

Meade, J. E. (1973) *The Theory of Externalities*. Geneva: Institute Universitaire de Hautes Etudes Internationales.

Mincer, J. (1974) *Schooling, Experience, and Earning* (New York: National Bureau of Economic Research).

Moav, O. and Neeman, Z. (2012) 'Saving Rates and Poverty: The Role of Conspicuous Consumption and Human Capital', *Economic Journal*, 122 (563): 933–56.

Moore, G. E. (1903) *Principia Ethica*, Cambridge: Cambridge University Press.

Myers, N. and Kent, J. (2000) *Perverse Subsidies: How Tax Dollars Undercut our Environment and Our Economies*, Washington, D.C.: Island Press.

Oswald, A. J. (1997) 'Happiness and Economic Performance', *Economic Journal*, 107: 1815–31.

Ravallion, M. (2012) 'Troubling Tradeoffs in the Human Development Index', *Journal of Development Economics*, forthcoming.

Rawls, J. (1972) *A Theory of Justice*, Oxford: Clarendon Press.

Reid, W. V., Mooney, H. A., Cropper, A. et al. (2005) *Ecosystems and Human-Wellbeing: Synthesis*, Washington, D.C.: World Resources Institute.

Repetto, R., Magrath, W., Wells, M. Beer, C., and Rossini, F. (1989) *Wasting Assets: Natural Resources and the National Income Accounts*, Washington D.C.: World Resources Institute.

Ridley, M. (2010) *The Rational Optimist: How Prosperity Evolves*, London: 4th Estate.

Royal Society (2012) *People and the Planet*, London: Royal Society.

Ryder, H. E. and Heal, G. M. (1973) 'Optimal Growth with Intertemporally Dependent Preferences', *Review of Economic Studies*, 40(1): 1–31.

Solorzano, R., de Camino, R., Woodward, R., Tosi, J., Watson, V., Vasquez, A., Villalobos, C., Jimenez, J., Repetto, R., and Cruz, W. (1991) *Accounts Overdue: Natural Resource Depreciation in Costa Rica*, Washington, D.C.: World Resources Institute.

Solow, R. M. (1974) 'Intergenerational Equity and Exhaustible Resources', *Review of Economic Studies*, 41 (Symposium Issue): 29–45.

Southerton, D. (2012) 'Temporal Rhythms, Habits and Routines: from consumer behaviour to the temporalities of practice', *British Journal of Sociology*, forthcoming.

Southerton, D., Olsen, W., and Warde, A. (2012) 'Practices and Trajectories: A Comparative Analysis of Reading in France, Norway, the Netherlands, the UK, and the USA', *Journal of Consumer Culture*, 12 (3): 237–362.

Starrett, D. A. (1972) 'Fundamental Non-Convexities in the Theory of Externalities', *Journal of Economic Theory*, 4(1): 180–99.

Steffen, W., Sanderson, A., Tyson, P. D., Jäger, J., Matson, P. A., Moore III, B., Oldfield, F., Richardson, K., Schellnhuber, H. J., Turner II, B. L., and Wasson, R. J. (2004) *Global Change and the Earth System*, Berlin: Springer.

Sunstein, C. R. and Ullmann-Margalit, E. (2001) 'Solidarity Goods', *Journal of Political Philosophy*, 9(2): 129–49.

UNDP (2010) *Human Development Report: The Real Wealth of Nations*, New York: Palgrave Macmillan.

Veblen, T. (1899, [1925]) *The Theory of the Leisure Class: An Economic Study of Institutions*, London: George Allen & Unwin.

Vermeulen, F. (2012) 'Foundations of Revealed Preference: Introduction', *Economic Journal*, 122 (566: Conference Papers): 287–94.

Vincent, J. R., Ali, R. M., and Associates (1997) *Environment and Development in a Resource-Rich Economy: Malaysia under the New Economic Policy*, Cambridge, Mass.: Harvard Institute for International Development.

Vitousek, P. M., Ehrlich, P. R., Ehrlich A. H., and Matson, P. (1986) 'Human Appropriation of the Product of Photosynthensis', *BioScience*, 36: 368–73.

Vitousek, P. M., Mooney, H. A., Lubchenco, J., and Melillo, J. M. (1997) 'Human Domination of Earth's Ecosystem', *Science*, 277: 494–9.

Warde, A. (1997) 'Consumption, Taste, and Social Change', in *Consumption, Food, and Taste: Culinary Antinomies and Commodity Culture*, London: Sage.

Warde, A. and Martens, L. (2000) *Eating Out: Social Differentiation, Consumption, and Pleasure*, Cambridge: Cambridge University Press.

Warde, A. and Southerton, D. (eds) (2012) *The Habits of Consumption*, Helsinki: Open Access Book Series of the Collegium of Advanced Studies.

World Bank (2010) *World Development Report*, Washington, D.C.: World Bank.

World Commission on Environment and Development (1987) *Our Common Future*, New York: Oxford University Press.

3

The Value to the Environmental Movement of the New Literature on the Economics of Happiness

Andrew J. Oswald[1]

3.1 Introduction

Economics textbooks continue to teach students that humans are happier if they consume more goods. In almost every country in the world, on almost all weekdays in a year, someone somewhere will be writing u = u(c) on a blackboard or whiteboard. Utility rises with consumption.

Students rarely ask for empirical proof. Yet a new research literature in economics—indeed broadly across social science—has started to scrutinize this idea using proxy data on 'utility'. The new literature uses information from happiness and well-being surveys. Because consumption can be hard to observe in data sets, the research has focused on the closely related question of whether 'utility' is an increasing function of income. Technically, this is the idea that the indirect utility function u = v(y) is increasing in income. Money makes people happier.

Early pioneers in well-being research were Richard Easterlin (1974) from the University of Southern California (from economics) and Ed Diener (Diener et al., 1999) from the University of Illinois (from psychology). This literature finds that there is plenty of support in the data for the idea that richer people

[1] This work was supported by the ESRC. I wrote the first draft of this chapter while at the Institute for the Study of Labour (IZA) in Bonn and am deeply grateful to that Institute for its stimulating hospitality. For valuable discussions, I thank colleagues at 'Sustainable Consumption: A Multifaceted Approach' (Sustainable Consumption Institute, University of Manchester, 8–9 March 2012), especially Paul Fletcher and Alistair Ulph. I have also received invaluable advice from some of the major scholars in this area—including Arik Levinson, Simon Luechinger, Mirko Moro, and Heinz Welsch.

tend to be happier. However, crucially, and of relevance most especially for policy-makers and environmental economists, there is a lot of evidence that it is not true at the macroeconomic level that a country gets happier as it gets richer. This is the Easterlin Paradox and has been the subject of debate since the seminal 1974 paper.

A natural interpretation of Easterlin's finding that happiness survey numbers run flat as countries get richer is the following: humans care about their relative position and status, and unfortunately the great tide of GDP growth lifts (the size and speed and glamour of) all boats together, so on average nobody feels better off. Indeed a fine paper by Fliessbach et al. (2007) has recently shown that there is brain-science evidence for relative-income effects in the human brain. Their work showed, in a laboratory setting with two side-by-side fMRI scanners, that activity in a key node in brain reward circuitry is sensitive not just to the value of an outcome but to how that outcome compares with that received by someone else in the laboratory. It thus provides a modern underpinning for the various relative-income hypotheses that have been advocated through the decades by Easterlin and other thinkers.

Here it should be pointed out that the work of Arrow and Dasgupta (2009) has made the important conceptual point that to jump immediately—as some researchers like to—from a relativistic utility function to the conclusion that there is an inefficient rat-race for consumption does require a set of other assumptions (especially about the value of leisure and its observability). The idea of a 'rat race' is that people as a group may compete too hard for promotion and the pursuit of possessions—too hard, that is, from the point of social optimality. They can get locked into an inefficient Nash equilibrium. Arrow and Dasgupta (2009) make it clear that an inefficient rat-race equilibrium is not inevitable (intuitively, even envious humans will bear in mind that they do not want to be relatively poor in their old age, and that may slow their 'Keeping up with the Joneses' while young). Despite their important and correct caveats, Arrow and Dasgupta (2009) would probably agree that in western society there is now a distinct possibility that such a rat-race exists. That possibility deserves further empirical scrutiny.

3.2 Evidence about the World

One area in which modern economics textbooks are particularly weak is real examples of the world of consumption. Say we forget equations for a moment and, bearing in mind the earlier paragraphs, simply take an inductive approach and look at the modern world.

An unusual but potentially interesting starting point for a practical discussion of happiness and consumption is the example of men's watches. Men's watches seem particularly useful as examples, because in general in western society it is unusual for men to wear jewelry; watches—unlike, say, fast cars—can in principle be evaluated purely for their narrow, functional value. However, it is perfectly possible to find a price difference between men's watches of 100,000-fold—say between £5 and £500,000—whilst those watches are almost identical in their ability to tell the time. There may be a few economists in the world who wish to tell a story to try to justify such a price difference in some rational way consistent with standard economics textbooks, but the common sense view is surely that the price difference between these two watches can only be sensibly understood by thinking of one watch as carrying huge 'relative status' that is nothing to do with time-keeping.

This takes us back to the ideas in the literature on the economics of happiness. It complements an older way to think. For nearly a century, policy debate has been dominated by cost–benefit analyses in which monetary gains and losses are summed. A project or policy is viewed by HM Treasury as good if it makes more income and jobs than it loses. By its nature, such an approach ignores a range of less tangible, but potentially extremely important, influences on human life. Yet economists have had few ways of allowing for those non-monetary variables. So calculations about money have ruled the day. That is now changing—and fundamentally.

This chapter describes some of the ideas in the new research on the economics of happiness and human well-being. Its focus is on how the environmental movement will benefit from this new branch of social science. The chapter suggests that the results in policy debate may be dramatic.

In this new literature, clean air, for example, has been shown to be worth more (in terms of happiness) to people than is a large pay rise. There is also much evidence that the pursuit of higher GDP is close to pointless in a country that is already wealthy. More broadly, it is probably not currently realized by the green movement around the world that the new research literature provides conceptual and empirical methods for anyone who believes that a particular feature of the environment matters to human beings—and it has demonstrated that green factors influence human happiness just as much as, or more than, material prosperity.

These new statistical methods make it possible to measure a fuller range of the forces that shape humans' mental well-being.[2] In principle, and remarkably, these techniques allow researchers to calculate subtle things such as the happiness value from different economic, social, and environmental factors. 'Green' variables in the economics of happiness turn out empirically to be especially important.

[2] An introduction to the happiness literature, and these methods, can be found in Oswald (1997) and Clark and Oswald (2002).

Some readers may think that the words 'economics' and 'happiness' do not deserve to go together in a sentence, but research is starting to link those two notions. The field of quantitative social science has changed in the last twenty years and social scientists are drawing closer to subjects like medicine. For example, economists have begun to publish in epidemiology journals, in science journals, and more broadly. Some observers will see this as a good step for the economics profession, although it is inevitable that the borders between economics (officially defined) and other social science disciplines are going to become increasingly blurred.

To do this kind of work, researchers take random samples of people from nations across the world and are interested in understanding what it is that explains—in a statistical sense—the patterns of happiness or mental health across different sorts of people. They try, second, to explain the levels of happiness and mental health across different nations. Some researchers are optimistic that it may eventually be possible to learn how to make whole countries happier. Of course some of the people who would agree that maximizing GDP is not a sensible objective may not yet be persuaded that, even if it can be accurately measured, maximizing well-being (or happiness) is a legitimate goal (e.g. liberals might argue that this is not a legitimate goal for public policy). These issues merit future debate. Nevertheless, the new literature has reached the point where it seems to offer a tractable alternative to GDP maximization. Moreover, papers like Oswald and Wu (2010) have shown that there is a match between happiness measures and some of the traditional economic ways of measuring utility.

In this area of intellectual inquiry, two questions are central. One is: should our goal for the rest of this century be, as it more or less has for the past fifty years, to try to maximize GDP? Should we have the aim of four BMWs for everybody, by the end of the century? The spirit of the Stiglitz Commission report (2009) on the measurement of human well-being was that such a path would be the wrong one, and that emotions not just pound notes should be measured. Second, at the individual level, what determines human well-being? This is the subject matter of an empirical literature in which many different sorts of researchers estimate multiple regression equations with well-being as a dependent variable. In plainer English, researchers search for—and find—interesting patterns in data on what makes people happy.

Reasonably enough, many readers who encounter the field for the first time ask the question: well how on earth can you study happiness anyway? Research is normally done in the following way. First, economists take a large random sample of people, as in the British data captured in Figure 3.1. Second, each of those individuals is asked how they feel about the quality of their own life. Each gives an answer to a question like 'Taking everything into account, how happy do you feel overall?' where people can answer on a scale

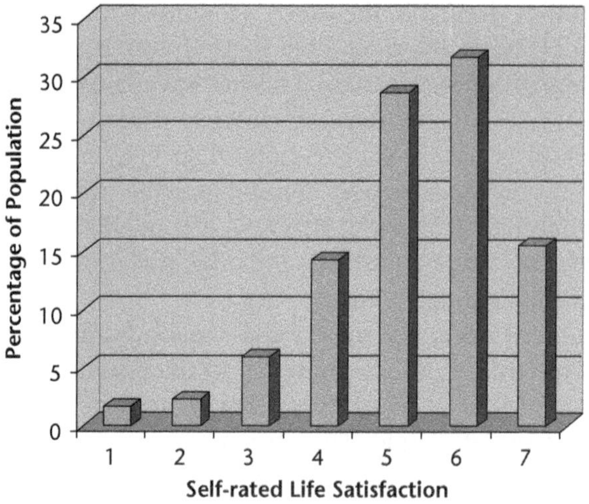

Figure 3.1. The distribution of life-satisfaction in Britain

Notes: British Household Panel Study data—sample size approx 75,000 observations: where 7 is Completely Satisfied

Source: http://www.iser.essex.ac.uk/bhps

from, say, a low of one to a high of seven. Third, each person answers many other questions, such as about their age, gender, marital status, job type, earnings, educational qualifications, and so on. By using normal statistical methods (of the sort used to study how smoking or eating fresh vegetables affects the chance of long life, say), it is then straightforward to examine the patterns in people's life-satisfaction or happiness answers.

This approach might seem too simple or potentially just unreliable. The trick to understanding the method intuitively is to think—behind the equations themselves—of people's idiosyncrasies as averaging out. Different people care about different things and may even use language differently from one another. But by taking information on large enough numbers of human beings, most of that statistical 'noise' washes out. What is then left behind is an underlying pattern for the typical individual human (just as in medical science, where a few people can actually smoke safely until they are ninety-five and survive it, but the average person cannot). The assumption that much of the variation in the individual determinants of happiness can be treated as 'noise' might sound a draconian one, but almost all empirical research in economics and epidemiology makes technically equivalent assumptions, and the robustness of happiness patterns in different countries provides a reasonable degree of reassurance.

Researchers work empirically with a kind of *happiness equation*. Happiness can be thought of as being captured by an expression like:

Happiness depends on $x + y + z$

where x is a group of economic variables, y a group of social variables, and z a group of environmental variables. Crucially, in this research, it is possible to *measure* the separate effects on happiness of having clean air in the environment, of being married, of having a high income, of having lots of friends of living in Scotland, of having a long commuting time, and so on, and on.

3.3 Possible Concerns

Various sensible objections come to mind. One is that, surely, asking a simple happiness question of this type produces special answers, and ones that are not very believable? In fact, the research indicates that this worry seems to be incorrect. When human beings give answers in these surveys, what appears to be going on is that they are providing a rough sense of the quality of their own life as they themselves perceive it. Critics sometimes argue that people's happiness answers are untrustworthy because those answers may be influenced by those people's perceptions of others' happiness; but we know from Fliessbach et al. (2007) that relative effects are genuine, in the sense that others' incomes matter objectively in the brain and not just as revealed subjectively (as critics might say) in happiness answers. Moreover, the precise language of the question does not turn out to make a big difference. Intriguingly, the econometric structure of well-being equations seems to be similar across the world and largely unaffected by the exact wording of survey questions.

Another natural objection is probably the most famous in the whole of social science (and perhaps even science). Can we really sort out cause-and-effect here? The latest evidence suggests that we can. One way of doing so is to follow the same people through time—and watch what happens to their mental well-being as good and bad events strike them. Then we can measure longitudinally the changes in happiness in response to things like marrying, becoming disabled, winning money in a lottery, and so on. Much more needs to be understood here scientifically, but important progress is being made.

Finally, and crucially, researchers have developed ways to put monetary values on the good and bad events in life.

It is hard to explain fully intuitively how that is done, but one attempt is the following. Think of the different points on the happiness scale that people are given in a survey question. They can answer from a low of one to a high of seven, let us imagine. By averaging across everyone's answers, it is then possible to work out (i) that, say, an extra £40,000 a year will move people on average up the happiness scale by one point, and (ii) that being married rather than single gives people one and a half points on the same happiness scale. Then, on average, the happiness 'value' of marriage is £60,000 a year.

3.4 Recent Findings

Large effects on human well-being are found to stem from the quality of the environment. The happiness literature offers a new way to assess that. The new approach offers a method that is additional to the conventional approach where people are asked their willingness to pay, reviewed in sources such as Horowitz and McConnell (2002). It does not require individuals to be able to value complex hypothetical scenarios and respond to non-trivial questions like 'how much would you pay to have air that is 10 per cent cleaner?' Recently, for instance, a substantial number of papers (see References) have shown that clean air and lack of noise have strong and statistically significant consequences. In some of the best research, Luechinger (2009) uses German data to show that people's reported happiness depends sensitively upon the level of SO_2 in the air they breathe (probably without those individuals realizing that). To demonstrate a causal relationship, he uses information on the direction of the wind and on the installation of certain kinds of power plants in different parts of Germany. His latest work (2010) is on US air pollution. Luechinger[3] finds that, on his best estimate, *a halving of air pollution would make the same contribution to a typical citizen's happiness as a 25 per cent rise in that person's income.*

Levinson (2012) does something similar for the United States. He takes data on daily air pollution across the regions of the USA. He matches those numbers with the happiness levels of randomly sampled Americans in the data different areas of the country. Again, after controlling for other influences on people's lives, the quality of the air turns out to have strong effects on personal happiness.

Both researchers use an equation approximately of the following form:

$$\begin{aligned} \textit{Human happiness} &= a + b(\textit{Income}) + c(\textit{Air quality}) \\ &\quad + d(\textit{Other factors affecting people's happiness}). \end{aligned}$$

These and other researchers (such as Welsch, 2002, 2006, 2009; Van Praag and Baarsma, 2005; Rehdanz and Maddison, 2005; MacKerron and Mourato, 2009;

[3] I am grateful to Simon Luechinger for providing me with the following interesting calculations. According to his 2009 paper, an income increase by 10 per cent is equivalent to a reduction in sulfur dioxide pollution by 67 per cent (OLS estimate) or 39 per cent (IV estimate) at the mean income of €21,500 and mean pollution concentration of 17 mcm. According to Luechinger (2010), the respective figures are 44 per cent (OLS estimate) and 21 per cent (IV estimate) at the means of $27,300 and 39 mcm.

Frey et al., 2010) are able to measure the coefficients *b* and *c*. The first of these coefficients gives economists an estimate of the extra happiness that humans get from a rise in their income. The second gives an estimate of the extra happiness they obtain from better air quality. The true value of air quality—namely, the happiness value of clean air expressed as a monetary value—is then given by the ratio of *c* to *b*. This method is the way in which the different, subtle, intangible forces in people's lives can be measured and weighed within a statistical cost–benefit equation of a more accurate kind than the traditional one that looks only at narrow monetary influences on human well-being.

3.5 Conclusions

What the research suggests—repeatedly and from different research teams—is that environmental quality matters enormously to people's feelings of happiness and satisfaction with their life. Green variables are more important to human well-being than many economists have realized, and these variables operate on people's well-being in subconscious as well as conscious ways (for example, at the conscious level, individuals do not appreciate how much they are affected by, say, the quality of the air, so it is hard for them to act wisely if asked to vote on giving more of their tax money towards cleaning up the environment).

By offering formal ways to assess the contribution to human well-being of non-pecuniary variables, the economics of happiness seems likely to change the future of the environmental movement and of policy debate in the world. That is not widely realized by environmentalists. I believe that it is a matter of time before these methods come to figure in public debate about our environment and its true 'happiness' value to human beings.

References

Arrow, K. J. and Dasgupta, P. S. (2009) 'Conspicuous Consumption, Inconspicuous Leisure', *Economic Journal*, 119, F497–F516.

Clark, A. E. and Oswald, A. J. (2002) 'A Simple Statistical Method for Measuring How Life Events Affect Happiness', *International Journal of Epidemiology*, 31: 1139–44.

Diener, E., Suh, E. M., Lucas, R. E., and Smith, H. L. (1999) 'Subjective Well-being: Three Decades of Progress', *Psychological Bulletin*, 125: 276–302.

Easterlin, R. A. (1974) 'Does Economic Growth Improve the Human Lot? Some Empirical Evidence', in P. A. David and M. W. Reder (eds) *Nations and Households in Economic Growth: Essays in Honor of Moses Abramowitz*. New York: Academic Press.

Fliessbach, K., Weber, B., Trautner, P., Dohmen, T., Sunde, U., Elger, C., and Falk, A. (2007) 'Social Comparison Affects Reward-Related Brain Activity in the Human Ventral Striatum', *Science,* 318: 1305–8.

Frey, B., Luechinger, S., and Stutzer, A. (2010) 'The Life Satisfaction Approach to Environmental Valuation', *Annual Review of Resource Economics,* 2: 139–60.

Horowitz, J. K. and McConnell, K. E. (2002) 'A Review of WTA/WTP Studies', *Journal of Environmental Economics and Management,* 44: 426–47.

Levinson, A. (2012) 'Valuing Public Goods using Happiness Data: The Case of Air Quality', *Journal of Public Economics,* 96: 869–80.

Luechinger, S. (2009) 'Valuing Air Quality using the Life Satisfaction Approach', *Economic Journal,* 119: 482–515.

Luechinger, S. (2010) 'Life Satisfaction and the Transboundary Problem', *Economics Letters,* 107: 4–6.

MacKerron, G. and Mourato, S. (2009) 'Life Satisfaction and Air Quality in London', *Ecological Economics,* 68: 1441–53.

Oswald, A. J. (1997) 'Happiness and Economic Performance', *Economic Journal,* 107: 1815–31.

Oswald, A. J. and Wu, S. (2010) 'Objective Confirmation of Subjective Measures of Human Well-being: Evidence from the USA', *Science* 327: 576–9.

Rehdanz, K. and Maddison, D. (2005) 'Climate and Happiness', *Ecological Economics,* 52(1): 111–25.

Stiglitz, J. (2009) *International Commission on the Measurement of Economic Performance and Social Progress.* <http://www.stiglitz-sen-fitoussi.fr>

Van Praag, B. M. S. and Baarsma, B. E. (2005) 'Using Happiness Surveys to Value Intangibles: The Case of Airport Noise', *Economic Journal,* 115(500): 224–46.

Welsch, H. (2002) 'Preferences over Prosperity and Pollution: Environmental Valuation based on Happiness Surveys', *Kyklos,* 55: 473–94.

Welsch, H. (2006) 'Environment and Happiness: Valuation of Air Pollution using Life Satisfaction Data', *Ecological Economics,* 58: 801–13.

Welsch, H. (2009) 'Implications of Happiness Research for Environmental Economics', *Ecological Economics,* 68: 2735–42.

4

Consumption, Stability, and Sustainability in Social-Ecological Systems

Ann Kinzig and Charles Perrings

4.1 Stability and Sustainability

The Brundtland Commission's definition of sustainable development—development that meets the needs of the current generation without compromising the ability of future generations to meet their own needs—implies that per capita consumption should be non-declining over time (World Commission on Environment and Development, 1987). The broad problem addressed by the Commission was the fact that consumption in many parts of the world had historically been supported by the depletion of natural resources and the degradation of ecosystems. Economists concerned with this problem had already considered the conditions on investment that would be sufficient to assure non-declining consumption in a world that depended on the exploitation of exhaustible resources. They had established that consumption could be held constant over time if the rents (surplus returns) generated through the extraction of exhaustible resources were reinvested in reproducible capital (Hartwick, 1977, 1978; Solow, 1986).

Following publication of the Brundtland report these results were generalized to cover renewable natural resources (Dasgupta and Mäler, 2000; Arrow et al., 2003; Dasgupta, 2009). They gave rise to the more general proposition that the sustainability of current consumption depends on maintaining investment at levels which assure that per capita wealth is non-declining (Arrow et al., 2004), where wealth is defined to be inclusive of environmental assets—natural capital. Much effort has since gone into the development indicators of investment (adjusted to account for changes in natural capital stocks) (World Bank 2006, 2010) and inclusive wealth (UNU-IHDP and UNEP, 2012).

Part of the problem addressed in these exercises is that the efforts to increase the value of produced assets have simultaneously reduced the value of natural assets (Arrow et al., 1995). While there is some scope for substituting produced for natural capital there are limits to the extent of environmental change that is consistent with constant consumption. These limits may be sensitive to changes in both technology and environmental conditions, but they exist. Maintaining the value of critical natural capital—the value of environmental assets that are essential to life support—requires investment in the ecosystems that provide critical life support services to offset the impacts of ecosystem degradation.

More particularly, it requires investment in the capacity of such ecosystems to function over the expected range of environmental conditions. An ecosystem, like an economic system, comprises a combination of biotic and abiotic assets. These include the species in a system, the abiotic elements of the system such as soils or nutrients, and the way they interact. The ability of the system to function over a range of environmental conditions then depends on the relative performance of different assets as environmental conditions vary. As with a portfolio of financial assets, the covariance in the performance of distinct ecological assets is what determines the value of the system as a whole. In many systems the capacity to function over a range of conditions reflects the degree to which it is anthropogenically stressed. Increasing levels of stress can induce changes in the state of the system. A common measure of the capacity of ecological systems to function over a range of environmental conditions is the resilience of the system.

The concept of resilience has been defined in two rather different ways in the ecological literature: one relating to the speed of return to a given equilibrium (Pimm, 1984), the other relating to the size of a perturbation that can be absorbed before the system is displaced from one state to another (Holling, 1973). The latter supposes that the system is characterized by multiple locally stable equilibria, and that the measure of a system's resilience in any one local stability domain is the extent of the shocks it can absorb before being displaced into some other local stability domain. Factors that increase the likelihood that a system will lose resilience include the accumulation of biomass (which makes the system more susceptible to shocks), and high or low levels of stress due to predation, competition or habitat change, and the size and nature of the shocks (moderate perturbations can increase the resilience of ecological systems). Change in the composition and relative abundance of species is frequently implicated in loss of resilience. There is long-standing evidence, for example, that deletion of some species has little effect on the short-term functioning of ecosystems, whilst the deletion of others triggers a fundamental change (Allison and Martiny, 2008; Laliberté et al., 2010). This switches attention from the impact of consumption on the size of capital stocks at the steady state to the impact of consumption on the stability of the system (potentially the stability of each of multiple states). Levin et al. (1998) make the point that in an evolving system sustainability might best be measured by system resilience whether at or away from equilibrium.

In what follows we approach the sustainability of consumption in social-ecological systems via the stability of those systems. Consumption, as it affects the environment, is measured in terms of the ecosystem services described by the Millennium Ecosystem Assessment (MEA): that is, it is measured by the provisioning, cultural, regulating, and supporting services (MEA, 2005c). The modern notion of ecosystem services was developed by Holdren, Ehrlich, and Westman in the 1970s (Holdren and Ehrlich, 1974; Ehrlich et al., 1977; Westman, 1977). The central idea in these contributions was that humankind benefited from a set of services that were the free gifts of nature. Westman (1977) described them as:

> [T]he absorption and breakdown of pollutants, the cycling of nutrients, the binding of soil, the degradation of organic waste, the maintenance of a balance of gases in the air, the regulation of radiation balance and climate, and the fixation of solar energy—the functions, in short, that maintain clean air, pure water, a green earth, and a balance of creatures; the functions that enable humans to obtain the food, fiber, energy, and other material needs for survival

He referred to the ecological functions underpinning these benefits as 'nature's free services'.

The list and characteristics of such services were elaborated in several papers over the next decade (Ehrlich and Ehrlich, 1992; Myers, 1996; Daily et al., 1997, 1999) before being systematized in the MEA (MEA, 2005c).

The services that most directly connect to system stability are the regulating services. These affect the variability in production of the goods and services that enter directly or indirectly into final demand. The examples described by the MEA included the following: air quality regulation (by affecting the chemicals contributed to and extracted from the atmosphere); climate regulation (through the way that ecosystem processes affect climate both locally and globally); water regulation (through the impact of land cover and soil micro-organisms on flooding, or aquifer recharge); erosion regulation (through the role of plants, insects, and other soil biota in soil retention); water purification and waste treatment services (through impacts of the biota on water pollution and filtration in inland waters and coastal ecosystems); disease regulation (through the impact of changes in the abundance of human pathogens, such as cholera, or disease vectors such as mosquitoes); pest regulation (through the effect of predators and competitors on the prevalence of crop and livestock pests and diseases; and natural hazard regulation (through a wide range of buffering functions of biota, e.g. in coastal ecosystems where mangroves and coral reefs can reduce the damage caused by hurricanes and storm surges) (MEA, 2005a). More generally, wherever there is natural variability in the conditions governing ecosystem functioning and hence the supply of ecosystem services, the system heterogeneity that moderates that variability provides a regulating service.

In many cases, heterogeneity refers to biodiversity. Of all of the ecosystem services, the regulating services are most affected by levels of biodiversity—genetic, species, and landscape diversity. In general, higher levels of genetic and species diversity will enhance the capacity of ecosystems to remain 'stable' or operate within certain bounds. However, if it is the stability of yield of a particular target species that is being sought, then increasing species diversity can increase variability of focal-species (May, 1973). The relationship between landscape diversity and regulating services is more complex—at times, higher levels of landscape diversity can enhance regulating services while at other times it can erode regulating services. So the problem we wish to consider is the relation between consumption and the stability of time-varying social-ecological systems. We take the sustainability of such systems to be satisfied if the time-varying system is stable in the sense that a bounded input generates a bounded response. It follows that the investment in natural capital required for the sustainability of the coupled system should be sufficient to assure the stability of that system.

4.2 Stability of Ecological Systems

There has been a long and contentious debate in ecology concerning the relationship between species diversity and the stability of ecological communities or ecosystems. The divergence of views depends in part on what component of the system stability is being measured against (e.g. population dynamics versus some system-level property like net primary production), in part on what type of stability is being considered (e.g. capacity to remain within a particular basin of attraction versus capacity to resist fluctuations), and in part on theoretical and empirical treatments, among other things.

It is not our intent here to sort through these complexities of the diversity–stability debate. Ives and Carpenter (2007) reviewed 52 empirical studies of diversity–stability relationships giving 64 different relationships; of those relationships, the majority (69–85 per cent) showed positive relationships between diversity and stability, depending on the measure of stability used. This would lend some support to the general assertion that diversity and stability are positively related. Nonetheless, Ives and Carpenter note that (i) the studies themselves are not diverse (e.g. the majority of studies are focused on grassland or herbaceous communities, or on a single trophic level); and

(ii) that fewer than half of the theoretically employed definitions of stability were examined. Few of the studies elucidate the mechanisms underlying the relationships.

Ives and Carpenter also generated a simple model of randomly constructed competitive communities (single trophic level) and used it to test the relationship between diversity and stability for 13 different definitions of stability. Of the 13 relationships, four were positive (diversity enhanced stability), six were negative, and three were neutral or close to neutral. They did not directly evaluate the stability of ecosystem processes related to regulating services, but two positive relationships are instructive for our purposes: in communities with a stable equilibrium, higher diversity enhanced the ability of a community to rapidly return to that equilibrium following a pulse perturbation, and reduced the variation in community density. On the other hand, increasing diversity increases both the number of alternative stable states and the rate at which the system is repelled away from the unstable stationary point between stable states and (in systems with non-point attractors) the probability of chaotic dynamics, implying that diversity may undermine regulating services in some cases.

Of course, Ives and Carpenter's model of population dynamics is not connected to a model of ecosystem processes. So stability is measured relative to, for example, abundances or persistence of particular species in the system, or some community level indicator such as biomass. Stability of these features may or may not be related to stability in the capacity of the system to, for example, resist fire or disease. In general, increasing stability with diversity is held to depend on a 'portfolio effect' (also called the insurance effect). When some species in a community are performing poorly, others are performing well.

The nature of interactions between species has less ambiguous effects on the stability of ecological systems. Many theoretical papers examining the relationship between diversity and stability have assumed a constant 'correlation coefficient' (r) for all species responses to environmental change (positive r means all species respond similarly to environmental perturbation; negative r represents strong competitive interactions and anti-varying responses to environmental conditions) (see e.g. Doak et al., 1998; Tilman et al., 1998; Lhomme and Winkel, 2002). These papers show, not surprisingly, that negative values of r enhance community stability, and that (with negative r) stability is generally enhanced the more species present in the system (though the requirement of identical correlation coefficients also limits mathematically the number of species that can coexist in the system). Yachi and Loreau (1999) relax the constraint of equal correlation coefficients, and find that unless species are perfectly correlated ($r = +1$ or -1) mean productivity rises and temporal variance in productivity falls as species richness increases. We note, though, that as correlation coefficients are randomly assigned in this work, as species richness rises, so too does the probability of at least one negative correlation coefficient.

Of course there is no a priori reason to assume either constant, or random, correlation coefficients; these assumptions are made for mathematical tractability. If communities were randomly assembled we would expect a greater probability of counter-varying responses to perturbations the larger the number of species selected (Doak et al., 1998), but communities are not assembled randomly (Levin, 1999). Thus, a small number of species with strong counter-varying responses to environmental perturbations may well generate a more stable system than a large number of species with weak co-varying responses. This said, a fundamental theory in ecology—the theory of 'niche differentiation' or 'limits to similarity'—suggests that responses should be counter-varying. This theory suggests that natural selection serves to reduce competition by driving co-existing species into different patterns of resource use or environmental response—different niches. Two species that are 'too similar' in response or resource use cannot coexist. One will competitively exclude the other (Schoener, 1974). Thus, we would generally expect co-existing species to have *either* differential resource acquisition strategies (think Darwin's finches) or differential responses to environmental perturbations, or both.

Counter-varying effects have been found in various systems. For example, functionally similar species have been shown to have dissimilar responses—in this case, grazing—to perturbation in grasslands (Walker et al., 1999). This is referred to as 'response diversity'—the variability of responses to disturbances or changing conditions among species that have similar contributions to ecosystem function. It has been found that response diversity is a widespread, perhaps even universal, feature of ecological systems (Elmqvist et al., 2003a). However, response diversity may be sensitive to the disturbance on a landscape. A meta-analysis of 18 different biomes distributed globally and subject to gradients of land-use intensity considered the impacts on functional and response diversity, and found that response diversity declined with increasing land-use intensity in five of the 18 datasets (Laliberté et al., 2010). These measurements of response diversity, however, differ from the correlation coefficients used in the theoretical literature, and so make it difficult to connect empirical and theoretical insights to search for broader generalizations (Freckleton and Watkinson, 2001).

The third characteristic of ecological systems that affects their stability is the degree of modularity within the system, which is a property of the internal structure or patchiness of the system. Modularity captures the notion that spatial or temporal compartmentalization of processes may be essential for enhancing resilience (Levin, 1999). In the resilience literature, the lack of modularity is often called 'hypercoherence' or 'overconnectedness' (see e.g.

Gunderson and Holling, 2002). Systems at all levels of ecological organization are seen as going through characteristic cycles of change, and systems are most vulnerable to 'flipping' into a new state (or cycle of change) at particular stages in cycle development (Holling, 2001). If all sub-systems at a particular level of organization—for example, all patches within a forest—are completely connected (not modular) and reach this vulnerable stage simultaneously, then a disturbance (such as fire or pest outbreak) that might previously have been contained at the patch scale can explode to the larger landscape scale.

In contrast, complete isolation of patches (complete modularity) would mean lack of genetic exchange, low local diversity through establishment of competitive dominants, and inability to maintain function under environmental change (Loreau et al., 2003). Intermediate levels of modularity that allow some independence in dynamics but exchange of critical resources will best serve resilience.

These conceptual observations are supported by both theoretical and empirical studies. Turner et al. used simple landscape models derived from percolation theory to show that landscapes with fragmented spatial patterns tended to contain disturbances, and reduce their propagation (Turner et al., 1989). In the case of fire regulation, for example, it has been shown that numerous irregularly-shaped patches of different types reduced fire spread (Ryu et al., 2007). The same thing has been observed in disease regulation. The severity of sudden oak death in forest plots in Northern California, for example, was shown to be greatest in plots surrounded by the largest patches of contiguous forest (Condeso and Meentemeyer, 2007). Real and Biek developed a discrete-event simulator to explain a 30-year record, at the county level, of rabies outbreaks within raccoon population in eastern United States. Their stochastic spatial simulator was only able to capture patterns of disease outbreaks in cases where the environmental heterogeneity (in this case, distribution of rivers, which acted as inhospitable territory) was explicitly considered. The effect of the spatial heterogeneity was quite large; townships separated by rivers had a seven-fold reduction in local transmission rates relative to those that were not (Real and Biek, 2007). These examples highlight the capacity of spatially heterogeneous (diverse) landscapes to contain endogenous disturbances. Landscape-level diversity is likely less important in containing damage from exogenous disturbances such as floods or windstorms.

4.3 The Controllability, Observability, and Sustainability of the Coupled System

To see how these determinants of ecosystem stability may affect the stability and hence sustainability of consumption in coupled human–ecological systems, we construct a simple model of the general system. This establishes the formal conditions required for an imperfectly observed or controlled system to be stabilizable (managed sustainably). The formal conclusions of this section are summarized in the discussion offered in section 4.4. Our model reflects the following stylized facts. All ecosystems have been affected by human activity to some degree, and more than a third of the Earth's land area has been fundamentally transformed by human activity. All ecosystems are, for example, affected by anthropogenic climate change. Many are affected by depositions of reactive nitrogen. Most terrestrial ecosystems have been affected by changes in land use and land cover. Of the 14 major terrestrial biomes only tundra and boreal forests have been left relatively intact. All others have been transformed to some degree, and in six (temperate grasslands, Mediterranean forests, tropical dry forests, temperate broadleaf forests, tropical grassland, and flooded grasslands) the area converted to agriculture, forestry or urban industrial, commercial, domestic, or other activities currently lies somewhere between one half and two thirds (MEA, 2005c).

The primary driver of change in terrestrial systems has been the conversion of habitat for a range of human uses, mostly for the production of foods, fuels and fibres, and for industrial and domestic uses. Conversion of habitat leads to the destruction of directly affected sessile species, as well as those mobile species dependent on undisturbed ranges of particular sizes. The extensive growth of agriculture—growth that depends on expanding the area of land committed to agriculture—generally involves clearance of all existing vegetation and the species that depend on that vegetation (MEA, 2005c). Conversion of particular pieces of land leads to the fragmentation of habitat. As the habitat remnants become smaller, the size of the populations of plants and animals that can be supported falls. This in turn makes them more vulnerable to variation in climatic conditions, resource availability, and the introduction of new species. Moreover, the greater the distance between remnants the lower is the likelihood that the sub-populations will mix, and the greater is the likelihood that each will experience genetic erosion. Indeed, habitat fragmentation is recognized to be a significant cause of extinction, with the effect of fragmentation depending on both the size and remoteness of habitat fragments (Rosenzweig, 1995; Reed, 2004) and the nature of the habitat itself (Fagan, 2002).

Interactions between converted and unconverted land lead to offsite effects on biodiversity. This includes the effects of nutrient flows, pesticide applications, and the appropriation of available water, as well as biotic exchange between different patch types. For example, the global flux of nitrogen has roughly doubled due to the effects of agricultural activity, and the global flux of phosphorus has roughly tripled over background levels (MEA, 2005b). The dead zone in the Gulf of Mexico, for example, is an offsite effect of excess nutrient applications on farms in the Mississippi basin (Dodds, 2006; Turner et al., 2008). Similar effects can be observed in many other parts of the world (Diaz and Rosenberg, 2008). Introduction of domesticated species in agriculture, and the accidental introduction of pests and pathogens along with traded agricultural inputs and outputs, have led to establishment and spread of many invasive species, frequently with negative effects on native biodiversity (Perrings et al., 2010).

We describe the 'resources' of the general system by the components of the n-dimensional vector $x(t) = x_1(t), \ldots, x_n(t)$, a 'resource' being any element of the system that contributes to its general functioning. So 'resources' include both those things recognized to contribute directly to human well-being (produced capital, durable consumer goods, and so on) and the biotic and abiotic elements of the natural environment that underpin it's functioning (frequently referred to as natural capital). The latter accordingly includes abiotic resources, such as mineral reserves, water bodies and the like, and the species responsible for ecosystem processes such as photosynthesis or nutrient cycling. Some components of the vector may be subject to claims by people, others not.

We suppose that the system is observed through a k-dimensional vector of prices $p(t) = p_1(t), \ldots, p_k(t), p_i(t)$ defining people's beliefs about the marginal contribution of the ith resource to human well-being at time t. Since not all resources in the system are either subject to claims by people, or even recognized to contribute to human well-being, we suppose that k is strictly less than n. Indeed we suppose k to be quite small relative to n: only a few resources in the coupled system are priced. We suppose that people use the information provided by $p(k)$ to determine which resources to grow and which to contract, which to conserve and which to use. In other words, we suppose that people use $p(k)$ to determine patterns of investment and consumption.

We describe the level of investment in or consumption of the resources of the system by the n-dimensional vector $B(t)u(t)$. The $n \times m$ matrix $B(t)$ determines the impact of investment or consumption on the resources of the system, and so reflects the 'technology' of investment, consumption, and waste disposal. The m-dimensional vector $u(t)$ describes the level of investment or consumption: $u_i(t) > 0$ if people invest in the ith resource, and $u_i(t) < 0$ if people consume the ith resource.

We describe the dynamics of the coupled system by

$$\begin{aligned} \dot{x}(t) &= A(t)x(t) + B(t)u(t) \\ p(t) &= C(t)x(t) \end{aligned} \quad (1)$$

in which the n x n matrix $A(t)$ describes the production processes of both the economy and supporting ecosystems. Specifically, a_{ij} denotes the amount of the jth resource used per unit of output of the ith process at time t. If $(I - A(t))x(t) > 0$ then the system generates 'residuals'—resources available for consumption, investment, or waste. The $n \times m$ matrix $B(t)$, already defined, describes the investment, consumption, and waste disposal processes of the economy at time t. The stylized facts about the way that human activities affect and are affected by ecosystem processes are reflected in the dimensions and structure of $A(t)$ and $B(t)$. Suppose, for example, that economic activities depended on the extraction of resources from the environment, but that there was no return flow. The matrix $A(t)$ could then be decomposed into a form $A(t) = \begin{bmatrix} A_{11} & A_{12} \\ 0 & A_{22} \end{bmatrix}(t)$ in which the elements of A_{11} describe the processes of the socio-economic system, A_{12} describes the contributions of the environmental system to the socio-economic system, A_{21} describes the impacts of the socio-economic system on the environment, and A_{22} describes the processes of the natural environment. Since $A_{21} = 0, A_{22} \neq 0$ there is no impact of production and consumption on the processes of the natural environment, but the resources of the natural environment do affect the processes of the socio-economic system. If $A(t)$ were indecomposable, on the other hand, $A_{21} \neq 0$, implying that the ecosystem is affected by production and consumption. Depending on the sign of the elements of that submatrix, the ecological system would be affected by the harvesting of other species (a trophic relationship), the negative effects of habitat conversion, waste disposal and so on (a competitive relationship), and the positive effect on commensals (a symbiotic relationship).

We suppose that the general system is controlled through the application of residuals and the technology governing their application, $B(t)u(t)$, and is observed through the vector of resource prices, $p(t)$. Prices depend on the set of resources, $x(t)$, and the $k \times n$ matrix of system observers, $C(t)$, C_{ij} denoting the observed impact of the jth resource on the price of the ith process. Note that $C_{ij} = 0$ implies that there is no observed impact. It does not necessarily imply that there is no actual impact. We suppose that $u(t)$ is a linear function of $p(t)$.

We take the economic problem to be to maximize some index of well-being over some finite time horizon through choice of investment/consumption, subject to the system dynamics (and structure) indicated in equation (1). Our index of well-being is a concave function of the resources of the system, and investment/consumption $W(x(t), u(t))$. The formal problem for society is to maximize well-being over the time horizon by choosing the level of investment and consumption, given the production possibilities of both the economic and the ecological system:

$$Max_{u(t)} \int_{t=0}^{T} e^{-\delta t} W(x(t), u(t))dt \qquad (2)$$

where δ is the rate at which future flows are discounted.

First consider the necessary conditions for choice of $u(t)$ to maximize $W(x(t)u(t))$. It can be shown that along the optimal trajectory $W_{u(t)}B^{-1} = \mu^*(t)$, where the co-state vector $\mu^*(t)$ defines the user cost of resources—often referred to as the shadow or accounting price of those resources. Furthermore, it can be shown that $\mu^*(t)$ evolves according to $\mu^*(t) = \mu^*[\delta - A(t) + B(t)K(t)C(t)]$. These conditions require that along the optimal trajectory the marginal benefit of investment/consumption should be equal to the marginal user cost. They do not, however, guarantee that an optimal trajectory can be attained. For that we need to consider the sufficient conditions. It is these that determine whether or not the impacts of economic activity on the processes of the environment are sustainable.

Note that the solution of $\dot{x}(t) = A(t)x(t) + B(t)u(t)$ is $x(t) = \Phi(t, t_0)$ $\left[x_0 + \int_{\tau - t_0}^{t} \Phi(t_0, \tau)B(\tau)u(\tau)d\tau\right]$, where $\Phi(t, t_0)$ is a matrix relating the state of the system at time t to its state at t_0 (called a state transition matrix) and that x_0 gives the initial state of the resources of the system. For linear feedback control it follows that $y(t) = C(t) \int_{\tau - t_0}^{t} \Phi(t, \tau)B(\tau)u(\tau)d\tau$. The system is said to be completely controllable if for any initial time, t_0, and state, x_0, and for any final state, x_T, there exists a control, $u(t)$, such that $x(T) = x_T$. It can be shown that this condition is satisfied only if the symmetric controllability matrix

$$U(t_0, T) = \int_{\tau=t_0}^{T} \Phi(t_0, \tau)B(\tau)B'(\tau)\Phi'(t_0, \tau)d\tau \qquad (3)$$

is non-singular. Similarly, the system is said to be completely observable if for any initial time, t_0, and state, x_0, there exists a finite time T such that knowledge of $p(t)$ in the interval $t_0 \leq t \leq T$ is sufficient to determine x_0. It can be shown that the condition is satisfied only if the symmetric observability matrix

$$V(t_0, T) = \int_{\tau=t_0}^{T} \Phi(t_0, \tau)C(\tau)C'(\tau)\Phi'(t_0, \tau)d\tau \qquad (4)$$

is non-singular. More importantly, the system will be completely controllable only if it is completely observable. Since the non-singularity of a matrix implies that all of its rows and columns are linearly independent (of full rank), and therefore that the matrix is invertible, these sufficiency conditions imply that there exists an investment/consumption sequence, $u(t)$, where

$$u(t) = -B'(\tau)\Phi'(t_0, \tau)U^{-1}(t_0, T)[x_0 - \Phi(t_0, \tau)x(T)] \tag{5}$$

such that will be possible to achieve a target $x(T)$ from initial conditions x_0. Similarly, there exists a sequence of prices, $y(t)$, such that observation of those prices and the investment/consumption sequence, $u(t)$, is sufficient to determine the initial stock of resources, x_0,

$$x_0 = V^{-1}(t_0, T) \int_{\tau=t_0}^{T} \Phi(t_0, \tau)C'(\tau)p(t)d\tau \tag{6}$$

If these sufficiency conditions are satisfied—if the system is completely observable (through prices) and completely controllable (through investment/consumption)—then there will exist an optimal policy that is also sustainable.

To see the intuition behind this consider a time invariant system. The sufficient condition for the controllability of the time invariant pair, (A, B), where A is $n \times n$ and B is $n \times m$, is that the $n \times m$ controllability matrix, $U = [B, AB, \ldots, A^{n-1}B]$ is of rank n. What this means is that every resource in the system can be reached and managed by a control. Similarly, a sufficient condition for observability is that every resource in the system is measured by a price. If these conditions are satisfied, it follows immediately that the system can be made stable (and hence sustainable) through price-informed investment/consumption decisions. More particularly, it can be shown that controllability is equivalent to the condition that for the pair (A, B) and the arbitrary set, Λ, there exists a matrix K such that elements of Λ are the eigenvalues of $A + BK$. Since the stability of the controlled system depends on the eigenvalues of $A + B$, this ensures that the pair (A, B) can be made stable. In other words, if the pair (A, B) is completely controllable it is also stabilizable—and so can be rendered sustainable by the adoption of a suitable feedback control (Aoki, 1973).

If the coupled human–ecological system is neither completely observable or completely controllable, then whether or not it is sustainable depends entirely on the stability of the parts of the system that lie beyond human control. If A is decomposable, and if the controls reach only some of the processes of the coupled system, then the sufficient conditions for controllability will not be satisfied. Similarly, if only a small subset of resources is measured through prices, it will not be observable. Whether or not it is sustainable then depends on the effect of human activities on the processes of the natural environment—the effect on diversity, modularity, and heterogeneity.

Note that a system that is neither completely controllable nor completely observable may still be stabilizable, and if it is, then it may still be sustainable. In fact, problems of this kind have a long history in both engineering and economics, the first results on the necessary and sufficient conditions for the stabilization of uncontrollable time-invariant systems appearing in the 1960s (Wonham, 1967), with applications to economic systems following some years later (Aoki, 1973; Turnovsky, 1973). These show that if (A, B) is not completely controllable it may still be stabilizable. However, this will be true if and only if all unstable modes of the system are completely controllable—and so can be made stable (Wonham, 1967).

The results have subsequently been extended to time-varying deterministic and stochastic systems, and to systems involving non-linear controls (Davis et al., 2010; Leonov and Shumafov, 2010). They show that if a time varying system is completely controllable, application of the optimal control can bring the eigenvalues of the time varying closed loop matrix $A(t) + B(t)K$ close to some arbitrary set. It can be made stable (and hence sustainable). In a time varying system that is not completely controllable or observable, by contrast, there will be processes that cannot be affected through $B(t)u(t)$ or observed through $C(t)x(t)$. In such circumstances a control strategy (a pattern of consumption and investment) that satisfies the necessary conditions for optimality may be stable and hence sustainable only if the processes that are neither observed nor controlled are themselves stable over time. This is the central insight of the result reported in Wonham (1967) and Aoki (1973), but applied to time varying systems.

4.4 Discussion

How does this relate to the problem of sustainable consumption? Recall that the choice of $u(t)$ determines how income earned in the activities of the economic system is allocated between consumption and investment, and which activities are promoted to meet people's consumption goals. The effect of the choice of $u(t)$ on the dynamics of the environment then depends on structure of and linkages between the two components (social and ecological) of the coupled system. The most direct environmental effect of consumption has been to change the structure and functioning of landscapes as people have promoted some species (the sources of valued foods, fuels, fibres, pharmaceuticals, etc.) and suppressed others (pests, predators, competitors, and pathogens). The conversion of wildlands to farmland, grazing land, production forests, residential, commercial, and industrial use has reduced the habitat available to other wild species. The development of transport, energy, and water infrastructures has fragmented remaining habitats, diverted water resources, and established barriers to the movement of wild species. All these trends have caused a very well documented decline in the richness of all species, and a dramatic change in the relative abundance of domesticated over wild species (MEA, 2005a).

Human consumption in fact depends directly on a very small subset of existing species (less than 1 per cent) (though indirectly on a greater proportion of species). Plant and animal breeding programs have narrowed the genetic base of agriculture to the point where more than 90 per cent of global food supply derives from only 11 species: wheat, rice, corn, oats, tomato, potato, cattle, sheep, pigs, chickens, and ducks. Moreover, within each of these species there has been substantial loss of intraspecific genetic diversity. The adoption of high yielding rice varieties, for example, has led to the abandonment of traditional varieties bred to meet local conditions over millennia. In India, where there were some 30,000 varieties in cultivation before the twentieth century's Green Revolution, with no one being dominant, ten varieties accounted for some 75 per cent of production by the beginning of the twenty-first century (Cervigni, 2001).

These trends have implications for the stability of ecosystems, and hence the sustainability of the coupled system. We have noted that even if the coupled system is neither controllable nor observable, it is potentially stabilizable through consumption-investment decisions as long as the processes of the environment are stable. However, patterns of consumption that have suppressed large numbers of species in the interests of promoting those whose attributes suit humans potentially compromise the stability of many environmental processes.

There is a substantial body of experimental evidence on the relationship between biodiversity and ecosystem functioning showing that the stability of many functions is increasing in the number of species within the functional group (Cardinale et al., 2012). If environmental conditions are not constant, for example, net primary productivity may increase with the number of species providing that those species have different niches, and hence have different responses to disturbances or changes in environmental conditions. The same response diversity helps stabilize production. Predator–prey systems typically exhibit 'boom-and-bust' dynamics, but complex predator–prey systems operating at several trophic levels, have much smoother dynamics (Thébault and Loreau, 2006). The loss of biodiversity accordingly tends to affect the regulating services (which stabilize production) more than the provisioning or cultural services. These services include such things as control over the gaseous mix of the atmosphere, control of soil erosion, control of pests and diseases, pollution buffering, and the mitigation of storm damage (Ehrlich and Ehrlich, 1992).

Beyond the effects of declining biodiversity, the stability of ecosystems, and the goods and services they provide, are affected by the homogenization of ecosystems through the dispersal of species and the adoption of common patterns of production and consumption, and the increasing connectedness of ecosystems through trade. From an ecological perspective a reduction in the heterogeneity and modularity of the system adversely affects both its capacity to function over a range of environmental conditions, and its capacity to adapt to new conditions (Elmqvist et al., 2003). Modularity, or the spatial (and temporal) compartmentalization of processes, enhances the capacity of the system to accommodate spatial (and temporal) variation in environmental conditions. Heterogeneity allows a greater range of responses to new conditions.

In principle, the effects of tighter connections between system components can be either positive or negative. The development of trade links between autarkic economies, for example, can add to the biological diversity of each ecosystem through the dispersal of species, and hence to their capacity to function over a range of environmental conditions. At the other end of the scale, full integration of the world's economies can have exactly the opposite effect, reducing both biodiversity and the stability of local ecosystems. There are several mechanisms at work. The most important of these, however, is the dispersal of pests and pathogens, and the introduction of alien species that competitively exclude native species (Daszak et al., 2000; Daszak et al., 2007; Hubalek, 2003; Jones et al., 2008; McNeely, 2001; Williamson, 1996, 1999). From an ecological perspective, intermediate dispersal rates offer most insurance against the spatial distribution of risks (Loreau et al., 2003).

An additional effect of tighter connections between the system components is an increase in the speed with which disturbances, such as a disease outbreak, propagates through the system (Gunderson and Holling, 2002; Perrings, 2006). Where tighter connections lead to the homogenization of ecosystems (in terms of the set of species they contain) they will also become sensitive to the same set of disturbances, and will lose the functional redundancy needed to withstand disturbance.

So where specialization in the production of commodities that people wish to consume affects the capacity of the uncontrolled parts of the coupled system to cope with disturbance and change, it potentially affects the stability of ecosystem functioning and thus ecosystem services. This gives us a rather different perspective on the problem of consumption than that discussed in the literature. Instead of the balance between consumption levels and the carrying capacity of the environment implicit in many discussions of overconsumption or the use of metrics such as the ecological footprint, it focuses our attention on the impact of interventions on the stability and hence sustainability of the ecological components of the coupled system.

We have argued that whether or not consumption affects the sustainability of the coupled system depends on the controllability and observability of that system—the sufficient conditions for optimization of the coupled system. From an economic perspective, the unobservability of components of the system is frequently evidence of market failure. System components will be unobservable if they are not priced in the market. If those same system components are scarce, in the sense that their use has a positive social opportunity cost, then reliance on available market signals will cause them to be misallocated. The consequences of such a misallocation of resources will be external to the market.

We suggest that the destabilization of ecosystems is amongst the most important externalities of current consumption and investment patterns. There are many mechanisms involved—those affecting the diversity, heterogeneity, modularity, and connectedness of ecosystems—each of which has different impacts on the capacity of those systems to function over a range of environmental conditions or to adapt to changes in conditions. Development strategies that affect the diversity, heterogeneity, modularity, and connectedness of ecosystems also affect their sustainability. They accordingly determine the degree to which the system can tolerate stress or shock. The planetary boundaries that constrain our ability to sustain economic development may therefore be endogenously determined. While stabilization of the system in any given state does imply that human activities should be confined to the 'safe operating space' it allows, there is potentially scope for managing the sensitivity of the system to environmental fluctuations. But this can only happen to the extent that the currently uncontrolled parts of that system become observable and hence controllable.

References

Allison, S. D. and Martiny, J. B. H. (2008) 'Resistance, Resilience, and Redundancy in Microbial Communities', *Proceedings of the National Academy of Sciences*, 105: 11512–19.

Aoki, M. (1973) 'On Sufficient Conditions for Optimal Stabilization Policies', *Review of Economic Studies*, 40: 131–8.

Arrow, K., Bolin, B., Costanza, R., Dasgupta, P., Folke, C., Holling, C. H., Jansson, B.-O., Levin, S. A., Mäler, K.-G., Perrings, C., and Pimentel, D. (1995) 'Economic Growth, Carrying Capacity, and the Environment', *Science*, 268: 520–1.

Arrow, K., Dasgupta, P., Goulder, L., Daily, G., Ehrlich, P., Heal, G., Levin, S., Mäler, K.-G., Schneider, S., Starrett, D., and Walker B. (2004) 'Are We Consuming Too Much?', *Journal of Economic Perspectives*, 18: 147–72.

Arrow, K. J., Dasgupta, P., and Mäler, K.-G. (2003) 'The Genuine Savings Criterion and the Value of Population', *Economic Theory*, 21: 217–25.

Cardinale, B. J., Duffy, J. E., Gonzalez, A., Hooper, D. U., Perrings, C., Venail, P., Narwani, A., Mace, G. M., Tilman, D., Wardle, D. A., Kinzig, A. P., Daily, G. C., Loreau, M., Grace, J. B., Larigauderie, A., Srivastava, D. S., and Naeem S. (2012) 'Biodiversity Loss and its Impact on Humanity', *Nature*, 486: 59–67.

Cervigni, R. (2001) *Biodiversity in the Balance: Land Use, National Development and Global Welfare*, Cheltenham, UK: Edward Elgar.

Condeso, T. E. and Meentemeyer, R .K. (2007) 'Effects of Landscape Heterogeneity on the Emerging Forest Disease Sudden Oak Death', *Journal of Ecology*, 95: 364–75.

Daily, G., Söderqvist, T., Aniyar, S., Arrow, K. J., Dasgupta, P., Ehrlich, P., Folke, C., Jansson, A., Jansson, B.-O., Kautsky, N., Levin, S., Lubchenco, J., Mäler, K.-G., Simpson, D., Starrett, D., Tilman, D., and Walker, B. (1999) *Valuing Resources*, Stockholm: Beijer International Institute of Ecological Economics.

Daily, G. C., Alexander, S., Ehrlich, P. R., Goulder, L., Lubchenco, J., Matson, P. A., Mooney, H. A., Postel, S., Schneider, S. H., Tilman, D., and Woodwell, G. M. (1997) 'Ecosystems Services: Benefits Supplied to Human Societies by Natural Ecosystems', *Issues in Ecology*, 1: 1–18.

Dasgupta, P. (2009) 'The Welfare Economic Theory of Green National Accounts', *Environmental and Resource Economics*, 42: 3–38.

Dasgupta, P. and Mäler, K.-G. (2000) 'Net National Product, Wealth, and Social Well-Being', *Environment and Development Economics*, 5: 69–93.

Daszak, P., Cunningham, A. A., and Hyatt, A. D. (2000) 'Emerging Infectious Diseases of Wildlife: Threats to Biodiversity and Human Health', *Science*, 287: 443–9.

Daszak, P., Jones, K., Levy, M., Gittleman, J., Patel, N., Mara, V., Nakielny, S. F., Chan, J., and Labo, M. N. (2007) 'Global Trends in Emerging Infectious Diseases', *American Journal of Tropical Medicine and Hygiene*, 77: 284–5.

Davis, J. M., Gravagne, I., Jackson, B., and Marks, R. J. (2010) 'State Feedback Stabilization of Linear Time-Varying Systems on Time Scales', in *42nd Southeastern Symposium on System Theory*, IEEE: 9–14.

Diaz, R. J. and Rosenberg, R. (2008) 'Spreading Dead Zones and Consequences for Marine Ecosystems', *Science* 321: 926–9.

Doak, D. F., Bigger, D., Harding, E. K., Marvier, M. A., O'Malley, R. E., and Thomson, D. (1998) 'The Statistical Inevitability of Stability–Diversity Relationships in Community Ecology', *The American Naturalist*, 151: 264–76.

Dodds, W. K. (2006) 'Nutrients and the Dead Zone: The Link between Nutrient Ratios and Dissolved Oxygen in the Northern Gulf of Mexico', *Frontiers in Ecology and the Environment*, 4: 211–17.

Ehrlich, P. R. and Ehrlich, A. H. (1992) 'The Value of Biodiversity', *Ambio*, 21: 219–26.

Ehrlich, P. R., Ehrlich, A. H., and Holdren, J. P. (1977) *EcoScience: Population, Resources, Environment*, San Francisco, Calif.: W. H. Freeman.

Elmqvist, T., Folke, C., Nystrom, M., Peterson, G., Bengtsson, J., Walker, B., and Norberg, J. (2003) 'Response Diversity, Ecosystem Change, and Resilience', *Frontiers in Ecology and the Environment*, 1: 488–94.

Fagan, W. F. (2002) 'Connectivity, Fragmentation, and Extinction Risk in Dendritic Metapopulations', *Ecology*, 83: 3243–9.

Freckleton, R. P. and Watkinson, A. R. (2001) 'Predicting Competition Coefficients for Plant Mixtures: Reciprocity, Transitivity, and Correlations with Life-history Traits', *Ecology Letters*, 4: 348–57.

Gunderson, L. H. and Holling, C. S. (eds) (2002) *Panarchy: Understanding Transformation in Human and Natural Systems*, Washington, D.C.: Island Press.

Hartwick, J. (1977) 'Intergenerational Equity and the Investing of Rents from Exhaustible Resources', *American Economic Review*, 66: 972–4.

Hartwick, J. (1978) 'Substitution among Exhaustible Resources and Intergenerational Equity', *Review of Economic Studies*, 45: 347–54.

Holdren, J. P. and Ehrlich, P. R. (1974) 'Human Population and the Global Environment', *American Scientist*, 62: 282–92.

Holling, C. (1973) 'Resilience and Stability of Ecological Systems', *Annual Review Ecology and Systematics*, 4: 1–23.

Holling, C. S. (2001) 'Understanding the Complexity of Ecological, Economic, and Social Systems', *Ecosystems*, 4 (5): 390–405.

Hubalek, Z. (2003) 'Emerging Human Infectious Diseases: Anthroponoses, Zoonoses and Sapronoses', *Emerging Infectious Diseases*, 9: 403–4.

Ives, A. and Carpenter, S. (2007) 'Stability and Diversity of Ecosystems', *Science*, 317: 58–62.

Jones, K. E., Patel, N., Levy, M., Storeygard, A., Balk, D., Gittleman, J. L., and Daszak, P. (2008) 'Global Trends in Emerging Infectious Diseases', *Nature*, 451: 990–3.

Laliberté, E., Wells, J. A., DeClerck, Metcalfe, D. J., Catterall, C. P., Queiroz, C., Aubin, I., Bonser, S. P., Ding, Y., Fraterrigo, J. M., McNamara, S., Morgan, J. W., Sánchez Merlos, D., Vesk, P. A., and Mayfield, M. M. (2010) 'Land-use Intensification Reduces Functional Redundancy and Response Diversity in Plant Communities', *Ecology Letters*, 13: 76–86.

Leonov, G. A. and Shumafov, M. M. (2010) 'Stabilization of Controllable Linear Systems', *Nonlinear Dynamics and Systems Theory*, 10: 235–68.

Levin, S., Barrett, S., Aniyar, S., Baumol, W., Bliss, C., Bolin, B., Dasgupta, P., Ehrlich, P., Folke, C., Gren, I.-M., Holling, C. S., Jansson, A., Jansson, B.-O., Mäler, K.-G., Martin, D., Perrings, C., and Shenshinski, E. (1998) 'Resilience in Natural and Socioeconomic Systems', *Environment and Development Economics*, 3: 222–62.

Levin, S. A. (1999) *Fragile Dominion: Complexity and the Commons*, Cambridge, Mass.: Perseus Publishing.

Lhomme, J. P. and Winkel, T. (2002) 'Diversity–Stability Relationships in Community Ecology: Re-examination of the Portfolio Effect', *Theoretical Population Biology* 62: 271–9.

Loreau, M., Mouguet, N., and Gonzalez, A. (2003) 'Biodiversity as Spatial Insurance in Heterogeneous Landscapes', *Proceedings of the National Academy of Sciences*, 100: 12765–70.

May, R. M. (1973) *Stability and Complexity in Model Ecosystems*, Princeton: Princeton University Press.

McNeely, J. A. (2001) 'An Introduction to Human Dimensions of Invasive Alien Species' in J. A. McNeely (ed.) *The Great Reshuffling: Human Dimensions of Invasive Alien Species*, Gland, Switzerland and Cambridge, UK: IUCN.

MEA (Millennium Ecosystem Assessment) (2005a) *Ecosystems and Human Well-Being: Biodiversity Synthesis*, Washington, D.C.: World Resources Institute.

MEA (Millennium Ecosystem Assessment) (2005b) *Ecosystems and Human Well-Being: Current State and Trends*, Washington, D.C.: Island Press.

MEA (Millennium Ecosystem Assessment) (2005c) *Ecosystems and Human Well-being: General Synthesis*, Washington, D.C.: Island Press.

Myers, N. (1996) 'Environmental Services of Biodiversity', *Proceedings of the National Academy of Sciences of the United States of America*, 93: 2764–9.

Perrings, C. (2006) 'Resilience and Sustainable Development', *Environment and Development Economics*, 11: 417–27.

Perrings, C., Fenichel, E., and Kinzig, A. (2010) 'Globalization and invasive Alien Species: Trade, Pests and Pathogens' in C. Perrings, H. A. Mooney, and M. Williamson (eds) *Globalization and Bioinvasions: Ecology, Economics, Management and Policy*, Oxford: Oxford University Press.

Pimm, S. L. (1984) 'The Complexity and Stability of Ecosystems', *Nature*, 307: 321–6.

Real, L. and Biek, R. (2007) 'Spatial Dynamics and Genetics of Infectious Diseases on Heterogeneous Landscapes', *Interface*, 4: 935–48.

Reed, D. H. (2004) 'Extinction Risk in Fragmented Habitats', *Animal Conservation*, 7: 181–91.

Rosenzweig, M. L. (1995) *Species Diversity in Space and Time*, Cambridge: Cambridge University Press.

Ryu, S.*R*., Chen, J., Zheng, D., and Lacroix, J. J. (2007) 'Relating Surface Fire Spread to Landscape Structure: An Application of FARSITE in a Managed Forest Landscape', *Landscape and Urban Planning*, 83: 275–83.

Schoener, T. W. (1974) 'Resource Partitioning in Ecological Communities', *Science*, 185: 27–39.

Solow, R. M. (1986) 'On the Intergenerational Allocation of Exhaustible Resources', *Scandinavian Journal of Economics*, 88: 141–9.

Thébault, E. and Loreau, M. (2006) 'The Relationship between Biodiversity and Ecosystem Functioning in Food Webs', *Ecological Research*, 21: 17–25.

Tilman, D., Lehman, C. L., and Bristow, C. E. (1998) 'Diversity–Stability Relationships: Statistical Inevitability or Ecological Consequence?' in *The American Naturalist*, 151: 277–82.

Turner, M. G., Gardner, R. H., Dale, V. H., and O'Neill, R. V. (1989) 'Predicting the spread of disturbance across heterogeneous landscapes', *Oikos*, 55: 121–9.

Turner, R. E., Rabalais, N. N., and Justic, D. (2008) 'Gulf of Mexico Hypoxia: Alternate States and a Legacy', *Environmental Science and Technology*, 42: 2323–7.

Turnovsky, S. J. (1973) 'Optimal Stabilization Policies for Deterministic and Stochastic Linear Economic Systems', *Review of Economic Studies*, 40: 79–95.

UNU-IHDP and UNEP (2012) *Inclusive Wealth Report 2012: Measuring Progress toward Sustainability*, Cambridge: Cambridge University Press.

Walker, B. H., Kinzig, A. P., and Langridge, J. (1999) 'Plant Attribute Diversity, Resilience, and Ecosystem Function: The Nature and Significance of Dominant and Minor Species', *Ecosystems*, 2: 95–113.

Westman, W. E. (1977) 'How Much Are Nature's Services Worth?' *Science*, 197: 960–4.

Williamson, M. (1996) *Biological Invasions*, London: Chapman and Hall.

Williamson, M. (1999) 'Invasions', *Ecography*, 22: 5–12.

Wonham, W. M. (1967) 'On Pole Assignment in Multi-Input Controllable Linear Systems', *IEEE Transactions on Automatic Control*, 12: 660–5.

World Bank (2006) *Where is the Wealth of Nations?: Measuring Capital for the 21st Century*, Washington, D.C.: The World Bank.

World Bank (2010) *The Changing Wealth of Nations: Measuring Sustainable Development in the New Millennium*, Washington, D.C.: The World Bank.

World Commission on Environment and Development (1987) *Our Common Future*, Washington D.C.: Island Press.

Yachi, S. and Loreau, M. (1999) 'Biodiversity and Ecosystem Productivity in a Fluctuating Environment: The Insurance Hypothesis', *Proceedings of the National Academy of Sciences*, 96: 1463–8.

5

How Should Benefits and Costs Be Discounted in an Inter-generational Context?

Maureen L. Cropper[1]

5.1 Introduction

Many of the decisions we make today have implications for future generations. This includes decisions to invest in physical capital or in research and development of knowledge, as well as decisions that affect environmental capital. Perhaps the most salient example of the latter is the stock of greenhouse gases (GHGs) in the earth's atmosphere: GHGs emitted to the atmosphere today will affect the earth's climate for generations to come. There is, internationally, a debate about what fraction of the world's resources should be devoted to reducing carbon emissions. In the academic literature this debate is reflected in arguments about the optimal carbon tax. According to Nordhaus (2007), the optimal carbon tax should currently be less than $10 per ton of carbon. The Stern Review (2006) argues for a carbon tax that is ten times as large. Much of this discrepancy can be attributed to differences in the rate at which the authors discount future climate damages. Stern suggests that a discount rate of 1.4 per cent is appropriate; Nordhaus uses a rate closer to 5 per cent.

In project analysis, the rate at which future benefits and costs are discounted often determines whether a project passes the benefit–cost test. This is especially true of projects with long horizons, such as projects to reduce GHG emissions. Whether such projects pass the benefit–cost test is especially sensitive to the rate at which future benefits are discounted. In the United States

[1] I would like to thank Partha Dasgupta, Randy Lutter, Dale Southerton, Alistair Ulph, and Hal Wilhite for comments and members of the USEPA National Center for Environmental Economics for helpful discussions.

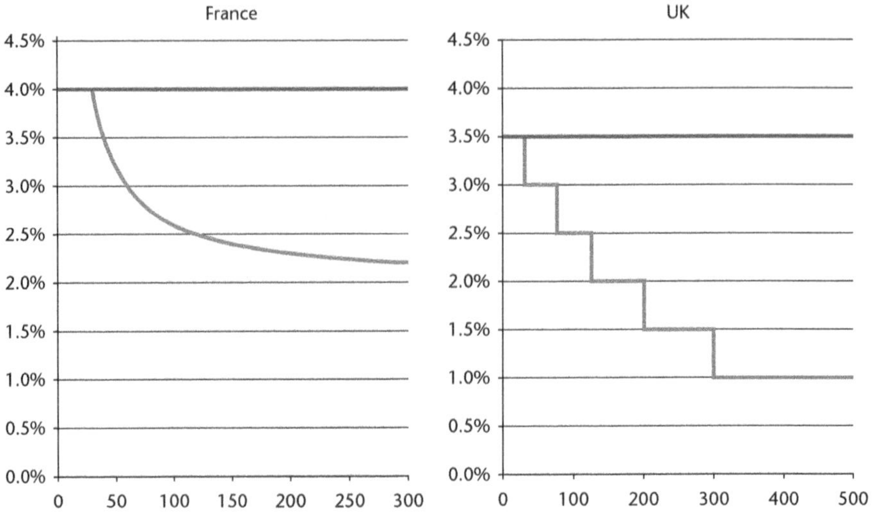

Figure 5.1. Declining discount rates in France and the UK
Source: Sterner (2011)

the Office of Management and Budget (OMB) recommends that project costs and benefits be discounted at a constant exponential rate, although this rate may be lower for projects that affect future generations (OMB, 2003). In contrast, France and the United Kingdom use discount rate schedules, pictured in Figure 5.1, in which the discount rate applied to benefits and costs in future years declines over time: the rate used to discount benefits in year 50 to year 10 is lower than the rate used to discount benefits in year 10 to the present. In the United Kingdom, for example, a rate of 3.5 per cent is used to discount benefits in year 10, but a rate of 2.5 per cent is used to discount benefits in year 70, falling to 1 per cent in year 300.

Whether the use of a declining discount rate (DDR) is more present-oriented than the use of a constant discount rate depends, of course, on the levels of each. It is clear, however, that the use of a DDR schedule that begins at 4 per cent will yield a higher net present value of whatever is being discounted than the use of a constant exponential discount rate of 4 per cent. This raises two questions. Firstly, should governments, in discounting the future benefits and costs of public projects, use a discount rate that declines over time? Secondly, how should the discount rate—or discount rate schedule—be set?

This chapter focuses on the first question: should governments, in discounting the future benefits and costs of public projects, use a discount rate that declines over time? To answer this question we review the arguments for a DDR. The basic argument is a simple one: if there is persistence in the discount rates that will be applied in the future and if we can assign probabilities to these discount rates, this will result in a declining schedule of certainty-equivalent discount rates. In the economics literature, this argument was first advanced by Weitzman (1998, 2001) in an expected net present value (ENPV) framework. If an analyst is evaluating the net present value of the benefits of a project using a constant exponential discount rate and if the discount rate is uncertain, taking the expected value of the discount factor will yield a declining certainty-equivalent discount rate. This has led to a growing empirical literature that estimates reduced-form models of interest rate determination and their implications for the shape of the DDR schedule. We briefly review this literature, focusing on models of interest rate determination for the United States and their implications for calculating the marginal social cost of carbon—the present value of damages from emitting an additional ton of carbon.

The ENPV literature has, however, been criticized for lack of connection to the economics literature on project evaluation. In benefit–cost analysis, the net benefits of a project in year t (in consumption units) are to be discounted to the present at the rate at which society would trade consumption in year t for consumption in the present. This approach leads to the Ramsey discounting formula, in which the discount rate applied to net benefits at time t, ρ_t, equals the sum of the utility rate of discount (δ) and the rate of growth in consumption between t and the present (g_t), weighted by the elasticity of marginal utility of consumption (η).[2] The Ramsey formula can also lead to a DDR if there is uncertainty about rate of growth in consumption (g_t) and if shocks to consumption are correlated over time. Uncertainty about the mean and variance of the rate of growth in consumption can also lead to a declining certainty-equivalent discount rate.

The chapter is organized as follows. Section 5.2 discusses the ENPV approach and summarizes empirical estimates of certainty-equivalent discount rates for the United States. Section 5.3 focuses on the consumption rate of discount as represented by the Ramsey formula. We discuss conditions under which uncertainty in the rate of growth in consumption, as reflected in the extended Ramsey formula, leads to a declining certainty-equivalent discount rate. Section 5.4 addresses the issue of how, empirically, the parameters of the Ramsey formula might be estimated. Section 5.5 summarizes the arguments for using a DDR in project analysis and discusses the difficulties in determining empirically how the discount rate schedule should be set.

[2] Formally, $\rho_t = \delta + \eta \cdot g_t$.

5.2 The Expected Net Present Value Approach to Discounting

In performing a cost–benefit analysis an analyst must typically discount a stream of net benefits to the present. If $Z(t)$ denotes net benefits at time t and net benefits are discounted at a constant exponential rate r, $Z(t)\exp(-rt)$ is the present value of net benefits at time t.[3] If the discount rate r is uncertain then the expected value of net benefits is given by

$$A(t)Z(t) = E(\exp(-rt))Z(t) \qquad (1)$$

where expectation is taken with respect to r. $A(t)$ is the expected value of the discount factor and $R_t \equiv -(dA_t/dt)/A_t$ is the instantaneous certainty-equivalent discount rate. If the probability distribution over r is stationary, then, because the discount factor is a convex function of r, the certainty-equivalent discount rate, R_t, will decline over time (Weitzman, 1998; 2001).[4]

This is illustrated in Table 5.1, which contrasts the present value of £1,000 received at various dates using a constant discount rate of 4 per cent versus a constant discount rate that equals 1 per cent and 7 per cent with equal probability. Jensen's inequality guarantees the present value computed using the mean discount rate of 4 per cent is always smaller than the expected value of the discount factor, that is,

$$E(\exp(-rt)) > \exp(-E(r)t)). \qquad (2)$$

This effect is magnified as t increases, implying that R_t declines over time.

This was first pointed out in the context of inter-generational discounting by Weitzman (1998; 2001). In a seminal article, 'Gamma Discounting',

Table 5.1. Present value of a cash flow of £1000 received after *t* years

t	Scenario A: 4%	Scenario B: 1% or 7%	Certainty-Equivalent Discount Rate (R_t)
1	960.7894	961.2218	0.0394
10	670.3200	700.7114	0.0313
50	135.3353	318.3640	0.0128
100	18.3156	184.3957	0.0102
150	2.4788	111.5788	0.0101
200	0.3355	67.6681	0.0101
300	0.0061	24.8935	0.0101
400	0.0001	9.1578	0.0101

Source: Gollier et al. (2008)

[3] We assume that $Z(t)$ represents certain benefits. If benefits are uncertain we assume that they are uncorrelated with r and that $Z(t)$ represents certainty-equivalent benefits.

[4] Gollier and Weitzman (2010) discuss the theoretical underpinnings for the ENPV approach. The approach is consistent with utility maximization in the case of a logarithmic utility function.

Table 5.2. Discount rate schedule

Time period	Name	Marginal discount rate (per cent)
Within year 1 to 5 hence	Immediate future	4
Within year 6 to 25 hence	Near future	3
Within year 26 to 75 hence	Medium future	2
Within year 76 to 300 hence	Distant future	1
Within year more than 300 hence	Far-distant future	0

Source: Weitzman (2001)

Weitzman (2001) showed that, if r follows a gamma distribution with mean μ and variance σ^2, the certainty-equivalent discount rate is given by

$$R_t = \mu/[1 + t\sigma^2/\mu]. \tag{3}$$

The gamma distribution provides a good fit to the responses Weitzman obtained when he asked over 2,000 PhD economists what rate should be used to discount the costs and benefits associated with programs to mitigate climate change. The associated mean (4 per cent) and standard deviation (3 per cent) of responses lead to the schedule of instantaneous certainty-equivalent discount rates in Table 5.2.

The declining certainty-equivalent discount rate in gamma discounting follows directly from Jensen's inequality and the fact that the distribution over the discount rate is constant over time. In the more general case in which the discount rate varies over time, so that

$$A(t) = E[\exp(-\textstyle\sum_{\tau=1\ldots t} r_\tau)], \tag{4}$$

the shape of the R_t path depends on the distribution of the $\{r_\tau\}$. If $\{r_\tau\}$ are independently and identically distributed, the certainty-equivalent discount rate is constant. In equation (4), there must be persistence in uncertainty about the discount rate for the certainty-equivalent rate to decline. If, for example, shocks to the discount rate are correlated over time, as in equation (5),

$$r_t = \pi + e_t \quad \text{and} \quad e_t = ae_{t-1} + u_t, \quad |a| \leq 1, \tag{5}$$

the certainty-equivalent discount rate will decline over time (Newell and Pizer, 2003).[5]

This suggests that it is important to consider the underlying source of uncertainty about discount rates. In gamma discounting there is disagreement among experts about a constant rate of discount. In Weitzman (2001) the views of experts are treated as equally valid and used to estimate the parameters of a true, underlying distribution of the interest rate. As Freeman and Groom (2010) have shown, viewing the responses of experts as forecasts of the true mean interest rate leads to a different method of combining

[5] In equation (5) the interest rate follows an $AR(1)$ process. In estimating (5) it is typically assumed that $\pi \sim N(\mu_\pi, \sigma_\pi^2)$ and $\{u_t\} \sim$ i.i.d. $N(0, \sigma_u^2)$.

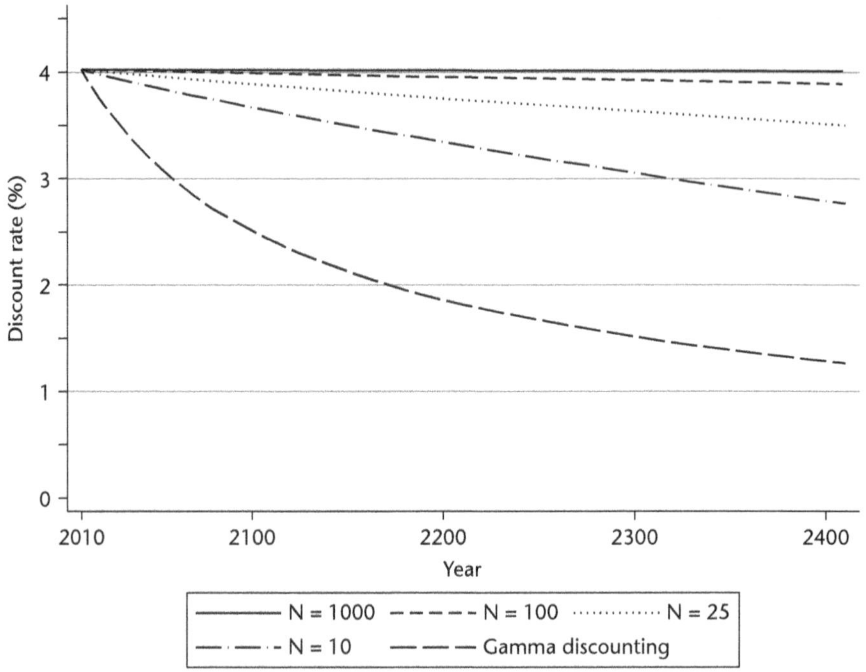

Figure 5.2. Certainty-equivalent discount rates: Freeman-Groom vs. Weitzman
Source: Groom (2011)

expert responses than Weitzman used. When experts' forecast errors are independently and identically distributed, the decline in the certainty-equivalent discount rate is attenuated, compared to gamma discounting, since each expert provides additional information that reduces the variance of the true mean interest rate. This is illustrated in Figure 5.2, which shows how increasing the number of experts whose opinion is aggregated alters the path of the certainty-equivalent discount rate and contrasts the aggregation approaches used by Freeman and Groom (2010) and Weitzman (2001).

A criticism of both Weitzman (2001) and Freeman and Groom (2010) is that the authors view the appropriate discount rate as constant. As Dasgupta (2008) has pointed out, this is an especially inappropriate assumption when discounting over long horizons. It is also true that, in the context of gamma discounting, the source of the uncertainty that gives rise to a DDR is disagreement among experts. Whether the discount rate represents the return to capital or the consumption rate of discount, it is likely to change over time. And, a more satisfying approach is to model the underlying economic source of the uncertainty.

5.2.1 *Empirical Estimates of the DDR Schedule for the United States*

The predominant approach followed in the empirical DDR literature is to view r_t as representing the return to risk-free capital at time t, and to develop econometric models to forecast r_t. The empirical DDR literature includes models of interest rate determination for the United States (Newell and Pizer, 2003; Groom, et al., 2007), Australia, Canada, Germany, and UK (Hepburn, et al., 2009; Gollier, et al., 2008), and France, India, Japan, and South Africa (Gollier, et al., 2008). We focus on the empirical DDR literature as applied to the United States. Newell and Pizer (2003) estimate reduced-form models of bond yields for the United States, using two centuries of data on Treasury bonds, and use them to estimate certainty-equivalent discount rates over the next 400 years. The authors assume that interest rates follow an autoregressive process. This is given by equation (5) in the case of $AR(1)$.[6] Equation (5) implies that the mean interest rate is uncertain, and that deviations from the mean interest rate will be more persistent the higher is a.

The authors demonstrate that the instantaneous certainty-equivalent interest rate corresponding to (5) is given by

$$R_t = \mu_\pi - t\sigma_\pi^2 - \sigma_u^2 f(a,t), \qquad (6)$$

where $f(a,t)$ is increasing in a and t. How fast the certainty-equivalent interest rate declines depends on the variance in the mean interest rate, as well as on how persistent shocks are to the mean interest rate (i.e. on a). When $a = 1$, interest rates follow a random walk model. To illustrate the implications of persistence, if $a = 1$, $\mu_\pi = 4\%$, $\sigma_\pi^2 = 0.52\%$ and $\sigma_\mu^2 = 0.23\%$, the certainty-equivalent discount rate declines from 4 per cent today to 1 per cent 100 years from now. In contrast, a value of $a < 1$ (a mean-reverting model) implies that interest rates will revert to μ_π in the long run. When $a = 0.96$, $\mu_\pi = 4\%$, $\sigma_\pi^2 = 0.52\%$ and $\sigma_u^2 = 0.23\%$, the certainty-equivalent discount rate is 4.0 per cent today and 3.6 per cent 100 years from now (Newell and Pizer, 2003).

Newell and Pizer use results from their preferred specifications of random walk and mean reverting models to simulate the path of certainty-equivalent discount rates.[7] In the random walk model (see Figure 5.3) the certainty-equivalent discount rate falls from 4 per cent today to 2 per cent in 100 years; in the mean reverting model a certainty-equivalent discount rate of 2 per cent is reached only in 300 years. The authors cannot reject the random walk hypothesis, but investigate the implications of both models for

[6] The authors estimate autoregressive models in the logarithms of the variables ($lnr_t = ln\pi + e_t$) to avoid negative interest rates. Their preferred models are $AR(3)$ models in which $e_t = a_1e_{t-1} + a_2e_{t-2} + a_3e_{t-3} + u_t$.

[7] The preferred models are $AR(3)$ models, estimated using the logarithms of the variables (see footnote 2). The random walk model imposes the restriction that $a_1 + a_2 + a_3 = 1$.

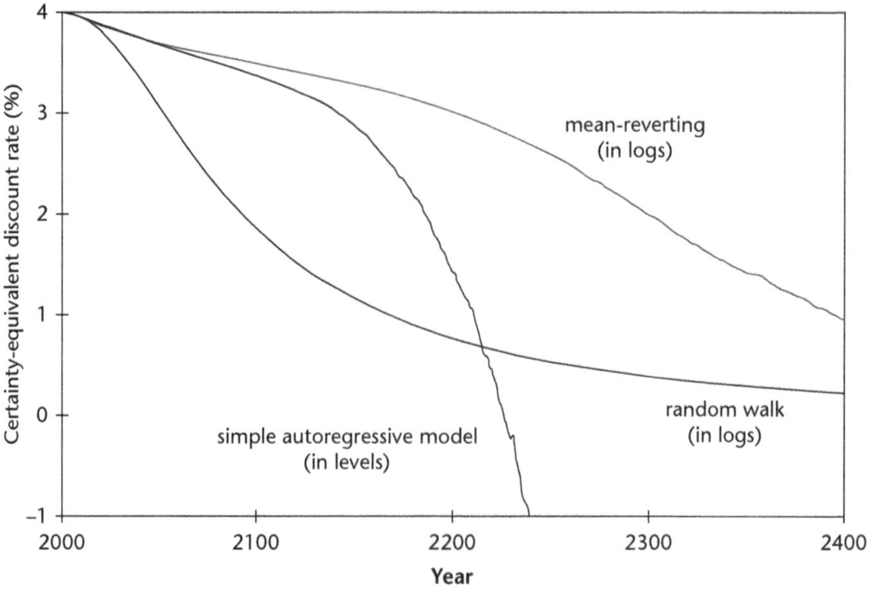

Figure 5.3. Forecasts of certainty-equivalent discount rates
Source: Newell and Pizer (2003)

calculating the marginal social cost of carbon.[8] Using damage estimates from Nordhaus (1994), the marginal social cost of carbon is computed as the present discounted value of global damages from emitting a ton of carbon in 2000, discounted at a constant exponential rate of 4 per cent and using certainty-equivalent rates from the two models. The marginal social cost of carbon increases from \$5.29 using a constant rate of 4 per cent to \$10.44 (1989 USD) using the random walk model.

The subsequent literature, following the literature in finance, has estimated more flexible reduced-form models of interest rate determination. Groom et al. (2007) estimate five models for the United States using the same data as Newell and Pizer (2003). The first two are random walk (RW) and mean-reverting (MR) models identical to those in Newell and Pizer (2003). The third is an autoregressive IGARCH model that allows the conditional variance of the interest rate (held fixed in equation (5)) to vary over time. The fourth is a regime-switching model that allows the interest rate to shift randomly between two regimes that differ in their mean and variance. The final model, which outperforms the others in within-sample and out-of-sample predictions, is a state

[8] The point estimate of $a_1 + a_2 + a_3 = 0.976$ with a standard error of 0.11. The authors also note that the mean-reverting model, when estimated using data from 1798 through 1899, over-predicts interest rates in the first half of the twentieth century.

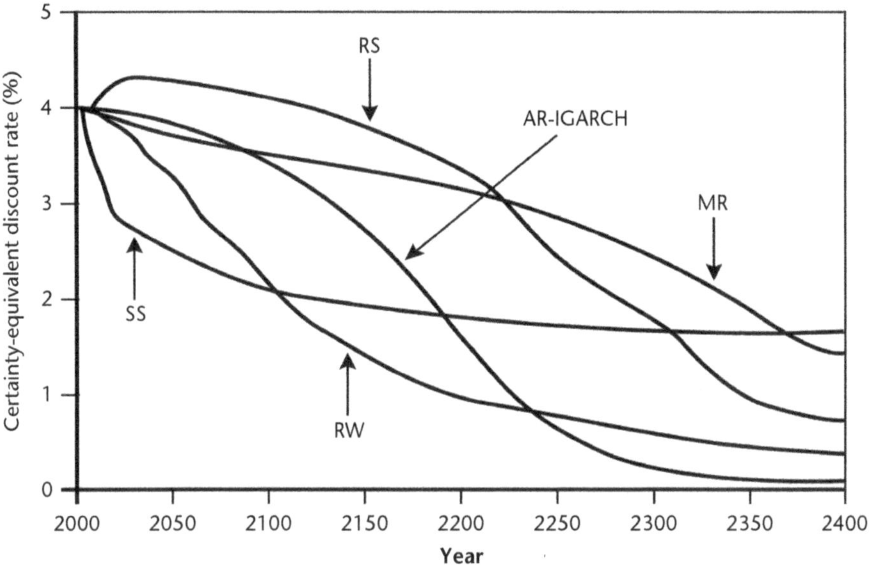

Figure 5.4. Forecasts of certainty-equivalent discount rates

Note: RS = Regime Switching, MR = Mean-Reverting, SS = State Space, RW = Random Walk, AR-IGARCH = Autoregressive Integrated Generalized Autoregressive Conditional Heteroskedasticity

Source: Groom et al. (2007)

space model. This is an autoregressive model that allows both the degree of mean reversion and the variance of the process to change over time.[9]

Groom et al. (2007) use their estimation results to simulate certainty-equivalent discount rates and use these in turn to compute the marginal social cost of carbon using data from Nordhaus (1994). Figure 5.4 displays the paths of certainty-equivalent discount rates based on all five models, starting from a discount rate of 4 per cent. The certainty-equivalent rates from the state space model decline more rapidly than rates produced by the random walk model (see Figure 5.4) for the first 100 years, levelling off at about 2 per cent. The random walk model yields a certainty-equivalent discount rate of 2 per cent at 100 years and 1 per cent in year 200, declining to about 0.5 per cent when t = 400. The social cost of carbon is, however, higher using discount rates produced by the state space model due to initial rapid decline in the certainty-equivalent rate and the path of climate change damages: $14.44 per ton of

[9] In the state-space model $r_t = \pi + a_t r_{t-1} + e_t,$ where $a_t = \sum \lambda_i a_{t-1} + u_t e_t$ and u_t are serially independent, zero-mean, normally distributed random variables, whose distributions are uncorrelated. The authors compare the models using the root mean squared error of within-sample and out-of-sample predictions.

carbon using the state space model versus \$10.32 per ton using the random walk model (1989 USD).

Results from the empirical DDR literature are sensitive to the model estimated, the data series used to estimate the model, and how the data are smoothed and corrected for inflation. However, these models clearly make a difference. Using the certainty-equivalent discount factors from Groom et al.'s (2007) preferred model increases the social cost of carbon, based on Nordhaus' damage estimates, by 250 per cent (from \$5.74 to \$14.44) compared to using a constant exponential discount rate.

The appropriateness of using these estimates for policy depends on one's view of what the discount rate represents. The empirical literature forecasts the risk-free rate of return on capital, as measured by the yield on long-term government bonds. The literature on cost–benefit analysis dictates that the net benefits of a project in year *t*—in consumption units—are to be discounted to the present at the rate at which society would trade consumption in year *t* for consumption in the present. The consumption rate of discount may not equal the risk-free rate of return on capital. Section 5.3 presents arguments for a DDR following the consumption rate of discount approach.

5.3 DDRs Based on the Ramsey Formula

In the context of inter-generational discounting, the consumption rate of discount is usually approached from the perspective of a social planner who wishes to maximize the social welfare of society (Dasgupta, 2008; Goulder and Williams, 2012).[10] In evaluating investment projects, a social planner would be indifferent between £1 received at time *t* and £ϵ today if the marginal utility of £ϵ today equalled the marginal utility of £1 at time *t*.[11]

$$u'(c_0)\epsilon = e^{-\delta t} u'(c_t) \tag{7}$$

Equation (7) assumes that the utility received from a given level of consumption is constant over time, but that future utility is discounted at the rate δ. Solving equation (7) for ϵ yields

[10] Dasgupta (2011) suggests an alternative approach in which an infinitely lived representative agent is replaced by dynasties of agents with finite lives. This model distinguishes between an individual's preferences for allocating consumption across his/her own lifetime from that person's preferences to bequeath resources to future generations.

[11] In this chapter c_t represents the average consumption of people alive at time *t*. In an inter-generational context *t* is often interpreted as indexing different generations; however, it need not be. It can simply represent average consumption in different time periods, some of which may contain the same people.

$$\epsilon = \frac{e^{-\delta t}u'(c_t)}{u'(c_0)} = e^{-\rho_{tt}} \tag{8}$$

where ρ_t denotes the consumption rate of discount. If we assume that $u(c)$ exhibits constant relative risk aversion (CRRA)$[u(c) = c^{(1-\eta)}/(1-\eta)]$ then ρ_t can be written using the familiar Ramsey formula

$$\rho_t = \delta + \eta \cdot g_t \tag{9}$$

where η is the coefficient of relative risk aversion (also minus the elasticity of marginal utility with respect to consumption) and g_t is the annualized growth rate of consumption between time 0 and time t.

In equation (9) δ is the rate at which society discounts the utility of future generations. A value of $\delta = 0$ says that we judge the utility of future generations to be equal to our utility, holding consumption constant. η describes (for any generation) how fast the marginal utility of consumption declines as consumption increases. Higher values of η imply that the marginal utility of consumption declines more rapidly as η increases. The standard interpretation of equation (9) is that the planner (society) will discount the utility of consumption of future generations at a higher rate because future generations are wealthier (i.e. the higher is the rate of growth in consumption, g_t). To illustrate, if g_t = 1.3 per cent per capita consumption in 200 years will be over 13 times higher than today. So, it makes sense to discount the utility of an extra dollar of consumption received 200 years from now. And, the planner will discount it at a higher rate the faster the marginal utility of consumption decreases as consumption rises.

We defer the discussion of how a planner should choose the parameters δ and η to section 5.4, and focus now on conditions under which equation (9) will yield a consumption discount rate that declines over time. Assuming that δ and η are constants and g_t is certain, a DDR requires the rate of growth in consumption to decline over time. The rate of growth in consumption is, however, uncertain—especially over long horizons.

If shocks to consumption are independently and identically normally distributed, uncertainty about g_t reduces ρ_t, but ρ_t will be constant. Suppose that $ln\ (c_t/c_0) = \sum_{i=1,t} ln\ (c_i/c_{i-1})$, where $ln\ (c_i/c_{i-1})$, the proportionate change in consumption at i, is independently and identically normally distributed with mean μ_g and variance $\sigma_g^{\ 2}$. This leads to the extended Ramsey rule (Gollier, 2007):[12]

$$\rho = \delta + \eta\mu_g - 0.5\,\eta^2\sigma_g^{\ 2}. \tag{10}$$

The last term in equation (10) is a precautionary effect: uncertainty about the rate of growth in consumption reduces the discount rate, causing the social

[12] This result goes back at least as far as Mankiw (1981).

planner to save more in the present.[13] The magnitude of the precautionary effect is, however, likely to be small, at least for the United States. Suppose that $\delta = 0$, and $\eta = 2$, as suggested by Dasgupta (2008). Using annual data from 1889 to 1978 for the United States Kocherlakota (1996) estimated μ_g to be 1.8 per cent and σ_g to equal 3.6 per cent. This implies that the precautionary effect = 0.002592 and that ρ = 3.34 per cent (rather than 3.6 per cent, as implied by equation (9)).[14]

As equation (10) illustrates, independently and identically normally distributed shocks to consumption with known mean and variance result in a constant consumption rate of discount. The consumption rate of discount may decline if shocks to consumption are correlated over time, or if the rate of change in consumption is independently and identically distributed with unknown mean or variance.

Gollier (2007) proves that if shocks to consumption are positively correlated and $u(c)$ exhibits CRRA, ρ_t will decline.[15] The intuition behind this is that positive shocks to consumption make future consumption riskier, increasing the strength of the precautionary effect in equation (10) as t increases. A possible form that shocks to consumption could take is for $ln\ (c_t/c_{t-1}) \equiv x_t$, the percentage growth in consumption at t, to follow an $AR(1)$ process

$$x_t = \varphi x_{t-1} + (1 - \varphi)\mu + u_t \qquad (11)$$

where u_t is independently and identically normally distributed with constant variance. Mathematically, equation (11) will generate a DDR, provided $0 < \varphi < 1$. To be precise, the precautionary effect is multiplied by the factor $(1 - \varphi)^{-2}$ as t goes to infinity (Gollier, 2008).

Various models of per capita consumption growth have been estimated for the United States (e.g. Cochrane, 1988; Cecchetti, Lam, and Mark, 2000) and these could be used to empirically estimate a DDR using the extended Ramsey formula. It is, however, the case that there is less persistence in the rate of change in per capita consumption in the United States than in the yield on the long-term bond reported in section 2. This approach is therefore unlikely to yield a certainty-equivalent rate that declines as rapidly as shown in Figures 5.3 and 5.4. In the case of equation (11) Gollier (2008) reports an estimate of φ = 0.3, based on the literature, which implies a very gradual decline in the certainty-equivalent discount rate. The same is true of the certainty-equivalent discount rate based on the regime-switching model of

[13] A necessary condition for this to hold is that the planner be prudent (i.e. that the third derivative of $u(c)$ be positive), which is satisfied by the CRRA utility function.

[14] Gollier (2011a) finds that the size of the precautionary effects is much larger for other countries, especially developing countries.

[15] Formally Gollier shows that if $ln\ (c_i/c_{i-1})$ exhibits positive first-order stochastic dependence and $u'''(c) > 0$, ρ_t will decline as t increases.

Cecchetti, Lam, and Mark (2000). The certainty-equivalent rate in the positive growth regime declines from 4.3 per cent today to 3.4 per cent after 100 years.

The approach to parameterizing the extended Ramsey formula described in this section is based on the assumption that the nature of the stochastic consumption-growth process can be adequately characterized by econometric models estimated using historical data. The consumption-based asset pricing literature suggests that this is not the case.[16] To quote Weitzman (2007), 'People are acting in the aggregate like there is much more... subjective variability about future growth rates than past observations seem to support.' This argues for treating μ_g and σ_g as uncertain. Subjective uncertainty about the trend and volatility in consumption growth, as modelled in Weitzman (2004, 2007) and Gollier (2007), will lead to a declining certainty-equivalent discount rate.

Weitzman (2004) considers the case in which x_t is independently and identically normally distributed with mean μ_g and variance σ_g^2. The planner is uncertain about μ_g and updates his/her diffuse prior using n observations on x_t. This leads to the following equation for the certainty-equivalent discount rate:

$$\rho_t = \delta + \eta\,\mu_g - 0.5\,\eta^2\sigma_g^2 - 0.5\,\eta^2\sigma_g^2(t/n). \tag{12}$$

Bayesian updating adds a fourth term to the extended Ramsey rule—a 'statistical forecasting effect'—which causes ρ_t to decline with t, conditional on n and σ_g^2. Intuitively, Bayesian learning generates positive correlation in the perceived growth of consumption.[17]

The form of the planner's subjective uncertainty about the mean rate of growth in consumption clearly influences the path of the certainty-equivalent discount rate. The assumptions in Weitzman (2004) cause the certainty-equivalent discount rate to decline linearly, eventually becoming negative (see equation (12)). Gollier (2007; 2008) presents examples that yield non-negative paths for the certainty-equivalent discount rate.

Gollier (2007) proves that, when the rate of growth in log consumption follows a random walk and the mean rate of growth depends on θ [$\mu_g = \mu_g(\theta)$], the certainty-equivalent discount rate, R_t, is given by

$$R_t = \delta + \eta\,M_t \tag{13}$$

where M_t is defined by

[16] The extended Ramsey formula does a poor job of explaining the equity premium puzzle: the large gap between the mean return on equities and risk-free assets.

[17] Weitzman (2007) also considers the case where $\sigma_g{}^2$ is unknown and is assumed to have an inverted Gamma distribution. In this case, Bayesian updating transforms the distribution of x_t from a normal into a student-t distribution, which has fatter tails. The certainty-equivalent discount rate also declines to $-\infty$ in this case.

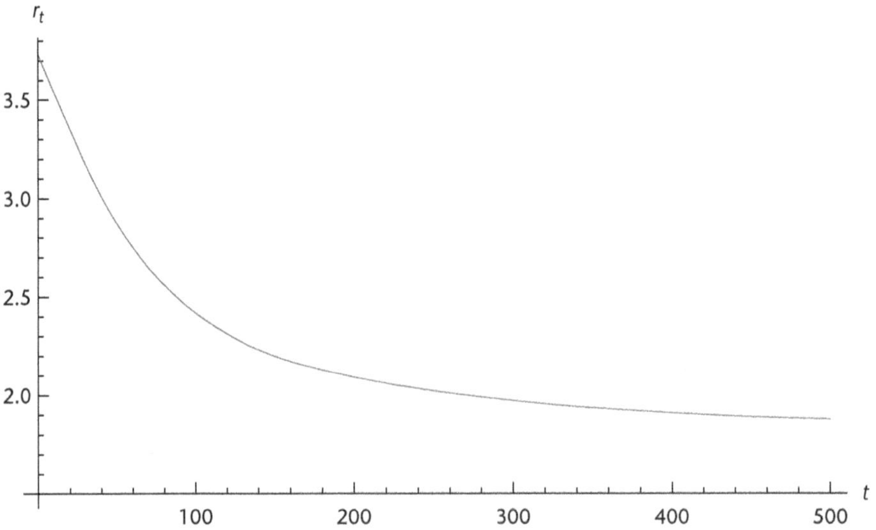

Figure 5.5. Certainty-equivalent discount rate assuming per capita consumption follows a random walk with uncertain mean ($\mu = \mu(\theta)$)
Source: Gollier (2011b)

$$\exp(-\eta t\, M_t) = E_\theta \exp\left[-\eta t\left(\mu_g(\theta) - 0.5\eta\sigma_g^2\right)\right]. \tag{14}$$

Due to Jensen's inequality, M_t (and R_t) will decline over time. Figure 5.5 demonstrates the path of R_t for case of $\delta = 0$, $\eta = 2$ and $\sigma_g = 3.6\%$. The mean rate of growth in consumption is assumed to equal 1 per cent and 3 per cent with equal probability. This yields a certainty-equivalent discount rate that declines from 3.8 per cent today to 2 per cent after 300 years—a path that closely resembles the French discounting schedule in Figure 5.1. The choice of other distributions for θ will, of course, lead to other DDR paths.

Uncertainty about the future rate of growth in per capita consumption can lead to a declining consumption rate of discount, assuming that shocks to consumption are positively correlated. Econometric models of per capita consumption growth can be used to parameterize the extended Ramsey formula, or subjective uncertainty about the trend and volatility of consumption growth can be used to derive a DDR. Econometric models of per capita gross domestic product (GDP) growth (Cochrane, 1988; Cicchetti, Lam, and Mark, 2000) are similar in form to the models used in the empirical ENPV literature. For the United States, however, these models do not suggest significant persistence in shocks to per capita consumption growth, implying that they will not generate a DDR that declines as rapidly as the DDRs in Figures 5.3 and 5.4.

Subjective uncertainty about the trend and volatility in consumption growth will also lead to a declining certainty-equivalent discount rate. The issue with this approach, from the perspective of policy-makers, is how to use it to obtain a numerical DDR schedule. As the examples in this section illustrate, the shape of the DDR is very sensitive to distributional assumptions about μ_g and σ_g. And, the fact that these distributional assumptions reflect subjective uncertainty makes it difficult to estimate them empirically.

5.4 How to Parameterize the Extended Ramsey Formula?

To parameterize the DDR using the consumption rate of discount requires estimates of δ and η as well as information about the process governing the growth of per capita consumption. The Ramsey approach to discounting, which underlies the theory of cost–benefit analysis, is a normative approach. This implies that its parameters should reflect how society values consumption by individuals at different points in time; that is, that δ and η should reflect social values. The question is how should these values be measured?

5.4.1 *δ and η as Ethical Parameters*

Many people would agree with Ramsey that it is ethically indefensible to discount the utility of future generations, except possibly to take account of the fact that these generations may not exist. This implies that $\delta = 0$, or a number that reflects the probability that future generations will not be alive. Stern (2006), for example, assumes that the hazard rate of extinction of the human race is 0.1 per cent per year.

The parameter η, which determines how fast the marginal utility of consumption declines as consumption increases, can be viewed as a measure of inequality aversion: it reflects the maximum sacrifice one generation should make to transfer income to another generation. To make this more concrete, Table 5.3 describes the maximum sacrifice that society believes a higher income group (A) should make to transfer £1 pound to the poorer income

Table 5.3. Maximum acceptable sacrifice from group A to increase income of group B by £1

η	Group A Income = 2*Group B Income	Group A Income = 10*Group B Income
0	1.00	1.00
0.5	1.41	3.16
1	2.00	10.00
1.5	2.83	31.62
2	4.00	100.00
4	16.00	10,000.00

Source: Gollier (2011b)

group (B), as a function of η. When group A is twice as rich as group B and $\eta = 1$ the maximum sacrifice is £2; when $\eta = 2$, the maximum sacrifice is £4.

How, empirically, should η be determined? One approach is to examine the value of η implied by decisions that society makes to redistribute income, such as through progressive income taxes. In the United Kingdom, socially revealed inequality aversion, based on income tax schedules, is pictured in Figure 5.6. As the figure reveals, η has fluctuated considerably since the Second World War, with a mean of 1.6 (Groom, 2011). It is also possible to elicit values of η and δ using stated preference methods. The issue here is whose preferences are to be examined and how. As Dasgupta (2008) has pointed out, it is important to examine the implications of the choice of η and δ for the fraction of output that a social planner would choose to save. *Ceteris paribus*, a lower value of η implies that society would choose to save a larger proportion of its output to increase the welfare of future generations.[18] The implications of the choice of δ and η would need to be made clear to the subjects queried.

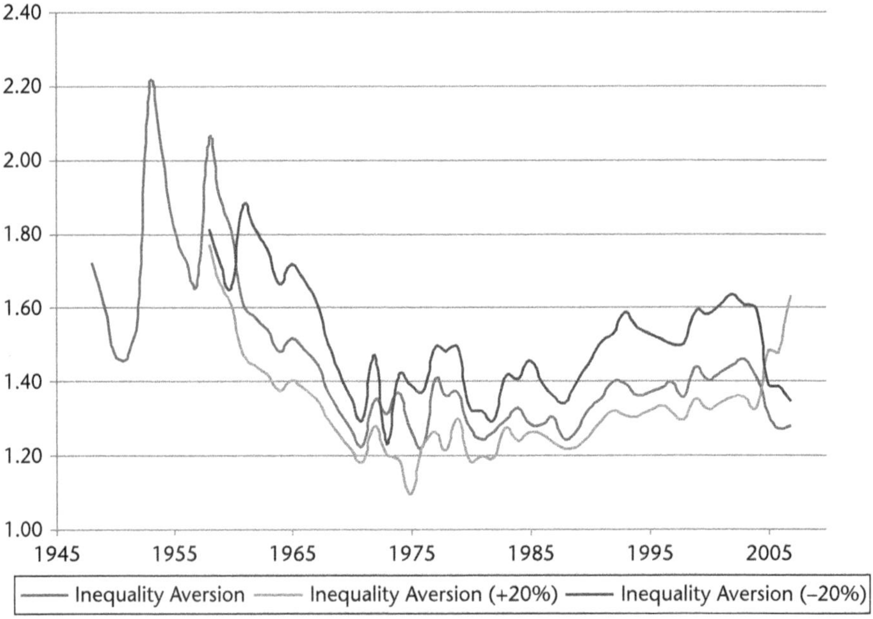

Figure 5.6. Estimates of inequality aversion (η) based on the UK income tax
Source: Groom (2011)

[18] Dasgupta (2008) criticizes the Stern Review's (2006) choice of $\eta = 1$ because it leads to an absurdly high rate of saving along an optimal consumption path. Higher values of η lead to more reasonable ratios of saving to output.

In equations (9) and (10) η also represents the coefficient of relative risk aversion. There is a large literature in which empirical estimates of η are inferred from savings and investment decisions in financial markets; however, these estimates do not reflect inter-generational consumption tradeoffs and are inappropriate as estimates of η in a social welfare function. It would, however, be possible to choose the coefficient of relative risk aversion from a social perspective by confronting respondents with lotteries over consumption.

5.4.2 *Should δ and η be Based on Observed Behaviour in Financial Markets?*

The suggestion that η be estimated from observed behaviour in financial markets raises the broader issue of whether the consumption rate of discount should reflect observed behaviour and/or the opportunity cost of capital. The 'descriptive' approach to social discounting (Arrow et al., 1996) epitomized by Nordhaus (1994, 2007), suggests that δ and η should be chosen so that ρ_t approximates market interest rates. In base runs of the Nordhaus DICE model, $\delta = 1.5$ and $\eta = 2$. DICE is an optimal growth model in which g_t and ρ_t are determined endogenously. ρ_t ranges from 6.5 per cent in 2015 to 4.5 per cent in 2095 (Nordhaus, 2007).

This raises the question: should we expect the consumption rate of discount in equation (8) to equal the rate of return to capital in financial markets, and, if not, what should we do about this? From a social welfare perspective, the consumption rate of discount in equation (9) will equal the marginal product of capital along an optimal consumption path. If, for example, the social planner chooses the path of society's consumption in a one-sector growth mode, ρ_t will equal the marginal product of capital along an optimal path. What if society is not on an optimal consumption path? Then theory (Dasgupta, Marglin, and Sen , 1972; Dasgupta, 2008) tells us that we need to calculate the social opportunity cost of capital—we need to evaluate the present discounted value of consumption that a unit of capital displaces—and use it to value the capital used in a project when we conduct a cost–benefit analysis. But, once this is done—once all quantities have been converted to consumption equivalents—the appropriate discount rate to judge whether a project increases social welfare is ρ_t.

5.5 Should Governments use a DDR in Cost–Benefit Analyses?

In cost–benefit analysis, the net benefits of a project in year t (in consumption units) are to be discounted to the present at the rate at which society would trade consumption in year t for consumption in the present. If utility of consumption exhibits CRRA the consumption rate of discount (ρ_t) is given by the Ramsey formula, $\rho_t = \delta + \eta g_t$, where δ is the utility rate of discount, η is the elasticity of marginal utility of consumption and g_t is the average rate of growth in consumption between t and the present. If there is persistence in uncertainty about the rate of growth in consumption, the certainty-equivalent consumption rate of discount will decline as t increases. This uncertainty in future consumption growth rates may be estimated econometrically based on historic observations, or it can be derived from subjective uncertainty about the mean rate of growth in mean consumption or its volatility.

The path from theory to a numerical schedule of the certainty-equivalent consumption rate of discount is, however, difficult. It requires estimates of δ, η and the process generating g_t. These are all difficult to estimate and to defend (or to explain!) to regulators. This suggests that a second-best approach may be called for.

The ENPV approach is less theoretically elegant, and does not measure the consumption rate of discount as given by the Ramsey formula. It is, however, empirically tractable and corresponds to the approach currently recommended by the United States Office of Management and Budget (OMB) for discounting net benefits, when expressed in consumption units (OMB, 2003). OMB acknowledges that 'the effects of regulation do not always fall exclusively or primarily on the allocation of capital. When regulation primarily and directly affects private consumption . . . a lower discount rate is appropriate.' A discount rate of 3 per cent is meant to represent this possibility and is approximated by the real rate of return on long-term government debt.[19] The empirical ENPV literature has focused on models of the rate of return on long-term government debt. And, in the United States, the literature suggests that the certainty-equivalent rate is declining over time.

For the DDR to be implemented empirically would require re-analysis of the choice of OMB's consumption rate of discount. Use of a DDR schedule would, however, avoid problems that arose in a recent benefit–cost analysis of fuel economy standards in the United States. The social cost of capital was calculated using a discount rate of 2.5 per cent while the fuel savings associated with the rule were discounted at 3 per cent. Different categories of benefits received in the same year were discounted at different rates, leading to inconsistency in the calculation of benefits. This problem could be avoided by using a DDR schedule.[20]

[19] Interestingly, OMB (2003) indicates that this rate is sometimes referred to as the 'social rate of time preference' and 'simply means the rate at which "society" discounts future consumption flows to their present value.'

[20] It could, of course, also be avoided by using the same constant discount rate (e.g. 3 per cent) to discount both sets of benefits.

It is also important to ask whether time consistency may be an issue in using a DDR for project analysis. It is well known that the decisions of a planner who discounts the utility of future consumption at a constant exponential rate will make time-consistent decisions even though the consumption rate of discount may decline over time (Gollier et al., 2008). The situation is somewhat different in the case of an analyst who is faced with an uncertain discount rate in an ENPV context. If an analyst were to evaluate future net benefits using the discounting schedule in gamma discounting (Weitzman, 2001) in 2012 and, if the schedule did not change over time, a program that passed the cost–benefit test in 2012 would not necessarily pass it in 2022, depending on the time pattern of net benefits.

Of course, if new information becomes available that alters the DDR schedule, the analyst will want to re-evaluate the ENPV of the program. Because new information is available, a reversal of the outcome of the cost–benefit analysis would not constitute time inconsistency. Newell and Pizer (2003) argue that an analyst, when using historical data to estimate a DDR, will naturally update estimates of the DDR as more information becomes available. This obviates the problem of time inconsistency. In a regulatory setting, however, such updating may occur only infrequently.[21] This is an issue to which more thought should be given.

5.6 Further Thoughts

The overarching theme of this volume is sustainable consumption. Choosing an appropriate discount rate schedule for project evaluation is an important part of promoting sustainable consumption—and it is certainly crucial to evaluating policies that will affect climate change. But, it is only part of the story. The design of policies to control GHG emissions involves important distributional issues that this chapter has ignored. As Dasgupta (2008) has noted, 'η is the index of the aversion society ought to display toward consumption inequality among people—be they people in the same period or in different periods'. But, the Ramsey formula does not adequately capture intragenerational distributional issues, and these are especially important in the case of climate change.[22]

[21] The United Kingdom discount rate schedule in Figure 5.1 has been in place since 2003 (HM Treasury, 2003).

[22] As my discussant, Hal Wilhite, has eloquently stated 'One of the problems with discounting global warming is that the consequences are separated from the source of the problem, not only in time but also in space. Western consumers emit climate gases, the most severe consequences of which will be experienced in other parts of the world.'

One way to capture the fact that poor countries are likely to bear the brunt of the damages associated with climate change is to assign equity weights when aggregating these damages. The marginal social cost of carbon, which, in a simple world of no tax distortions, would equal the tax on carbon, is the present value of climate change damages. But, these damages need to be assigned equity weights. Poor countries, where the marginal utility of income is higher than in rich countries, would receive higher weights in these calculations. As Anthoff and colleagues have demonstrated (Anthoff, Hepburn, and Tol, 2009) the use of equity weights may raise the marginal social cost of carbon by a factor of four or more. In integrated assessment models time discounting matters greatly, but so do distributional considerations.

References

Anthoff, D., Hepburn, C., and Tol, R. S. J. (2009) 'Equity Weighting and the Marginal Damage Costs of Climate Change', *Ecological Economics*, 68: 836–49.

Arrow, K. J. et al. (1996) 'Intertemporal Equity, Discounting, and Economic Efficiency', in J. P. Bruce, H. Lee, and E. F. Haites (eds), *Climate Change 1995: Economic and Social Dimensions of Climate Change, Contribution of Working Group III to the Second Assessment Report of the Intergovernmental Panel on Climate Change,* Cambridge: Cambridge University Press.

Cecchetti, S. G., Lam, P., and Mark, N. C. (2000) 'Asset Pricing with Distorted Beliefs: Are Equity Returns Too Good to Be True?', *American Economic Review*, 90(4): 787–805.

Cochrane, J. H. (1988) 'How Big is the Random Walk in GNP?', *Journal of Political Economy*, 96: 893–920.

Dasgupta, P. (2008) 'Discounting Climate Change', *Journal of Risk and Uncertainty*, 37: 141–69.

Dasgupta, P. (2011) 'Time and the Generations' Mimeo, Sustainable Consumption Institute, University of Manchester, April 2011.

Dasgupta, P., Marglin, P. A., and Sen, A. (1972) *Guidelines for Project Evaluation*, New York: United Nations.

Freeman, M. and Groom, B. (2010) 'Gamma Discounting and the Combination of Forecasts', available at: <http://papers.ssrn.com/sol3/papers.cfm?abstract_id=1676793>.

Gollier, C. (2007) 'The Consumption-Based Determinants of the Term Structure of Discount Rates' in *Mathematics and Financial Economics*, 1(2): 81–101.

Gollier, C. (2008) 'Discounting with Fat-Tailed Economic Growth', *Journal of Risk and Uncertainty*, 37: 171–86.

Gollier, C. (2011a) 'On the Understanding of the Precautionary Effect in Discounting', CESifo Working Paper.

Gollier, C. (2011b) Presentation. Workshop on Intergenerational Discounting, available at: <http://www.rff.org/Events/Pages/Intergenerational-Discounting-Workshop.aspx>.

Gollier, C., Koundouri, P., and Pantelidis, T. (2008) 'Declining Discount Rates: Economic Justifications and Implications for Long-run Policy', *Economic Policy*, 23: 757–95.

Gollier, C. and Weitzman, M. (2010) 'How Should the Distant Future be Discounted when Discount Rates are Uncertain?', *Economics Letters*, 107(3): 350–3.

Goulder, L. H. and Williams, R. (2012) 'The Choice of Discount Rate for Climate Change Policy Evaluation', *Climate Change Economics*, 3(4): 1–18.

Groom, B. (2011) Presentation. Workshop on Intergenerational Discounting, available at: <http://www.rff.org/Events/Pages/Intergenerational-Discounting-Workshop.aspx>.

Groom, B., Koundouri, P., Panopoulou, E., and Pantelidis, T. (2007) 'Discounting the Distant Future: How Much Does Model Selection Affect the Certainty Equivalent Rate?', *Journal of Applied Econometrics*, 22: 641–56.

H.M. Treasury (2003) *Green Book*, available at: <http://www.hm-treasury.gov.uk/data_greenbook_index.htm>.

Hepburn, C., Koundouri, P., Panopoulous, E., and Pantelidis, T. (2009) 'Social Discounting Under Uncertainty: a Cross-Country Comparison', *Journal of Environmental Economics and Management*, 57: 140–50.

Kocherlakota, N. R. (1996) 'The Equity Premium: It's Still a Puzzle', *Journal of Economic Literature*, 34: 42–71.

Mankiw, G. (1981) 'The Permanent Income Hypothesis and the Real Interest Rate', *Economics Letters*, 7: 307–11.

Newell, R. and Pizer, W. (2003) 'Discounting the Distant Future: How Much Do Uncertain Rates Increase Valuations?', *Journal of Environmental Economics and Management*, 46(1): 52–71.

Nordhaus, W. D. (1994) *Managing the Global Commons: The Economics of Climate Change*, Cambridge, Mass.: MIT Press.

Nordhaus, W. D. (2007) 'The Stern Review on the Economics of Climate Change', *Journal of Economic Literature*, 45(3): 686–702.

OMB (Office of Management and Budget) (2003) *Circular A-4: Regulatory Analysis*. Executive Office of the President, Washington, D.C., available at: <http://www.whitehouse.gov/omb/circulars/>.

Stern, N. (2006) *The Economics of Climate Change: The Stern Review*, Cambridge: Cambridge University Press.

Sterner, T. (2011) Presentation. Workshop on Intergenerational Discounting, available at: <http://www.rff.org/Events/Pages/Intergenerational-Discounting-Workshop.aspx>.

Weitzman, M. (2004) 'Discounting a Distant Future Whose Technology Is Unknown', available at: <http://www.sv.uio.no/econ/forskning/aktuelt/arrangementer/torsdagseminaret/2004/torsdag-v04/weitzman-1.pdf>.

Weitzman, M. L. (1998) 'Why the Far-Distant Future Should be Discounted at Its Lowest Possible Rate', *Journal of Environmental Economics and Management*, 36: 201–8.

Weitzman, M. L. (2001) 'Gamma Discounting', *American Economic Review*, 91: 260–71.

Weitzman, M. L. (2007) 'Subjective Expectations and Asset-Return Puzzles', *American Economic Review*, 97: 1102–30.

Part II

Challenging the Assumption that Individual Consumers Always Act Rationally

6

The Hungry Brain

Paul Fletcher

6.1 Introduction

Consumption should be easy to understand. Our primary requirements are for the maintenance of homeostatic balance—an avoidance of extremes of temperature or pH—and reproduction. These requirements, along with the periodic need to escape danger, require energy—and energy requires consumption. Maintaining this balance would be a simple matter in an environment in which our needs could be met without effort or exposure to danger. But for much of our history rewards have been sparse and costly in terms of energy. Moreover, their acquisition has entailed competition, in the forms of fellow reward-seekers and predators.

This observation leads us to a slightly more complex (though still simplistic) view of successful consumption. One that should be underpinned by separate sets of processes: those that govern what we wish to consume; and those that determine how we get it. That is, we must be sensitive to our needs and we must have a repertoire of behaviours allowing those needs to be met. Behaviours are optimized to maximize attainment of rewards. I think that the enormously complex development of these behaviours has created a hungry brain, driven towards consumption by salient and predictive environmental stimuli. This has led to a situation in which acquisitive behaviours are often dissociated from needs and in which actions can shift from reflective, flexible, and goal-directed to rapid, rigid, and habitual.

Put another way, we can consider consumption as being driven both by internal (homoeostatic) drives or *pushes* and external (environmental) *pulls*. The internal drive can modulate the impact of environmental pulls (profound hunger may make the blandest of foods desirable) and the environmental pull can over-ride internal drive, or lack of it (an attractive desert may be hard to resist even in the absence of hunger).

Hovering over this interactive set of motivating factors is the basic necessity of ensuring that the input of energy to the body is sufficient both to maintain survival (which itself is metabolically costly) and to expend energy in pursuit of further consumption. This introduces a further challenge to the inhabitant of the impoverished environment: if energy reserves are low, they must be replenished but this act of replenishment will itself deplete them further. At the other extreme, the brain is presented with quite a different challenge, and one that, it may plausibly be argued, it is ill-evolved to meet: the ready availability of high-energy foods with minimal outlay of physical, mental, or financial resources. In this latter situation, we might consider ourselves at the mercy of external pulls, or highly rewarding stimuli that drive, even in the absence of internal drives, what neuroscientists call acquisitive or consummatory behaviour.

Clearly, the simple act of consumption of food entails a complex and delicate balance of internal and external factors. This prompts some potentially useful observations. First, our environment can be considered not merely as a storehouse of potential rewards, each available in varying amounts and with varying degrees of availability depending on one's circumstances. Rather, it must been seen to contain numerous, potentially strong and sometimes irresistible, cues to consumption. These cues are linked in complex ways and mere proximity to a rewarding stimulus can render an otherwise neutral cue highly alluring and even enjoyable in itself. Furthermore, the rewarding properties of the stimuli that surround us and compete for our attention may lie, at least in part, in what they predict or promise. After all, a behavioural response to a stimulus occurs in the context of an association between that stimulus and some salient outcome. This goes well beyond food, which is just one among many rewards. In fact, it offers us a set of principles for considering highly complex reward-related behaviours, in many domains, in terms of association and reinforcement: terms that can be applied at the level of basic neuroscience but also at the level of individuals and groups of individuals. This perspective is therefore complementary to, and complemented by, for example, Andrew Oswald's consideration in Chapter 3 of how a non-food object (a watch) may become highly motivating through its associations. In recognizing the extent to which our environment is packed with external cues to behaviour, we can gain an understanding of how our actions may become led more my stimuli (to which we automatically respond) than by goals or desires. I will discuss this insight at some length. This perspective is central, too, to Geoffrey Beattie's and Laura McGuire's consideration of so-called type I and type II thinking in Chapter 8.

While the perspectives here have some overlap with those offered in the other chapters in this volume, they differ in a number of ways. Firstly, the remit of this work is very narrow. It largely consists of careful and repeated observations in small groups of individuals in highly constrained situations. Though I will allude to some exceptions, in which an individual's behaviour is viewed in the context of others, this is not considered in detail. This is in contrast to, for example, Andrew Oswald's chapter (Chapter 3) which considers the importance of social comparison in evaluating experimentally-administered rewards and the chapter by Richard Correia and Catarina Roseta-Palma (Chapter 9), which addresses factors such as social comparison in demand for water consumption. I am thus cautious in assuming that my observations translate easily or linearly to the real world. Secondly, in focussing on consumption of food (one of the 'primary' goals or rewards) I might be accused of neglecting sustainable consumption, the organizing theme of this volume. Focussing on the individual necessarily drives attention away from the bigger picture. Moreover, my focus is on the act of, rather than consequences of, consumption in distinction to most of the other chapters in this volume. But nonetheless, in the concluding section I speculate on how the perspective of neuroscience offers insights that may stimulate ideas for population-level changes in consummatory behaviour.

Further, in emphasizing the automaticity of behaviour, the ways in which it is initiated, governed, and shaped by incidental cues, I am concerning myself with an aspect of consumption that contrasts with notions of rationally-acting agents. The transition that I will explore, between goal-directed (and perhaps more rational) and habitual behaviours, is one that I believe must be taken into account in deriving as full as possible a picture of the drives towards consumption in humans.

I will begin by outlining a number of behavioural distinctions drawn by neuroscientists. Foremost in my consideration are food-related behaviours though I will extend some of the key neuroscientific insights to secondary rewards such as money.

6.2 Pushes and Pulls

Although there is growing concern over obesity, it is worth reminding ourselves that our ability to balance energy intake with expenditure, and thereby to maintain a fairly stable weight over a lifetime, is actually remarkable. Even in cases of severe obesity, the imbalance between intake and expenditure is not marked and most instances of obesity reflect a relatively subtle but persistently excessive intake (O'Rahilly, 2009). This suggests an exquisitely tuned ability to sense and respond to our nutrient needs—an ability that is determined by neural and hormonal factors. A key brain structure involved in this is the hypothalamus, which is sensitive to nutrient levels and hormones in the blood. That the hypothalamus is involved not just in sensing nutritional status but also in driving hunger and satiety is demonstrated by the fact that hypothalamic damage in the medial and lateral regions (just a couple of millimetres apart) leads to life-threatening over-eating and under-eating respectively. Furthermore, the congenital absence of hormonal signals to the hypothalamus (or dysfunction of the receptors for these hormones) has a profound influence on eating and weight. For example, the fat-derived hormone, leptin, normally rises following a meal and decreases with fasting. It is thought to be critical to the control of eating behaviour. People in whom this hormone is missing experience a continual drive to eat and a correspondingly severe obesity from an early age, a condition which resolves dramatically with hormone replacement (Farooqi et al., 1999).

Clearly, hypothalamic sensitivity to metabolic signals is an important origin of internal pushes towards food consumption. But even at this fundamental level, there is a striking interaction with higher level brain circuits known to be critical to reward, motivation, and learning. A functional neuroimaging study in two leptin-deficient adolescents (Farooqi et al., 2007) helped us to understand this interaction: in both people, observation of food images was associated with elevated responses in brain regions that form part of the dopamine reward circuit. These brain responses, unlike those found in healthy people, were large even when they had just eaten a large meal. Following a week of leptin treatment, the neural responses were significantly reduced (though weight, at this point, had not changed). Importantly, prior to treatment, both the subjective experience of foods and the neural responses to food images was relatively non-specific, with heightened reactions even to bland, unappetizing foods. Following treatment, the neural response became more selective, showing heightened response to pictures of more appetizing foods. These data are compatible with an interaction between internal pushes towards food and external pulls. In the leptin-deficient state, when the drive is high and persistent, neural circuitry known to be sensitive to attractive environmental stimuli shows heightened but unselective responses to food stimuli. Following replacement of the hormone, function in this circuitry is normalized and its responses appear to be more sensitive to the reward value of the depicted food.

These case studies indicate an intimate relationship between basic processes governing hunger and higher level experience of environmental stimuli, a relationship repeatedly confirmed by functional neuroimaging experiments showing heightened sensitivity of brain reward circuitry to food-related stimuli in fasted subjects. That this sensitivity is attenuated by satiety, strongly suggests that, as the internal drive abates, the stimuli become less motivationally salient.

In many ways, these observations are unsurprising. They are highly compatible with the everyday experience that our drive state modifies our experience of the attractiveness, or pull, of stimuli. Severe hunger and thirst increase the desirability even of foods and drinks that we otherwise dislike. But this relationship is not unidirectional. The pull of stimuli can create or curb the inner drive to consumption. We eat when we are not hungry and drink when we are not thirsty. This is an important observation. Consumption that arises solely in response to homeostatic need is not the problem. Rather, it is externally-driven consumption, the behaviour that goes beyond the simple need to fulfil our homeostatic requirements that seems more problematic.

In section 6.3 I will consider another important distinction, one that helps us to understand this externally-driven consumption: the distinction between *appetitive* and *consummatory* behaviours. Describing this will form a prelude to a description of the nature and neural bases of appetitive behaviours, detailed considerations of which are, I believe, very important to our understanding of consumption.

6.3 Meeting Our Needs: Appetitive and Consummatory Behaviours

Neuroscientists like to distinguish between two sets of behaviours related to our interactions with reward. Firstly, those aimed towards coming into contact with the reward; that is, the collection of often complex and strategic actions that may be necessary before, say, a food is acquired. These are referred to as *appetitive behaviours*. And secondly, those that entail a direct interaction with the reward itself, referred to as *consummatory behaviours*.

This is not merely a convenient, descriptive distinction: there is a great deal of evidence that the behaviours are dissociable and that this dissociation is seen at the neural level. Broadly speaking, damage to hypothalamus and its inputs from the brain stem leads to changes in consummatory behaviours but does not impair appetitive behaviours. Damage to higher level structures, including the amygdala and ventral striatum, on the other hand, leads to disrupted appetitive behaviours while consummatory behaviours persist. Thus, for example, with respect to sexual behaviours in the rat, damage to the hypothalamus may lead to a failure to copulate even when the animal has engaged in a complex train of preliminary behaviours in order to create an opportunity to do so (Everitt, 1990). This extends to temperature regulation: the animal will not shiver when the temperature is lowered but it remains able to learn to press a lever if such an action turns on the heat. Conversely, following amygdala damage, the animal appears unable to engage in the necessary chain of behaviours that brings it into contact with the reward: it will not learn to navigate its way towards a mate though it will show copulatory behaviour once presented with the opportunity.

For completeness, it is worth pointing out that this distinction is relevant to another influential dichotomy in animal neuroscience, that between *liking* and *wanting* (Berridge and Robinson, 1998). This will not be discussed here but, in brief, it emerges from observations that the liking (often called 'hedonic') responses to rewards in animals can be dissociated from the behaviours that seem to indicate a motivation towards (wanting) those rewards. Thus, for example, an animal experiencing temporary dopamine blockade makes no effort to acquire food but, if the food is presented directly, it shows every sign of relishing it.

6.4 Interim Summary

In order to understand the neural bases of consumption—whether of food, drink, or sex—it helps to remember that we are not just pushed by inner drives but pulled by external attractors. Ideally, these may be integrated so that our drive state reflects what we actually need and these needs therefore motivate and modulate behaviours that may be chained in complex ways in order to negotiate an environment that does not necessarily yield its rewards easily or safely. This integration is bidirectional. It is not that the attractive sheen of environmental stimuli is simply a reflection of primary need. Rather, these stimuli can create and shape such drives. A further distinction—between appetitive and consummatory behaviours—offers important insights to the neural bases for consumption. Appetitive behaviours are the array of actions concatenated in pursuit of reward. While they are sensitive to the organism's current and future needs, they are strongly driven too by environmental places, stimuli, and events, the effects of which may be both conscious and unconscious.

In section 6.5 I will consider the appetitive behaviours in more detail in the hope that this may offer useful insights to the arcane and indirect, yet potent, drivers of consumption.

6.5 Appetitive Behaviour and the Human Brain

Consummatory behaviours are relatively straightforward. Though by no means simple, they are largely instinctive and automatic, a matter of reflex requiring little if anything in the way of higher cognitive function. They proceed even in the context of widespread cortical and subcortical damage.

At their simplest appetitive behaviours also seem straightforward, requiring little more than the correct choice of action in order to obtain the desired reward. But a sparse, competitive, uncertain, volatile, and dangerous environment demands that the successful organism must develop a repertoire of more complex behaviours. An exploration of the neural basis of these behaviours has formed a large part of human and animal neuroscientific work. A number of important insights have emerged about how the brain enables these behaviours, drawing particularly on problems originally framed within fields such as machine learning and artificial intelligence (Sutton and Barto, 1998). Central to this work is, firstly, the idea that the brain seeks to maximize reward and to minimize punishments (i.e. to maximize the value of outcomes). In order to do this, the brain must learn associations between stimuli in the environment and between behaviours and outcomes, in order to predict consequences and select the actions that are most likely to bring about valued outcomes. The brain can be viewed as a learning and predicting device. Successful learning engenders accurate prediction, which in turn enables optimal evaluation of possible actions. Interactions with the environment can therefore become more rapid, efficient, and fruitful. But there is a price to be paid too. A system that is sensitive to the stimuli that predicts rewards, and that increases the capacity of those stimuli to drive rapid, vigorous actions, is also a system that may allow the usurpation of goal-directed actions (those that support the individual's needs) by stimulus-driven, inflexible, habitual responses. The latter, though they have the advantage of being rapid and efficient, may place the organism at the mercy of its environment—with behaviours driven more by external pulls than internal pushes.

This is a greatly simplified summary of a very big field of research. In section 6.6 I outline the ideas in more detail and selectively discuss experimental evidence for them, focusing mainly on human behavioural and neuroimaging studies.

6.6 The Learning Brain: Associations and Predictions

The connections between neurons (synapses) have long been recognized as providing a potential mechanism by which neuroplasticity may occur. Neuroplasticity refers to experience-dependent changes in brain structure and function. Repeated demonstrations of its ubiquity have refuted previous views that, after adolescence, these attributes of the brain remain fairly static. The first glimmer of a mechanistic understanding of neuroplasticity came from Hebb's work showing that 'neurons that fire together, wire together'.

That is, if two neurons have contact through a synapse and if each fires in response to separate stimuli that tend to co-occur (i.e. are associated) then the simultaneous firing of these neurons will lead to a change in the strength of their synaptic connection. While views of synaptic plasticity have become much more sophisticated than is captured in this early formulation, this simple insight points to an obvious mechanism for how the brain may code stimuli or events that are associated. Indeed, work from chimpanzees (Kawai et al., 2004) shows that even in the womb associations are formed between events occurring in the outside world. From its earliest stages, the brain is changing its microstructure to encode structural relationships in the environment.

But the mere occurrence of an association is insufficient to drive learning. New learning can be blocked by pre-existing knowledge. Suppose that I eat beetroot for the first time and discover that my tongue has turned red. Having established this, suppose that I make an (admittedly, unlikely) meal of beetroot and cherries. Once again my tongue turns red but I will not have updated my learning about the tongue-altering properties of cherries, despite the fact that the two events (eating cherries and tongue turning red) are strongly associated. This phenomenon, known in the associative learning field as 'blocking', has been demonstrated across a number of species and stimuli and it tells us something very important about whether and how the brain learns an associative relationship. That relationship must entail surprise. There must be an accompanying violation of expectancy—a so-called 'prediction error' (Schultz and Dickinson, 2000). The prediction error signal is a cornerstone of our understanding of learning: it is an internal signal that our current expectation (our current model of the world) is wrong and must be updated, with the reallocation of attention and the formation or adjustment of our associations.

Prediction error has been explored at the neural level for the last two decades and a widely, though not universally, accepted theory is that the prediction errors relating to reward are underpinned by a collection of neurons in an area of the midbrain called the ventral tegmental area (VTA). The VTA receives signals from the hypothalamus and related areas (thought to reflect the current drive state), from higher level structures including the frontal lobes (thought to relate to overall goals and motivations), and, indirectly, from a key memory structure, the hippocampus (signals emanating from here have been suggested to relate to, among other things, novelty). The output signals of VTA, involving the neurotransmitter dopamine, are widespread and include a region called the nucleus accumbens as well as frontal lobe areas. Some of the output travels in a collection of fibres called the median forebrain bundle (MFB), damage to which produces a state in which all appetites appear to be lost. Conversely, an animal that is given the capacity to provide electrical stimulation to its own MFB will do so repeatedly and enthusiastically. In addition, it is worth noting that dopamine is a key contributor to the long-term changes in synaptic efficacy that are critical to long-term learning.

Taken together, we have the components of a system which is sensitive to novelty, drives, and overall goals and which can, in the context of these attributes, translate unexpected occurrences into synaptic change (i.e. learning) and, ultimately, into motivated behaviours. This system is spread widely across the brain.

6.7 The Goal-Directed Brain: Stimuli Driving Actions

Much of the neuroscientific experimentation on reward-predicting stimuli has used what is known as operant or instrumental conditioning (such conditioning entails learning by doing and can be contrasted with Pavlovian conditioning, which entails learning more passively). During instrumental conditioning, the animal or person learns that, if they respond to a stimulus in a particular way, a reward will be obtained or a punishment avoided. Anticipated outcomes, whether positive or negative, are dominant drivers or reinforcers of action and simple principles of reinforcement have proven powerful and flexible in explaining an array of behaviours, both useful and harmful. For example, the escalation of drug use can be explained with reference to positive reinforcement. The desire for a pleasurable outcome—the high—drives the behaviour, namely drug-taking). Further, the persistence of drug use entails negative reinforcement: the desire to avoid an unpleasant outcome—withdrawal symptoms—drives the behaviour. This is almost trivially self-evident: we do what we can to get what we like and avoid what we don't like. But there is something more subtle, potent, and, crucially, resistant to control that accompanies instrumental, goal-directed actions: incidental stimuli that have no direct implications for choosing or motivating action can themselves become associated with the reinforcers and can come to govern behaviour. A clue to how this comes about arises from observations of the dopamine learning signal, referred to already and described in more detailhere.

The dopaminergic prediction error signal drives associative learning. Repeated experience results in an interesting pattern of activity. Initially, the presence of a reward increases the level of neural responding. But when another stimulus becomes a reliable predictor of that same reward, this stimulus appears to take on the reward's desirable properties. If we look closely at the response of dopamine neurons, their activity appears, with learning, to move forwards in time so that, rather than responding to the expected reward, they respond to anything that predicts it (Schultz, 1998). Once a reward is highly predicted, then its (unsurprising) receipt appears to engender little change in dopamine neuron firing. The (surprising) omission of the rewards, however, *is* associated with a reduction in dopamine neuron firing.

In short, key neurons begin to respond to predictors of outcomes, not just the outcomes themselves. This neural response is mirrored by behavioural change. It is as though the predictor has taken on the role of the outcome. This effect has been demonstrated in studies of second order conditioning, a situation in which the predictor of a reward comes to be treated as though it were the reward. If a light predicts a tasty treat, that light becomes a powerful motivator of responding and an animal will work hard for it even if it is no long associated with the treat. Indeed, the animal may come to interact with the light (licking or pecking at it) as though it were the treat itself. Such second order conditioning is regularly observed in humans. Money and air miles are nice examples of second order reinforcers. Such commodities retain their incentive motivation of behaviour even when their value recedes. This is illustrated nicely in *Robinson Crusoe* when the hero expends a great deal of energy in lugging bags of money to his shelter despite the fact that this money has no value in his isolation. In drug dependence, the paraphernalia of drug-taking (needles, packets, powder, mirrors) can become extraordinarily attractive to the user and functional neuroimaging in cocaine-dependent people suggests that the sight of such drug-taking accoutrements powerfully stimulates the components of the dopamine system discussed here (Volkow et al., 2006).

A brief digression is in order to make the point that, as is implicit in this section, the fundamental principles under discussion here are suggested to hold across different reward domains. Though particular rewards may have widely differing capacities to drive, for example, the release of dopamine (a drug such as cocaine produces a much more marked effect than, for example, a slice of chocolate cake), nonetheless, the speculation is that there is a common, or at least overlapping, system of brain reward circuitry that makes it possible to generalize the assertions made here to other primary rewards, such as sex, as well as secondary rewards like money, status, and possessions. On a related note, given that we are in every instant confronted with numerous stimuli, each predictive to differing degrees of relatively rewarding (or punishing) outcomes or associates, the question of which stimuli actually win the competition to drive behaviour is an interesting and complex one. Several factors will determine this and these include factors emerging out of the individual's current goals (a ravenous person may rapidly allocate attention to a familiar logo indicating food), or perhaps the insistence of a particular stimulus in comparison to those around it (brightly coloured signs indicating a sale may prove relatively alluring). Moreover, individuals' likelihood of attending to particular cues may be highly sensitive to how reliably predictive those cues are of an outcome.

Of course, if we consider a role of the system is motivating actions that acquire a reward (appetitive behaviour)—rather than the actions associated with its consumption (consummatory behaviour)—it seems very sensible that predictors gain our attention, inform our choices, and invigorate our responses. However, in favouring predictive stimuli like this, the brain does something very important and dangerous: it loosens the relationship between actions and desired outcomes. While this leads to an enhancement in the speed and efficiency of responding, it also allows the external pulls to exert a greater effect than the internal pushes towards consumption.

This effect—that stimuli can capture behaviour—has been well-demonstrated, in humans and animals, by the phenomenon of Pavlovian-Instrumental Transfer (PIT). As the name suggests this involves a transfer from a Pavlovian conditioned response to an instrumental conditioned response. Firstly, suppose that an incidental stimulus predicts a reward, as in Pavlovian conditioning—for example, a bell is rung and a dog is presented with food. Secondly, suppose the dog is placed in a chamber where it can press a lever to obtain food. This latter case is instrumental conditioning: the dog learns that the action of pressing the lever leads to the reward of food. Now suppose the food reward is removed from the experiment but the bell is rung. It is found that the rate and vigour with which the dog presses the lever increases when the stimulus of the bell is introduced. This happens even though the stimulus previously predicted reward without any need for any action. In brief, if cue C predicts outcome O, and action A brings about outcome O, then C will provoke A. The incidental but predictive stimulus comes to shape the selection of actions and the vigour with which those actions are performed. The sight of an old drinking partner may trigger the irresistible urge to drink in an abstaining alcoholic. Furthermore, the motivational effect of the predictive cue extends to other behaviours which, in its presence, are performed with greater vigour than in its absence. Thus, the McDonalds logo enhances a three year old's consumption and enjoyment of raw carrot (Robinson et al., 2007).

This is not to say that the environmental stimuli completely over-ride current needs or goals. But it is increasingly clear that such stimuli, even when they are not consciously perceived, shape consummatory behaviour. We have recently observed the degree to which even the briefest presentation of relevant stimuli can change motivation and how this effect can also be modulated by current drive state (Ziauddeen et al., 2011). Healthy people, in a fasted state, played a game in which stimuli appearing on a screen prompted them to squeeze a grip force transducer in order to win the item depicted by that stimulus. Importantly, these stimuli included pictures of muffins and pizza, which, in their fasted state, participants found very attractive. Unsurprisingly, grip force exerted in response to these food pictures was greater than that evoked by other non-food items. The hungry participants were then given a substantial portion of one of the foods before recommencing the task. While their responding remained strong for the item that they had *not* been given, it was significantly reduced for the one that they *had* eaten. Again, this is unsurprising: this phenomenon whereby one no longer desires a food that one has just eaten but retains a desire for other foods is well known and is referred to as 'sensory-specific satiety' (Rolls et al., 1981). What was interesting about our study, however, was that, in half of the cases, images were presented subliminally: below the level of conscious awareness, such that the subjects were aware only of a flicker on the screen but did not consciously perceive the stimulus depicted. In such cases the same effects were observed even though none of the images were consciously perceived. The experiment clearly demonstrates the measurable impact of even the most subtle and fleeting stimulation on motivation towards foods. It shows, too, that the metabolic state, the sensory properties of consumed foods, and the internal valuation of foods can interact below the level of conscious awareness. It is noteworthy that elevated grip responding has been found in response to subliminally presented reward stimuli, notably money (Pessiglione et al., 2007). Intriguingly, if the image is presented to one cerebral hemisphere, the increased grip occurs only in the hand controlled by that hemisphere (Schmidt et al., 2010).

Perhaps this should make us pause. The evidence clearly indicates that even stimuli that are not consciously perceived can have a measurable impact on our choices and actions towards food. Importantly, these influential stimuli are not the rewards themselves but rather environmental associates of the rewards. It seems to be a simple matter to alter someone's behaviour by populating their environment with incidental but predictive stimuli. This, of course, has not escaped the notice of advertisers and shopkeepers whose adornment of their products with the colours and symbols of Christmas will, they seem to believe, elevate consumption even in September. The existing studies suggest that they are probably right.

6.8 When Environmental Stimuli take Complete Control: The Transition from Goal-directed Actions to Habitual Behaviours

I have considered the brain in terms of its sensitivity to environmental stimuli (even those below the level of consciousness), with this sensitivity forming the basis for accurate associative learning. This learning is driven by prediction error signals and, in turn, forms the basis for future predictions. A system in which prediction errors engender alterations in synaptic efficacy (i.e. learning) enables optimization of future predictions (assuming, of course, that the environment is not excessively volatile). Optimizing predictions is useful because it allows optimal action selection, and this maximizes the opportunity for obtaining rewards and avoiding harm. The system is further enhanced by the fact that predictive stimuli seem to have a fast track to action—they shape and invigorate it even when those actions may be unnecessary. Ultimately, and perhaps of greatest relevance to the emergence of aberrant and harmful consumption, these stimuli may come to drive actions that produce undesired outcomes. Such stimulus-driven actions may persist even when the outcomes prove detrimental to one's health, happiness, or bank account. At this stage one may say that actions are no longer directed towards a goal but are habitual. I consider this distinction here.

Habits are often not terribly well defined. Perhaps most commonly, they are used to describe actions that are routinely and frequently performed. In my view, and in the view of many neuroscientists, this idea is not entirely helpful. A more useful definition, and one that is supported by observations of the brain (de Wit and Dickinson, 2009), entails a distinction between actions that are made with a goal in mind (goal-directed action) and those that are divorced from the goal, being performed automatically in response to a stimulus (habit). Notwithstanding my preference for this definition, it is important to note that it is not the only one and some would consider habits in terms of how routine and practised they are, rather than in terms of any specific change in the degree to which they are cued or resistant to altered outcome value. However, in many instances the precise definition reflects a theoretical rather than a practical concern given that more routine and practised behaviours are also more likely to be inflexible and resistant to change (even when negative consequences occur).

Habits are extremely efficient. They bypass thoughts of goals and they automatize and speed up responses to stimuli. In many instances, the introduction of reflective cognitive processing renders behaviour less efficient ('the native hue of resolution is sicklied o'er with the pale cast of thought'). The ambition of an optimally predictive brain must surely be to produce as many habitual responses as possible, freeing up cognitive resources and allowing appropriate actions to occur with as little interference as possible. It is noteworthy that stressful situations drive our responses towards the habitual. Imagine driving home along an intimately familiar route: a hugely complex series of actions and reactions may occur while one's thoughts are elsewhere. One may arrive with no recollection of the journey. But this speed and efficiency sacrifices flexibility. A goal-directed action is one that is made in the belief that it will produce an outcome and in the context of a drive state in which that outcome is desired. These are no longer considerations in the setting of habitual actions. So-called 'slips of action' (de Wit and Dickinson, 2009) occur when a habitual behaviour becomes intrusive rather than helpful. It is not unknown for someone to move house and find themselves obliviously driving to their old house. Of course, such an error is unlikely to recur given that one rapidly develops a new set of behaviours. Nonetheless, these slips of action give us an insight into the situations in which the actual goal seems to play very little role in shaping a complex train of behaviours. Critically, given the right (or wrong) circumstances, the persistence of the behaviour goes well beyond a single slip and this may be associated with subtle but long-lasting change in the neurocircuitry controlling the behaviour.

Given this key distinction—that the desire for, and prediction of, outcomes drives goal-directed behaviour and that stimuli drive habitual behaviour—an important and potentially harmful characteristic of the latter emerges. Habits persist. They are insensitive to a devaluation of the outcome. This can easily be demonstrated in animals. If a particular response, say, a lever press, leads to a reward, and if the animal receives repeated training on this contingent relationship, the behaviour becomes habitual: it persists when the predicted reward no longer arrives and even when that reward is no longer desired (e.g. when the animal has been fed to satiety or when the reward has been paired with a nauseating chemical). In humans, it is less easy to set up the intensive and prolonged training that transforms goal-directed into habitual actions. However, building upon a conflict procedure that has successfully produced this transformation in rats (de Wit et al., 2007) we developed an experimental manipulation in healthy volunteers undergoing functional magnetic resonance imaging (fMRI) (de Wit et al., 2009). In brief, the manipulation was based on the fact that goal-directed actions occur when a cueing stimulus prompts the thought of the goal and this thought prompts the relevant action. Over a series of trials, it was set up so that a particular stimulus served, in some cases, as a predictive cue and, in others, as an outcome. Critically, the conflict was produced by ensuring that the action required when that stimulus served as a cue was different to when it served as the subsequent outcome. Under these experimental circumstances when someone sees a cue this will produce two competing processes. On the one hand, he/she will recall the action associated with that cue in its role as a predictive stimulus. On the other, that cue will remind him/her of its status as an outcome and therefore of the action that obtained it. These two actions conflict and lead to performance difficulties. Rats resolve this conflict by ignoring outcomes and engaging in stimulus-driven (habitual) behaviour. Humans, too, it transpired, abandon goal-directed behaviour. We were able to observe the neural changes that accompanied this transition. An area of medial prefrontal cortex showed reduced responding under these action–conflict circumstances. Moreover, when we subsequently devalued the status of stimuli as outcomes, they showed the outcome insensitivity classically associated with habitual responding and the degree to which this occurred was predicted by the level of attenuation in frontal activity. It appears therefore that the transformation to habit-based responding is associated with reductions in frontal activity. This observation resonates with general ideas that integration of frontal and striatal responses shape and modify behaviour according to current goals; and that people in whom such integration is disrupted may be prone to more impulsive, automatic, and unreflective behaviour (Volkow et al., 2008). It is highly appropriate that drug use is sometimes referred to as habitual, given that it happens even when the individual desperately tries to avoid the behaviour and when the drug itself no longer gives pleasure. It is striking too that relapse in drug use may be precipitated not by the immediate proximity of the drug but by an incidental and unfortunate exposure to people, places, or objects that were previously intimately linked with the drug experience. These stimuli retain a powerful capacity to drive behaviour despite the fact that they may not have been confronted for months or even years. Coverage of the elegant neuroscientific studies exploring the neural underpinnings of these habits is beyond the scope of this chapter. The work of Everitt and Robbins (e.g. see 2005) is highly recommended.

6.9 Further Considerations: Beyond the Here and Now—Time and Uncertainty in Human Reward Learning

I have concentrated in this chapter so far on the simplest case, where current stimuli inform actions aimed at obtaining immediately valuable outcomes. Clearly this gives a very partial view of how we seek and interact with rewards. A further important characteristic of the successful organism lies in the capacity to anticipate future needs and to act accordingly. Such needs, as they become dissociated from current drives, may lack the immediate value of outcomes that are closer in time. The classic *temporal discounting* phenomenon suggests that, as rewards become more distant, capacity to motivate choice and behaviour is correspondingly attenuated. Interestingly, this appears to be related to dopamine function (Pine et al., 2010). The availability of fast food, when someone is in a ravenous state, can trump the less immediate desire for healthy eating and weight control. An important consideration in modulating behaviours is whether and how health-promoting decisions (to cook, to exercise, to abstain) can be made rewarding not just in the long term but now. Perhaps the observations of second order conditioning discussed in section 6.7 may offer hope in this respect. These observations suggest that a stimulus that is not primarily rewarding can come to acquire reward value by dint of its proximity to other stimuli.

We should remember too that the system needs to deal with a variable degree of uncertainty: sensory inputs are noisy; environments are dynamic;

resources are finite. A stimulus or action that precedes a desired outcome today will not necessarily do so next week. Recent observations using fMRI in humans has suggested a well-developed behavioural and neural sensitivity to such volatility and a sophisticated capacity to change learning depending on whether the environment in which one finds oneself can be predicted accurately and reliably (Behrens et al., 2007).

6.10 Beyond the Individual: The Influence of Social Factors

Individuals differ in their capacity to resist impulsive behaviours. Such resistance correlates with responses in brain reward circuitry and it has been considered as a factor that protects against health-harming consumption of food or drugs. But it is critical to consider too phenomena that emerge in the interaction between individuals. That such a consideration is current in neuroscience is demonstrated by a large and growing body of work in social neuroscience. While a consideration of the field is beyond the scope of this chapter, it is worth pausing to remember that our learning and valuation of stimuli, as well as the decisions and actions that they provoke, is highly determined by social factors. A few simple observations are worth making in this respect. First, the reinforcement learning models that successfully capture an individual's capacity to learn from his/her interaction with the environment are also able to capture that person's capacity to learn from observing other individuals interacting with that environment. Moreover, the neural circuitry that serves this learning is highly overlapping but not identical. The latter observation has led to some contention over whether socially-based learning entails the functioning of dedicated, socially-specific brain systems or whether it is simply the case that social learning demands additional processes that are not themselves specific to the social domain. This remains unresolved. However, one striking finding is that the brain response to environmental uncertainty in a reward-learning task is close to, but distinct from, the response to social uncertainty; though both forms of learning appear to thereafter employ the same circuitry in evaluating the ensuing rewarding outcomes (Behrens et al., 2008).

That decisions concerning reward and consumption are socially influenced is both intuitively and empirically compelling. To select just one example, the willingness of an individual to accept menu advice from a waitress is dependent on whether that waitress is considered overweight and this effect is pre-determined by whether the recipient of the advice is him/herself on a diet or not (McFerran et al., 2010). It should be noted too that one's behaviour and the subjective evaluation of reward is heavily influenced by the observation of the behaviour (and attendant success or failure), a point that is clearly made by Andrew Oswald in Chapter 3 of this volume. This introduces a further, and clearly important, perspective on the social influence on human behaviour: that of what other people value and what other people do. Here the factors, and interactions between factors, become far more complex than can currently be encompassed by human neuroscience research but recognition of the need for work in this area is emphasized by the growing field of social cognitive neuroscience. It is notable too that these ideas form key components of other chapters in thisvolume; notably a fascinating historical perspective on the relationship between inequality and consumption from Richard Wilk in Chapter 14 and an economic perspective from Partha Dasgupta in Chapter 2. Alan Warde (Chapter 12) shows clearly the importance of social practice in consumption albeit he offers a markedly different, though I feel a highly complementary, perspective on habitual behaviours and their importance.

6.11 Summary and Further Thoughts

The perspective that the brain is a predicting device whose goal is to select actions in pursuit of valuable outcomes, captures a number of interesting characteristics of consumption. Particularly interesting is the notion that environmental cues, which are not rewarding in themselves but come to be reliable predictors of rewards, can come to usurp our inner drives and enslave our choices and consumption. The speed and efficiency of such a system is helpful up to a point, but it comes at a cost. Specifically, it can become inflexible, persistent, and dissociated from outcome value. This is the essence of habitual behaviour—extremely useful but potentially harmful.

Are these insights of any practical value in thinking of ways to modify consumption? Perhaps. There are grounds for optimism given the wide influence that basic associative models of behaviour have had in modifying certain forms of anxiety and phobia. Such conditions themselves may be precipitated and maintained by the capacity for previously neutral environmental cues to drive behaviours to such an extent that an individual is distressed and incapacitated by an inability to shake off the effects of these cues. The distress and incapacity are not ameliorated by the conscious knowledge that the cues have little real value or power other than that with which they are invested by the sufferer. With this in mind, therapeutic strategies tend to involve re-learning the significance of these cues and experiencing them in the absence of outcomes in order that their effects may be extinguished. Perhaps the appetitive cues in the environment may be similarly viewed as a prelude to developing therapeutic strategies. Given our growing knowledge of the neurotransmitters that are key to consumption, the possibility of specifically targeting these systems in order to modify appetitive drives is an intriguing possibility

(Fletcher et al., 2010). Though this may be done successfully it is difficult to do it specifically and it is likely that the pharmacological approach will be limited. We should consider the possibility of using individually-tailored, learning-based treatment regimens to establish and diminish the key motivators to consumption, but this is unlikely to prove easy. We should consider too whether those who wield these powerful tools and populate our environment with irresistible cues in the form of brands and logos should be subject to stricter constraints.

But, as I confessed at the outset, this has largely been a consideration of individual behaviours in unique and specific situations. Perhaps admitting this is tantamount to acknowledging that, currently, cognitive neuroscience has little to say about consumption at the population level. However, one recurring theme in this view of human behaviour is that it is driven predominantly by automatic and habitual responses, rather than reflective and goal-directed processes. Thus, when non-legislative interventions are under consideration as a strategy to modify or reduce the preponderance of health-harming over-consumption, this should be taken into consideration. Given that the majority of such interventions currently target reflective processes (by seeking to change values and to educate potential consumers), this is not yet an insight that is helping to shape policies. It has been pointed out that this should change (Marteau et al., 2012) and that interventions targeting automatic behaviours may prove more effective, tractable, and scalable to larger groups.

Finally, and perhaps most importantly, another approach is one that does not emphasize the desire to curb health-harming consumption by devaluing the reward that it brings, but rather one that nurtures health-promoting consumption by maximizing its value. Choices depend on predicted value. If unhealthy foods are not only an isolated source of reward but also an economic necessity, their relative value will be high and the alternatives few. Under such circumstances, choices will become stereotyped and, as I have tried to outline in this chapter, environmental cues are potentized and goal-directed behaviours transform easily into habits.

References

Behrens, T. E., Hunt, L. T., Woolrich, M. W., and Rushworth, M. F. (2008) 'Associative Learning of Social Value', *Nature*, 456(7219): 245–9.

Behrens T. E., Woolrich, M. W., Walton, M. E., and Rushworth, M. F. (2007) 'Learning the Value of information in an Uncertain World', *Natural Neuroscience*, 10(9): 1214–21.

Berridge, K. C. and Robinson, T. E. (1998) 'What is the Role of Dopamine in Reward: Hedonic Impact, Reward Learning, or Incentive Salience?', *Brain Research Review*, 28(3): 309–69.

de Wit, S., Corlett, P. R., Aitken, M. R., Dickinson, A. and Fletcher, P. C. (2009) 'Differential Engagement of the Ventromedial Prefrontal Cortex by Goal-directed and Habitual Behavior toward Food Pictures in Humans', *Journal of Neuroscience*, 29 (36): 11330–8.

de Wit, S. and Dickinson, A. (2009) 'Associative Theories of Goal-directed Behaviour: A Case for Animal–Human Translational Models', *Psychological Research*, 73(4): 463–76.

de Wit, S., Niry, D., Wariyar, R., Aitken, M. R. and Dickinson, A. (2007) 'Stimulus-Outcome Interactions during Instrumental Discrimination Learning by Rats and Humans' Journal of Experimental Psychological Animal Behavior Processes', 33(1): 1–11.

Everitt, B. J. (1990) 'Sexual Motivation', *Neuroscience and Biobehavoural Reviews*, 14(2): 217–32.

Everitt, B. J. and Robbins, T. W. (2005) 'Neural Systems of Reinforcement for Drug Addiction: From Actions to Habits to Compulsion', *Natural Neuroscience*, 8(11): 1481–9.

Farooqi, I. S., Bullmore, E., Keogh, J., Gillard, J., O'Rahilly, S. and Fletcher, P. C. (2007) 'Leptin Regulates Striatal Regions and Human Eating Behavior', *Science*, 317: 1355.

Farooqi, I. S., Jebb, S. A., Langmack, G., Lawrence, E., Cheetham, C. H., Prentice, A. M., Hughes, I. A., McCamish, M. A., and O'Rahilly, S. (1999) 'Effects of Recombinant Leptin Therapy in a Child with Congenital Leptin Deficiency', *New England Journal of Medicine*, 341: 879.

Fletcher, P. C., Napolitano, A., Skeggs, A., Miller, S. R., Delafont, B., Cambridge, V. C., de Wit, S., Nathan, P. J., Brooke, A., O'Rahilly, S., Farooqi, I. S., and Bullmore, E. T. (2010) 'Distinct Modulatory Effects of Satiety and Sibutramine on Brain Responses to Food Images in Humans: A Double Dissociation across Hypothalamus, Amygdala, and Ventral Striatum', *Journal of Neuroscience*, 30(43): 14346–55.

Kawai, N., Morokuma, S., Tomonaga, M., Horimoto, N., and Tanaka, M. (2004) 'Associative Learning and Memory in a Chimpanzee Fetus: Learning and Long-Lasting Memory Before Birth', *Developmental Psychobiology*, 44(2): 116–22.

Marteau, T., Hollands, G. J., and Fletcher, P. C. (2012) 'Changing Human Behaviour to Prevent Disease: The Importance of Targeting Automatic Processes', *Science*, 337: 1492–5.

McFerran, B., Dahl, D. W., Fitzsimons, G. J., and Morales, A. C. (2010) 'Might an Overweight Waitress Make You Eat More? How the Body Type of Others is Sufficient to Alter Our Food Consumption', *Journal of Consumer Psychology*, 20: 146–51.

O'Rahilly, S. (2009) 'Human genetics illuminates the paths to metabolic disease', *Nature*, 462: 307–14.

Pessiglione, M., Schmidt, L., Draganski, B., Kalisch, R., Lau, H., Dolan, R. J., and Frith, C. D. (2007) 'How the Brain Translates Money into Force: A Neuroimaging Study of Subliminal Motivation', *Science*, 316(5826): 904–6.

Pine, A., Shiner, T., Seymour, B., and Dolan, R. J. (2010) 'Dopamine, Time, and Impulsivity in Humans', *Journal of Neuroscience*, 30(26): 8888–96.

Robinson, T. N., Borzekowski, D. L., Matheson, D. M., and Kraemer, H. C. (2007) 'Effects of Fast Food Branding on Young Children's Taste Preferences', *Archives of Pediatric Adolescent Medicine*, 161(8): 792–7.

Rolls, B. J., Rolls, E. T., Rowe, E. A., and Sweeney, K. (1981) 'Sensory Specific Satiety in Man', *Physiological Behaviour*, 7(1): 137–42.

Schmidt, L., Palminteri, S., Lafargue, G., and Pessiglione, M. (2010) 'Splitting Motivation: Unilateral Effects of Subliminal Incentives', *Psychological Science*, 21(7): 977–83.

Schultz, W. (1998) 'Predictive Reward Signal of Dopamine Neurons', *Journal of Neurophysiology*, 80(1): 1–27.

Schultz, W. and Dickinson, A. (2000) 'Neural Coding of Prediction Errors', *Annual Review of Neuroscience*, 23: 473–500.

Sutton, R. and Barto, A. (1998) *Reinforcement Learning*, Cambridge, Mass.: MIT Press.

Volkow, N. D., Wang, G. J., Telang, F., Fowler, J. S., Logan, J., Childress, A. R., Jayne, M., Ma, Y., and Wong, C. (2006) 'Cocaine Cues and Dopamine in Dorsal Striatum: Mechanism of Craving in Cocaine Addiction', *Journal of Neuroscience*, 26(24): 6583–8.

Volkow, N. D., Wang, G. J., Telang, F., Fowler, J. S., Thanos, P. K., Logan, J., Alexoff, D., Ding, Y. S., Wong, C., Ma, Y., and Pradhan, K. (2008) 'Low Dopamine Striatal D2 Receptors are Associated with Prefrontal Metabolism in Obese Subjects: Possible Contributing Factors', *Neuroimage*, 42(4): 1537–43.

Ziauddeen, H., Subramaniam, N., Gaillard, R., Burke, L. K., Farooqi, I. S., and Fletcher, P. C. (2011) 'Food Images Engage Subliminal Motivation to Seek Food', *International Journal of Obesity*, 36(9): 1245–7.

7

Consuming at the Wrong Rate

Lessons from the Harvard Game

Drazen Prelec[1]

> 'I should have drunk more champagne.' attributed to John Maynard Keynes'

7.1 Introduction

A lifetime of consumption, that is, a personal consumption *history*, is built up from a myriad of choices, some deliberate and some less so. This holds not only for purchases of goods and services, but also for daily investments of time into work, exercise, family life, or the solitary pleasures offered up by the so-called 'social' media. Is it reasonable to expect that these moment-by-moment choices should produce a history that maximizes personal welfare? If consumption is too high or low, how would a person come to realize this?

Maximization requires knowing the correct rate of consumption, as well as an ability to implement that rate through repeated choices. Over the last several decades, behavioural economists and psychologists have challenged our competence on both counts. Behavioural economists have studied problems of implementation that arise when agents have incomplete self-control (Thaler and Shefrin, 1981; Fudenberg and Levine, 2006), or exhibit hyperbolic discounting (Ainslie, 1975; Laibson, 1997). Psychologists have, in turn, uncovered biases and illusions in predicting one's own preferences (Loewenstein et al.,

[1] These ideas reflect many hours of discussion with Yonatan Loewenstein and Sebastian Seung. I am also grateful to Alistair Ulph for extended comments on the first draft of this chapter. The usual disclaimer applies.

2003; Gilbert, 2006). An ambitious agenda looms in the background, namely, to show that science can replace traditional sources of advice and establish objective principles for individual welfare. More modestly, experimental evidence might help diagnose generic, preventable sources of dissatisfaction, and leave the pursuit of the definition of happiness to others.

In this chapter I discuss the difficulties involved in setting a rate of consumption or allocating time across activities. Both are examples of *distributed choice* (Herrnstein and Prelec, 1991), a term that describes situations where utility is naturally defined on an aggregate scale, averaging consumption over some period of time, while choices take place on a local scale, occasion-by-occasion. As a result, each local choice—for example, to open a bottle of champagne—has a direct utility effect via the current consumption experience, and an indirect utility effect on satisfactions derived from future bottles, and perhaps satisfactions with other things as well.[2] If the indirect effect is not taken into account, we have an *internality* (Herrnstein et al., 1993), leading to consumption rates that the consumer might, upon reflection, recognize as sub-optimal. Internalities formally resemble externalities, which are the 'unacknowledged or unrecorded consequences for others (including future generations) of actions taken by one or more persons' (Dasgupta, Chapter 2). The key difference is whether the ignored consequences fall on other individuals (externalities) or the decision-maker him/herself (internalities).

Why might a consumer fall victim to an internality? Consider the difference between choosing how much to consume on a specific occasion and choosing a rate of consumption. Both decisions involve marginal utility. When deciding whether to consume one or two scoops of ice cream a persons knows, from experience, that the second scoop is likely to be less satisfying than the first, and can compare the reduced enjoyment of the second scoop against the (likewise lower) price. Here, the incremental utility of the second scoop is a surface phenomenon, traceable to a specific experience. In setting a rate of consumption, a person also needs to consider marginal utility, because more frequent consumption makes each occasion less satisfying or special. However, the net impact of increasing the rate by one unit combines two disparate effects, namely, (i) the satisfaction produced by one extra occasion, and (ii) the reduction in satisfaction distributed over many subsequent occasions. There is no

[2] Economists might view this as an example of habit formation, or taste change, but that would be an overly specific interpretation of the phenomenon. If one consumes champagne more often, so that some of the 'special occasion' feeling is lost, that would normally be treated as a simple illustration of the diminishing marginal utility principle. It is not necessarily the case that taste for champagne has been fundamentally altered. Of course, tastes could shift as a result of consumption—one might acquire a more discriminating palate or an alcohol problem—but those enduring changes in preference are a separate matter psychologically, formal similarities notwithstanding.

single moment at which one experiences the net marginal utility of an extra visit to the ice cream parlor. This makes the problem much more difficult.

The literature dealing with this problem is extensive, and I will focus on a single strand of evidence that has emerged from an experimental paradigm that has come to be known as the 'Harvard game'. The game simulates a utility machine, in which subjects make a long series of choices between two alternatives and experience a variable reward after each choice. The rewards may appear stochastic, but are in reality a purely deterministic function of the current choice and the choices made previously. The history dependence, that is, the functional relationship between reward and past choices, is designed to seduce subjects into a utility-minimizing pattern of choices. In effect, subjects learn to choose what is bad for them.

What can the artificial setting of a laboratory game teach us about sub-optimal consumption 'in the wild'? One can make an argument that the laboratory decision problem is easier than what one faces in real life, and also a case for the opposite view, that the laboratory problem is harder. I will examine both sides of the issue, and then consider three categories of potential internalities:

(1) Consumption that produces invidious changes in one's capacity for pleasure, with substance addiction being an extreme case.
(2) Dividing a fixed budget between superior, more expensive variants of an activity or product, and inferior, cheaper versions.
(3) Accumulation of stocks of goods.

7.2 History of the Game

The Harvard game was developed in the Harvard 'pigeon lab', at a time when B. F. Skinner's presence was still strongly felt. Skinner's ambition was to create an experimentally grounded science of human behaviour, based on universally valid principles of conditioning and learning. The studies were largely done with animals, on the assumption that the results would generalize to people.

In the 1970s and 1980s the lab was headed by Richard Herrnstein, a great experimental psychologist in his own right, who shared Skinner's vision but added a belief in the value of quantification. Herrnstein's key contribution was the discovery of a 'matching law' relating frequencies of response to simple parameters of reward, such as frequency and delay (Herrnstein, 1970). The matching law asserted that in a steady state one should observe equal average rates of return from all reward sources. The average rate of return was defined by a simple ratio: the number of rewards, divided by effort or time invested in an activity. Faced with different average rates of return, subjects would put more time into activities with higher average rates of return, continuing until either one activity displaced all others or until the average rates of return became approximately equal. The dynamic process tending toward an equality of average rates of return was called *melioration* (Vaughan Jr., 1981; Herrnstein and Prelec, 1992).

The matching equations worked nicely in practice. One could sit down the night before an experiment and predict quite well what the pigeons would do the next day, much the way that one might plan out a physics or chemistry experiment. However, about 1980, several researchers developed an alternative approach, based on applying economic demand theory to animal experiments (Rachlin et al., 1976). Subjects pressing levers or pecking keys for food or drink were assumed to maximize a function of effort and consumption, given the constraints imposed by the experimental procedure. The implication of this optimizing approach is that consumers, whether human or animal, should equalize the marginal return per unit of income or effort, rather than the average return assumed by Herrnstein. This was an interesting idea, but it failed to explain certain robust features of animal choice if the notion of optimization was taken literally. What seemed to be at issue is whether the animals were tracking average or marginal value (Prelec, 1982).

The Harvard game was an attempt to put the two principles in the sharpest possible contrast, so that someone who systematically shifted choices toward alternatives that delivered higher average value would thereby wind up with approximately the smallest possible total. Thomas Schelling's N-person's Prisoner's Dilemma game, as described in *Micromotives and Macrobehavior*, provided inspiration (Schelling, 2006). Here, strikingly, was a set up in which individual optimization produced the worst collective outcome. The internality was therefore constructed to be an exact analogue of the externality in Schelling's game, and when I first presented our results (Figure 7.2) I referred to it as an 'Intra-personal Prisoner's Dilemma' (Prelec, Herrnstein, and Vaughan Jr., 1986; see also Loewenstein et al., 2009).

7.3 The Harvard Game

Certain psychology findings are difficult to intuit from the armchair, from a mere description of the protocol. The game has some of this quality, so it may be helpful to indicate how a typical subject would experience it. The instructions are minimal: the experiment presents an opportunity for earning money by executing a long series of binary choices as rapidly as possible. Each choice involves pressing one of two buttons, after which a light stays on for what feels like several seconds, no more than ten. The choice of the left button leads to a red light, the right button to a blue light. When the light comes on, there is no indication how long it will stay on for. It might seem a bit like waiting for an elevator to come, or a webpage to load. Each choice earns 10 cents and the game lasts 10 minutes, so the time during which the light stays on is simply wasted. The objective, therefore, is to make the lights as short as possible. There are 100 practice choices at the start, allowing subjects to try a few strategies without cost.

A typical subject might make choices and experience delays that resemble those in Figure 7.1. The top panel shows delays that would accompany roughly equal exploration of the two sides, which is how one might start. The first order impression is that the red side is followed by shorter delays, and is therefore more attractive. It is apparent that the delay following a choice is not the same, and that the sequence of choices might therefore influence the outcome. This would cause a typical subject to favour the red side, and experience something like the delays displayed in the bottom panel. At this point, the delays seem somewhat longer than they were in the beginning, but attempts to try something different by sampling blue are punished by even longer delays.

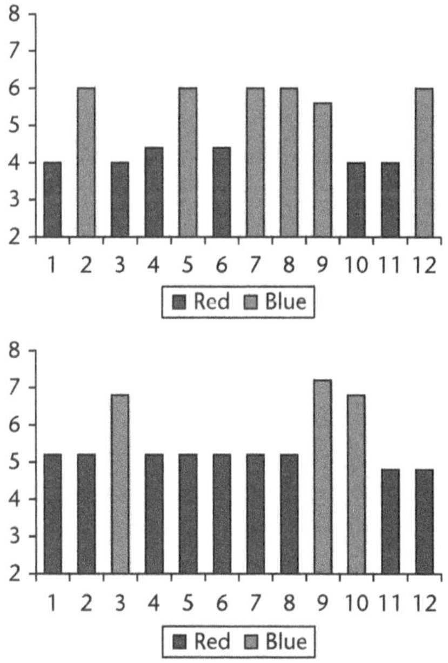

Figure 7.1. Typical pattern of delays experienced over a dozen choices early in a session of the Harvard game (top panel), and when choices stabilize (bottom panel)

Notes: Delays are displayed on the vertical axis, and range from 2 to 8 seconds. Shorter delays imply higher pay-off rate. The best strategy (Blue always) yields 4 second delays; the worst strategy (Red always) yields 6 second delays

Source: the author

The algorithm that governs delays is deterministic: on any given choice, and irrespective of the previous sequence of choices, the selection of red produces a delay that is faster by 2 seconds. However, as a side effect, each selection of red adds 0.4 seconds to each of the next ten delays, again irrespective of the particular choice sequence that follows. Therefore, a selection of red carries a total penalty of 4 seconds, distributed evenly over the next ten choices. The optimal strategy for someone who understands the algorithm is to never touch red, and always select blue. Conversely, exclusive preference for red is the worst possible strategy (ignoring a small end-game effect, where it pays to briefly return to red). Other strategies produce a rate of return that linearly interpolates between these two extremes, in proportion to the division of choices between red and blue.

7.4 Results and Variations

In this situation, most subjects do not recognize the hidden cost of the quicker alternative, and drift toward exclusive preference for the bad one (red). Earnings typically fall close to the theoretical minimum. In the original study, subjects preferred red by about a nine to one ratio. The best subjects, who presumably deduced something about the delayed costs, still could do no better than chance (Prelec, Herrnstein, and Vaughan Jr., 1986).

The Harvard game has been replicated many times with variations. Here are some stylized facts about the impact of different conditions. First, one can rule out impatience as an explanation. It is true that delays, even on the order of several seconds, are unpleasant (think of a slow internet connection). However, if this same experiment is conducted so that longer delays are good, signifying larger rather than smaller pay-offs, the results remain unchanged (Herrnstein et al., 1993). Second, transforming the game into one of loss minimization tends to improve performance (Herrnstein et al., 1993), and especially improves the performance of depressive subjects (Maddox et al., 2012). Third, and perhaps most important, there is significant improvement if pay-offs are conveyed quantitatively as the amount earned per choice, rather than qualitatively as delay (Herrnstein et al., 1993). In the former case, the subject merely learns the outcome of each choice, in the latter case he/she also endures an extended experience, which may be pleasant or unpleasant in itself, apart from any financial consequences. This would be consistent with a dual 'hot–cold' decisional architecture, where the delay experience causes the hot system to be engaged. The experiential delay version might therefore be a better approximation to actual consumption.

The simplest version of the Harvard game limits history-dependence to only the single previous choice (rather than ten previous choices), so that a choice of red improves the current delay by 2 seconds but exacts a cost of 4 seconds on the next round, and has no further consequences. As in the original game, the optimal strategy remains exclusive preference for blue. In this relatively more transparent setting, the typical subject divides choices about equally between two alternatives, which is considerably better than in the original version but still far from optimal. However, one does find a few subjects who 'solve' the problem, and prefer the blue side almost exclusively (Prelec, Herrnstein, and Vaughan Jr., 1986).

As expected, performance can be influenced by providing information about the algorithm. Telling subjects that their current choice determines future outcomes, without specifying the nature of the impact, raises efficiency from 14 per cent to 25 per cent, if efficiency is measured by the per cent correct Blue choices. Going one step further and specifying the structure of the algorithm, namely, that selecting one option reduces the subsequent quality of *both* options, raises efficiency to 58 per cent. With this strong hint, subjects know that the red choice harms future pay-offs unambiguously, yet are still unable to compute the trade-off between present and future pay-offs (Herrnstein et al., 1993).

That people find the problem hard need not in itself be suprising. The reward function in Figure 7.2 may be easy to define, but it is only one of

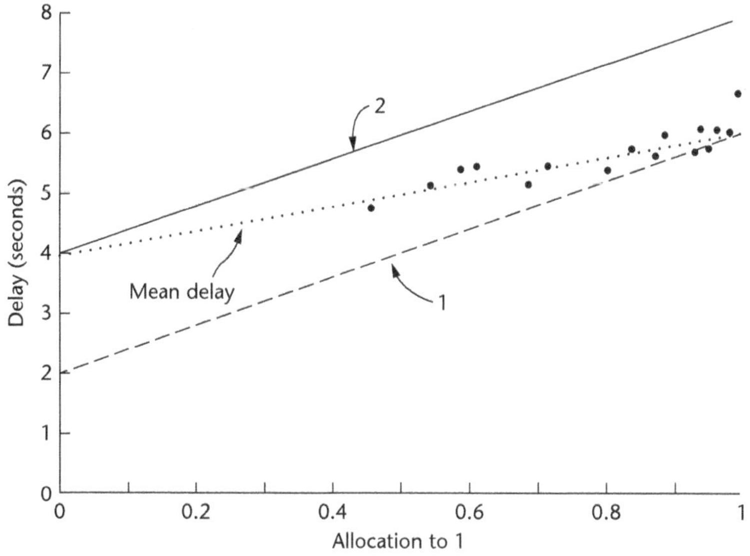

Figure 7.2. Results from the original Harvard game (Prelec, Herrnstein, and Vaughan Jr. 1986), as shown in Herrnstein and Prelec, 1991

Notes: Pay-off is a negative linear function of Delay. Most subjects' earnings approximated the theoretical minimum

Source: Herrnstein and Prelec (1991)

infinitely many possible history-dependent schemes, and subjects have little information about the relevant search space.

How would state-of-the-art optimization methods perform in the same environment? Given enough trials, machine learning techniques would certainly arrive at the correct solution (Baxter and Bartlett, 2001; Loewenstein, Prelec, and Seung, 2011). Such algorithms distribute credit for the current pay-off to a running average of past choices (the 'eligibility trace'); if the running average has a long memory, the algorithm is guaranteed to eventually converge to the optimum, but the speed of convergence is slow.

Recent simulations have tested a powerful Bayesian learning model in the Harvard game, and shown that finding the correct strategy remains difficult (Sims et al., 2013). In the implementation of Sims et al., the rational learner starts with a prior over all possible history-dependent algorithms that keep track of no more that ten past responses (this prior is biased toward functionally simpler algorithms, with smaller state spaces). The rational learner has complete memory and uses past data on choices and outcomes to compute a posterior distribution over possible algorithms by Bayes' rule. If this past data matches the history of 400 trials produced by experimental subjects, the rational learner would make the correct directional inference only about half the time. In the remaining cases, the pattern of exploration that a particular subject exhibited is not sufficiently informative to deduce the directional structure of the game. If the past data is itself generated by an exploration algorithm (e.g. choosing randomly), the learner will eventually deduce that blue is the correct strategy, but it may take thousands of trials to do so.

One should note that Sims et al. (2013) implement the Harvard game as a two-armed bandit: the pay-off functions in Figure 7.2 are treated as probabilities of a (binary) reward following each choice. The signal about the functions is therefore garbled by a random device, which is not the case in the original Harvard game. This caveat notwhitstanding, the simulation results suggest that a seemingly simple problem of history-dependent reward creates huge challenges for Bayesian learning if learning starts with a uniform prior. The performance of a Bayesian machine is of course not an absolute ceiling on human performance. I have noticed that in classroom presentations of the Harvard game a naïve volunteer player may, on a rare occasion, guess the correct strategy by a sheer contrarian insight, namely, that the obvious strategy must be incorrect in a demonstration of this type. There is no question that people could optimize if their prior beliefs are strongly biased in the right direction. This brings up the crucial question of ecological validity of the game as a model for actual consumption inefficiency.

7.4.1 *Example One: The Harvard Game as a Model for Soft Addictions*

Consider a pill that improves the quality of sleep on the night it is taken by 20 per cent, that is, it leaves the individual 20 per cent more energetic on the following day. The pill also has a delayed side effect in that sleep quality will deteriorate by 4 per cent for each of the next ten days after it is taken, irrespective of what happens on those days. The example is not far fetched, requiring only a reasonable assumption of habituation to sleeping aids. If the positive and negative percentages add up, the optimal strategy is to avoid the pill altogether. Taking the pill nightly results in a 20 (= 40 – 20) per cent reduction in quality of sleep relative to baseline. Occasional use yields a linear interpolation between these two extremes.

We can think of this as a mild addiction, an example of the sorts of bad habits and mistakes potentially present in real life (Herrnstein and Prelec, 1992; Heyman, 2009). Formally, the values in the example reproduce exactly the pay-off structure of the Harvard game. Which situation is more likely to trap people in the sub-optimal corner?

There are several reasons why the lab setup might be easier. First, the number of trials is large, the choices are massed in a short period of time, without distractions or exogeneous 'shocks' to utility. Second, the practice rounds in the lab provide opportunities for costless exploration of alternative choice patterns; in the pill case, experimentation is costly. Third, and perhaps most important, in the experiment time discounting and self-control play no role. The duration of the experiment is held constant, and the payout is received at the end of the session. The subject cannot speed up the task, the only thing that will be affected is how much money he/she makes at the end. In the sleeping example case, a subject who understood the algorithm would still need to balance the discounted value of the future costs in sleep quality against the immediate benefit of improved sleep on the very next day. The individual might understand that pill taking is a bad idea, but because of hyperbolic discounting, would not be able to implement this.[3]

Against this view, one could point out that the stakes in the experiment are small, and the person does not have too much incentive to carefully record outcomes, nor too much time to consider systematic approaches to the problem. Perhaps more importantly, in the real world one is not limited to learning from personal experience. There are formal and informal sources of information, one can absorb advice and learn by watching others.

[3] In essence, the Becker-Murphy model of addiction takes this view (Becker and Murphy, 1988). The additional feature of the Becker-Murphy model is that the lines in Figure 7.2 must have different slope, being further apart in the bad corner.

7.4.2 *Example Two: Consuming Too Much, Too Quickly*

Example One presented a choice between two alternatives, one exhibiting increasing returns to consumption and the other exhibiting decreasing returns. What about more standard cases of diminishing marginal utility on both sides? Here, too, we can find internalities, if the consumer chooses according to the principle of equal average value.

Many pleasures rest on a foundation of desire or appetite, which depends, in turn, on consumption frequency. There is experimental evidence that people burn appetite by consuming too rapidly, even when they understand the general relationship between consumption and appetite (Galak et al., 2013). This bears directly on choices between frequent consumption of cheap goods (e.g. snacks) and less frequent consumption of more expensive ones. Indeed, I now derive a new implication of melioration, namely, that it produces a bias in favour of cheap, lower quality items within a category of goods serving a common need.

To give concreteness to the example, imagine a wine and champagne drinker with a fixed monthly budget for both beverages, hence facing a trade-off between enjoying the cheaper one (wine) more often or the more expensive one (champagne) less often. Let us denote the respective monthly rates of consumption, x_c, x_w, and assume that the average satisfaction derived from beverage *i* is a decreasing function,$v_i(x_c + x_w)$, of combined consumption of both drinks,$(x_c + x_w)$. Desire thus depends on total intake, not on the source. This is a reasonable approximation for rate-dependent satiation, not just for alcohol but also for any collection of goods serving a common appetite. For example, hunger depends primarily on calories consumed, and secondarily, if at all, on the price and quality of the meal.

Suppose that the consumer has fixed budget for both drinks, and settles into a meliorating allocation of income where the average utility per dollar is the same for both drinks, $v_c(x_c + x_w)/p_c = v_w(x_c + x_w)/p_w$, with p_c, p_w denoting prices. This might seem sensible, yet it will leave the person drinking too little champagne. The implication follows from a comparison of marginal utilities per dollar for the drinks. At an optimal allocation, the two marginal utilities per dollar should be the same. However, at the meliorating allocation, the marginal utility of champagne per dollar will be greater.

Observe that total utility for a month of consumption is the product of rate and the satisfaction experienced on an average occasion, at that rate: $u(x_c, x_w) = x_c v_c + x_w v_w$, hence the difference between the marginal utilities per dollar for champagne and wine is:

$$\frac{\partial u}{\partial x_c}/p_c - \frac{\partial u}{\partial x_w}/p_w = (v_c + x_c v_c' + x_w v_w')/p_c - (v_w + x_c v_c' + x_w v_w')/p_w > 0 \qquad (1)$$

The inequality follows from (i) the equality of average utilities per dollar at the meliorating allocation: $v_c/p_c = v_w/p_w$, (ii) the assumption of satiation:$v_i' < 0$, and (iii) the fact that champagne is more expensive: $p_c > p_w$. Therefore, the consumer would do better to cut back on cheap wine in favour of champagne.

The internality arises because the consumer squanders a scarce resource—appetite or desire—on the cheaper commodity. Given a fixed budget, the more expensive commodity will necessarily restrain consumption and promote total satisfaction. The expensive item succeeds purely as a rationing device.

That overconsumption is a chronic problem has been conjectured, but direct experimental evidence is less available. An interesting recent study has shown that experimental subjects enjoy simple experiences (snacks, or video games) more when consumption is paced by an external clock, with extended time pauses, than when they are allowed to freely choose how fast to consume (Galak et al., 2013). Moreover, subjects whose consumption is yoked to a schedule chosen by others likewise enjoy things less than subjects whose experiences are paced further apart, showing that the critical variable is speed of consumption, not whether consumption is under voluntary control or externally rationed.

7.4.3 *Example Three: Accumulating Too Much, or Too Little*

The internalities described so far are best described as neglect of an internal psychological or physiological state, such as appetite. However, internalities may arise with respect to observable quantities or characteristics, in situations where the impact of a single decision on the relevant quantity is difficult to assess or very small (Prelec, 1991). Thus a single session at the study desk may have little impact on the test score, a single savings deposit will not materially affect well-being in retirement, and though a 'moment on the lips' may 'stay forever on the hips', the weight gain due to one portion of dessert is likely to be negligible, in terms of appearance or health. The consequences of many everyday actions may appear lost in the noise.

An important class of distributed choice internalities arise from stock-and-flow interactions, when utility depends both on consumption and on the stock of an item, but the impact of individual purchase and consumption decisions on stock is ignored (again, because a single purchase has a small impact on stock). For example, a wine drinker derives pleasure from consumption and also from having a cellar. The ideal cellar should reflect a balance of different considerations, such as carrying cost, wine aging, variety, and so on. Suppose, however, that the person does not think about this problem at all, but rather lets the size and composition of the cellar emerge gradually through individual purchase and consumption decisions, which are assessed on a one-off basis (this would be called 'narrow bracketing' of choice consequences (Read and Loewenstein, 2000)).

To simplify further, let us concentrate on a decision whether to drink an expensive, rare bottle of wine that is already in the cellar. There is a tension between the desire to consume now, and the desire to preserve it for future contemplation or display. Someone who consumes such bottles rarely will feel that by drinking it now he/she is destroying years of expected ownership. Conversely, a person who tends to drink the best bottles quickly will suspect that this particular bottle will not last irrespective of what happens today. This creates a positive feedback loop, where a low rate of consumption increases the perceived benefits of ownership relative to consumption, promoting an even lower rate. Conversely, a high rate of consumption reduces the value of ownership for any single item, promoting an even higher rate. As a result, one individual may accumulate a large cellar, with expensive bottles surviving past their prime, while the other has no cellar at all.

The two individuals could of course have different preferences, but that is not essential to the example. Even with identical preferences, the outcome of the dynamic process depends on initial conditions, leaving at least one, and possibly both individuals with a cellar of wrong size.

7.5 Conclusion

We have seen how a simple history-dependent reward scheme—simple in the sense of being easy to define—can prove intractable, unless the solver, whether a human or a Bayesian algorithm, has some prior information about its nature. This is perhaps the main lesson of the Harvard game. To the extent that the bodily processes of satiation, adaptation, and taste formation exhibit similar history dependence and are similarly opaque, the individual will be vulnerable to negative utility traps: stable allocations that not only fall short of the optimum, but may indeed approximate a local utility minimum.

This bears directly on the normative status of revealed preference and the merits of paternalistic policy interventions. I will not say much about paternalism, except to point out the following. It is significant that even with an agent as rational as the Bayesian learner of Sims et al. (2013), we can easily find ourselves in a situation where 'revealed preferences' do not reveal preference in any substantive sense, in a reasonable period of time. If we take the choices of experimental subjects in the game at face value, we might reach an absurd conclusion that they prefer to earn less money with more effort. And, if we cannot trust the revealed preference principle in simple laboratory games, why should we trust it elsewhere?

The real world internalities of our three examples here have been in large part conjectural. In the absence of a utility meter, it is hard to convict someone of utility inefficiency. But, this is also true for externalities that are based on psychological rather than physical side effects, such as, for example, the Veblen externalities created by social comparisons (Dasgupta and Erhrlich, 2013). From the standpoint of policy, the fundamental difference between internalities and externalities lies elsewhere. Since internalities are based on sheer neglect of side effects, and the person who is responsible for them also suffers the consequences, it seems that they should be curable by information alone. Plainly, this is not the case. Instead, any internality is likely to require two separate stories, one explaining why individuals fall into the trap and another why it is so difficult to climb out of it, after the scales have fallen from the proverbial eyes. The Harvard game, and indeed any laboratory experiment of this type, may only shed light on 'Chapter One'.

References

Ainslie, G. (1975) 'Specious Reward: A Behavioral Theory of Impulsiveness and Impulse Control', *Psychological Bulletin*, 82(4): 463–96.

Baxter, J. and Bartlett, P. L. (2001) 'Infinite-horizon Policy-gradient Estimation' *Journal of Artificial Intelligence Research*, 15(4): 319–50.

Becker, G. S. and Murphy, K. M. (1988) 'A Theory of Rational Addiction', *The Journal of Political Economy*, 96(4): 675–700.

Dasgupta, P. S. and Erhrlich, P. R. (2013) 'Pervasive Externalities at the Population, Consumption, and Environment Nexus', *Science*, 340(6130): 324–8.

Fudenberg, D. and Levine, D. K. (2006) 'A Dual-self Model of Impulse Control', *The American Economic Review*, 96(5): 1449–76.

Galak, J., Kruger, J., and Loewenstein, G. (2013) 'Slow Down! Insensitivity to Rate of Consumption Leads to Avoidable Satiation', *Journal of Consumer Research* 39(5): 993–1009.

Gilbert, D. T. (2006) *Stumbling on Happiness*, New York: Alfred A. Knopf.

Herrnstein, R. J. (1970) 'On the Law of Effect 1', *Journal of the Experimental Analysis of Behavior*, 13(2): 243–66.

Herrnstein, R. J., and Loewenstein, G. F., Prelec, D., and Vaughan, W., Jr. (1993) 'Utility Maximization and Melioration—Internalities in Individual Choice', *Journal of Behavioral Decision Making*, 6(3): 149–85.

Herrnstein, R. J. and Prelec, D. (1991) 'Melioration—A Theory of Distributed Choice', *Journal of Economic Perspectives*, 5(3): 137–56.

Herrnstein, R. J. and Prelec, D. (1992) 'A theory of addiction' in G. Loewenstein and J. Elster (eds) *Choice Over Time*, New York: Russell Sage.

Heyman, G. M. (2009) *Addiction: A Disorder of Choice*, Cambridge, Mass.: Harvard University Press.

Laibson, D. (1997) 'Golden Eggs and Hyperbolic Discounting', *The Quarterly Journal of Economics*, 112(2): 443–78.

Loewenstein, G., O'Donoghue, T., and Rabin, M. (2003) 'Projection Bias in Predicting Future Utility', *The Quarterly Journal of Economics*, 118(4): 1209–48.

Loewenstein, Y., Prelec, D., and Seung, H. S. (2009) 'Operant Matching as a Nash Equilibrium of an Intertemporal Game', *Neural Computation* 21(10): 2755–73.

Maddox, W. T., Gorlick, M. A., Worthy, D. A., and Beevers, C. G. (2012) 'Depressive Symptoms Enhance Loss-minimization, but Attenuate Gain-maximization in History-dependent Decision-making', *Cognition*, 125(1): 118–24.

Prelec, D. (1982) 'Matching, Maximizing, and the Hyperbolic Reinforcement Feedback Function', *Psychological Review*, 89(3): 189–230.

Prelec, D. (1991) 'Values and Principles—Some Limitations on Traditional Economic-analysis', in A. Etzioni and P.R. Lawrence (eds) *Socio-Economics: Toward a New Synthesis,* Armonk, N.Y.: M.E. Sharpe.

Prelec, D., Herrnstein, R. J., and Vaughan, W., Jr. (1986) 'An intra-personal prisoners' dilemma'. Paper presented at the IX Symposium on Quantitative Analysis of Behavior: Behavioral Economics, Harvard University.

Rachlin, H., Green, L., Kagel, J. H., and Battalio, R. C. (1976) 'Economic Demand Theory and Psychological Studies of Choice', in G.H. Bower (ed.) *The Psychology of Learning and Motivation, Volume 10,* New York: Academic Press.

Read, D. and Loewenstein, G. (2000) 'Choice Bracketing', in B. Fischhoff and C.F. Manski (eds) *Elicitation of Preferences,* Norwell, Mass.: Kluwer Academic Publishers.

Schelling, T. C. (2006) *Micromotives and Macrobehavior,* New York: WW Norton.

Sims, C. R., Neth, H., Jacobs, R. A., and Gray, W. D. (2013). 'Melioration as Rational Choice: Sequential Decision Making in Uncertain Environments', *Psychological Review* 120(1): 139–54.

Thaler, R. H. and Shefrin, H. M. (1981) 'An Economic Theory of Self-control', *The Journal of Political Economy*, 89(2): 392–406.

Vaughan, W., Jr. (1981) 'Melioration, Matching, and Maximization,' *Journal of the Experimental Analysis of Behavior*, 36(2): 141–9.

8

The Psychology of Sustainable Consumption

Geoff Beattie and Laura McGuire

8.1 Introduction

What we consume, how we consume it, and why we consume it in the first place are central to the psychological make-up of each and every individual. Our concept of who we are, our perception of our status, our class, our social and reference group, plus our understanding of our needs, aspirations, compulsions, habits, and even our individual psychopathologies, in other words many aspects of our basic identity, are all bound up inextricably with our patterns of consumption. We know vaguely that these patterns of consumption are influenced by the worlds of fashion, marketing and advertising, and great social trends, but we also think that some of it goes much deeper than this and somehow reflects aspects of our 'true selves', and, by implication, the 'true selves' of others. We look at the car of a neighbour, or we stare into their supermarket trolley or into their living room, and we sometimes assume that we can somehow read aspects of the real person underneath the material veneer (regardless of what else they say or do). And they sometimes feel that way as well, as if they have revealed too much, vulnerable and on show through their pattern of consumption. This occurs not just with 'significant' consumption involving degrees of reflection (houses, cars, fashion, music), that is, those types of consumption disproportionately focussed on by sociologists interested in the culture of consumption (see Warde, Chapter 12), but with more mundane consumption as well (own brand corn flakes versus Kellogg's corn flakes, 'they're exactly the same, you know', says the self-ascribed discerning shopper and self-constructed cynic). And yet there is much of this endless cycle of consumption that we, the consumer, do not understand, even when we are in the throes of it. Indeed, most people offer little insight into their own consumer behaviour, except when they assert that we are all just 'creatures of habit', driven by habitual and repeated action, rarely reflecting, merely consuming. But of course, this is a very limited insight; it merely reminds us that much of this consumptive behaviour occurs without any real thought or conscious awareness, like so much else in our everyday, busy lives.

In terms of the narrative and intellectual history of psychology, consumption has been very much at the margins rather than centre stage, of passing interest to social psychologists with particular connections with economics, sociology, anthropology, media, or fashion, and sometimes of interest to clinical psychologists trying to understand the process, but then only when it goes wrong (for instance in the compulsive behaviour of the 'shopaholic'). This position of the study of consumption relative to the main focus of academic psychology has been acknowledged by many in the past.

> Those of us interested in economic psychology could not claim that our concerns lie at the heart of our discipline... Even within social psychology, interest in economic psychology is, at best, an emerging field. Moreover, very few of the social psychologists who study economic beliefs and behaviour have an awareness of and interest in consumption... My focus, therefore, concerns the potential of what is a point on the periphery, at the margins of the discipline. (Lunt, 1995, p. 237)

But these days the intellectual landscape of psychology and consumption has changed for one simple reason, our physical landscape has changed, as environmental problems, in the words of the Stakeholder Forum and the Commonwealth Secretariat (2012), 'have intensified globally'. This has now made the psychology of consumption particularly interesting and potentially important and put it very much centre stage, but still perhaps the juvenile lead amongst a more experienced cast.

According to the 2005 Millennium Ecosystem Assessment (MEA) 'over the past 50 years, humans have changed ecosystems more rapidly and extensively than in any comparable period of time in human history' (2005, p. 2). In the words of Cruickshank, Schneeberger, and Smith (2012):

> The Intergovernmental Panel on Climate Change (IPCC) has found that global CO_2 emissions grew by 70 per cent between 1970 and 2004. This is despite the overwhelming scientific consensus that increasing levels of CO_2 in the atmosphere caused by human activity pose a serious threat to human well-being. This time frame also corresponds to the period during which the global community has come to understand human impacts on the environment better than ever before, and has developed an ever-expanding system of global governance to address these problems. (2012, p. 9)

The authors add a coda that 'It is important to recognize that coincidence does not imply causality. The continued degradation of the global environment has not been caused solely by government weaknesses, but rather by a multitude of drivers, including prevailing economic models and patterns of consumption and production' (Cruickshank, Schneeberger, and Smith, 2012, p. 9). Clearly, patterns of consumption are crucial to this change in CO_2 emissions (along with prevailing economic models and patterns of production, as well as, quite probably, the absence of effective global governance) because, in many ways these everyday behaviours are at the centre of everything. Change the patterns of consumption, and therefore the demand for certain products (and, of course, the needs, habits, and aspirations of the consumer), and many other things will fall into place. As a consequence of this logic the psychology of consumption is now, at last, moving towards the centre ground. But what light can psychology shine on consumption and on the likelihood of changing some of our most deeply rooted patterns of behaviour, which connect to our identity, our perceived personality, and our reference group?

8.2 Challenges

There is often something quite frustrating about consumer behaviour in the context of environmental problems and climate change. People say one thing but do something else. They say that they care about the environment and recognize the threat of climate change and yet they are not changing their behaviour in the way that one might expect in order to do anything about this (despite the fact that they acknowledge that certain changes would have a significant effect). The science is clear and unambiguous that our climate is changing and that human behaviour in all its many forms, has played, and *is playing*, a very significant role in this (see e.g. the Stern Review, 2006, p. 1). Even by 1995 the IPCC had come to the conclusion that human activity was significantly influencing our climate. By 2001, the IPCC in their Third Assessment Report stated that the evidence was now 'strong' and by 2007, in the IPCC's Fourth Assessment Report, the evidence was said to be 'unequivocal'. And this scientific message seems *at some level* to have got through to people, because they do seem aware of the issue and they report that 'they are prepared to change their behaviour to help limit climate change' (Downing and Ballantyne, 2007).

It is perhaps not that surprising, of course, that the message has seeped through because it has the backing of many heads of state and senior politicians from across the globe. Indeed, climate change would seem to be towards the very top of the global political agenda. The UN Framework Convention on Climate Change (UNFCCC) is almost certainly the most high profile of all global environmental conventions and the Fifteenth Conference of Parties

(COP15) in Copenhagen in December 2009 saw heads of state from all over the world convene to negotiate (or rather try to negotiate) an agreement to limit global carbon emissions (the 'fair and legally binding deal', of course, did not actually materialize). The underlying message about climate change also has the backing of many leading figures from the commercial world. They have had significant success in addressing environmental issues within their business and supply chains, but have, it would seem, struggled to influence effectively consumer behaviour in this regard. They have developed many high profile campaigns for the public to 'do their bit', be it by using bags for life, buying low energy light bulbs, or shifting to low carbon alternatives in their weekly shop. Some of these campaigns were, one might argue, largely symbolic (and highly visible), both for the commercial organization and the consumer concerned, but this was intended to be at the vanguard of a major shift in consumer behaviour. However, this major shift in consumer behaviour seems not to have occurred in quite the way anticipated and there is growing evidence that people seem to be very slow to change their everyday behaviour to ameliorate the possible effects of climate change, apart from, that is, the symbolic and public displays of using a bag for life (or at least for one or two shops). Indeed they often display very little *genuine* concern about this whole issue of climate change (see Weber, 2006). We, the consumers, still seem to require the same range and types of products that we always have, and we have stuck with the same consumer habits that have led to dangerously higher levels of carbon emissions. Many have suggested that in this area appropriate behaviour change is actually highly problematic. According to Darnton, Verplanken, White, and Whitmarsh (2011) reporting on behalf of the Department for Environment, Food and Rural Affairs (DEFRA) in the UK, 'Habit is especially important in the context of advancing sustainability, as many behaviours with the biggest environmental impacts are habits' (2011, p. 2). The problem would seem to be, according to the same authors, that because 'habits are "less rational" behaviours, it follows that interventions which run along rational lines (e.g. relying on information or incentives) may not be able to influence these behaviours effectively' (2011, p. 2).

There are clearly many changes in our lifestyle that are possible, which would have some impact on the process of climate change, although exactly how significant this would be is fiercely debated. Indeed Warde (Chapter 12) argues that: 'Regular, routine, and habitual behaviour, on a global and mass scale—like having a shower every day, driving to work, or eating meat daily—is more the source of the problem than what design of shower, which car, or the price and quality of meat'. He finishes this point by asserting that 'Buying greener products is not the solution, or rather not a sufficient solution'. It may not be *the* solution, or a sufficient solution, but it could be part of a solution. And perhaps more importantly it could be the start of a solution, with knock-on effects for other behaviours and practices, a move towards a potential tipping point. But even this limited goal has been frustratingly difficult to achieve. We, as consumers, seem rooted in our habits. And we may not even have the right type of thinking to start this basic process of change (if a change in thinking is indeed relevant to changing habitual behaviours of this sort). Walker and King (2008) noted that 'It's easy to believe that global warming is somebody else's problem—other people will suffer and other people will come up with the solution... it's as individuals that we live our lives and make our choices... now we will have to adapt our choices to the new realities of the twenty-first century' (2008, p. 238). But this adaptation has been slow and the 'urgent global response', which many influential commentators have identified as being essential, has quite simply not materialized.

This is the nature of the problem that we face and the reason why the current volume brings together leading economists, sociologists, anthropologists, neuroscientists, and others, all in search of a common solution (or set of solutions). All of these disciplines are concerned with attempting to understand human behaviour when it comes to consumption and identify the 'levers' that might work, be they financial, societal, social, cognitive, emotional, or some complex combination of these and other factors. But what can psychology offer?

The first thing that it can offer is a range of evidence from a number of domains that change here will unfortunately be very difficult, for good theoretical reasons. In other words, it brings a degree of (theoretically driven) realism to the challenge. The changes in our climate that are already occurring cannot be reversed immediately and we know that *delayed* contingent reinforcement and punishment is highly problematic for behaviour change from a traditional behaviourist and Skinnerian perspective (see Skinner, 1938, 1963). So how do you reinforce and change people's everyday behaviour when the reinforcement (actual reversals in the climate data) will only occur at some vague ill-defined point in the future? Climate change also requires a 'global response', in other words, a response from many individuals more or less simultaneously, all acting 'cooperatively'. But the problem in this domain would seem to be that many people are leaving it up to others. They do not want to make changes in case others do not bother; it is a question of trust, or rather more accurately mistrust. In many ways, this is the classic prisoner's dilemma where the optimal outcome depends upon a particular course of joint action, but if one person makes a change and the other does not, this may lead to the worst possible outcome, in this particular case, inconvenience in one's personal life and no change to the climate (see Rapoport and Chammah, 1965). How do you promote genuine cooperative action in this domain? What mechanisms can be employed? Is it through the encouragement of community action with public displays of who is now doing what for the environment, as some have suggested? And for many people climate change is still a bit abstract. How do you get people to really *care* about this and provide an appropriate emotional response to it? How do you instil an appropriate emotion, which could guide behaviour, irrespective of any rational thoughts, or even subconscious doubt? These are just three questions out of a set of many, but all connect back to issues at the very heart of academic psychology (but not necessarily addressed by the discipline so far).

8.3 The Manufacture of Doubt and its Effects

We must also remember that for many people there is still a nagging doubt at the backs of their minds about climate change, and this can impact on their behaviour. Doubts have been raised by some about the scientific evidence underpinning the whole climate change debate (so called 'Climategate' in the UK was one manifestation of this) even though some of those who are most vociferous in raising objections to the data may have a particular stake in the whole matter (including the oil lobby and its numerous spokespersons). Of course, we have all been here before and because of this we know how insidious and effective this process of the deliberate manufacture of doubt really can be, and we now know more about its impact on patterns of consumption in other domains. It is incredible to think now that in the 1960s and 1970s many ordinary people were not more alarmed by smoking, and its impact on health, and they continued to smoke furiously, given that the relationship between cigarettes and lung cancer was already widely known and openly discussed for several decades. How could ordinary people not have seen the dangers it posed at that time? Indeed, as far back as 1953, *Reader's Digest* had run an article entitled 'Cancer by the Carton', where they described the work of Ernest Wynder and colleagues (1953), showing that cigarette tar painted on the skin of mice caused fatal cancers. The final sentence of this article read 'Such studies, in view of the corollary clinical data relating smoking to various types of cancer, appear urgent. They may not only result in furthering our knowledge of carcinogens, but in promoting some practical aspects of cancer prevention.' The tobacco industry, perhaps not surprisingly, fought back. In the words of Oreskes and Conway (2011) '"Cancer by the carton" was not a slogan the tobacco industry would embrace . . . The decision was to hire a public relations firm to challenge the scientific evidence that smoking could kill you'. The method of the tobacco industry in the words of Oreskes and Conway was to 'fight science with science—or at least with the gaps and uncertainties in existing science, and with scientific research that could be used to deflect attention from the main event' (2011, p. 13). Perhaps the ambivalence of ordinary people is more understandable when famous academics, even famous psychologists, were openly disputing the connection between smoking and lung cancer. Hans Eysenck, perhaps Britain's foremost psychologist, even in the mid 1990s (see also Eysenck 1965), was still saying that the apparent statistical link between smoking and lung cancer was really just an artefact of personality. He argued that certain personalities were prone to lung cancer and certain personalities were prone to smoking and it was this underlying personality dimension which was the significant factor here. It wasn't smoking that gave you lung cancer; it was your genetically-determined personality which gave you lung cancer (and made you smoke).

But there is one other thing that is important to know about his research. According to *The Independent* newspaper on the 31 October 1996, Eysenck received more than £70,000 in 'consultancy' funds through a secret United States tobacco fund called Special Account Number 4. Eysenck apparently was not alone. According to Oreskes and Conway (2011) on 15 December 1953 the presidents of four of America's largest tobacco companies, American Tobacco, Benson and Hedges, Philip Morris, and U.S. Tobacco met with John Hill, the CEO of the public relations firm Hill and Knowlton, at the Plaza Hotel in New York to challenge the scientific evidence that smoking could kill you. In the words of the authors:

> They would work together to convince the public that there was 'no sound scientific basis for the charges,' and that the recent reports [about cigarette tar and cancer] were simply 'sensational accusations' made by publicity-seeking scientists hoping to attract more funds for their research. They would not sit idly by while their product was vilified; instead they would create a Tobacco Industry Committee for Public Information to supply a 'positive' and 'entirely pro-cigarette' message to counter the anti-cigarette one. As the U.S. department of Justice would later put it, they decided to deceive the American public about the health effects of smoking. At first, the companies didn't think they needed to fund new scientific research, thinking it would be sufficient to 'disseminate information on hand.' John Hill disagreed, 'emphatically warn[ing] . . . that they should . . . sponsor additional research,' and that this would be a long-term project. He also suggested including the word 'research' in the title of their new committee because a pro-cigarette message would need science to back it up. At the end of the day, Hill concluded, 'scientific doubts must remain'. (Oreskes and Conway, 2011, pp. 15–16)

And some academics made sure that scientific doubts did remain for decades.

And so it is the case with climate change, where doubt still lingers at the back of some people's minds about exactly what is happening to our climate and what our role in the whole thing really is. *Time* magazine in 2006 reported that only just over half of Americans polled thought that average global temperatures had actually risen; an ABC news poll that same year reported that more than half of its respondents did not think the science behind climate change was settled. According to Oreskes and Conway (2011) this is largely attributable to a small set of well-placed and very eminent academics who have forcefully argued the opposing case, against the overriding scientific consensus, blaming global warming on the sun (see e.g. Jastrow, Nierenberg and Seitz, 1989). Once we were cognitively conflicted on the issue of smoking, but now some are conflicted on the issue of anthropogenic climate change. Oreskes and Conway (2011) called their excellent book *Merchants of Doubt* for very good reasons. How do we remove this doubt?

8.4 So What Can Psychology Actually Offer?

So issues to do with consumer behaviour and climate change are to do with breaking habits, establishing new more sustainable and appropriate forms of consumer behaviour, encouraging trust in others, promoting cooperation, attempting to modify consumer behaviour in the context of significantly delayed reward, overcoming doubt lodged in the subconscious from whatever source (with whatever original stake or interest), promoting immediate, emotional responding to certain cues (as a guide to action), and ultimately (and most importantly) transforming core underlying values.

Some other disciplines, not surprisingly, see the challenge somewhat differently, whilst having significant points of contact. Warde (Chapter 12), from a sociological perspective, argues that we need to focus primarily on the social practices underpinning consumption. He maintains that construing the failure to modify consumer behaviour by conceptualizing it in terms of a 'value-action' gap is not adequate because 'the principal models of action... are flawed'. Warde recognizes, as we and many others would, that much of consumer behaviour is not reflective but then says that we must focus on the actions themselves, 'doing rather than thinking, habits rather than decisions, embodied procedures and the affordances of material equipment rather than deliberative acts, collective guidance over individual choice—all moves that enhance the understanding of processes of appropriation in ordinary consumption' (Warde, 2005). The solution of the sociologist would be that we need a transformation of routine social practices, no more and no less.

There is much to agree with in all of this from our psychological point of view. But can psychology actually offer anything which would allow the two distinct conceptual approaches from these neighbouring disciplines to converge (rather than continuing on separate and parallel tracks)? Our argument will be that classic social psychology deriving from the work and inspiration of its founder, Gordon Allport (1935), does not really help here because it has placed far too much emphasis on what people say as the way into understanding where human action springs from (which is highly problematic for much of routine action), and has clearly not succeeded in drawing the disciplines together after nearly 80 years. But there is new research in psychology on implicit cognition, including research in social psychology on identifying underlying implicit attitudes, which might just help. This research could lead us to think about the 'value-action' differently, because we may be able to identify and measure *implicit* values, a measure with potentially greater predictive force for habitual everyday behaviour than those we are used to, and rethink the relationship between value and action, and perhaps even (one day) close the 'value-action' gap altogether. Once we have a reliable and valid measure of implicit attitudes we become empowered in a number of ways. We have potentially a way into the basis for action. We can see whether any of our communicative strategies designed to impact on minds and behaviour are actually working. Do they impact on implicit values? We could segment the population in new and innovative ways (using measures of both implicit and explicit attitudes), instead of relying just on self-report measures of attitudes, to work out how to target any communicational strategies. This all could be very practical (perhaps easier than just trying to do something about social practices), as well as theoretically extremely interesting. The same implicit attitude, after all, might underpin a number of quite different social practices and it could be highly parsimonious to begin with that underlying value, and a test of its readiness or robustness to change.

This approach necessitates taking a fresh look at one of the cornerstones of psychology, the 'attitude', and reworking it in a way that is more relevant to habits, social practices, and consumer behaviour. The classic definition of 'attitude' was, of course, introduced by Allport in 1935, and defined as 'a mental and neural state of readiness organised through experience, exerting a directive or dynamic influence upon the individual's response to all objects and situations with which it is related' (1935, p. 810). In other words, an attitude is an internal state of mind affected by what we do which affects our behaviour towards the world around us. But the question is how do we conceptualize and measure attitudes in a way that allows a high degree of predictive validity? This is a very difficult and important question because there is no reason why a 'mental and neural state of readiness' should be fully, or even partially, conscious. This was even recognized by Allport, and many of the other early pioneers. Indeed in 1935 Allport wrote 'The meagreness with which attitudes are represented in consciousness resulted in a tendency to regard them as manifestations of brain activity or of the unconscious mind'. The persistence of attitudes which are totally unconscious was demonstrated by Muller and Pilzecker (1900), who called the phenomenon 'perseveration' (Allport, 1935, p. 801). Allport himself, however, focussed on the measurement of attitudes with self-report questionnaires (because we are then dealing with publically observable behaviour) where people indicate whether they agree or disagree with a series of statements or propositions presented to them, which, of course, completely neglects any probing of the unconscious mind whatsoever.

When it comes to attitudes towards climate change and environmental behaviour the explicit attitudes that are reported tend to be very positive, see, for example, Table 8.1 (from Beattie, 2010, p. 31).

In a similar vein, Beattie and Sale (2009) measured explicit attitudes towards carbon footprint and again drew some very similar (and similarly optimistic) conclusions, using both the traditional Likert scale and a measure called the Feeling Thermometer (where people rate how warm or cold they feel towards high and low carbon products). The Likert scale revealed that 70 per cent of participants reported some preference for products with a low carbon footprint and the Feeling Thermometer revealed that 67 per cent of participants showed a preference for low carbon products. So if attitudes are 'a mental and neural state of readiness' to act then it would seem (from these measures) that many people are indeed ready. So why then do they not act in appropriate ways, and check out the carbon footprint on products to find the low carbon alternatives (Beattie, 2012a), and buy the low carbon products rather than their high carbon competitors?

The most obvious answer to this is that self-report measures of attitude do not reflect their real attitude because quite simply they are subject to the constraints of social desirability. In other words, the participants in our and others' research may want to appear 'greener' than they actually are. This is a plausible explanation given that people who are environmentally friendly are perceived as 'considerable', 'thoughtful', 'caring', 'knowledgeable', 'selfless', and 'nice' (see Beattie, 2010, p. 36), but it may not be the whole story. The research of Greenwald (1990) suggests that in order to predict actual behaviour in a range of situations it may not be wise to restrict ourselves to such self-reported attitudes. He says that much of our 'mental and neural state of readiness' may not be available to introspection and may be represented unconsciously in the human brain. Indeed, as we have already noted, there

Table 8.1. Explicit attitudes towards climate change and environmental behaviour

Explicit Measure Source	Findings
70% of people agree that if there is no change in the world, we will soon experience a *major environmental crisis*	Downing and Ballantyne (2007)
78% of people say that they are *prepared to change* their behaviour to help limit climate change	Downing and Ballantyne (2007)
85% of consumers want *more information* about the environmental impacts of products they buy	Berry, Crossley, and Jewell (2008)
84% say retailers should do more to *reduce the impact* of production and transportation of their products on climate change	Ipsos MORI (2008); see Beattie 2010, p. 31

Source: the authors

is nothing in Allport's original definition of an attitude that excludes a possible unconscious component. The problem with possible unconscious components of an attitude was that we had no way to access them (or measure them), until Greenwald developed the Implicit Association Test (IAT) (Greenwald, McGhee, and Schwartz, 1998). The IAT is a computerized classification task that appears to be highly reliable and resistant to the kinds of faking driven by a desire to produce a socially appropriate response. The basic premise behind the test is that when participants categorize items into two sets of paired concepts, then if the paired concepts are strongly associated, participants should be able to categorize the items faster (and with fewer errors) than if they are not strongly associated.

The IAT is now widely used in psychology, and has revealed some extraordinary (and, on occasion, controversial) results. It yields a measure of implicit attitude (called a 'difference' or 'D' score) that is often discrepant with the scores that emerge from explicit measures like the Likert scale. So, for example, the IAT has revealed that people are consistently faster at categorizing 'black' and 'white' images and 'pleasant' and 'unpleasant' words when the target categories are grouped 'white'/'pleasant' and 'black'/'unpleasant' than when they are grouped 'white'/'unpleasant' and 'black'/'pleasant' suggesting that the former concepts 'white' and 'pleasant' and 'black' and 'unpleasant' are more strongly associated than the converse. The IAT tends to reveal that although the majority of participants report that they have no racial preference in their self-reported attitudes; the vast majority of participants (including surprisingly a significant proportion of black participants) seem to have an implicit pro-'white' preference (reflected in a positive D Score, often above + 0.8). A high positive D score also predicts a bias towards selecting just white candidates in a simulated shortlisting task when the white and black and minority ethnic candidates are presenting with identical CVs (see Beattie, 2012b; Beattie, Cohen, and McGuire, 2013).

In a number of domains, it has been found that there is little correlation between the scores that derive from the explicit measures and the scores that derive from the IAT (see Greenwald and Nosek, 2008; Hofmann, Gawronski, Gschwendner, Le, and Schmitt, 2005; Nosek, 2005) and this has led Greenwald and Nosek to say that the concepts of explicit and implicit attitude are 'dissociated'. But there is considerable evidence that the IAT is a better predictor of actual behaviour in many domains, especially where the behaviour in question is spontaneous and unplanned (see e.g. Beattie, 2010). Indeed, some theorists have argued that implicit and explicit attitudes have structurally distinct mental representations (see Chaiken and Trope, 1999; Wilson, Lindsey, and Schooler, 2000) and a number have argued that it is parsimonious to model the human mind as comprising two important subsystems; a familiar foreground where processing is 'conscious', 'controlled', 'reflective', 'intentional', and 'slow' (the explicit system), and a hidden background, our implicit system, where processing is 'unconscious', 'automatic', 'impulsive', 'unintended', and 'fast' (see Gregg, 2008; see also Kahneman, 2011), which may, nevertheless, interact in significant ways (see Beattie, 2012b).

8.5 Our Implicit System and the Dangers We See

The advantage of this new theorizing is that it may hold the key to why we are not doing more about climate change, and it may link better to the theorizing in other disciplines. Perhaps our implicit system is not in tune with our explicit system and, despite what the measures of explicit attitudes tell us, the implicit system is not directing us towards the right kind of action. Research in psychology has only recently begun to tackle this issue in the area of those aspects of consumer behaviour relevant to the environment. Preliminary research in this area suggests that implicit attitudes may appear to be quite positive to low carbon footprint products in the small samples analysed so far (see Beattie and Sale, 2009, 2011; Vantomme, Geuens, De Houwer, and De Pelsmaker, 2006). But these studies also reveal a lack of correlation between implicit and explicit attitudes and the fact that many respondents, in terms of implicit attitude, are not really as green as they say they are.

The concept of implicit attitude gives us a new way of thinking about the motivational basis for human action and could be a critical element in the fight against climate change. Implicit, rather than explicit attitudes may well be underpinning everyday habitual behaviours. Such behaviours may be 'sticky', in sociological jargon, because attempts to change attitudes and behaviour just focus on the explicit self-report attitudes, leaving the implicit attitude intact and undisturbed. Financial incentive may, on occasion, be effective in changing behaviour because it impacts on underlying implicit attitude, but if and only if it does impact on implicit attitude. Neuroscience, one day, may reveal the separate neural pathways that mediate implicit attitudes and implicit processing separately from explicit processing, in many ways the two great systems of the human mind in action (see Kahneman, 2011).

But, of course, the first task for psychology is to attempt to understand this concept more fully and to investigate how this measure relates to other aspects of behaviour. For example, how does it relate to how we process information relevant to climate change, assuming that the processing of relevant information is the start point of the whole process of behavioural action in context? There are many persuasive messages available about climate change, including films like Al Gore's *An Inconvenient Truth*, and research done in our laboratory has demonstrated that sections of this film can produce a significant impact on how people think and feel about environmental issues (see Beattie, 2010, 2011a; Beattie, Sale, and McGuire, 2011). In this research, clips from the film were played to participants and then their mood states were assessed as well as any changes in explicit attitudes and social cognitions towards climate change. We found the film to be very influential on a whole host of measures in this experimental setting. And there are many other films, documentaries, and TV news reports that should be galvanizing the public in terms of behaviour change, so why are they not working in the way intended? Perhaps the reason is that our experiment (and others like it) missed a level of subtlety in the whole process. In our experimental setting, participants were compelled to watch clips from the Gore film; in real life there is no such compulsion. People can choose to go to the cinema to watch *An Inconvenient Truth*, or not, people can watch television documentaries on climate change, or ignore them, people can attend to images of climate change, or miss them entirely (and this whole process does not have to be conscious either). Indeed, it could potentially be the case that different individuals are drawn, or not drawn, to the same set of images with major implications for their subsequent behaviour. What happens if you never see the evidence for climate change? The factors that affect attentional focus could be of immense theoretical and practical concern in this area. This issue formed the basis for our recent investigation (Beattie and McGuire, 2012). Indeed, this study represented the first attempt to investigate the effects of implicit (as well as explicit) attitude on gaze behaviour in the area of sustainability where this implicit measure might well be a better determinant of *unconscious* eye movements. In this study, we attempted to determine how eye movements towards or away from iconic images of environmental damage and climate change are affected by different attitudinal measures (implicit/explicit). The theoretical justification for this work really derives from the early research of Kahneman (1973) on attention and effort. In Kahneman's words 'In the absence of a specific instruction to search for visual information, spontaneous looking is controlled by enduring dispositions that determine which parts of the field of view should attract and hold the gaze' (Kahneman, 1973, p. 52). In this investigation we wanted to find out whether implicit or explicit attitudes were a good measure of 'enduring dispositions' here. We did this by projecting slides onto a computer screen, each slide containing three images, one positive image of nature, one negative image of climate change and environmental damage, and one neutral image (things like pictures of cups, plates, and other everyday objects).

We found that people do not focus inordinately on the negative images of environmental damage when there are other positive images and neutral images available. They usually look less than 40 per cent of the time at the negative images. But very importantly those who the IAT reveals have strong positive implicit attitudes to carbon footprint are significantly more likely to focus on the negative images of environmental damage and climate change than positive images, and focus more on these images than those who do not have such strong implicit attitudes.

But what we also found was that this even occurs in the first 200 milliseconds of viewing the slide (see Figure 8.1). Those with a positive implicit attitude to low carbon footprint products (high implicit group) looked more at the negative images of climate change and environmental damage in the first 200 milliseconds compared with those with less strong positive implicit attitudes to low carbon footprint products (low implicit group). Measures of explicit attitude do not, however, predict patterns of eye movement towards the negative images in this way (see Figure 8.2). It would seem that those who have strong implicit pro-low carbon attitudes are primed to attend to these sorts of images, whereas those with strong explicit attitudes are not (they actually look less).

This is both a novel and exciting finding in that we clearly build our representations of the world using those features of scenes that we notice and some significant association between attitudes and attentional focus might give us some insight into how and why people develop quite different representations of the world and the dangers it faces. This exploratory eye tracking research suggests that there is a significant connection between implicit attitudes and gaze fixations. But, of course, all that we have observed here is an association between attitudes and behaviour—however, one that opens up intriguing theoretical and practical possibilities. One interpretation of the results would be that those who have got a strong implicit attitude

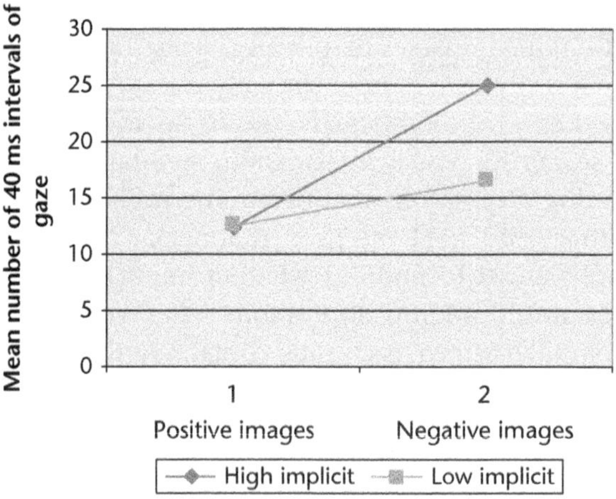

Figure 8.1. Mean number of 40 ms intervals of gaze at positive and negative images for high and low implicit groups (first 200 ms only)

Source: the authors

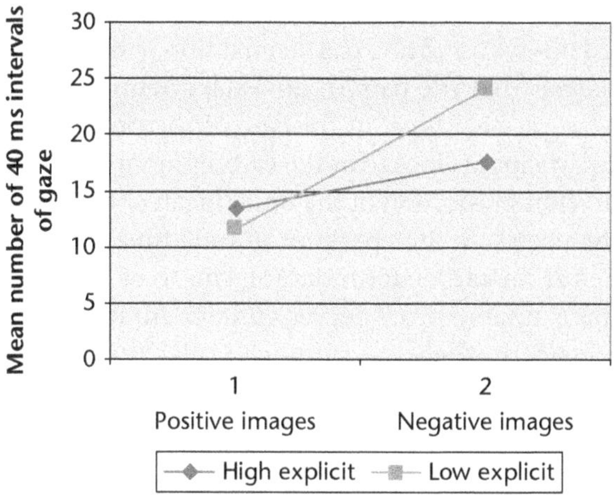

Figure 8.2. Mean number of 40 ms intervals of gaze at positive and negative images for high and low explicit groups (first 200 ms only)
Source: the authors

towards low carbon footprint products (i.e. are more environmentally friendly) focus more on negative images of environmental damage and climate change and because of this essential 'priming' are in a position to receive other appropriate environmental messages (see Beattie, 2011b for a more general discussion of priming).

This significant pattern of 'primed' eye movement occurs in such a short interval (one fifth of a second) that it is pre-conscious. Therefore, those with positive implicit attitudes, the kinds of attitudes that could direct their non-reflective consumer behaviour (Beattie, 2010; Beattie and Sale, 2011), could potentially direct attention to appropriate imagistic representations relevant to sustainability on products in supermarkets (for example, carbon footprint, see Beattie, 2012a). Why is this significant? It is potentially significant because many high profile campaigns aimed at behaviour change have involved presenting information to consumers, for example, carbon footprint information on products, and hoping that they would notice it in the relevant time frame, to make a 'rational' decision about choice of product. There was, after all, evidence from elsewhere that the provision of other types of information on products could significantly affect consumer choice, for example, the Guideline Daily Amounts (GDA) nutritional labelling scheme. But the results of the carbon labelling scheme were somewhat disappointing by comparison. One reason was that people *generally* did not fixate on the carbon labels (Beattie, McGuire, and Sale, 2010). There is, of course, a lot of competing information on products so we showed simultaneous front and back views of each product on a computer screen and analysed point of gaze on a 40 millisecond frame-by-frame basis, for 10 seconds. We analysed level of fixation in the first and second 5 second interval, and also the first fixation period of 200 milliseconds. What we found was that the pattern of visual attention varied considerably depending on the product type. In the case of the clearly 'green' low energy light bulb, our participants looked at the carbon footprint (icon plus information) for a significant proportion of the time (mean of 65.3 frames across both right–left rotated views, or 26.1 per cent of total time). In the case of orange juice they looked at the carbon footprint for a mean of 24.9 frames (or 10.0 per cent of total time), dipping to 5.7 per cent for one stimulus view. In the case of the 'non-bio' detergent, there was minimal visual attention to any aspect of the carbon footprint. Importantly, in less than 7 per cent of all cases did the participants fixate first on the carbon footprint.

But could carbon footprint ever have had the impact that GDA nutritional information does have? The answer is probably not. Firstly, because nutritional information, like calories and fat content, have a certain *emotional* significance for us and we know that emotions are very important for guiding behaviour. The neuropsychologist Damasio (1994) demonstrated that in choice experiments non-conscious biases guide behaviour before conscious knowledge does. Furthermore, he suggested that without the help of such biases overt knowledge may be insufficient to ensure advantageous behaviour. Damasio found that activation of the emotional system precedes activation of any conceptual system with the neural connection between the two systems located in the ventromedial prefrontal cortex. It is, at the present time, very unlikely that carbon footprint information would produce the same kind of emotional response that information about calories and fat content does. Calories and fat content mean something emotionally because we know what they do to the human body: *our* body. We can see its effects, sometimes more or less immediately. But carbon footprint information is much more abstract (the effects will only be seen in the future), much less under our personal control, and, hence, much less emotional. Of course, with shopping, time is often of the essence so we need to be engaged immediately; emotional responses are good for immediate responding.

So is carbon labelling doomed for all time as a way of guiding consumer choice? Not necessarily. The new research on implicit attitudes might suggest that it could potentially work for *some proportion* of the population, that is, those with a strong positive implicit attitude to carbon footprint. But how many of these are there and where can they be found? The answer is that we do not know but potentially we could find out and we may want to do a different kind of segmentation analysis that might look more like that shown in Figure 8.3. Carbon labelling might well work for 'true greens' (positive on both implicit and explicit measures) and 'hidden greens' (individuals with a strong positive implicit attitude to the environment but who do not care to

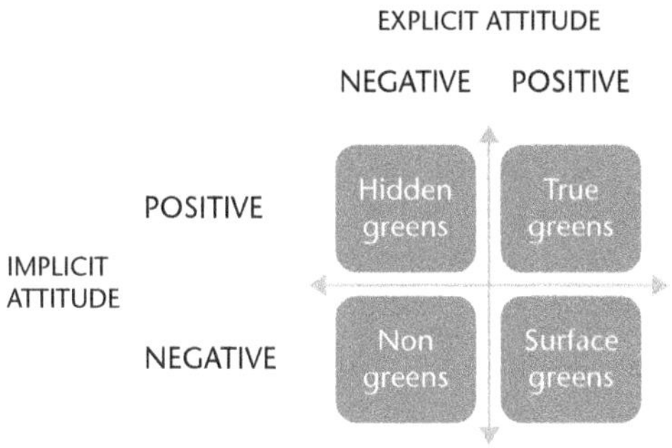

Figure 8.3. A new kind of segmentation analysis based on the concept of implicit/explicit attitudinal convergence and divergence
Source: the authors

report it routinely). But what proportion of the population does each of the segments represent? How are each of these segments distributed across social classes and income groups? What media do they consume and how, therefore, could they be targeted? It should be remembered that DEFRA has spent a considerable amount of time and effort engaged in segmentation analysis of the United Kingdom population as a whole, without once trying to incorporate any measure of attitude, which does not rely solely on self-reports (see DEFRA, 2008). It is easy to imagine a different sort of approach here that could prove more fruitful.

One other important point is that we know from other domains that we can induce changes to our implicit system. This has been demonstrated in changing automatic responses to people from different racial or ethnic groups. Here Olson and Fazio (2006) used 'implicit evaluative conditioning' (a form of classical conditioning) to reduce automatically activated responses to people from different races, but it would take time (and effort) to induce different emotional responses to high/low carbon items through, presumably, a mixture of marketing, advertising, and education (see also Beattie, 2012b). But importantly it can be done, and this could be a very practical proposal with some real merit in the area of green consumerism.

8.6 Some Implications for the Future

This work on implicit attitudes and behaviour could have major implications for understanding and changing consumer behaviour in the light of the threat posed by climate change. It would suggest that some approaches to changing consumer behaviour in the past may have been extremely well-intentioned but they may also have been a little naïve. We may well need to consider implicit processes and System 1 (Kahnemann, 2011) responses when we are dealing with everyday routine, quick behaviours like shopping 'decisions' (decisions often with no thought whatsoever). We may also need to consider more carefully the role of emotion in directing our behaviour in this domain and others. This could lead psychological approaches to play some role in the identification and analysis of the attributes of different types of social practices connected with consumption.

At the start of this chapter we said that the psychology of consumption had always resided towards the edges of the discipline of psychology. However, consumer behaviour, especially in the light of the issues raised by climate change, is now far too important to remain there. This particular area raises some very important and challenging questions but much of the new theorizing in psychology by Greenwald, Kahneman, and others could potentially shed real light on this critically important area. But, as is so often the case, we end with a plea for further work. For example, we do need further research to unravel the statistical association described here between implicit attitudes and attention. If we were to find that the association really worked the other way around and that attentional focus directs implicit attitudes, then we may want to think much more strategically about how to make sure that images of climate change hit the attention of more of the people more of the time. On the other hand, if it is the case (as we have anticipated) that certain individuals are 'primed' to notice certain things because of their implicit attitudes then we might need to think with great urgency about the best ways of getting that information to them, in order to target this implicit and unconscious system with so much potential power. Either way round, these could be research topics of major significance not just for psychology but, much more importantly, for tackling consumer behaviour and climate change (and, of course, if the truth is a mixture of the two hypotheses, then they both become equally urgent for investigation and further development). And this sort of work and thinking could potentially place psychology at the very heart of this multidisciplinary effort to do something about consumers and their everyday behaviour. And finally, of course, there is always the possibility that this new understanding of ways of detecting and measuring implicit values could input into the thinking of other disciplines who like us recognize the 'mindlessness' of much of everyday behaviour, including consumer behaviour, but are looking, sometimes in vain, for how to get a firm handle on it. Psychology might, perhaps, just be able to help.

References

Allport, G. W. (1935) 'Attitudes', in C. Murchison (ed.), *Handbook of Social Psychology*, Worcester, Mass.: Clark University Press.

Beattie, G. (2010) *Why Aren't We Saving the Planet? A Psychologist's Perspective*, London: Routledge.

Beattie, G. (2011a) 'Making an Action Film. Do Films Such as Al Gore's *An Inconvenient Truth* Really Make Any Difference to How We Think and Feel about Climate Change?', *Nature Climate Change*, 1: 372–4.

Beattie, G. (2011b) *Get the Edge: How Simple Changes Will Transform Your Life*, London: Headline.

Beattie, G. (2012a) 'How Effective is Carbon Labelling for the Consumer?', *Nature Climate Change*, 2: 214–17.

Beattie, G. (2012b) *Our Racist Heart? An Exploration of Unconscious Prejudice in Everyday Life*, London: Routledge.

Beattie, G., Cohen, D., and McGuire, L. (2013) 'An Exploration of Possible Unconscious Ethnic Biases in Higher Education: The Role of Implicit Attitudes on Selection for University Posts', *Semiotica*, 197: 217–47.

Beattie, G. and McGuire, L. (2012) 'See No Evil? Only Implicit Attitudes Predict Unconscious Eye Movements towards Images of Climate Change', *Semiotica*, 192: 315–39.

Beattie, G., McGuire, L., and Sale, L. (2010) 'Do We Actually Look at the Carbon Footprint of a Product in the Initial Few Seconds? An Experimental Analysis of Unconscious Eye Movements', *International Journal of Environmental, Cultural, Economic and Social Sustainability*, 6: 47–65.

Beattie, G. and Sale, L. (2009) 'Explicit and Implicit Attitudes to Low and High Carbon Footprint Products', *International Journal of Environmental, Cultural, Economic and Social Sustainability*, 5: 191–206.

Beattie, G. and Sale, L. (2011) 'Shopping to Save the Planet? Implicit rather than Explicit Attitudes Predict Low Carbon Footprint Consumer Choice', *International Journal of Environmental, Cultural, Economic and Social Sustainability*, 7: 211–32.

Beattie, G., Sale, L., and McGuire, L. (2011) 'An Inconvenient Truth? Can Extracts of a Film Really Affect Our Psychological Mood and Our Motivation to Act Against Climate Change?', *Semiotica*, 187, 105–25.

Berry, T., Crossley, D., and Jewell, J. (2008) *Check-Out Carbon: The Role of Carbon Labelling in Delivering a Low-Carbon Shopping Basket*, London: Forum for the Future.

Chaiken, S. and Trope, Y. (eds) (1999) *Dual Process Theories in Social Psychology*, New York: Guilford.

Cruickshank, E. W., Schneeberger, K., and Smith, N. (2012) *A Pocket Guide to Sustainable Development Governance*, second edition, London: Commonwealth Secretariat Stakeholder Forum.

Damasio, A. R. (1994) *Descartes' Error: Emotion, Reason, and the Human Brain*, New York: Putnam Publishing.

Darnton, A., Verplanken, B., White, P., and Whitmarsh, L. (2011) *Habits, Routines and Sustainable Lifestyles: A Summary Report to the Department for Environment, Food and Rural Affairs*, London: AD Research & Analysis for DEFRA.

DEFRA (2008) *A Framework for Pro-Environmental Behaviours*, London: Department for Environment, Food and Rural Affairs.

Downing, P. and Ballantyne, J. (2007) *Tipping Point or Turning Point? Social Marketing and Climate Change*, London: Ipsos MORI.

Eysenck, H. J. (1965) *Smoking, Health and Personality*, London: Weidenfeld and Nicolson.

Greenwald, A. G. (1990) 'What Cognitive Representations Underlie Attitudes?', *Bulletin of the Psycholonomic Society*, 28: 254–60.

Greenwald, A. G., McGhee, D. E., and Schwartz, J. L. K. (1998) 'Measuring Individual Differences in Implicit Cognition: The Implicit Association Test', *Journal of Personality and Social Psychology*, 74: 1464–80.

Greenwald, A. G. and Nosek, B. A. (2008) 'Attitudinal Dissociation: What Does it Mean?', in R.E. Petty, R.H. Fazio, and P. Brinol (eds) *Attitudes: Insights from the New Implicit Measures*, Hillsdale, N.J.: Erlbaum.

Gregg, A. P. (2008) 'Oracle of the Unconscious or Deceiver of the Unwitting?', *The Psychologist*, 21: 762–6.

Hofmann, W., Gawronski, B., Gschwendner, T., Le, H., and Schmitt, M. (2005) 'A Meta-Analysis on the Correlation between the Implicit Association Test and Explicit Self-Report Measures', *Personality and Social Psychology Bulletin*, 31: 1369–85.

Jastrow, R., Nierenberg, W., and Seitz, F. (1989) *Global Warming: What Does the Science Tell Us?*, Washington D.C.: George C. Marshall Institute.

Kahneman, D. (1973) *Attention and Effort*, New Jersey: Prentice Hall.

Kahneman, D. (2011) *Thinking Fast and Slow*, London: Allen Lane.

Lunt, P. (1995) 'Psychological Approaches to Consumption', in Miller, D. (ed.) *Acknowledging Consumption*, London: Routledge.

Millennium Ecosystem Assessment (2005) Review Editors: J. Sarukhán and A.Whyte (co-chairs) and MA Board of Review Editors *Ecosystems and Human Well-Being: Synthesis*, Washington, D.C.: Island Press.

Müller, G. E. and Pilzecker, A. (1900) 'Experimentelle Beiträge zur Lehre vom Gedächtnis', *Zeitschrift für Psychologie, Erganzungsband*, 1: 1–128.

Nosek, B. A. (2005) 'Moderators of the Relationship between Implicit and Explicit Evaluation', *Journal of Experimental Psychology: General*, 134: 565–84.

Olson, M. A. and Fazio, R. H. (2006) 'Reducing Automatically Activated Racial Prejudice through Implicit Evaluative Conditioning', *Journal of Personality and Social Psychology*, 32: 421–33.

Oreskes, N. and Conway, E. M. (2011) *Merchants of Doubt: How a Handful of Scientists Obscured the Truth on Issues from Tobacco Smoke to Global Warming*, London: Bloomsbury.

Rapoport, A. and Chammah, A. M. (1965) *Prisoner's Dilemma: A Study in Conflict and Cooperation*, Michigan: University of Michigan Press.

Skinner, B. F. (1938) *The Behavior of Organisms: An Experimental Analysis*, New York: D. Appleton-Century.

Skinner, B. F. (1963) 'Operant Behaviour', *American Psychologist*, 18: 503–15.

Stern, N. H. (2006) *The Economics of Climate Change: The Stern Review*, Cambridge: Cambridge University Press.

Vantomme D., Geuens M., De Houwer J., De Pelsmacker P. (2006) 'Implicit Attitudes toward Green Consumer Behavior', *Psychologica Belgica*, 45(4): 217–39.

Walker, G. and King, D. (2008) *The Hot Topic: How to Tackle Global Warming and Still Keep the Lights On*, London: Bloomsbury.

Warde, A. (2005) 'Consumption and Theories of Practice', *Journal of Consumer Culture*, 5: 131–53.

Weber, E. U. (2006) 'Experience-Based and Description-Based Perceptions of Long-Term Risk: Why Global Warming Does Not Scare Us (Yet)', *Climate Change*, 77: 103–20.

Wilson, T., Lindsey, S., and Schooler, T. Y. (2000) 'A Model of Dual Attitudes', *Psychological Review*, 107: 101–26.

Wynder, E. L., Graham, E. A., and Croninger, A. B. (1953) 'Experimental Production of Carcinoma with Cigarette Tar', *Cancer Research*, 13: 855–64.

9

Behavioural Economics in Water Management

An Overview of Behavioural Economics Applications to Residential Water Demand

Ricardo Correia and Catarina Roseta-Palma[1]

9.1 Introduction

Water consumption is an essential component of human activities, yet it has only recently been acknowledged as an economic good that can be provided through markets, albeit imperfect or incomplete ones. Traditionally, water management was mostly held to mean supply management, such as the provision of reservoirs, distribution networks and other infrastructure, whereas demand management is now understood to be crucial. Moreover, the quantity and quality of water decisively affect all ecosystems on Earth, which means that the costs and benefits of water use are rarely captured fully in market mechanisms. Economists have therefore focused both on market analysis (pricing, demand estimation, costs) and on the study of external effects such as the negative impacts of human-induced scarcity and the losses brought about by water pollution. In the European Union, the Water Framework

[1] We would like to thank Alistair Ulph, Dale Southerton, and all the participants at 'Sustainable Consumption: A Multifaceted Approach' (Sustainable Consumption Institute, University of Manchester, 8–9 March 2012). The benefits of multi-disciplinary interaction were on clear display at the workshop. A special thanks to Geoff Beattie for his discussion of this chapter and to Partha Dasgupta for inspiring the work of so many economists like ourselves. We also thank conference participants at ISEE 2012 Conference (Rio de Janeiro, Brazil), V AERNA Conference (Faro, Portugal) and 11° Congresso da Água (Porto, Portugal) for helpful comments. This research is supported by FCT—Fundação para a Ciência e a Tecnologia (Science and Technology Foundation), project PTDC/EGE-ECO/114477/2009 and project PEst-OE/EGE/UI0315/2011.

Directive (European Parliament and Council, 2000) Article 9 requires that water prices provide an appropriate incentive for the efficient use of the resource as well as recover costs, including environmental and scarcity costs. Nonetheless, recent evaluations (European Commission, 2007) show that economic instruments still play a very limited role in water management, while significant problems persist in ecological water status. The European Commission has thus identified the promotion of economic instruments as a priority action.

On the other hand, economists have also come to accept that traditional utility-maximization models often do not appropriately describe actual decisions of economic agents. Through the influence of many significant experiments and insights provided by psychologists, an interesting cross-fertilization process took place between the two fields, giving rise to what is now known as behavioural economics. To ascertain the potential of economic instruments in a new light, in this chapter we use the behavioural economics framework to identify possible implications for water management, using references from psychology and marketing that we believe have been overlooked. We suggest four behavioural economic applications (hereafter behavioural applications), namely: reference block pricing; asymmetric elasticities; reference transaction; and social comparison through reference consumption.

There are some surveys with extremely well-organized information which discuss water demand models, both generally, at a global level (Worthington and Hoffman, 2008) and at a European level (Schleich and Hillenbrand, 2009), and focus on price specifications and price elasticities (Arbués et al., 2003). Nevertheless, they all implicitly exhibit a common feature: the absence of behavioural economics in the residential water demand literature. In this work we corroborate this finding through a brief review of similar studies over the last decade, which differs from the previous surveys in that our analysis focuses on the behavioural perspective. We refer to the existing (slender) literature about behavioural economics in water management and sketch our proposals for the four behavioural applications mentioned already. Furthermore, we stress the importance of experimental data versus non-experimental data, besides the usual division between aggregate data and household data.

First we discuss reference block pricing, which relates primarily to the issue of choosing the most appropriate price structure. There is a significant amount of literature on block-tariff structures in regulated water utilities, yet none of it explains the popularity of increasing block tariffs, since the nature of the water supply infrastructure recommends constant or decreasing tariff structures (Elnaboulsi, 2009; 2001). In Portugal, for example, most utilities charge prices with a fixed and a variable component, and the latter is usually an increasing block tariff (IBT) of three or more blocks, especially for residential use, where the IBT structure is seen by water managers as a way to signal scarcity and promote resource conservation.

Recent work on residential water demand (Monteiro and Roseta-Palma, 2011) has shown that if water demand and costs respond to weather conditions, increasing marginal prices could indeed be explained by water scarcity and customer heterogeneity in a setting where utilities maintain a balanced budget. However, the implications for tariff design of asymmetric value functions with loss aversion (Kahneman and Tversky, 1979) have never been considered, and we believe such a framework can shed new light on the issue. In particular, if water consumers react to a reference price, which may be that of the initial block or their actual block, the following block price can be interpreted as a loss or a discount, depending on whether the block tariff structure is increasing or decreasing, respectively.

A closely related topic is that of behavioural responses to price changes. We will investigate the implications of prospect theory (Kahneman and Tversky, 1979) on the optimal pricing policy and on the frequency of price updates, given that consumers seem to value losses more highly than gains, which should generate asymmetric price elasticities (i.e. higher price elasticities with price increases than with price reductions). This asymmetry was first corroborated by the pioneering study of Putler (1992). More recently this topic has been studied in the energy literature (Adeyemi and Hunt, 2007), but it is yet untested for water demand. The third topic deals with the implications of the reference-transaction framework (Kahneman et al., 1986) for water management. The concept of reference transaction is based on the dual entitlement principle, under which firms are entitled to a (positive) reference profit and individuals are entitled to reference terms (i.e. price, salary, rent). This concept was recently applied in a comparison of allocation rules for scarce resources (Raux et al., 2009) as well as in the marketing literature, which has analysed the issue of perceived price fairness (for recent reviews see Diller, 2008 and Krishna, 2009). In the case of water, since a reference transaction could imply fairness constraints, the utilities could be inhibited from proposing reference terms (i.e. prices) that would be perceived as unfair. This may indeed be the case in Portugal, where 71 per cent of water utilities are held by municipalities or associations of municipalities (INAG, 2011). Recent social protests against the rise of water bills highlight consumers' concerns and could lead to the maintenance of artificially low cost-recovery levels by the municipalities due to price fairness constraints. To illustrate, note that the revenues of Portuguese water utilities in 2009 covered only 80 per cent of the financial costs of providing the service,[2] for water supply, and an even lower 46 per cent for

[2] The financial costs of water services include the operation and maintenance costs, capital costs, administrative costs, and other direct costs (European Commission, 2003, p. 118).

wastewater drainage and treatment (INAG, 2011). Given the characteristics of water as an essential good, indeed now a human right, perceived fairness could be one explanation for the insufficient cost-recovery levels attained by water utilities in many countries.

Finally, we will review the few existing papers on the impact of the information included in water bills, such as that on price, social norms, and resource saving campaigns, in particular the inclusion of reference consumption values that are used to frame consumers into social comparison. The water demand literature has emphasized the importance of incorporating information about the water price in water bills and its relevance to the effectiveness of water pricing policies (Frondel and Messner, 2008; Gaudin, 2006). Nevertheless, only recently has social comparison been tested as a water management tool (Ferraro and Price, 2011), and reference consumption information was the more effective tool of all the conservation strategies tested.

The remainder of the chapter can be summarized as follows. Section 9.2 contains a literature review of behavioural economics in water management. Section 9.3 describes the behavioural applications and their potential contribution to water policy and water resource economics. Section 9.4 concludes and examines potential paths for future research in water management shedding light on the behavioural applications suggested.

9.2 Literature Review of Behavioural Economics in Water Management

9.2.1 *Behavioural Economics*

Behavioural economics arguably started as early as the eighteenth century with Adam Smith's *The Theory of Moral Sentiments*, but economic theory gradually grew apart from psychology until the second half of the twentieth century with 'researchers like George Katona, Harvey Leibenstein, Tibor Scitovsky, and Herbert Simon... suggesting the importance of psychological measures and bounds on rationality' (Camerer, 2004a, p. 6).

In the mid-1970s Kahneman and Tversky (1974) identified some significant heuristics and biases of human behaviour, especially under uncertainty,[3] but their major contributions to economics were published a few years later. In one of *Econometrica*'s most cited papers the authors developed prospect theory as an alternative model to expected utility theory and the rational choice paradigm (Kahneman and Tversky, 1979). This article has had by far the

[3] For further information about departures from the standard economic theory see Kahneman et al. (1982).

most major influence in changing the conceptual framework of economics and establishing the growing field of behavioural economics.[4]

The field of behavioural economics is focused on empirical validation and identification of behavioural departures from the standard model (i.e. the neoclassical model) as well as on the interpretation of behavioural deviations using alternative economic frameworks. Furthermore, these deviations can be organized into three areas where human nature strays from standard assumptions: there are limits to the pursuit of self-interest, to cognitive abilities, and to self-control (Mullainathan and Thaler, 2000).[5]

Despite the obvious rivalry between behavioural economic theory and standard rational choice theory, we want the reader to bear in mind that these two competing theories are not a dichotomy, in spite of past (and current) conflicts among practitioners. Future economic theory could (and we dare say should) be based on a hybrid approach, with the co-existence of neoclassical and behavioural approaches (MacFadyen, 2006; Rabin, 2002). For instance, Matthew Rabin states that behavioural findings should be integrated into economics and that his research programme 'does not abandon the correct insights of neoclassical economics, but supplements these insights with the insights to be had from realistic new assumptions' (Rabin, 2002, p. 659).

The rivalry mentioned here is one barrier to the development of this field, but there is another one, related to the dissemination of behavioural economic findings. The recent literature has made several efforts to encourage use of behavioural economic models, either through analysis of field phenomena (Camerer, 2004b) or by pointing out potential applications of different behavioural models (Ho et al., 2006). Nonetheless, some subfields of economics have shown little evidence of the incorporation of behavioural economics. Water resource economics is one of these cases, as discussed in section 9.2.2.

9.2.2 *State of the Art of Behavioural Economics in Water Resource Economics*

Water resource economics deals with the efficient allocation of a scarce resource (water). It aims to develop water management policies and to study the decision-making process of economic agents that use water resources (Griffin, 2006). In surveying this literature we found there is almost no incorporation of concepts from behavioural economics.

[4] Behavioural economics could be defined as 'a commitment to empirical testing of neoclassic assumptions of human behaviour and to modifying economic theory on the basis of what is found in the testing process' (Simon, 2008, p. 221).

[5] For a more recent analysis of the types of departures see Zarri (2010).

The subfield of behavioural water economics should focus on the development of water resource economics through the application of the findings of behavioural economics, as well as insights from other related general fields (e.g. psychology, sociology, ecology, marketing) or more specific fields (e.g. behavioural environmental economics, experimental economics, environmental psychology, behavioural finance).

So far, there seem to be very few published papers in this subfield. The first paper to incorporate behavioural assumptions into water resource economics was Winkler and Winett (1982), which approaches resource conservation, namely residential energy and water, integrating the psychological (social-learning) and economic views. The authors discuss the importance of monetary rebates for conservation policies, emphasizing that those rebates[6] (i.e. economic approach) could allow changes in conservation behaviour, but also that they could be complemented by information technology that would influence consumer behaviour (i.e. psychological approach). Therefore, they argue for a combined approach in conservation policies, without overlooking the psychological framework in the policy-makers' agenda.

Additionally, the authors argue that changes in human behaviour are made through behavioural interventions which should be interpreted in the context of two systems of behaviours: an internal system (linked to the individual) and an external system (linking the individual and the society). Therefore, insofar we are analysing behaviours of households (the typical individual level used in residential water demand literature) we should account for these two systems when designing water policies.

More recently, Jorgensen et al. (2009) contribute to the residential water demand literature with a new socio-economic model to understand household water consumption, emphasizing the importance of trust. Their work stresses the demand side and summarizes the main direct and indirect drivers which determine human behaviour towards water conservation. Their model also emphasizes other behavioural variables besides trust (e.g. past water use behaviour, outdoor-area interest and use, and pricing attitude), although the authors advise that there could be other variables to discover.

Finally, another issue within the framework of behavioural economics is the impact of social comparison as a water conservation strategy (Ferraro and Price, 2011). The authors analyse the influence on water consumption of three types of experimental treatments (i.e. technical recommendation, pro-social message, and social comparison). These authors conclude that non-pecuniary strategies (i.e. psychological strategies) do influence water conservation, with a higher

[6] Nevertheless, the application of (monetary) rebates has since been criticized due to the low price elasticity of water demand (Foxall, 1995).

effectiveness of social comparison in the group of high-use households, and a larger effect in the short-term rather than the long-term.

One of the major issues in water resource economics is the potential unsustainability of use (i.e. demand exceeding water supply in a consistent manner leading to the degradation of the resource). Strategies to improve water management can be centred on demand management or on supply enhancement (Griffin, 2006). Perhaps due to the prevalence of the latter throughout the twentieth century, the last few years have seen demand-side strategies became the dominant paradigm both in the water and energy sectors (Strengers, 2011; Barberán and Arbués, 2009).[7] Naturally, demand analysis is also the purpose of the few published papers, described already, which incorporate behavioural insights into residential water consumption.

Further applications of behavioural economics in water management could also be developed for other sectors that contribute significantly to water demand, such as agriculture, industry, and tourism, although these are outside the scope of this chapter. Another possibility would be for supply-side analysis to take into account the biases of system managers within water utilities and understanding the behaviour of these utilities.[8]

At this point two questions could arise: (i) why is there so little work on behavioural economics in the water management literature? And (ii) why does behavioural economics matter in this context?

From our perspective, the underdevelopment of this subfield has some potential explanations:

- Neoclassical hegemony
  - Environmental economics models are underpinned by the hegemony of standard neoclassic economic theory (Shogren and Taylor 2008; Venkatachalam 2007), and water resource economics is not an exception, as will be described in section 9.2.3.
- Dearth of household data
  - Scarcity of social/psychological data about households (Jorgensen et al., 2009) and lack of 'readily available data' in environmental data (Smith, 2008, p. 141).
  - Difficulty in obtaining reliable (and real) variables (e.g. appropriate income per household) and in collecting information from several sources of household data.

[7] This one-sided approach can be criticized, for instance Merrett states that '[w]ith outstream water we should always integrate in our thinking and our practice both demand-side and supply-side strategies' (2005, p. 92).

[8] Very recent literature discusses the importance of understanding the behaviour of firms. See the work of Bandiera et al. (2011) for a review of field experiments with firms.

- Limited systematization and availability of detailed aggregate data
  - There are significant limitations in the available aggregate statistics, even those related to fundamental aspects of water supply and wastewater services at the country level (OECD, 2010).
- Little application of experimental design to residential water demand
  - Few water demand studies have used experimental data during the last decade (as discussed in section 9.2.3), possibly because many water utilities have not traditionally focused on demand management and so do not perceive the value of engaging in such activities.
- Status quo bias
  - Resistance to change of water resource economists to behavioural economic models,[9] which is in a broader sense connected to status quo bias in human behaviour. Or as stated by MacFadyen 'we are often reluctant to abandon the security of conventional construct systems, but there may be cascade effects as highly regarded practitioners adopt new ideas' (2006, p. 195).

In response to the second question, there are some arguments in favour of incorporation of psychological insights into water resource economics:

- Development of residential water demand models, using a behavioural perspective
  - A wider set of models to test would improve knowledge of demand determinants and contribute to water policy design.
- Impact of psychological strategies in water policy
  - Policy-makers have exhibited little understanding of psychological strategies, diminishing the potential role of demand management and leading to a lack of significant influence of resource management strategies on policy (Winkler and Winett, 1982).
- In the expression 'economic agents' behaviour', behaviour should stand first
  - That 'a major part of economics is concerned with the study of behaviour' (Winkler and Winett, 1982, p. 422) seems to be a trivial statement. However, the residential water demand literature is focused on the economic, leaving the behaviour on the sidelines.

If economics is about studying economic agents' behaviour (e.g. consumers, firms, and investors), there is indeed redundancy in 'behavioural economics' (Simon, 2008; Thaler, 1999). We think data play a major role in this issue.

[9] Note that water resource economists may not be aware of the existence of behavioural economics models and therefore in this case the idea of resistance to change is not applicable.

Shogren and Taylor state that data are essential because they are 'a necessary condition to fully understand the relevance of any behavio[u]ral bias to economic phenomena' (2008, p. 34). Arguably this is one of the major constraints to the development of behavioural environmental economics in general and behavioural water economics in particular.

There have been some recent improvements in aggregate environmental data, such as the creation of the Water Information System for Europe in 2007 (WISE, 2007). However, there are still no globally available micro-level data.

The scarcity of individual household consumption data and of potential conditioning factors which are difficult to measure (e.g. past water use patterns, or attitude towards restrictions) is another important issue (Jorgensen et al., 2009). At the household level additional information (i.e. economic, financial, and behavioural indicators) is also essential to improve water demand studies. However, the quality of the information used influences the significance and robustness of both statistical and economics results in water demand literature (Arbués et al., 2010). To illustrate the difficulties, it is interesting to consider the experience we have had in the research project we are currently developing.[10] We contacted many water utilities to ask for their cooperation, both in providing us with consumption data and customer telephone numbers so we could run a household survey. Some utilities could not provide organized information on household consumption levels, others did not have telephone numbers in their customer databases, and yet others did not agree to cooperate with the project because of data privacy concerns. In one case of a rural municipality with a small customer base, the utility was keen to participate and did give us the necessary data, but after we had collected a few surveys some of the customers complained to the utility that they thought we had asked for too much information on household characteristics (house size, garden, appliances, household income, number and age of household members, and so forth) and therefore they wondered whether the research team might possibly be running a scam! Naturally, the utility withdrew its cooperation.

Besides this household data problem, there is another scarcity problem (and we are not talking about water scarcity): the lack of information about water allocations and consumption levels. Some examples of lack of measurement can be found in all sectors (agriculture, households, and industrial water), as well as in water losses, not only the leakage but also the unmeasured waste and consumption of water (Brown, 2002).

After this overview of the state of the art of behavioural economics in water management and discussion of some problems that have negatively

[10] *Pricing and behavioural responses in the water sector* supported by Fundação para a Ciência e a Tecnologia (Portuguese Science and Technology Foundation), PTDC/EGE-ECO/114477/2009.

influenced the development of this subfield, we provide a brief literature review of residential water demand to highlight past contributions and bring out the absence of behavioural models. Then we discuss four behavioural applications that could contribute to water resource economics.

9.2.3 *Literature Review Based on a Behavioural Perspective*

There are a few recent literature reviews in the field of residential water demand (Schleich and Hillenbrand, 2009; Worthington and Hoffman, 2008; Arbués et al., 2003). We do not intend to provide another one. Instead, we will analyse the residential water demand literature in light of the potential applications of behavioural perspectives, to be developed in section 9.3.

Nonetheless, before starting that analysis we want to discuss the categorization of the type of data used in residential water demand studies. The literature reviews divide data between aggregate data and household data. In this literature review we will also take into account whether the data is experimental. Thus, the categorization of the data used by the studies includes: aggregate data (AD); household data (HD); experimental household data (EHD), where the data is collected directly from households through experiments and/or household surveys; and experimental aggregate data (EAD) where we have experimental data at the aggregate level related to one or more communities. These categories are summarized in Figure 9.1.

Table 9.1 summarizes 25 papers that estimate residential water demand that have been published since 2000. The great majority used panel data and the periodicity of the data is mostly annual or monthly, with some exceptions. Typically the price elasticity of residential water demand in these studies is inelastic and negative, whereas income elasticity is positive but has a small magnitude in general terms, which is in line with the findings of the literature (Worthington and Hoffman, 2008).

The use of aggregate data is more common than household data, as expected. A more interesting finding is that experimental procedures have not been used often in this literature. Also, there are differences in the way data are obtained through experimental design or surveys. Two studies use surveys to obtain aggregate data from water utilities, namely Bell and Griffin (2008), which asked water providers about tariff structures, and Mazzanti and Montini (2006), which obtained information on water consumption, tariff structure, and water users from water utilities. Nonetheless, these studies are not experiments and should not be misinterpreted as EAD studies just because the researchers used surveys to obtain the data. In order to understand what would fit in the EAD category, suppose there is a government funding programme to enforce the use of water-saving technology in some communities of the country's richest regions in income per capita during a given period.

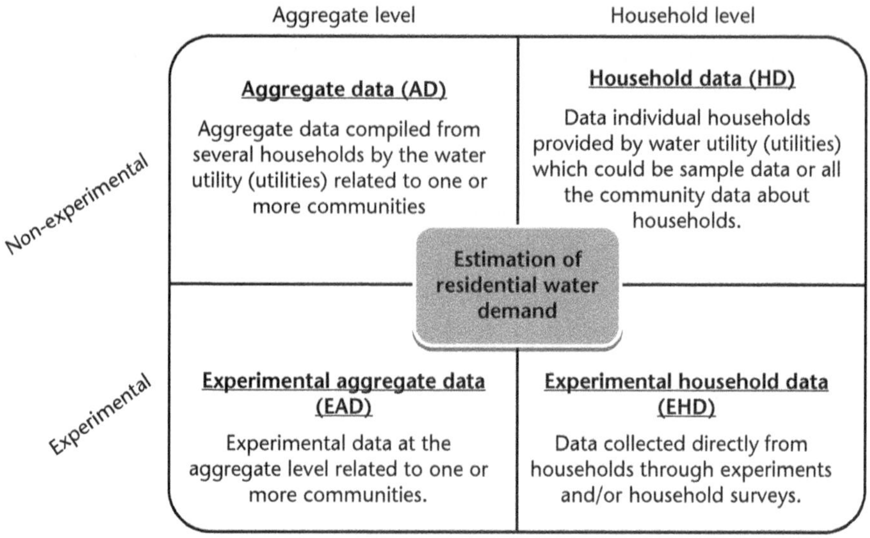

Figure 9.1. Type of data used in residential water demand studies
Source: the authors

A possible control group for this field experiment would be communities of the same regions, in which the use of the technology is not compulsory. Thus, analysing the aggregate data from each community the government can check whether the cost of the programme would compensate the water savings for a global implementation in all regions. In this case we would have EAD.

In the case of EHD some experiments have focused on residential water demand during the last decade (Martins and Moura e Sá, 2011; Frondel and Messner, 2008; Olmstead et al., 2007; Carter and Milon, 2005; Krause et al., 2003; Higgs and Worthington, 2001). A very recent work from Martins and Moura e Sá (2011) argues that water bills fail to spread environmental education among water consumers because they are too complex. They recommend the redesign of the bills with more clarity and simplicity, because current bills could compromise price signals and consequently the effectiveness of price strategies.

Frondel and Messner's work uses data from a household survey in Leipzig (Germany) to analyse price perceptions and their impact on residential water consumption. They conclude that water pricing policies will only have significant effects in sophisticated households (i.e. 'price-conscious'). Naïve households (i.e. 'price-ignorant'), the majority according to their sample, do not significantly diminish their water consumption with price increases. In a prior study, Carter and Milon (2005) also approached the issue of price knowledge, among other sources of heterogeneity. These authors used a 1997 survey of residential water consumers and monthly billing data of these

Table 9.1. Brief overview of residential water demand studies since 2000

Author(s) (year)	Study area	Data set	Periodicity	Type of data	Price elasticity	Income elasticity
Bell and Griffin (2011)	USA	Panel	Monthly data [Jan-95; Dec-05]	AD	Residential: −0.15 Commercial: −0.12 Aggregated: −0.27	n.a.
Martins and Moura e Sá (2011)	Madeira (Portugal)	Cross-sectional	Data obtained from 1 survey	EHD	n.a.	n.a.
Monteiro and Roseta-Palma (2011)	Portugal	Panel	Annual data [1998, 2000, 2002, 2005]	AD	[−0.13; −0.05]	[0.03;0.09]
Arbués et al. (2010)	Zaragoza (Spain)	Panel	Quarterly data (10 meter readings) [1996–1998]	HD	Aggregated: −0.57	Wealth semi-elasticity(1): 0.29×10^{-3}
Diakité et al. (2009)	Côte d'Ivoire	Panel	Annual data [1998–2002]	AD	−0.82	0.15
Schleich and Hillenbrand (2009)	Germany	Cross-sectional	Annual data [2003]	AD	−0.24	0.36
Bell and Griffin (2008)	Texas (USA)	Panel	Monthly data [Jan-99; Dec-03]	AD	−0.13	n.a.
Frondel and Messner (2008)	Leipzig (Germany)	Panel	Annual data [1998–2001]	EHD	[−0.49; −0.27]	[0.30; 0.31]
Kenney et al. (2008)(2)	Aurora (USA)	Panel	Monthly data [1997–2005]	HD	Pre-drought: −0.56 Drought: −1.11 Aggregated: −0.60	n.a.
Ruijs et al. (2008)	São Paulo (Brazil)	Time series	Monthly data [1997–2002]	AD	[−0.50; −0.45]	[0.39; 0.42]
Martínez-Espiñeira (2007)	Seville (Spain)	Time series	Monthly data [1991–1999]	AD	Short-run: −0.10 Long-run: −0.50	n.a.
Martins and Fortunato (2007)	Portugal	Panel	Monthly data [1998–2003]	AD	−0.56	n.a.
Musolesi and Nosvelli (2007)	Cremona Province (Italy)	Panel	Annual data [1998–2001]	AD	Short-run: −0.27 Long-run: −0.47	0.18
Olmstead et al. (2007)	USA and Canada	Panel	Daily data [four weeks]	EHD	Full sample: −0.33 IBT only: [−0.61; −0.59]	Full sample: 0.13 IBT only: [0.18; 0.19]
Arbués and Villanúa (2006)	Zaragoza (Spain)	Panel	Quarterly data (10 meter readings) [1996–1998]	HD	−0.08	0.79

(*Continued*)

Table 9.1. Continued

Author(s) (year)	Study area	Data set	Periodicity	Type of data	Price elasticity	Income elasticity
Gaudin (2006)	USA	Cross-sectional	Annual data [1995]	AD	Base model: −0.37 Price info given: −0.51 Price info not given: −0.36	Mean: 0.30 Median: 0.24
Hoffmann et al. (2006)	Brisbane (Australia)	Panel	Quarterly data [Sep-98; Jun-03]	AD	Short-run: −0.51 Long-run: −1.17	0.24
Mazzanti and Montini (2006)	Emilia-Romagna (Italy)	Panel	Annual data [1998–2001]	AD	[−1.33; −0.99]	[0.40; 0.71]
Carter and Milon (2005)	Florida (USA)	Panel	Monthly data [1997–1999]	EHD	**Marginal price short-run** Know price: −0.58 Don't know price: −0.21	**Short-run** Know price: −0.01 (not significant) Don't know price: 0.06
Garcia-Valiñas (2005)	Seville (Spain)	Panel	Quarterly data [Dec-91; Sep-00]	HD	Average: −0.49 Peak period: −0.55 Off-peak period: −0.46	0.58
Arbués et al. (2004)[3]	Zaragoza (Spain)	Panel	Quarterly data (10 time observations) [1996–1998]	HD	[−0.06; −0.03]	[0.07; 0.21]
Martínez-Espiñeira and Nauges (2004)	Seville (Spain)	Time series	Monthly data [1991–1999]	AD	−0.1	0.1
Garcia and Reynaud (2004)	Bourdeaux (France)	Panel	Annual data [1995–1998]	AD	−0.25	0.03 (not significant)
Krause et al. (2003)	New Mexico (USA)	Panel	Data obtained from 6 experiments	EHD	[−0.10; −0.02]	n.a.
Higgs and Worthington (2001)	Brisbane (Australia)	Cross-sectional	Annual data [n.a.]	EHD	n.a.	n.a.

Source: authors' analysis of the papers

Notes: aggregated data (AD) are the data compiled from several households by water utilities related to one or more communities; household data (HD) are data of individual households provided by water utilities, which could be sample data or all the community data about households; experimental household data (EHD) is the information collected directly from households through experiments and/or household surveys; experimental aggregated data (EAD) are experimental data at the aggregate level related to one or more communities. n.a.: not available or not applicable

(1) The wealth (income) semi-elasticity is the percentage change in water consumption when the income variable changes €1,000. (2) This study used community household data with all household data about single family homes available of the city of Aurora. (3) Almost all the data used in this study are household data, with the exception of the variable of availability of collective hot water facilities used in the water demand estimation that was obtained through a telephone survey

households and found that water users' behaviour is sensitive to price awareness, with price-conscious households exhibiting more responsiveness to both average and marginal prices. Additionally, the authors obtained a counterintuitive conclusion that price awareness increases water consumption which may be explained by price overestimation, in line with the literature on electricity demand.

Olmstead et al. (2007) use experimental household data from a previous study[11] and suggest that the difference between the price-elasticities under IBT and uniform rates could be explained by behavioural responses to price structures or city-level heterogeneity.

Krause et al. (2003) developed six laboratory experiments in New Mexico (United States) which combined experimental and survey data to analyse and estimate water demand. The authors found that consumer heterogeneity matters, since the heterogeneous responses of consumers are relevant to water policy effectiveness. Moreover, they criticized the limitations of studies that use aggregate data, which do not allow testing for this heterogeneity.

Higgs and Worthington (2001) used a household survey in the city of Brisbane (Australia) to study consumer preferences in a dual-pricing system (i.e. consumers can choose one of two systems). The authors conclude that consumers generally prefer a pricing system which minimizes the impact on payments of uncertain future demand, even if there are no clear reasons to do so considering only current consumption. This can explain the so-called 'flat-rate bias'.

To sum up, economists have not used experimental data very much in residential water demand studies. This could be explained by the resistance of social scientists to laboratory experiments,[12] which are criticized because of their lack of realistic features and lack of generalization to the real world (Falk and Heckman, 2009). Non-experimental data (i.e. AD and HD) are used by most of the studies, with laboratory experiments and field experiments left on the sidelines.[13]

Furthermore, none of the studies accounts for asymmetric price and income elasticities or reference block pricing. The use of the reference-transaction framework has likewise never been proposed, whereas the use of social comparison (and reference consumption) has just begun with the pioneering work of Ferraro and Price (2011).

[11] Household level data obtained through mail surveys and historic billing data (Mayer et al., 1999).

[12] Lab experiments are sometimes underestimated compared with field experiments due to the implicit assumption of the superiority of field data over lab data. However, Falk and Heckman argue that lab experiments should be done more often (see Falk and Heckman (2009) for further details).

[13] The discussion about non-experimental data versus experimental data is outside the scope of this research, although further research should focus on the advantages and limitations of different type of experiments within water resource economics.

We proceed to discuss the four behavioural applications we propose—reference block pricing, asymmetric elasticities, reference transaction, and social comparison—highlighting their potential contribution to the enrichment of this literature.

9.3 Discussion of Behavioural Applications and Their Effects in Water Management

In this section we suggest four applications of behavioural economics to water demand studies based on four different behavioural frameworks, namely prospect theory, asymmetric price elasticity (APE), reference transaction, and social comparison. Table 9.2 summarizes the main features of different behavioural economic frameworks that can have implications for water management. We stress that these potential applications are not exhaustive. Our approach is to focus on the introduction of some new methods into the residential water demand literature.

9.3.1 *Reference Block Pricing*

Prospect theory proposes a model of decision-making under risk which accounts for some behavioural biases, namely the certainty effect, the reflection effect, and the isolation effect (Kahneman and Tversky, 1979).[14] Prospect theory assumes an asymmetric value function with three characteristics: value depends on the deviation from the (neutral) reference point[15] (e.g. status quo or current asset position); the function is concave for gains and convex for losses; and it is steeper for losses than for gains (i.e. there is loss aversion). This means that individuals are more sensitive to changes seen as losses than to gains of the same magnitude, with respect to a reference point. Supported by the existence of loss aversion, the potential application suggested for this concept is reference block pricing. Notice that most pricing research in both economics and marketing has been focused on intrinsic prices, although the 'behavioural aspects of pricing', including reference-price effects, acquired some importance over the last three decades. For a categorization of these behavioural aspects see Krishna (2009).

[14] The certainty effect is the bias to underweight outcomes that are probable in relation to sure outcomes. Reflection effect is the aversion to risk in the domain of gains accompanied by risk seeking in the domain of losses. Finally, the isolation effect means that people display inconsistent preferences in the presence of the same choice with a change of framework (i.e. framing effects). For additional information see Kahneman and Tversky (1979).

[15] The reference point could shift and be different from the status quo. The location of the reference point and the form in which the choice is framed are essential determinants of decisions.

Table 9.2. Potential behavioural applications to water management

Seminal reference	Behaviour framework	Potential application	Policy implications	Current references in water management
Kahneman and Tversky (1979)	Prospect theory	Reference block pricing	– Redefinition of tariff structures – Revision of the effectiveness of pricing policy – Influence on price elasticities in terms of magnitude and persistence	–
Putler (1992)	Asymmetric price elasticity (APE)	Asymmetric elasticities of residential water demand	– Redefinition of tariff structures – Revision of the effectiveness of pricing policy – Influence on price elasticities in terms of magnitude and persistence	–
Kahneman et al. (1986)	Reference transaction	Reference transaction and tariff acceptability	– Understanding of the insufficient cost recovery achieved by water utilities through tariffs – Definition of economic criteria for equitable allocation – Implications in the definition of allocation rules for scarce resources – Redefinition of water policies	–
Festinger (1954)	Social comparison (and reference consumption)	Social comparison (and water reference consumption)	– Development of water conservation strategies – Redefinition of water policies – Influence on price elasticities in terms of magnitude and persistence	Ferraro and Price (2011)

Source: authors' analysis

As noted in the Introduction, the significant amount of literature on pricing structures in regulated water utilities does not explain the popularity of increasing block tariffs, given the theoretical efficiency of marginal-cost pricing in most situations. Some countries and regions do use decreasing block tariffs, predominantly for users with high consumption levels, due to their weight on the total revenues of water utilities. Since these large consumers ensure 'substantial revenues' and 'stable flows', the water utilities could be reluctant in such cases to apply tariff structures which promote water conservation (OECD, 2010, p. 11). On the other hand, Griffin and Mjelde (2011) have recently argued that low-consumption and low-income households are favoured with uniform block tariffs compared with increasing block tariffs.

Despite this extensive discussion of block-tariff settings in water, the impact of asymmetric value functions with loss aversion (Kahneman and Tversky, 1979) has never been proposed. We think that consumer responses could be based on a reference point which we call the consumer's reference block tariff. This may be the tariff of their actual block or, alternatively, the initial blocks of a tariff structure could be interpreted as reference points, so that framing effects would influence customers to view a change to the following block as a loss (increasing block tariffs) or discount (decreasing block tariffs).

Furthermore, loss aversion indicates that individuals are more sensitive to variations interpreted as losses and consequently IBT could lead water consumers to reduce consumption by more than higher flat rates. Therefore, the reduction on water consumption due to changing to a more expensive block tariff, which would be typically explained by the price effect, could also be explained by this loss aversion effect.

This behavioural application could have several implications to sectors with non-linear prices. The concept of reference block price could contribute to the redefinition of tariff structures, revision of the effectiveness of pricing policy, redefinition of water policies, and also influence the determination of price elasticities in terms of magnitude and persistence.

9.3.2 *Asymmetric Elasticities of Residential Water Demand*

APE can be defined as the asymmetric behaviour of consumers to price changes, according to the seminal work developed in the field of marketing (Putler, 1992). Typically if prices increase with respect to a reference price the price elasticities of demand will be higher, whereas we will have lower price elasticities with price reductions. The author argues that reference price influences consumer behaviour. Moreover, he corroborates the existence of loss aversion. We propose that both asymmetric price elasticity and the asymmetric income elasticity of demand are relevant issues in residential water demand.

Water pricing is one of the most important policy instruments to deal with scarcity and sustainability issues, allowing the implementation of demand management strategies (Griffin, 2006). Therefore, the study of the price elasticity of water demand is an essential measure for evaluation of the impact of pricing policies.

APE has been commonly applied in marketing studies according to Ho et al. (2006). More recently the study of APE has also been extended to the energy sector (Adeyemi and Hunt, 2007; Gately and Huntington, 2002), but it has not been approached so far in the domain of residential water demand, according to our previous literature review. Moreover, the study of asymmetric income elasticity (henceforth AIE) has not been analysed in this domain either. However, there is a piece of research in energy economics stating that income changes have asymmetric effects in the energy and oil demand in many non-OECD countries and these should be accounted for to mitigate biased estimations (Gately and Huntington, 2002).

The existence of APE could have several policy implications, of which we highlight the formation of reference prices, their effects on water consumption, implications for the design of tariff structures and impact on optimal water pricing policies.

Note that we argue that asymmetry in price and income elasticities should be tested, not assumed to exist. In this sense we believe that residential water demand studies should look into the issue instead of implicitly assuming that both price and income elasticities of water are symmetric.

9.3.3 *Reference Transaction and Tariff Acceptability*

The reference-transaction framework was first suggested by Kahneman, Knetsch, and Thaler during the 1980s. The concept is based on the dual entitlement principle under which firms are entitled to a (positive) reference profit and individuals are entitled to reference terms (i.e. price, salary, rent) (Kahneman et al., 1986). The most puzzling finding of the authors was that consumers and employees consider it acceptable for a firm to increase price and/or cut wages in order to ensure a positive reference profit. Additionally, firms' behaviour seems to be influenced by fairness constraints which lead to inefficient decisions according to standard rational theory. Using a framework with fairness constraints could explain many market anomalies. In particular, we believe the reference-transaction framework could provide a better understanding of the low levels of cost recovery in the water sector.

Notably, one of the major aims in the development of water policies has been the cost recovery of the services provided by water utilities through water prices (OECD, 2010). According to this report it is often difficult to reach full cost recovery exclusively through tariffs in water sector, with this concern reflected in Article 9 of the Water Framework Directive (European Parliament and Council, 2000). Given this difficulty the core debate has changed from full cost recovery to sustainable cost recovery, which implies a mix of tariffs, taxes, and transfers (i.e. three types of revenues, also known as '3Ts') to achieve that aim.

According to our perspective, the use of the reference-transaction framework (Kahneman et al., 1986) could be tested using an experiment to assess the attitudes of water users and managers of water utilities in at least two different ways. First, how does framing influence individual perceptions of fairness in water pricing? Second, why do water utilities so often seem to be financially unsustainable if they ought to be entitled to a positive reference profit? Both questions seem important in order to develop new approaches to cost recovery, at least for countries in which water services are a political issue for municipalities, such as Portugal. In the first question the underlying idea is to understand how different frameworks influence the application of water pricing policies, especially tariff increases aimed at ensuring full cost recovery. The second question is more puzzling. On the one hand, the concept of reference transaction implies the existence of fairness constrains which limit the water utilities' profit maximization and hence could explain (at least partially) the financial unsustainability. On the other hand, water utilities, as firms, should be entitled to a positive reference profit, which would minimize the issue of insufficient cost recovery. The essential nature of the good in question and traditionally low prices may provide clues to answer these questions. The marketing literature provides one avenue for solving this puzzle by identifying price fairness as a multifaceted concept, with possibly conflicting components, such as firm reputation, inferred motive of firm and price comparison (Krishna, 2009) or price honesty and credibility (Diller, 2008).

The reference transaction framework has not been applied to water resource economics as far as we know, although it seems appealing to understand whether water utilities could be a counter-evidence of the reference profit entitlement. This topic has been explored in experimental research, with a recent application in the comparison of allocation rules related to two scarce resources, seats in a high-speed train and parking spaces (Raux et al., 2009). The authors tested different allocation rules and conclude that they depend on the educational level of the individuals, the type of good, and the type of scarcity (exceptional or recurrent).

This framework could have some policy implications for water management, such as understanding why prices charged by water utilities are often insufficient to cover their costs, defining economic criteria for equitable allocation of scarce resources and general redefinition of water policies, in particular those related to public versus private ownership of utilities, since the reference transaction could be seen differently by consumers in each case.

9.3.4 *Social Comparison (and Water Reference Consumption)*

The theory of social comparison was developed in the seminal work of Festinger (1954). Typically, social comparisons are based on framing individuals with comparative information in order to promote a specific behaviour. Since Festinger's findings there have been several studies on this issue, but only recently has the theory been applied to residential water demand. In particular, the use of social comparison as well as pro-social information and technical advice given to the members of a household can influence their water consumption (Ferraro and Price, 2011). The authors show that social comparison has the strongest impact on consumer behaviour, using as reference consumption neighbours' consumption levels. Households in a randomized field experiment were provided with their own consumption along with two types of comparison: the median household consumption of their region and the percentile of that household considering all households of the region.

In this sense, the neighbours' consumption levels could be seen as the reference consumption, defined as a reference value of consumption (normally the average or median consumption) which frames the consumers into a social comparison framework. Consequently, if consumers have household consumptions above average (or median) they will categorize their actual situation in the domain of losses (i.e. these consumers will try to save water in order to achieve the domain of gains) and vice versa. In the field of energy economics the reference consumption framework has also been applied recently in a field experiment with the aim of promoting energy conservation by consumers through two reference consumption set-ups: an average consumption level of neighbours and an efficient consumption level of neighbours (Allcott, 2011). The author concludes that non-pecuniary strategies of energy savings can change consumer behaviour in a significant and cost-effective manner. Moreover, there is also another avenue of research focused on environmental conservation in hotels. A recent study (Goldstein et al., 2008) concludes that guests of hotels react more to social-comparison frameworks (e.g. 'the majority of quests reuse their towels'), than to the typical appeals to environmental protection.

Gaudin (2006) underpins the importance of the information provided to water consumers through the water bill and the relevance of this information in the effectiveness of water pricing policies. Frondel and Messner (2008) corroborate the importance of incorporating information in the water bill (e.g. price and cost perception) and argue that pricing policies need to be complemented by the availability of information to consumers in their bill, including price and cost information. More recently, Martins and Moura e Sá (2011) found that the clarity of water bills is a major issue in residential water sector. According to the authors the bills fail to have environmentally relevant impacts on consumers, namely in terms of fostering water conservation, thus their redesign to make them clearer and simpler could contribute to the effectiveness of price-based policies.

The social comparison measure could be tested in other ways. For example, the use of the typical average (or median) household consumption does not account for household size when framing the consumers. This fact could lead to biased conclusions if the household size has a significant impact on consumption. Arbués et al. (2010) recently argued that using household data which accounts for household size could matter in the estimation of residential water demand. Potential contributions of the social comparison framework to water management include the development of water conservation strategies, the redefinition of water policies, and influence over the price elasticities in terms of magnitude and persistence.

Framing effects are well-known to behavioural economists. Our aim in this section was to briefly explain some behaviour frameworks which we use to illustrate some of the applications and effects in water demand studies. In the section 9.4 we discuss further research of the suggested behavioural applications.

9.4 Conclusion and Future Research

At a basic level, water consumption cannot be considered sustainable until its costs are properly recovered. This issue has occupied many economists who have analysed customer demand, on the one hand, and service costs, on the other. However, financial cost recovery is not sufficient—truly sustainable use must respect ecosystem needs and be based on a good understanding of consumption patterns.

One of the aims of this chapter was to approach the scarcity issue. Surely, water scarcity is a topic dear to all water researchers; however our direct focus was on another type of scarcity: that of residential water demand studies that include behavioural economics, i.e. empirical testing of behavioural assumptions. Nowadays, the fields of behavioural economics and experimental economics, which arose from the collaboration between psychologists and economists, are an integral part of mainstream economics, as can be attested by many articles in top economic journals (Santos, 2011). However, the existing water demand literature exhibits a clear dominance of standard neoclassic economic theory. We argue that further research on water demand should use behavioural economics frameworks and account for behavioural failures.[16]

As argued by Thaler (1999) the logical evolution of economics as a field will be the incorporation of behavioural features into economic models. The challenge is to understand that the highway along which the herd of researchers is travelling could be the slowest way. Exploring alternative approaches and rethinking the frameworks could be the new alternative to that highway. New empirical results could promote discussion of new hypotheses and new lines of reasoning (Smith, 2008). Nevertheless, the development of environmental economics data along with social and psychological data (Jorgensen et al., 2009; Smith, 2008) is essential: without a proper vehicle, travelling will be a footslog.

In our view, this is one of the fundamental issues holding back the development of behavioural economics in the water domain. Information needs to be periodically collected, compiled, and organized, always respecting confidentiality constraints, especially in the case of household data. We believe that the development of more powerful databases and the growing importance of the sustainability issue will bring new researchers into water resource economics. The importance of data wealth has been proven by the developments of behavioural finance (Thaler, 1999). The challenge of development, collection, and systematization will be the first step in further research on behavioural applications in water management.

This chapter discussed some behavioural applications that could reshape the understanding of major issues in water management, through four different ideas: reference block pricing, asymmetric elasticities, reference transaction, and social comparison (and reference consumption). None of these lines of research have been analysed so far, with the exception of social comparison.

Reference block pricing could be empirically tested with the identification of reference blocks within different pricing structures (e.g. increasing and decreasing block rates) for each household and looking into their ex-post consumption behaviour after block shifts. Reference effects could help explain the stronger consumption reactions found by Olmstead et al. (2007) for IBT and thus provide a justification for the overwhelming use of such structures in Portugal, as well as in other countries.

Further research on asymmetric elasticities is essential due to the importance of price and income elasticities to evaluate pricing and affordability, which are core issues in water policy. If the typical assumption of symmetric

[16] Behavioural failures refer to situations where 'a person fails to behave as predicted by rational choice theory' as well as an 'anomaly, paradox, bias, heuristic misperception, fallacy, illusion, or paradigm' (Shogren and Taylor, 2008, p. 27).

elasticities does not hold this could reshape, to some extent, the pricing policies in the water sector.

The reference transaction framework could be an explanation for insufficient levels of cost recovery by emphasizing how perceived price fairness hinders tariff increases. Then again, limitations to profit maximization through fairness constraints contradict the idea that water utilities, as firms, are entitled to a positive reference profit. Although both ideas come from the reference transaction framework, they have antagonistic effects and the study of their combined impact is a further avenue of research.

Lastly, social comparison (and reference consumption) is a recent topic with several promising lines of research: the comparative study of different social comparison treatments (e.g. sending users the average household consumption in their neighbourhood, region, or country) and the application of findings from energy conservation literature, such as efficient consumption information, are two potential options for further research in this area. Furthermore, the use of different household sizes in experimental design could result in new findings.

There are other areas of water resource economics in which behavioural applications could also be applied, such as supply analysis, including investment decisions in water infrastructures, policy design, cost–benefit analysis, resource efficiency, water losses, and water markets, among others. For instance, in water markets, Garrido (2007) used a laboratory experiment to test specific market regulations of the water reform in Spain and concluded that eliminating the existing trading restrictions would imply welfare gains for senior users of water rights.

Simon (2008) argued that the development of behavioural research (and theory) is based on testing economic theories through empirical methods, namely survey research and experiments based on direct observation, either in laboratory context or through observation of the decision-making process in natural environments (e.g. case studies based on individual decisions or decisions in business firms). These methods are not common tools for economists, who are challenged by the techniques of experimentation and individual data collection as well as by interpretation of survey data. Thus, economists who aim to implement empirical tests of economic theory will probably have to invest time to develop skills in at least one of the aforementioned methods. These additional skills give an edge to behavioural economists and contribute to the redesign of consumption theory in general and water resource economics in particular. Further research could focus on the advantages and limitations of different types of experiments (e.g. laboratory experiments and field experiments) in contrast with the typical use of non-experimental data.

If water resource economists were to grasp the differences between the 'rational consumer' and the 'normal consumer'[17] through empirical behaviour analysis, that could improve water management practices and prevent scarcity, while possibly gaining insights that would be applicable to other natural resources. This conceptual framework could also be important to understand the supply side, with the analysis of existing water utilities as 'rational' or 'normal' in terms of corporate decisions (e.g. operational decisions, or investment decisions).

Although behavioural economics was originally based on empirical research it is not to be dismissed as some sort of 'reverse engineering' field based only on empirical analysis. Since the seminal work of Kahneman and Tversky (1979), behavioural economics is based on both empirical and theoretical foundations. Therefore, the development of residential water demand argued for in this chapter is implicitly based on a dual approach which tries to incorporate both.

The behavioural applications proposed in this chapter are based on the seminal works of psychologists such as Daniel Kahneman, Amos Tversky, and Leon Festinger, as well as on the price fairness research in marketing literature. We believe this highlights the relevance of a multidisciplinary approach to provide new research ideas and improve our understanding of water consumption.

We would like to end the chapter by noting that one of its primary aims is to promote brainstorming, not necessarily to be exhaustive in our analysis of possible applications of behavioural economics in water management. To conclude, our timeless question is: are economists thinking outside the box in their fields?

References

Adeyemi, O. I. and Hunt, L. C. (2007) 'Modelling OECD Industrial Energy Demand: Asymmetric Price Responses and Energy-Saving Technical Change', *Energy Economics*, 29(4): 693–709.

Allcott, H. (2011) 'Social Norms and Energy Conservation', *Journal of Public Economics*, 95(9–10): 1082–95.

Arbués, F., Barberán, R., and Villanúa, I. (2004) 'Price Impact on Urban Residential Water Demand: A Dynamic Panel Data Approach', *Water Resources Research*, 40, W11402.

[17] This draws on the dichotomy rational investor and normal investor suggested by Statman (1999), which can be similarly applied to consumer behaviour.

Arbués, F., Garcia-Valinas, M. A., and Martinez-Espineira, R. (2003) 'Estimation of Residential Water Demand: A State-of-the-Art Review', *Journal of Socio-Economics*, 32 (1): 81–102.

Arbués, F. and Villanúa, I. (2006) 'Potential for Pricing Policies in Water Resource Management: Estimation of Urban Residential Water Demand in Zaragoza, Spain', *Urban Studies*, 43(13): 2421–42.

Arbués, F., Villanúa, I., and Barberán, R. (2010) 'Household Size and Residential Water Demand: An Empirical Approach', *Australian Journal of Agricultural and Resource Economics*, 54(1): 61–80.

Bandiera, O., Barankay, I., and Rasul, I. (2011) 'Field Experiments with Firms', *Journal of Economic Perspectives*, 25(3): 63–82.

Barberán, R. and Arbués, F. (2009) 'Equity in Domestic Water Rates Design', *Water Resources Management*, 23(10): 2101–18.

Bell, D. R. and Griffin, R. C. (2008) 'An annual quasidifference approach to water price elasticity', *Water Resources Research*, 44, W08420.

Bell, D. R. and Griffin, R. C. (2011) 'Urban Water Demand with Periodic Error Correction', *Land Economics*, 87(3): 528–44.

Brown, K. (2002) 'Water Scarcity: Forecasting the Future with Spotty Data', *Science*, 297 (5583): 926.

Camerer, C. F. (2004a) 'Behavioral Economics: Past, Present, Future' in C. F. Camerer, G. Lowenstein, and M. Rabin (eds) *Advances in Behavioral Economics*, Princeton and Oxford: Princeton University Press.

Camerer, C. F. (2004b) 'Prospect Theory in the Wild: Evidence from the Field' in C. F. Camerer, G. Lowenstein, and M. Rabin (eds) *Advances in Behavioral Economics*, Princeton and Oxford: Princeton University Press.

Carter, D. W. and Milon, J. W. (2005) 'Price Knowledge in Household Demand for Utility Services', *Land Economics*, 81(2): 265–83.

Diakité, D., Semenov, A., and Thomas, A. (2009) 'A Proposal for Social Pricing of Water Supply in Côte d'Ivoire', *Journal of Development Economics*, 88(2): 258–68.

Diller, H. (2008) 'Price Fairness', *Journal of Product and Brand Management*, 17(5): 353–5.

Elnaboulsi, J. C. (2009) 'An Incentive Water Pricing Policy for Sustainable Water Use', *Environmental and Resource Economics*, 42(4): 451–69.

Elnaboulsi, J. C. (2001) 'Nonlinear pricing and capacity planning for water and wastewater services', *Water resources management*, 15(1): 55–69.

European Commission (2003) *Common Implementation Strategy for the Water Framework Directive (2000/60/EC) Guidance Document No 1*, Luxembourg: European Commission.

European Commission (2007) *Communication from the Commission to the European Parliament and the Council: Towards sustainable water management in the European Union—First stage in the implementation of the Water Framework Directive 2000/60/ EC. COM (2007) 128 final*, Brussels: Commission of the European Communities.

European Parliament and Council (2000) 'Council Directive 2000/60/EC of the European Parliament and of the Council of 23 October 2000 Establishing a Framework for Community Action in the Field of Water Policy', *Official Journal of the European Communities*, 22(12).

Falk, A. and Heckman, J. J. (2009) 'Lab Experiments are a Major Source of Knowledge in the Social Sciences', *Science*, 326(5952): 535.

Ferraro, P. J. and Price, M. K. (2011) 'Using Non-Pecuniary Strategies to Influence Behavior: Evidence from a Large Scale Field Experiment', *NBER Working Paper No. 17189*: 1–34.

Festinger, L. (1954) 'A Theory of Social Comparison Processes', *Human Relations*, 7(2): 117–40.

Foxall, G. R. (1995) 'Environment-Impacting Consumer Behavior: An Operant Analysis', *Advances in Consumer Research*, 22: 262–68.

Frondel, M. and Messner, M. (2008) 'Price Perception and Residential Water Demand: Evidence from a German Household Panel', in *16th Annual Conference of the European Association of Environmental and Resource Economists in Gothenburg*, Venice: European Association of Environmental and Resources Economists, pp. 1–13.

Garcia, S. and Reynaud, A. (2004) 'Estimating the Benefits of Efficient Water Pricing in France', *Resource and Energy Economics*, 26(1): 1–25.

Garcia-Valiñas, M. A. (2005) 'Efficiency and Equity in Natural Resources Pricing: A Proposal for Urban Water Distribution Service', *Environmental and Resource Economics*, 32(2): 183–204.

Garrido, A. (2007) 'Water Markets Design and Evidence from Experimental Economics', *Environmental and Resource Economics*, 38(3): 311–30.

Gately, D. and Huntington, H. G. (2002) 'The Asymmetric Effects of Changes in Price and Income on Energy and Oil Demand', *Energy Journal*, 23(1): 19–55.

Gaudin, S. (2006) 'Effect of Price Information on Residential Water Demand', *Applied Economics*, 38(4): 383–94.

Goldstein, N. J., Cialdini, R. B., and Griskevicius, V. (2008) 'A Room with a Viewpoint: Using Social Norms to Motivate Environmental Conservation in Hotels', *Journal of Consumer Research*, 35(3): 472–82.

Griffin, R. C. (2006) *Water Resource Economics: The Analysis of Scarcity, Policies, and Projects*, Cambridge, Mass.: MIT Press.

Griffin, R. C. and Mjelde, J. W. (2011) 'Distributing Water's Bounty', *Ecological Economics*, (72): 116–28.

Higgs, H. and Worthington, A. (2001) 'Consumer Preferences and Water Charging Options in a Large Urban Municipality: A Case Study', *Public Works Management and Policy*, 5(3): 209–17.

Ho, T. H., Lim, N. and Camerer, C. F. (2006) 'Modeling the psychology of consumer and firm behavior with behavioral economics', *Journal of Marketing Research*, 43(3): 307–31.

Hoffmann, M., Worthington, A., and Higgs, H. (2006) 'Urban Water Demand with Fixed Volumetric Charging in a Large Municipality: The Case of Brisbane, Australia', *Australian Journal of Agricultural and Resource Economics*, 50(3): 347–59.

INAG, I. P. (2011) *Relatório do Estado do Abastecimento de Água e Drenagem e Tratamento de Águas Residuais. Sistemas Públicos Urbanos INSAAR 2010 (dados 2009)*, Lisboa: INAG.

Jorgensen, B., Graymore, M., and O'Toole, K. (2009) 'Household Water Use Behavior: An Integrated Model', *Journal of Environmental Management*, 91(1): 227–36.

Kahneman, D., Knetsch, J. L., and Thaler, R. (1986) 'Fairness as a Constraint on Profit Seeking: Entitlements in the Market', *The American Economic Review*, 76(4): 728–41.

Kahneman, D., Slovic, P., and Tversky, A. (1982) *Judgement under Uncertainty: Heuristics and Biases*, Cambridge: Cambridge University Press.

Kahneman, D. and Tversky, A. (1974) 'Judgment under Uncertainty: Heuristics and Biases', *Science*, 185(4157): 1124–31.

Kahneman, D. and Tversky, A. (1979) 'Prospect Theory: An Analysis of Decision under Risk', *Econometrica: Journal of the Econometric Society*, 47(2): 263–92.

Kenney, D. S. et al. (2008) 'Residential Water Demand Management: Lessons from Aurora, Colorado', *Journal of the American Water Resources Association (JAWRA)*, 44(1): 192–207.

Krause, K., Chermak, J. M., and Brookshire, D. S. (2003) 'The Demand for Water: Consumer Response to Scarcity', *Journal of Regulatory Economics*, 23(2): 167–91.

Krishna, A. (2009) 'Behavioral Pricing' in V.R. Rao (ed.) *Handbook of Pricing Research in Marketing*, Massachusetts: Edward Elgar Publishing.

MacFadyen, A. J. (2006) 'Beliefs in Behavioral and Neoclassical Economics' in M. Altman (ed.) *Handbook of Contemporary Behavioral Economics*, New York: M.E. Sharpe.

Martínez-Espiñeira, R. (2007) 'An Estimation of Residential Water Demand Using Co-Integration and Error Correction Techniques', *Journal of Applied Economics*, 10(1): 161–84.

Martínez-Espiñeira, R. and Nauges, C. (2004) 'Is All Domestic Water Consumption Sensitive to Price Control?' *Applied economics*, 36(15): 1697–703.

Martins, R. and Fortunato, A. (2007) 'Residential Water Demand under Block Rates: A Portuguese Case Study', *Water policy*, 9(2): 217–30.

Martins, R. and Moura e Sá, P. (2011) 'Promoting Sustainable Residential Water Use: A Portuguese Case Study in Ownership and Regulation', *Policy Studies*, 32(3): 291–301.

Mayer, P. W. et al. (1999) *Residential End Uses of Water*, Denver: American Water Works Association Research Foundation.

Mazzanti, M. and Montini, A. (2006) 'The Determinants of Residential Water Demand: Empirical Evidence for a Panel of Italian Municipalities', *Applied Economics Letters*, 13 (2): 107–11.

Merrett, S. (2005) *The Price of Water: Studies in Water Resource Economics and Management*, London: IWA Publishing.

Monteiro, H. and Roseta-Palma, C. (2011) 'Pricing for Scarcity? An Efficiency Analysis of Increasing Block Tariffs', *Water Resources Research*, 47(6): W06510.

Mullainathan, S. and Thaler, R. (2000) *Behavioral Economics*, Cambridge: National Bureau of Economic Research.

Musolesi, A. and Nosvelli, M. (2007) 'Dynamics of Residential Water Consumption in a Panel of Italian Municipalities', *Applied Economics Letters*, 14(6): 441–4.

OECD (2010) *Pricing Water Resources and Water and Sanitation Services*, Paris: Organisation for Economic Co-operation and Development Publishing.

Olmstead, S. M., Michael Hanemann, W., and Stavins, R. N. (2007) 'Water Demand under Alternative Price Structures', *Journal of Environmental Economics and Management*, 54(2): 181–98.

Putler, D. S. (1992) 'Incorporating Reference Price Effects into a Theory of Consumer Choice', *Marketing Science*, 11(3): 287–309.

Rabin, M. (2002) 'A Perspective on Psychology and Economics', *European economic review*, 46(4–5): 657–85.

Raux, C., Souche, S., and Croissant, Y. (2009) 'How Fair is Pricing Perceived to Be? An Empirical Study', *Public Choice*, 139(1): 227–40.

Ruijs, A., Zimmermann, A. and Van den Berg, M. (2008) 'Demand and Distributional Effects of Water Pricing Policies', *Ecological Economics*, 66(2–3): 506–16.

Santos, A. C. (2011) 'Behavioural and Experimental Economics: Are They Really Transforming Economics?' *Cambridge Journal of Economics*, 35(4): 705–28.

Schleich, J. and Hillenbrand, T. (2009) 'Determinants of Residential Water Demand in Germany', *Ecological Economics*, 68(6): 1756–69.

Shogren, J. F. and Taylor, L. O. (2008) 'On Behavioral-Environmental Economics', *Review of Environmental Economics and Policy*, 2(1): 26–44.

Simon, H. A. (2008) 'Behavioural Economics' in S. Durlauf and L. E. Blume (general eds) *The New Palgrave Dictionary of Economics*, Basingstoke, UK: Palgrave Macmillan.

Smith, V. K. (2008) 'Reflections on the Literature', *Review of Environmental Economics and Policy*, 2(1): 130–45.

Statman, M. (1999) 'Behavioral Finance: Past Battles and Future Engagements', *Financial Analysts Journal*, 55:18–27.

Strengers, Y. (2011) 'Beyond Demand Management: Co-Managing Energy and Water Practices with Australian Households', *Policy Studies*, 32(1): 35–58.

Thaler, R. (1999) 'The End of Behavioral Finance', *Financial Analysts Journal*, 55: 12–17.

Venkatachalam, L. (2007) 'Environmental Economics and Ecological Economics: Where They Can Converge?' *Ecological Economics*, 61(2–3): 550–8.

Winkler, R. C. and Winett, R. A. (1982) 'Behavioral Interventions in Resource Conservation: A Systems Approach Based on Behavioral Economics', *American Psychologist*, 37(4): 421–35.

WISE (2007) WISE—The Water Information System for Europe, available at: <http://water.europa.eu/>.

Worthington, A. and Hoffman, M. (2008) 'An Empirical Survey of Residential Water Demand Modelling', *Journal of Economic Surveys*, 22(5): 842–71.

Zarri, L. (2010) 'Behavioral Economics Has Two "Souls": Do They Both Depart From economic rationality?' *Journal of Socio-Economics*, 39(5): 562–7.

10

The Politics of Nudge

Dilemmas in Implementing Policies for Sustainable Consumption

Gerry Stoker[1]

10.1 Introduction

A new policy paradigm has emerged in the early years of the twenty-first century that offers a different way forward towards the challenge of changing consumer and citizen behaviour. It goes under the general heading of 'nudge' and is sometimes presented as a new science of behavioural change. The approach has been popularized in a book titled *Nudge* by Richard Thaler and Cass Sunstein (2008) (see also <http://nudges.org/>) which has been highly influential in the Anglo-Saxon world. Drawing on research from psychology, cognitive science, and behavioural economics there has been a paradigm shift in policy debates away from the straightforward use of regulation or persuasion to change consumer behaviour and towards the adoption of 'nudge' strategies that build on the essential insight that people are influenced by cognitive and social factors in their decision-making. Nudges often involve changing people's choices by bringing issues to their attention or through explaining what others are doing. By shifting the choice architecture in which people make decisions it might be possible to get them to make better decisions for themselves and more generally for society.

Nudge offers a potentially new way forward in a difficult terrain because stepping into the arena of sustainable consumption for policy-makers means

[1] This chapter draws on research work completed with colleagues from the following universities: Manchester, Southampton, UCL, and Exeter.

entering a world of wicked problems: in the sense that the challenges are complex and the solutions either not known or difficult to achieve. There are a complex mix of factors influencing consumer behaviour, uncertainties about the effectiveness of interventions, and queasiness in liberal democracies around interfering in citizens' 'lifestyle choices'. Yet policy-makers appear to have no alternative but to carry on down the path, as to do nothing about sustainable consumption appears to be impossible. As Jackson comments, the issue of consumption needs to be addressed given that 'the realisation that people's choices, behaviours and lifestyles will play a vital role in achieving sustainable development is one of the (relatively few) points of agreement to have emerged from international environmental policy debates over the last decade or so' (2005, p. 3). However, how does government influence the behaviour of citizens in order to either limit consumption or change its form? Regulations and financial incentives can play their part but this chapter explores whether the emerging idea of nudge policies provides a different and viable way of approaching the challenge.

The United Kingdom's Institute for Government, in an enthusiastic report about these nudge insights comments:

> For policy-makers facing policy challenges such as crime, obesity, or environmental sustainability, behavioural approaches offer a potentially powerful new set of tools. Applying these tools can lead to low cost, low pain ways of 'nudging' citizens—or ourselves—into new ways of acting by going with the grain of how we think and act. This is an important idea at any time, but is especially relevant in a period of fiscal constraint. (Dolan et al., 2010, p. 7)

The power of the nudge argument is that it provides the platform for policy-makers to free themselves from past policies and achieve behaviour change among citizens and consumers, drawing on accumulated insights from academic research, but in a way that is cognizant of the context of austerity in terms of public spending and concerns of politicians not to be seen as dictating individual choice but rather shaping it. Nudge policy might be 'smart' in two senses: low cost and sensitive to the need to avoid charges of government acting like 'Big Brother'. Is it going to provide a key tool for promoting sustainable consumption?

A policy paradigm can fail for many reasons. One possibility is that the evidence base for the policy is not strong enough: the casual connections that are claimed may not be robustly established and missing factors could be overlooked, with both in turn explaining policy failure. In this brief introductory section to the chapter I note that there may well be some weaknesses to the evidence base for nudge and the conceptual framing offered alongside it, but that those issues could be overcome by properly trialling any interventions. Indeed there is considerable evidence that such an experimental and rigorous approach is to the fore at least in applications from the UK government. The evidence base for nudge is not perfect but it is good enough.

The theme of this chapter is not the lack of an evidence base but how the process of translation of even strongly evidence-based understandings about human behaviour has to run the gauntlet of the politics of implementation. Several challenges of implementation can be identified. If nudge is presented—largely for ideological reasons—as a stand-alone policy it may be less effective than when it is developed as a complement to, rather than a replacement for, standard forms of regulation, overt persuasion, and fiscal incentive. The advocates of nudge have not convinced opponents that there are not normative blocks to what can be presented as governing by stealth, and these normative stumbling blocks can undermine the legitimacy of nudge interventions. Top-down nudge strategies are widely favoured but have their limitations around the trust and persuasive capacity that citizens are prepared to grant to government. Bottom-up nudge strategies offer another option but may be only available in localized settings and not such comfortable terrain for government officials to work in. Inevitably any new policy paradigm faces resistance from bureaucratic forces that were established prior to its arrival and bureaucratic politics can undermine effective implementation. The politics of nudge is sufficiently daunting to ensure that nudge is unlikely to provide a magic elixir to the challenges of developing policies to support sustainable consumption. Yet there remains hope of more effective policy implementation if the politics of nudge is better understood.

10.2 The Behavioural Revolution: The Emergence of the Nudge Paradigm

Several decades of social science research confirms that humans are less than perfect rational decision-makers. Below we highlight just a few of the key findings into the way that human beings make decisions influenced by their cognitive imitations and social factors. The robustness of these findings, I argue, provides a viable base on which to build public policy, yet it can be conceded that we are only in the foothills of understanding in this area.

Prospect theory (Kahneman and Tversky, 1979) alerts us to the 'endowment effect' which suggests that, when we are already in possession of something, we are very reluctant to lose it. Cognitively it is more important for us to hold onto what we have (i.e. prevent loss) than to gain something extra. Another facet of our cognitive architecture which displays our less than fully rational behaviour is our use of psychological discounting (Frederick et al., 2002). We place more weight on the short-term than on the long-term effects of our decisions. A closely related phenomenon is our propensity for maintaining the status quo (Samuelson and Zeckhauser, 1988). Limited by time, intellectual energy, and resources, the majority of us, most of the time, prefer not to change our habits unless we really have to. In short we have a default position and we are often reluctant to move away from it. Using these insights might lead to thinking about new forms of policy intervention such as resetting the default to be something that is individually and socially desirable, for example, by obliging all employers to give employees five days a year free to engage in voluntary service to the community.

A further aspect of our behaviour, recognized by social psychologists is the issue of cognitive consistency. Following Festinger (1957) psychologists suggest that people seek consistency between their beliefs and their behaviour. However, when beliefs and behaviour clash (the phenomenon of cognitive dissonance), we frequently alter our beliefs instead of adjusting our behaviour. One way out of this difficulty is to extract commitments from people (Dawnay and Shah, 2005). Research indicates that when people make such a commitment they feel more motivated to adjust their behaviour to back up their expressed beliefs, particularly where commitments are made in public. Evidence in the field of environmental behaviour suggests that extracting public promises can help to improve water efficiency as compared to simple information provision (McKenzie-Mohr, 2000). Similar findings are reported in the area of voting behaviour, with those asked beforehand to predict their likelihood of voting more likely to vote than those not asked (Greenwald et al., 1987), and in blood donation decisions where exposing people to an 'active decision choice' (i.e. actively putting the choice before them) increases blood donation rates in people who display uncertainty on the subject (Stutzer et al., 2006).

Social pressure more generally appears to make a big difference to our decision-making (see Halpern et al., 2004 for a review). For instance, our perception of how others see us, particularly our peers, matters to us. In the context of promoting energy efficiency within offices, there is evidence that the technique of 'information disclosure' between firms creates a 'race to the top' amongst firms keen to display their green credentials (Thaler and Sunstein, 2008). Similarly, the concept of social proof suggests that when confronted with an ambiguous situation, we look to other people for cues on how to behave (Cialdini, 2007). Additionally, we will be most influenced by people with whom we identify, those we trust, and those who are seen as credible (Druckman, 2001). Peer support and community mentoring schemes which exploit these inter-personal influences, for instance programmes to increase breast feeding delivered by mothers (Bovaird, 2007), or bullying prevention schemes in schools where mentoring is provided by children who have suffered bullying (Cross et al., 2009).

These examples have only skimmed the surface of insights from social psychology and behavioural economics that could be applied. But this is sufficient to establish the potential rich hunting ground for translating evidence-based social science insights into policy interventions. This theme is helpfully developed in Thaler and Sunstein's *Nudge* (2008), which offers not only multiple examples of potential interventions but also a framework for thinking about the construction of policy.

Thaler and Sunstein (2008, p. 5–6) define nudge strategies in broad terms as focused on 'any aspect of the choice architecture that alters people's behaviour in a predictable way without forbidding any options or significantly changing their economic incentives' and go on to suggest that policy-makers can try 'to influence choices in a way that will make the chooser better off *as judged by themselves*'. The authors identify five further broad ways of changing social behaviour and pushing it in a positive direction. First, an understanding of choice architecture should lead policy-makers to understand that citizens often have a default option that they revert to in the absence of other strong signals. So a good nudge is one that leads people towards a positive choice by, for example, enrolling them on a pension scheme automatically unless they actively opt out. Second, policy-makers should expect error and design systems so that citizens learn immediately and effectively about mistakes that they will inevitably make. Third, it is important to give feedback in a timely and effectively way so that people understand the implications of their actions. For example, houses could be fitted with a light and sound indicator when a lot of energy is being used in order to get householders to consider taking measures to save energy. Fourth, policy-makers could support citizens by paying more attention to the way they construct mind maps when making decisions and encourage the adoption of mind maps that facilitate better decisions. Finally, given the problems that people have in making complex decisions, policy-makers could provide opportunities for collective filtering so that people can learn from others about what works or what choices might suit them as a person, given the tendency we all have to follow those we regard as like-minded people.

Nudge offers a framework for changing the 'choice architecture' of citizens in order to achieve alterations in their behaviour which constitute improvements for them and for society as a whole. Nudges are about framing our choices as individuals. We live in a complex world with competing signals about what is the best thing to do from both a practical and an ethical perspective. We use social cues to help us decide what to do: what are other citizens doing and should I follow? Can I work out the beneficial impact of a shift in behaviour quickly and easily? How much effort will it take to change my behaviour? Nudging, its advocates suggest, helps to reduce this complexity by simplifying choices, reducing the transaction costs of making decisions, and guiding people towards certain options.

Through Thaler and Sunstein's intervention these ideas are finding an increasingly strong grip on policy thinking and practice. Nor are Thaler and Sunstein alone in pushing this line of argument. There are a number of other books and pamphlets that offer policy lessons drawing on insights from behavioural economics and cognitive psychology and a number of corresponding programmes of policy activity are underway at the local and national level both in the United Kingdom and elsewhere (Halpern et al., 2004; Cialdini, 2007; Knott et al., 2007; Dolan et al., 2010). Thaler and Sunstein's *nudge* (2008), however, deserves particular credit because it has done much to bring out the possibilities of tackling issues of behaviour change in new ways.

The United Kingdom Government has taken up these insights with the Cameron-led coalition establishing in 2010 the Cabinet Office's Behavioural Insight Team, which is advised by Richard Thaler. Other behavioural change options have heavily featured in, for example, the United Kingdom Government's *Public Health White Paper* (Department of Health, 2010) and the *Giving Green Paper* (HM Government, 2010b). Local authorities and other public bodies in the United Kingdom have also pioneered the use of these techniques (Dolan et al., 2010). The Behavioural Insights Team (BIT) boasts several successes (for further information see the BIT web site <http://www.cabinetoffice.gov.uk/behavioural-insights-team>). It has introduced a compulsory choice for vehicle licence applicants of whether to join the organ donation scheme, in effect bringing a choice which many citizens claim they are happy to make to the forefront of their attention and requiring action from them. It is estimated that this may bring an extra million donors to the NHS register of donors in a four or five year time period. The BIT has worked with HM Revenue and Customs to produce letters that claim that most people in their local area had already paid their taxes—playing on the idea that people look to follow social norms—and have boosted repayment rates by around 15 percentage points. More generally BIT has shown how changes to wording can have an effect on combating fraud, collecting debt, and tax collection. Work has also been produced, although it appears less developed in impact, on improving the prospect of consumers making energy efficiency savings and on how providing information to consumers on their purchasing profiles and improving feedback on products and services might lead them to make different and better consumer choices.

10.3 Doubts about the Evidence Base for Nudge

As a policy paradigm nudge has a sound base because researchers, often in carefully controlled laboratory randomized control trials, have, in the last few decades, produced compelling evidence that people are less than perfect decision-makers and are driven by cognitive short-cuts as well as social norms and pressures. The nudge paradigm developed by Thaler and Sunstein helps in turning those disparate studies into a coherent framework for policy development. Moreover, there appears to be some evidence of effective policy interventions emerging. No wonder that nudge has been embraced by policy-makers: it is at first sight an approach that offers new ways forward to meet difficult challenges.

Doubts can be raised about whether nudge captures fully the complexities of behaviour change. There is general agreement that 'some actions are consciously planned, or deliberative, while others are governed by automatic, or non-deliberative, processes' (House of Lords, 2011, p. 16) and perhaps nudge focuses too much on the latter without fully understanding the interaction effects with the former. Maybe for substantial moves towards sustainable consumption there is more need for what Daniel Kahneman (2011) calls 'slow' decision making, rather than fast decision making. Cognitive scientists refer to Type 1 processes as fast and not requiring conscious thought, with Type 2 processes seen as slower and more careful; requiring time and effort to be put into evidence collecting, reflection, and deliberation. Both forms of thinking have their place but perhaps to get to long-term sustainable consumption we need space for consumers and citizens to think, not just be nudged (John et al., 2009, 2011).

There are other gaps and issues that would need to be taken into account in a complete approach to behaviour change. A House of Lords report (2011, p. 17) summarizes some of the core areas of uncertainty, suggesting that there is a lack of understanding 'in relation to how emotional processes regulate everyday behaviour; a lack of comparative research into the limits to the transferability of behaviour change interventions across cultural differences; uncertainty about how genes interact with environmental and social factors to cause behaviour; and, a lack of understanding about the effect of social dynamics on behaviour'. More generally, our actions are influenced by wider contextual factors, so even if there was a successful nudge to get people to ride bicycles to work this would not work so well if there were no bicycle lanes or the cost of a bicycle was prohibitive.

Though gaps in understanding exist; there is enough evidence to argue that nudge thinking is on to something. Yet a more general problem is that doubts remain about whether specific studies revealing specific behaviour traits (no matter how robustly they have been undertaken) can be translated into effective policy level interventions at a population level. As the House of Lords Report (2011, pp. 18–19) concludes: 'There is a lack of applied research at a population level to support specific interventions to change the behaviour of large groups of people (including a lack of evidence on cost-effectiveness and long-term impact). This is a barrier to the formulation of evidence-based policy'.

Results that come from the laboratory and that are supported by many iterations of a study may still not prove to be effective in the field. But in response to the challenge of developing applied policy measures the obvious thing to do is to go into the field and try out interventions and evaluate them rigorously. That is exactly what the Government in the United Kingdom in particular have done, led by the work from the BIT and using an explicit commitment to trialling interventions under the rubric of test, learn, and adapt experimental methods (Haynes et al., 2012). Being certain in the social sciences about the casual factors underlying complex phenomenon is perhaps asking too much, but nudge policy can claim a stronger evidence base than many policy initiatives and its exponents have developed an explicit trial dimension to their development of interventions. The seeds of implementation problems for nudge rest not so much in a lack of connection between evidence and policy as with a complex of policy implementation issues.

10.4 Implementation Problem One: To Nudge Alone or First?

There is a tendency on the part of the advocates of nudge and its adopters to present it as a smart solution to old-fashioned bureaucratic government. Thaler and Sunstein (2008, p. 15) state: 'if incentives and nudges replace requirements and bans, government will be both smaller and more modest. So, to be clear: we are not for bigger government, just for better governance'.

> Political advocates of nudge have emerged especially from the right of the political spectrum. Nudgers challenge the dominance of 'hard' tools of intervention that rely on command and control or financial incentives and argue for a range of 'softer' tool options. The UK's Conservative–Liberal Democrat Government frames nudge in the following terms: 'there has been the assumption that central government can only change people's behaviour through rules and regulations. Our government will be a much smarter one, shunning the bureaucratic levers of the past and finding intelligent ways to encourage, support and enable people to make better choices for themselves. (HM Government, 2010a, pp. 7–8)

Nudge then is presented as a non-coercive and smarter way forward.

But, as most researchers suggest, recognizing the importance of nudge mechanisms does not require a blind eye being turned to other influencing factors. Indeed many would argue that behaviour change would appear to demand a willingness to carry on using old 'bureaucratic' levers. Combining interventions to support behaviour change strategies would appear to be the best way forward and these interventions might include but go beyond the nudge spectrum. Successful design for behaviour change would need to address challenges in three conditions: capability, opportunity, and motivation (Michie et al., 2011). Capability is about the ability of an individual to engage in the activity that is the focus on attention and is likely to be driven by access to appropriate knowledge and skills. Opportunity captures, as noted section 10.3, how context can make a difference, such as the availability of cycle path for bicyclists. Motivation is the terrain of nudge in that it is about how individuals decide, although as noted in the discussion already there may be more scope for analytical or even deliberative thinking than nudge allows. The key constraints in promoting sustainable consumption may rest in the lack of capacity or opportunity for change among consumers. Consumers may lack the time and skills to shift their consumption patterns. The price of more sustainable consumption (e.g. as in organic foods) may limit the opportunities of some to adopt such a change. Nudge in that sense it not always going to be enough on its own.

Even if nudge strategies can be successfully devised there is no reason to abandon more 'conventional' tools of government intervention (see Hood, 1983) such as those based on authority/regulation and financial incentives. Moreover, regulations can themselves be used to underpin nudge-style choice architecture, such as a requirement to publish nutritional information on food products or for energy companies to publish information about average usage, thus facilitating behaviour change. The House of Lords report concludes:

> [T]he most effective means of changing behaviour at a population level is to use a range of policy tools, both regulatory and non-regulatory. Given that many factors may influence behaviour, this conclusion is perhaps unsurprising... We are concerned, however, that emphasising non-regulatory interventions will lead to policy decisions where the evidence for the effectiveness of other interventions in changing behaviour has not been considered. (2011, pp. 35–6)

In its response to this criticism the United Kingdom Government appears to be willing to offer a more nuanced position than in the original Coalition statement. It now argues:

> there are few circumstances in which the Government would argue that nudging *alone* is likely to be sufficient... It is not a question, therefore, of the use of regulation being ruled out altogether, rather that regulation is only used when satisfactory outcomes cannot be achieved by alternative approaches, or where alternative approaches would involve much higher costs. (Cabinet Office, 2012, p. 8)

In short there remains an ideological preference for nudge which is only to be trumped if (consistent with that ideological preference) the costs of nudging are considerably greater than using old-style bureaucratic regulation.

The evidence base argues for using the nudge spectrum of ideas, indeed it could be suggested that the evidence backs the view of nudge advocates that these insights have been over looked for too long. Yet political tension emerges not over the outright rejection of other forms of intervention but rather over the ideological preference for soft forms of intervention. The politics of behaviour change is less about disagreements over ends and more about implementation tactics. To opt for nudge first, or nudge alone, requires not only evidence that it works but also a value judgement that prioritizes a vision of the world in which free individuals choose their own lifestyle. Capabilities and opportunities are downgraded as part of the understanding. Nudge rests on a negative theory of freedom (you are free if you can choose) and downplays a more positive understanding (to be free you need skills and the right context) (Goodwin, 2012). Some may be happy with that emphasis but others may not. A barrier to the implementation of nudge policy as conceived is its association with certain value choices.

10.5 Implementation Problem Two: Normative Challenges to Nudge's Legitimacy

Nudge may be a soft form of government intervention but it is still a form of intervention. The problem is that all forms of intervention by government have a Janus-like quality when it comes to normative judgement. Bureaucratic forms of regulation and oversight can be criticized as inflexible and suffocating but they can be promoted as treating all equally, according to known and visible rules. Nudge strategies may be smarter and more fluid in style than bureaucratic regulation but they can appear to be more difficult to justify, and indeed, controversial. Forms of intervention that seek to trade on individuals' cognitive foibles, social practices, and moral convictions are, if anything, more open to challenge in comparison to standard forms of intervention based on regulation and incentives because they are relatively less open and explicit about their intentions. Even relatively favourable media coverage of nudge strategies prefaces itself with claims about 'lifting the lid on the secret Whitehall policy unit dreaming up psychological tricks to alter our behaviour' (Hickman, 2011). Others less supportive of nudge go for a more full-frontal attack. Dean (2010) describes it as 'a knowingly undemocratic way of doing business' while Perks (2008) comments that nudging is 'an underhand way of imposing solutions upon us, the very antithesis of choice'.

The perceived paternalistic or manipulative aspects of nudge create problems of implementation. These concerns go to the heart of nudge techniques as Goodwin (2012, p. 89) explains: 'by exploiting the imperfections in human judgement and decision-making, the choice architect is aiming to substitute his or her judgement of what should be done for the "nudgee's" own judgement. And this threatens an individual's control over his or her ability to choose'. Nudge may not be coercive because it still leaves room for much individual choice, but it does appear to be intrinsically manipulative. Of course, many citizens do not understand the details of tax laws or other regulations applied to them so in that sense they could be considered underhand as well, but nudge seems particularly open to this line of attack.

Nudge does open itself up to these criticisms partly because, as Anderson (2009) points out, Thaler and Sunstein (2008) demonstrate little concern with autonomy, either self-guidance or self-governance. Morally in some circumstances it may matter that we know why we are choosing (perhaps say over whether to join an organ donation register) and in others it is important that we endorse the constraints—soft nudges or hard regulations—imposed on our actions. One line of defence promoted by Thaler and Sunstein (2008) under the label of 'libertarian paternalism' is that at least choice does remain with the citizen, it is just the *architecture* of choice that is designed by democratically elected governments, to support what are judged by political representatives to be beneficial outcomes. We are free to dismiss the options offered to us and indeed to dismiss the government offering those options. A further suggestion, advanced by Thaler and Sunstein (2008) themselves, is for governments to publish all their nudges in order to increase transparency and thus to permit public challenge. Yet it remains the case that some choices need to be more consciously made and electoral sanction is a blunt instrument to check the behaviour of a government using expert judgement and managerial logic to influence the behaviour of citizens. These philosophical quibbles matter because they raise issues about values choices but also because they challenge the legitimacy of nudge.

10.6 Implementation Problem Three: Top-Down Approaches Can Fall at the Trust Hurdle

Nudge can be implemented in a top-down approach, in which citizens' decisions are influenced by a policy format that takes citizens as they are, but supports them towards certain decisions steered by expert nudgers. The top-down approach fits comfortably with much of the underlying thinking behind nudge. Public managers and expert psychologists dream up neat little nudges to try out on an unsuspecting public. The BIT in the United Kingdom exudes this sense of a team of top 'boffins' thinking up smart ways—using insights from cognitive science and behavioural economics—to shift social behaviour. In the world of nudge it is often government that takes on the role of framing citizens' choices.

However, there are clear constraints on the framing ability of governments or other elite actors. Research indicates that frames are only influential insofar as the people generating the frames are perceived as being trustworthy and credible by those they are attempting to influence (Druckman, 2001). Government agencies undoubtedly have the capacity to frame or nudge but they may not be trusted by citizens as credible sources of information or advice, and this constrains the capacity of interventions at this point to reach more challenging elements of citizen behaviour. There is a caveat here in that citizens are not always aware of the source of the framing; in many cases the source of information is not explicit and in other cases citizens may simply not notice where the information is coming from. In these cases trust in the source of the information does not play such a great role in the decision process. Nevertheless, regardless of whether the source of the information is explicit or not, it cannot be assumed that the trust needed to engage in effective framing will always be present.

There is evidence to suggest that nudges work best when citizens know that something is the right thing to do and just need to have that choice brought to the forefront of their mind (John et al., 2011). The key to a successful nudge is applying it to situations where people have already made up their minds and are willing to perform the action in question. This may limit the range of actions that nudges are capable of fostering, leaving out, for instance, issues which are more controversial or require more sustained consideration. Top-down approaches may sit more comfortably with government practice and may indeed be effective but only within limits. Bottom-up approaches demand a greater culture change from government but may enable the tackling of a wider range of issues than top-down approaches. Yet there are also limits to what bottom-up approaches can do.

10.7 Implementation Problem Four: Bottom-Up Approaches are Challenging to Deliver

Nudges could be developed in a more bottom-up way by fostering power to citizens to create their own social norms and expectations to steer behaviour. But the development of norms is difficult for policy-makers to influence because norms develop in an incremental and evolutionary way through a process of repeated interaction between groups. It would seem that the key is for government to cede power to citizens if the forces of norm-creation are to come to fruition. Groups themselves can find ways of overcoming 'tragedy of the commons' type scenarios (Hardin, 1968) in order to attain collective goals. As the late Nobel prize winning Ostrom notes: 'field research . . . shows that individuals systematically engage in collective action to provide local public goods or manage common-pool resources without an external authority to offer inducements or impose sanctions' (1998, p. 2). With repeated interactions, particularly face-to-face interactions, group members learn conditional co-operation and reciprocity, and develop norms of cooperation through the use of group sanctions and rewards, either material or reputational.

Government policy needs to work on the development of an institutional apparatus which will permit citizens to cooperate. In practice, this means building opportunities for face-to-face interaction, the development of trust, and the performance of reciprocal acts. It also implies that when governments are thinking about effecting behaviour change, citizens should play a role in defining what the appropriate behaviours, or norms, should be. And when citizens generate ideas about solving problems in their communities, government and local representatives should be responsive, allowing space in the political decision-making process for these ideas to be considered.

We have some evidence that bottom-up strategies can work. Our research team from the universities of Manchester and Southampton (John et al., 2011) tested the application of several nudges in a series of field trials aiming to promote civic behaviour. Our general finding was that nudges do have a modest impact in encouraging more pro-social and civic-minded behaviour. Nudges work precisely *because* government is not so directly involved. People trust a message when it is from a reliable third party source rather than from government itself. One of the ironies of our findings is that policy-makers can learn from our work that nudges are effective but also that they may find it hard to nudge by themselves. Public officials may find it advantageous to work with other partners in delivering nudge interventions at a local level. Such local experiments can complement a nationally rolled out programme. They show how innovations can work best when government is at one step removed from the general public and is not nudging them individually. The nudger needs to be believed, and this is a constraint in an era of large-scale distrust of government and government officials.

As Scott (1998) comments, the failings of grand social engineering projects are in part a reflection of the high-handed, uniform, centralizing, and codifying form of thinking that can dominate government approaches and a lack of respect for the local knowledge, craft understanding, and diversity of the practices and perspectives of citizens. A capacity to see like a citizen rather than seeing like a state is a considerable challenge for the effective development of new tools of intervention, but it is a critical component of being able to understand what is likely to motivate citizens to shift their behaviour. The issue then is not so much for policy-makers to see citizens as 'humans' rather than 'econs' but rather to see the world through the eyes of citizens.

10.8 Implementation Problem Five: Nudge Can be Limited by Bureaucratic Politics

Any new policy has to run the gauntlet of bureaucratic politics. It has to be sponsored by one agency or department and may in turn run the risk of being opposed by other agencies for no other reason than the source of its sponsorship; when that source is perceived to be a threat to the power, resources, or more generally the empire of other parts of the government machine. The Bureaucratic Politics model (Allison and Halperin, 1972) is an established framework for thinking about politics that rests on a set of related propositions. First the government is not unified but instead divided into a number of competing actors. These actors pursue their interests but also frame those interests in a reflexive way responding to the initiatives and demands of others: priorities are shaped by positions taken by other actors as well as those of home agency. Problems are multiple and ill-defined and responses to problems are often far from clear. Doing something requires a major effort and governance is more likely to focus on the management of a number of piecemeal choices rather than big strategic decisions. In this humdrum, everyday world of policy-making getting the government machine to do what is decided is the more challenging task than selecting the preferred solution.

Nudge is a relatively new policy kid on the block. Its sponsorship in the case of the UK Government rests on a small cadre of policy advisors, led by David Halpern, brought into the Cabinet Office, with direct support from Minister of State at the Cabinet Office Oliver Letwin, and it appears some backing from both the Prime Minister David Cameron and Chancellor of the Exchequer George Osborne. But other departments have not always welcomed the new unit's work or style. Tensions exist with the Department for Environment Farming, and Rural Affairs (DEFRA), which is resistant to having its own behaviour change programmes bent to the new demands of nudge, and other departments have been relatively disengaged from the process. Researchers exploring the implementation of nudge in Whitehall concluded: 'the overall attention to behaviour change policies at the moment tends to be patchy and dependent on departmental initiatives and ministerial interest' (John and Richardson, 2012, p. 20).

None of the difficulties created by bureaucratic politics are unique to nudge but recognizing their presence means identifying another classic implementation block on the introduction of a new policy, no matter how well evidenced or skilfully unfolded its advocates claim it is. Nudge does not enter a policy world that is empty. There are competing ideas and priorities and unless nudge is able to build a powerful enough base in the world of bureaucratic politics it will fail even if the evidence base for a nudge outlook on issues of behaviour change is strong.

10.9 Conclusions

The nudge-inspired debate has brought home the importance of recognizing that public policy interventions cannot be designed as if citizens were perfect rational decision-makers. The cauldron of new ideas and types of political intervention are particularly pertinent given a focus on changing consumers' lifestyle choices, both directly and indirectly to create the conditions for sustainability. But equally it is clear that we still have much to learn in order to turn psychological and social insights into viable policy interventions, and that we are only beginning to understand the politics and practices that would support the legitimization and effectiveness of those interventions.

Nudge draws on research driven ideas which are well founded and is being developed in a way that supports the idea of trialling initiatives to test what works. But it still faces a number of hurdles that regularly confront new policy developments and being aware of those hurdles could aid more effective implementation. In this chapter five hurdles are identified. In this conclusion I will briefly reflect on how to respond to each of the hurdles.

Nudge runs into an ideological trap by allowing itself to be framed as an approach that avoids the heavy hand of government intervention. Tackling the first hurdle is politically difficult but it is clear from the argument of this chapter that nudge would benefit from being freed from the neo-liberal framing as *the* preferred alternative to standard forms of governmental intervention. It would appear that nudge is more likely to be effective if it is seen as a partner to, rather than a replacement for, traditional mechanisms of regulation, persuasion and direct incentive provision. Nudge advocates also need to address normative doubts about the manipulative nature of its interventions by presenting a clearer and stronger framework for judging, prior to policy implementation, the ethical and value issues thrown up by particular intervention. Nudge advocates need to find a range of partners for the delivery of interventions that lessen the threat to legitimacy created by top down approaches. Similarly, steps could be taken to encourage and spread bottom-up approaches. The balance of implementation needs to be shifted away from schemes dreamed up by a 'nudging elite' towards the development of a set of tools and best practice guide that a range of governmental and non-governmental actors can use to address issues that matter to them. Finally the range of supporters and backers for the use of nudge insights needs to be extended to ward off the limitations of bureaucratic politics. A development of nudge that generalized its use through providing tools and practice guides would underwrite such a development. Nudge insights are powerful but if their benefit is to be best felt the message is that the politics of implementation matters as much as the rigour of the evidence base. Nudge advocates are more focused on the latter, for which they are to be congratulated, but they need to give more credence to the concerns raised by the former.

References

Allison, G. and Halperin, M. (1972) 'Bureaucratic politics: a paradigm and some policy implications', *World Politics*, 24: 40–79.

Anderson, J. (2009) 'Social norms as scaffolding for the will: Procrastination, distributed volition, nudges, and the politics of human irrationality', Workshop on 'Empires of Norms and Laws', Joint Sessions of the European Consortium on Political Research, Lisbon, 14–19 April 2009.

Bovaird, T. (2007) 'Beyond engagement and participation: User and community co-production of public services', *Public Administration Review*, Sept/Oct: 846–60.

Cabinet Office (2011) *Behavioural Insights Team Annual Update 2010–11*, available at: <https://www.gov.uk/government/uploads/system/uploads/attachment_data/file/60537/Behaviour-Change-Insight-Team-Annual-Update_acc.pdf>.

Cabinet Office (2012) *Government Response to the Science and Technology Select Committee Report on Behaviour Change*, available at: <http://www.cabinetoffice.gov.uk/sites/default/files/resources/Government-Response-House-of-Lords-Inquiry-Behaviour-Change.pdf>.

Cialdini, R. B. (2007) *Influence: The Psychology of Persuasion*, New York: Collins Business.

Cross, E. J., Richardson, B., Douglas T., and Vonkaenel-Flatt, J. (2009) *Virtual Violence: Protecting Children from Cyberbullying*, London: Beatbullying.

Dawnay, E. and Shah, H. (2005) *Behavioural Economics: Seven Principles for Policy Makers*, London: New Economics Foundation.

Dean, S. (2010) 'Alcohol pricing is not the "answer": the hypocrisy behind new drinking laws'. London: Institute of Ideas.

Department of Health (2010) *'Healthy Lives, Healthy People' Whitepaper: Our Strategy for Public Health in England*, London: HM Government.

Dolan, P., Hallsworth M., Halpern, D., King, D., and Vlaev, I. (2010) *MINDSPACE: Influencing Behaviour through Public Policy*. London: Cabinet Office/Institute for Government.

Druckman, J. N. (2001) 'On the limits of framing effects: Who can frame?', *The Journal of Politics*, 63(4): 1041–66.

Festinger, L. (1957) *A Theory of Cognitive Dissonance*, Stanford: University of California Press.

Frederick, S., Lowenstein G.. and O'Donoghue, T. (2002) 'Time discounting and time preference: A critical review', *Journal of Economic Literature*, 40(2): 351–401.

Goodwin, T. (2012) 'Why we should reject "nudge"', *Politics*, 32(2): 85–92.

Greenwald, A., Carnot, C., Beach, R., and Young, B. (1987) 'Increasing voting behavior by asking people if they expect to vote', *Journal of Applied Psychology*, 72: 315–18.

Halpein, D., Bates, C., Mulgan, G., Aldridge, S., Beales, G., and Heathfield, A. (2004) *Personal Responsibility and Changing Behaviour: The State of its Knowledge and its Implications for Public Policy*, London: Prime Minister's Strategy Unit, Cabinet Office.

Hardin, G. (1968) 'The tragedy of the Commons', *Science*, 162: 1243–8.

Haynes, L., Service, O., Goldacre, B., and Torgerson, D. (2012) *Test, Learn, Adapt: Developing Public Policy with Randomised Controlled Trials*, London: Cabinet Office.

Hickman, M. (2011) 'Nudge nudge wink wink: How the government wants to change the way we think', *The Independent*, 3 January 2011.

HM Government (2010a) *The Coalition: Our Programme for Government*, London: The Cabinet Office.

HM Government (2010b) *Giving Green Paper*, London: The Cabinet Office.

Hood, C. C. (1983) *The Tools of Government*, London and Basingstoke: Macmillan Press.

House of Lords (2011) *Behaviour Change. Second Report of Session 2010–12 of the Science and Technology Committee*, London: House of Lords.

Jackson, T. (2005) *Motivating Sustainable Consumption*, London: Sustainable Development Research Network, Policy Studies Institute.

John, P., Cotterill, S., Moseley, A., Richardson, L., Smith, G., Stoker, G., and Wales, C. (2011) *Nudge, nudge, think think: Experimenting with Ways to Change Civic Behavior*, London: Bloomsbury Academic.

John, P. with Richardson, L. (2012) *Nudging Citizens Towards Localism?*, London: British Academy.

John, P., Smith, G., and Stoker, G. (2009). 'Nudge, nudge, think think: Two strategies for changing civic behaviour', *The Political Quarterly*, 2009, 80(3): 361–9.

Kahneman, D. (2011) *Thinking, Fast and Slow*, London: Penguin.

Kahneman, D. and Tversky, A. (1979) 'Prospect theory: An analysis of decisions under risk', *Econometrica*, 47: 313–27.

Knott, D., Muers, S., and Aldridge, S. (2007) *Achieving Culture Change: A Policy Framework*, London: Prime Minister's Policy Unit.

McKenzie-Mohr, D. (2000) 'Promoting sustainable behaviour: An introduction to community-based social marketing', *Journal of Social Issues*, 56(3): 543–54.

Michie, S., van Stralen, M., and West, R. (2011) 'The behaviour change wheel: A new method for characterising and designing behaviour change interventions', *Implementation Science*, 6: 42.

Ostrom, E. (1998) 'A behavioural approach to the rational choice theory of collective action', *American Political Science Review*, 92(1): 1–22.

Perks, M. (2008) '"Nudging": the very antithesis of choice' *Spiked Review of Books*, Issue 19: 29 December 2008.

Samuelson, W. and Zeckhauser, R. (1988) 'Status quo bias in decision making', *Journal of Risk and Uncertainty*, 1(1): 7–59.

Scott, J. C. (1998) *Seeing Like a State*, New Haven: Yale University Press.

Stutzer, A., Goette, L., and Zehnder, M. (2006) 'Active decisions and pro-social behaviour: A field experiment in blood donation', Working paper No. 279, Institute for Empirical Research in Economics, Zurich: University of Zurich.

Thaler, R. H. and Sunstein, C. R. (2008) *Nudge: Improving Decisions about Health, Wealth, and Happiness*, New Haven: Yale University Press.

Part III

Looking Beyond the Individual Consumer: Socio-Cultural Explanations of Consumption

11

Past and Present

Historical Perspectives on Inequality and Collective Provision in Modern Consumption

Frank Trentmann

11.1 Introduction

The last three decades have seen a boom in the history of consumption. This chapter begins by briefly outlining the core questions and approaches that have emerged in historical research. Interestingly, sustainability has largely been marginal or missing altogether in the historical literature on consumption. This chapter seeks to show how a historical perspective might contribute to our understanding of sustainable (and unsustainable) consumption in the world today and tomorrow. In particular, I will focus on three themes where, I believe, historical knowledge can illuminate and revise conventional thinking about the dynamics driving unsustainable lifestyles. The first concerns the role of individual choice, which has been at the heart of current debates about behaviour change. A long-term view of the rise of consumption since the sixteenth century urges us to be cautious with such individualist and economistic views and, instead, to recognize the diverse cultural, political institutional forces that have stimulated and shaped materially-intensive behaviours. Secondly, I subject to scrutiny the ever popular idea that inequality and 'conspicuous consumption' are principal causes of material excess. Comparative historical analysis suggests this is limited to particular times and places and does not offer a generalizable, historically robust model. Finally, and more speculatively, I ask what happens if we take seriously that the rise in consumption is not a phenomenon limited to private choice and markets but also connected to collective provision by firms and states. Inequality and collective provision offer intriguing future lines of inquiry where historians might profitably engage in dialogue with social scientists.

11.2 Historical Matters

The 1970s were the springtime for historical studies of consumption. Since then, thousands of books and articles have appeared on a vast number of topics, from the taste for exotic foods and novelties in the seventeenth and eighteenth centuries to consumer credit, waste, and boycotts in the twentieth (Trentmann, 2012). It would be foolish to try and crystallize this diverse literature into a single essence, but it is possible to identify two broad concerns that have driven and organized historical work: one with the birth of consumer society in the early modern period, the other with the triumph of mass consumption, especially after 1945. The first was initially dated to mid-eighteenth century England by Neil McKendrick. Since then scholars have pushed it back to Stuart England, to Renaissance Italy, and even to the middle ages (McKendrick et al., 1982; Thirsk, 1978; Jardine, 1997; Dyer, 2005). The second research strand has been mainly concerned with the breakthrough of American 'affluent society' and its export to western Europe and beyond (de Grazia, 2005; Lüdtke et al., 1996; cf. Trentmann, 2009).

There are several interesting tensions between and within these two sets of approaches. The search for the 'birth' of consumer society initially started out with an emphasis on the precocious development of commercial culture and consumer choice. Advertising, marketing, branding, taste, shopping for pleasure, and a rising number of personal possessions—developments that are often seen as defining consumer culture (Lury, 2011; Slater, 1997)—are now well documented for seventeenth and eighteenth century Holland and Britain, so much so that some scholars argue that the industrial revolution was preceded by a consumer revolution. At the same time, historians have stressed that consumption meant something qualitatively different in earlier societies. Material desire, purchase, and use, they show, were not unknown in earlier periods but they operated within the context of communal bonds, traditions, and social customs that were fundamentally different from market exchanges today. Instead of choice and individual purchase, the emphasis has shifted to alternative systems of provision through which the rising volume of consumer goods passed into the hands of ever larger segments of society: gifting, loaning, and second hand sales (Styles, 2007; Welch, 2005). In Renaissance Florence, elite families like the Castellani shopped with certain retailers and loaned to others to cement their social networks. In eighteenth-century England, plebeian consumers displayed their newly acquired fashionable neckerchiefs in the context of customary fairs. Past cultures had their own customs and it was these, as much as commerce and purchasing power, that fuelled the rise of consumption in the early modern period.

Ironically, this rehabilitation of the past from the condescension of the present had the unfortunate side-effect of making twentieth-century consumer culture look more modern, commercial, and individualist than it probably ever was. The more customary older cultures looked, the less so did their modern successors. For the nineteenth and twentieth century, historians have largely focused on commercialization, charting how the department store, the mall, the TV, and Madison Avenue introduced a new culture of consumerism. Individual consumers and choice replaced class cultures and reciprocity. The telos of many of these histories is the triumph of the consumer, although in the long run this is mostly seen as a bad thing (de Grazia, 2005; Cohen, 2003; cf. Steigerwald, 2006). Needlework, cooking, and hand-me-downs disappear from the pages which are now crowded with branded clothing, fast-food, and self-service. Historians would be surprised to learn that, even though suffering a gradual decline, handiwork is still practised by one in five Americans today (Robinson and Godbey, 2005, p. 277). As the sociologist Viviana Zelizer has stressed, it is a fallacy to treat custom and commerce, morals and money, as separate islands (Zelizer, 2005).

A second asymmetry concerns space and the relation of the local to the global. Studies of eighteenth-century consumer culture have been seminal in unravelling the multiple transfers in global interactions. In particular, they have identified Asian luxuries (porcelain and cotton) as engines of emulation and innovation for western European societies (Berg, 2004, 2005). In the Atlantic world, slavery has been the model case for following commodity chains across space, from plantation to the breakfast table, connecting producers in one part of the world to consumers in another. With the exception of some food biographers, and in contrast to geographers and anthropologists, historians studying the twentieth century have largely eschewed such approaches and have either preferred local and national studies or they have followed one-way flows, such as the export of Americanization to post-war Europe. Comparative studies are few and far between (Haupt, 2002; Chessel, 2012).

At present, then, we have plenty of insights but also histories that are incongruent and with several blind spots and contradictions. Perhaps the biggest hole results from the centrifugal pull away from each other of the two research agendas: how do we get from the birth of consumer society in the seventeenth and eighteenth centuries to mass consumption in the twentieth? It is clearly more than a simple story of 'more, more, and more'. One attempt to connect the two has been Jan de Vries' thesis of the industrious revolution. De Vries, inspired by Gary Becker's extension of economics to the family, sees households as the decisive agents of change who arrange their labour in such a way to maximize their ultimate preferences (de Vries, 1994, 2008). In seventeenth-century Holland and eighteenth-century England, he argues, households shifted their energy from self-provisioning to wage labour in order to satisfy new consumer tastes. In the course of the nineteenth century, they split into the male breadwinner/female housekeeper model because their preferences shifted to higher standards of domestic comfort and hygiene. In the mid-twentieth century, in a second industrious revolution, households moved back to a double-earner model, albeit with fewer children.

De Vries' thesis is one of the few works which tries to take us from the early modern period to the present. It faces several problems. One is that rising purchases (effects) do not necessarily tell us about the underlying motives and causes. Urbanization and the erosion of wages and access to self-provisioning, especially from the mid-eighteenth century, might have pushed eighteenth-century labourers into the market for work, rather than them being pulled by choice and a desire to sip more sugared tea from china cups. Significantly, evidence for labourers working longer hours comes at the end of the eighteenth century *after* the volume of new objects of desire had been rising for many decades. There is, further, a problem with proportionality: is it reasonable to presume that a small shift in preferences, such as for sweetened tea, was enough to lead to a revolutionary transformation of household structures and family life? The middling classes played a much larger role in the diffusion of exotic things but they did not send their wives to work.

Evidence is equally conflicting at the other chronological end. De Vries, like Becker, presumes a trade off between unpaid work and paid work, and between home production and the purchase of consumer goods. Reality has been messier and more fascinating. A dual-earning American family, for example, cooks less than half a century ago but also spends more time with their children—in spite of finding cooking more pleasant than childcare. Home production has proved remarkably resilient in the twentieth century (Ramey, 2009). In their report on alternative ways of measuring wealth, Sen, Stiglitz, and Fitoussi estimate housework in the United States to be worth around 22 per cent of gross domestic product (GDP) in 2004—adding services performed by consumer durables would raise this number to 30 per cent; in France, for comparison, the share would be 30 per cent and 35 per cent respectively (Stiglitz et al., 2009, pp. 129). That is a lot of provisioning that is not handed over to the consumer economy. Methodologically, perhaps the most difficult feature of the 'industrious revolution' thesis is that the dynamics of change across time are left nebulous. Change takes place in sudden paradigm shifts generated by households from the inside, a kind of *deus ex machina*, or, rather, *deus ex domo*. Change follows on choice. The model echoes the current debate about behaviour change that is focused on individual choice. The family is rather bloodless, a site of production and consumption, drained of emotion and care, and lives almost outside politics and power, culture and community, ideology and passion—the stuff of history.

An alternative approach would be to focus on the changing interaction between households and the institutions, technologies, and values of the society in which they live. Urban networks, notions of comfort, and ways of living do not come about because individual consumers suddenly wish for them. It is better to view consumption as the outcome of the interplay between individual and collective forces. This would also enable us to make sense of the adoption of new technologies of consumption and comfort (including heating, bathing, and cooking) which have been and remain remarkably diverse across time, region, and classes. A detailed year-long analysis by the German energy giant RWE in 1974–5, for example, revealed that in neighbourhoods in the Ruhr 10 per cent still cooked with coal and that while 17 per cent bathed or showered once a week, another 11 per cent did so several times a day (RWE/Archive, 1975). These are significant contrasts that bear on radically different forms of sustainability and resource use, which do not fit into a more linear model of all-encompassing paradigm shifts.

The modern period, from around 1600, is characterized by a dual transformation. On the one hand, material desire, possessions, and rising standards of comfort and convenience have transformed the home, city, and politics. On the other hand, consumption was transformed by changes in housing, urbanization, and power at large. From such a dialogical view, the turn to coffee and exotic goods, cleaner homes, baths and toilets, electrified homes, and consumer durables is not so much a result of choice within the household as of a series of evolving interactions between households and their changing cultural, technical, and political environment. To view the modern expansion of consumption purely from the bottom-up, micro level of household behaviour produces a partial, distorted picture of the process by which consumption has expanded. Macro shifts have operated at a number of additional scales: the urban, national, imperial, and global. How to follow this interplay across time and place is the subject of a larger project (Trentmann, forthcoming). In the following pages, I can only illustrate the approach by turning briefly to two instances of this interplay: urban infrastructures and modern ideologies.

Alongside shopping and conspicuous consumption, the late nineteenth century witnessed a phenomenal increase in what sociologists have termed 'ordinary consumption': the use of water, gas, and, soon, electricity. Urban networks provided the material infrastructure for a new culture of comfort that relied on piped water, baths, and toilets. A micro approach understands its triumph as the result of a shift in household preferences. Encouraged by a new pre-occupation with cleanliness and hygiene, working-class families decided to have better, cleaner homes; and wives would devote themselves to keeping them clean rather than going out and earning additional income. It is doubtful whether households had a natural inclination to consume more water, for example, or a desire for constant supply. Into the 1920s and 1930s, after a century of crusades for hygiene, communities in rural England resisted the liquid march of progress and the idea that being civilized required having running water on demand. They had no problem getting by with a few litres a day and were fearful that being networked would multiply their tax bill. In London, the revolution of constant supply—with water on tap, day and night—was well under way in the 1880s, but here, similarly, it would be too simple to understand the new dynamics of consumption in terms of household agency without attention to politics, power, and norms. Urban households had been content with an intermittent supply of water to fill a cistern. The shift to constant supply was largely driven by the private monopoly water companies with the support of local government and landlords—cisterns posed a public health risk and took up valuable space. Once the new network was switched on, the old cisterns were torn out, especially in poorer neighbourhoods in the city's East End.

In the mid-1890s London and other regions were hit by several years of drought. The water companies responded by suspending constant supply and switching back to supplying water for a few hours a day (Taylor and Trentmann, 2011; Taylor et al., 2009). What is interesting to the historian is the public response. The droughts galvanized a wide network of agitation that stretched from ordinary working-class women to socialists and radicals urging a municipal take-over. Within a single generation, the network of constant supply had changed expectations of the 'normal' standard of consumption. Not having constant, running water had become unthinkable for late Victorian Londoners. The diffusion of constant supply and baths, in turn, exercised new pressure on the networks. Water companies at first treated baths as 'extras' for which they charged a higher tariff. In Sheffield, the propertied middle classes insisted that baths were a normal 'domestic' feature of clean, respectable living and organized a consumer boycott against paying more for their bathwater. Once water was flowing effortlessly from the tap, some households decided to let it run to water their gardens, causing water companies to complain about criminal 'waste'. Material networks facilitated the networking of citizens who led agitations about their rights as tax-paying property holders to expect the service they had paid for. The members of these consumer defence leagues would have been surprised to see themselves understood as purely private economic actors. Their call for cheaper, more plentiful water and for the recognition of consumer rights was informed by a political tradition of citizenship.

Political cultures, too, influenced how water companies and authorities tried to contain excessive and wasteful consumption; in the 1890s many

German cities simply imposed meters on households, whereas in liberal Britain compulsory metering was politically out of the question and only exceptional offenders received company approved standard fittings (Grahn, 1902; Royal Commission, 1900). The phenomenal rise in the volume of water resulted in no small part from poorly performing material actors: bad fittings and leaking pipes. Waste was pronounced in American cities, which were less compact than older European ones and, consequently, needed a disproportionately larger mileage of vulnerable service pipes. Whether such undesired forms of use should be included in consumption or not was something that already divided Victorian engineers. It certainly made no difference for the environment or network whether 100 gallons filled a bath tub or were lost thanks to leakage. Choice and individual preferences mattered little in this world of unseen, unintended consumption. The rising 'demand' for water really is little more than a vague label for everything that happened between consumers, providers, materials, landlords, and local government.

By the 1920s, running water, a clean kitchen—where the housewife could cook with clean fuels, standing upright—and a separate, private toilet were part of a standard western package of material civilization. In the west, they remained an ideal rather than reality for most urban working classes until the 1950s. In Asia, they were the ticket to modernity for the educated middle classes. Their diffusion and adoption had enormous consequences for habits, family life, the self, and for the material intensity of consumption. It is impossible to understand the global export of this material lifestyle from one small part of the world without reference to power and ideology. Household preferences were not formed in a vacuum but took shape in a force field of ideas, prescriptions and hierarchies of values shaped by states, experts, and social movements. People might have worked harder to consume more but not simply of their own volition. Industriousness was a normative project championed by enlightenment culture. In the nineteenth century, Britain's liberal empire put it on its flag as part of its global civilizing mission; Victorian missionaries actively promoted it on the ground in Africa and elsewhere. From Buenos Aires to Shanghai, the western concept of a comfortable, clean home gained ground among the middle classes and reformers through its association with British hegemony. Material culture signalled progress and civilization. In 1920s Japan, the Home Ministry launched a campaign to reform everyday life, with the help of middle-class reformers, women's schools, and architects. It reorganized domestic space, and with it domestic practices and identities. Cooking was to be upright in a clean separate kitchen fitted with gas, running water, and electricity. Instead of being shared between husband and wife, cooking and housekeeping became the domain of the modern housewife (Sand, 2003). By the 1930s totalitarian ideologies sought to harness the ideal and disciplines of personal cleanliness and comfort for their own collective purposes. Stalin looked to *kul'turnost'* (a cultured lifestyle) as a way to turn backward Russians into modern, productive communists. A clean shave, soap, and grooming would teach personal discipline. Radios, phonographs, and electric irons would generate higher material wants and higher levels of productivity to satisfy them (Fitzpatrick, 1999; Siegelbaum, 1988).

11.3 Inequality

Sections 11.1 and 11.2 give a compressed sketch of some of the larger historical forces—political economy, empire, and ideology—that tend to be missing from social science accounts that focus either on individual preferences or on interactions between groups at a particular moment in time. Conversely, there are a number of topics and approaches in the social sciences which have had surprisingly little resonance with the historical literature. With a few notable exceptions, historians have yet to engage with behavioural economics and the debate over well-being (Offer, 2006). The gap between historical research and the social sciences is probably wider today than it has been for a century, and certainly since the 1970s. There is one major reason for this: the cultural turn in history. As historians moved closer to anthropology and cultural studies they edged further away from sociology and economics. This movement had disproportionate consequences for the historical study of consumption because the world of goods served as a methodological passage from social to cultural history in the 1970s and 1980s, and from questions of class and work to those of representation and symbolic meaning (Schama, 1988; Brewer and Porter, 1993; Douglas and Isherwood, 1979); a notable exception of social science history is Savage (2011).

One victim in this shift has been inequality. The treatment of gender and youth is revealing. The appreciation of women as shoppers and homemakers was one of the major achievements of historians' turn to consumption. Taste and material desire, control of the family budget, and access to public spaces, all these gave female consumers agency and emancipatory qualities that had been missing in previous male-oriented accounts of class and production (de Grazia and Furlough, 1996; Rappaport, 2000; Vickery, 1998). Studies of youth sub-cultures reinforced this shift. Consumption was about transgression, resistance, and the creation of alternative spaces, styles, and identities (Hebdige, 1979; Mort, 1989, 1996). Notwithstanding their quite different political agendas, gender studies and post-modernism—like neo-liberalism—increasingly aligned consumption with choice. That consumption might also be about compulsion, restraint, passivity, and inequality was all but forgotten. By the 1990s, talk of 'Konsumterror', still intellectually respectable in the 1960s, had gone out of fashion.

The widening gulf between rich and poor in the last generation is an opportune moment to revisit the connection between inequality and consumption. Inequality, of course, comes in many forms. There are inequalities of wealth, status, health, and capabilities (Sen, 1999). Each involves further inequalities between regions, sexes, and generations. Very crudely speaking, the second half of the twentieth century has witnessed a widening of regional inequality and a narrowing of gender and generational divides. Globally, inequalities in life expectancy and infant mortality have fallen. Of course, this is a vast generalization and must not distract from significant regional differences. Sub-Saharan Africa does not mirror development in India. In 2006 the richest 1 per cent owned 40 per cent of the world's assets, the richest 10 per cent a staggering 85 per cent (Davies et al., 2006; UC Atlas, 2012; Milanovi, 2005; Hunter, 2007). The decline in generational inequality—at least in the affluent west—does deserve greater attention from consumption scholars than it has received. All of these forms matter and intersect at various points, shaping how (and how much) people consume. Longer education, for example, translates into higher material aspirations and activities as well as a longer, more prosperous life. French university graduates today own more audio-visual equipment and frequent a larger number of cultural and social events than early school leavers (Donnat, 1998). Sociologists have debated the influence of status for consumption patterns, and vice versa (Bourdieu, 1984/1979; Lahire, 2004; Bennett et al., 2009). Partha Dasgupta and fellow economists have examined the multiple forces that determine the well-being of people in poor, rural countries (Dasgupta, 1993). It would be presumptuous to try and offer a picture of the interplay between these vectors in the space of this chapter. Rather, I want to follow one particular vector: income inequality. After half a century of rising equality, incomes since the late 1970s have once again started to diverge sharply, both in Anglo-Saxon countries and, more recently, in Europe. Rising inequality has featured prominently in academic and popular explanations of consumerism and debt. It is thus a good way to illustrate the benefits a historical perspective can bring to current debates.

There is no single, ideal way of measuring economic inequality. Some economists prefer consumption over income because over the course of a lifetime consumption is smoother than current income, which can go up and down sharply. Nonetheless, income matters and, in the course of the twentieth century, came to matter ever more so for one's place in society. In 1900 America, as in Britain, self-made millionaires were a minority. The main ticket into the elite was inheritance and land. Almost one in two of the American rich came from a wealthy background (Sorokin, 1925). Wealth more than anything separated the classes from the masses. In Britain in 1901, it is worth recalling, only 17 per cent of the population left behind any wealth at all. The wide, if inequitable, distribution of home-ownership (and the inflation of property prices) since the 1970s has changed this. For rich and poor, income has become more important in the last two generations for several reasons. Income from stocks, property, investments, and performance-related pay acquired unprecedented significance, and has been assisted by the fall in top tax rates—hence the fascination with bankers' bonuses rather than country houses. Merely 9 per cent of the richest 1 per cent in the United States had inherited their wealth in 2001; as late as 1989, it had been 23 per cent (Frank, 2008, p. 107). For the less fortunate, the rise in part-time work, less effective tax redistribution, and the growing number of single-person households contributed significantly to earnings inequality (OECD, 2011, pp. 29–34, see now also Piketty, 2013). Between the mid-1980s and the late 2000s the Gini co-efficient increased by nearly 10 per cent in OECD countries. In the United States, the number of millionaires doubled in the decade after 1995. Rising inequality, however, is no longer an Anglo-Saxon disease but affects welfare states and social market societies like Sweden and Germany (see Figures 11.1 and 11.2). One in every hundred Germans is a millionaire today; the figure is probably an underestimate since it is based on the estimated number of high net worth individuals by the World Wealth Report, which

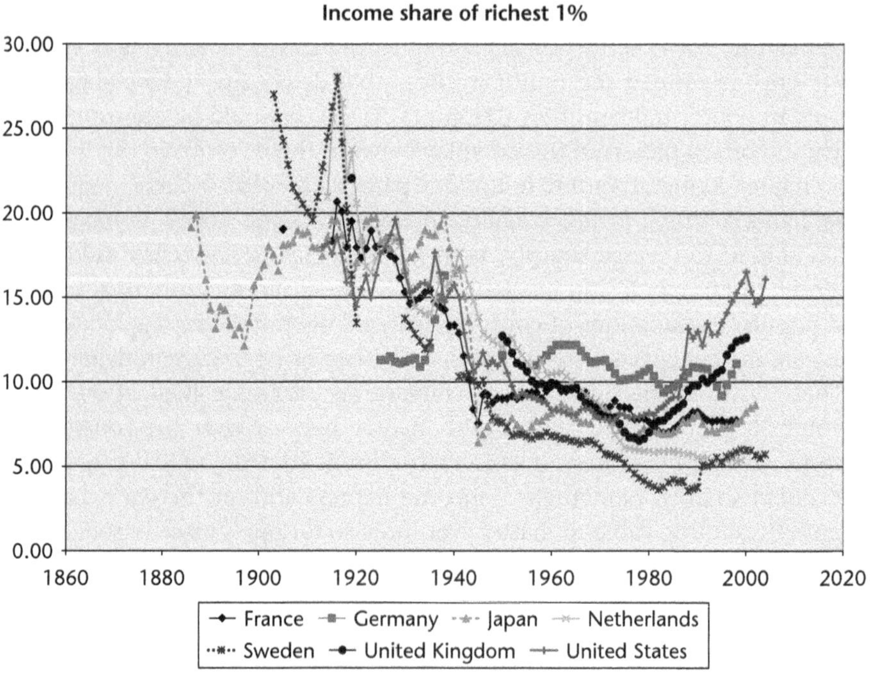

Figure 11.1. Income share of richest 1 per cent
Source: Adapted from Leigh (2007), with kind permission

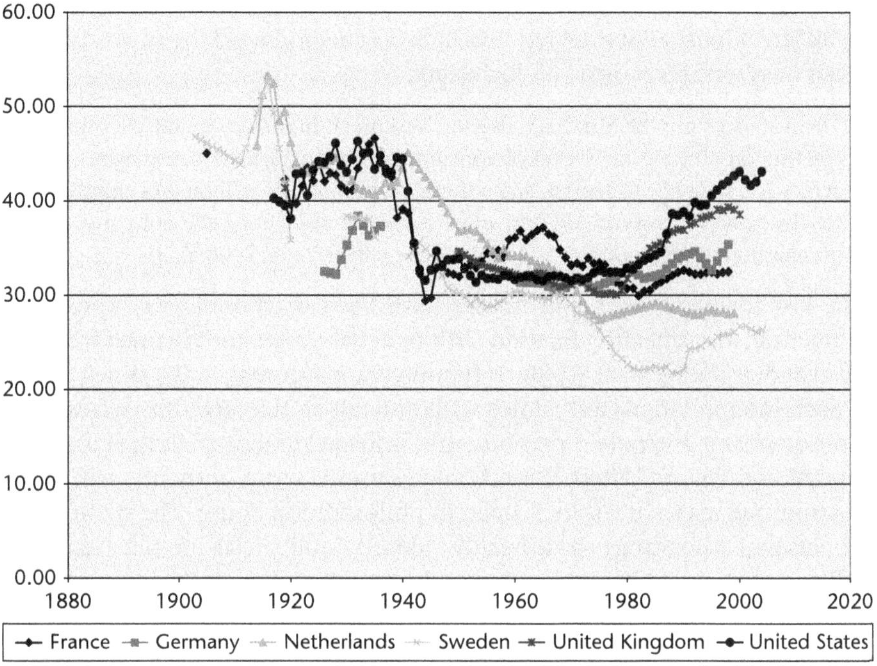

Figure 11.2. Income share of richest 10 per cent
Source: Adapted from Leigh (2007), with kind permission

does not include the value of the main home (Rickens, 2011). Concentration has been most pronounced at the very top. In the decade before the 2007 recession, the 400 richest Americans doubled their wealth.

11.3.1 *Luxury Fever?*

There are, then, good reasons for focusing on inequality and income inequality in particular. Most scholars would agree that inequality is bad for well-being, civic life, tolerance, and fairness (Wilkinson and Pickett, 2009). The question is what difference does inequality make for consumption and vice versa? Many commentators confidently find the answer in an excessive lifestyle and a popular culture of over-consumption. Greater riches have unleashed a 'luxury fever' (Frank, 1999). The economist Robert H. Frank details the growing size of American homes and luxury yachts, and the market for limited edition watches and other luxury articles. In this view, spending by the rich has set off a cascade of emulative consumption down the social hierarchy. Concern about the super-rich and the corrosive effects of inequality for mental health and personal finance has ensured such arguments wider public resonance. In a popular book, similarly named 'Wall Street Journal' special reporter Robert Frank followed the super-rich into 'their own virtual country' of 'Richistan'.

> There are so many Richistanis today, with so much money to spend, that they're creating an entirely new level of consumption. Being a truly conspicuous consumer has never been harder, since there are millions of millionaires competing for the same status symbols, and an even greater number of affluent consumers purchasing luxury goods to try to mimic the elite. (Frank, 2008, p. 3)

The lust for bigger cars and houses have been diagnosed as symptoms of 'affluenza', an unhealthy fixation with material possessions blamed for mental disorders (De Graaf et al., 2001; Hamilton and Denniss, 2006; James, 2007).

Such interpretations are riddled with difficulties. 'Luxury', like 'excess' and 'consumerism', is relative and normative, a loaded term with limited use as an analytical category. Whether we should yearn for a true, authentic self, separate from the material world, is open to philosophical doubt. The significance of personal belongings for a healthy identity and social life has been well documented by anthropologists (Csikszentmihalyi and Rochberg-Halton, 1981; Miller, 2008). In addition, we should also ask: how well does the argument for 'luxury fever' stand the test of history? Does the past lend support for a causal chain between inequality and an increased compulsion to consume? In addition to their own carbon footprint, are the 1 per cent responsible for the unsustainable lifestyle of the rest?

Anxieties about emulative consumption are as old as commerce. Luxury has been a moral lightning rod since ancient times. The arrival of exotic goods such as cotton, porcelain, tobacco, sugar, tea, and coffee in seventeenth- and eighteenth-century Europe rang in a new round in the so-called 'luxury wars'. Greater plebeian consumption triggered fears of moral decay and national stagnation. British observers warned of servant girls dressing above their station, always on the lookout for the newest cotton gown (McKendrick et al., 1982). In the early nineteenth century, factory girls were criticized for spending their hard-earned pennies on silk ribbons. A century later, middle-class reformers worried about workers living a champagne lifestyle on a lager budget.

Recent histories urge us to treat such diagnoses with caution. Certainly, plebeian consumers started to own more cotton goods, drink tea, and enjoy other novelties, but they did not automatically do so to emulate their superiors. A good deal of clothing was handed down from masters to servants. Ribbons and other accessories had their own symbolic meaning in plebeian culture. Fashionable clothes were markers of independence and identity, or an investment in landing a better job. Coffee houses provided spaces to do business, socialize, and learn about the newest discoveries. Drinking tea and coffee made good sense, providing urban workers with an easily prepared substitute for a hot meal, and a little boost on top. By the 1730s, workers in single rooms and lodging houses in London and Antwerp brewed their own. The thirst for hot beverages was habitual as much as emulative. Failed businessmen like the Dresden merchant Samuel Baker took the habit with them into the poorhouse when they fell on hard times. Tea, coffee, cocoa, and sugar were part of an expanding culture of domestic comfort and sociability. Its hub was the middling sort, and nowhere more so than in the society with the greatest appetite for goods at the time: Georgian Britain. Rather than aping aristocratic luxury, the middling classes were busy assembling possessions and discovering tastes that helped them define their own identity. Taste remained stratified. Furniture, wallpaper, and other possessions were positional goods but the reference group was primarily one's own peer group, not the nobility above, let alone the court. Taste and possessions had to be appropriate to one's status. Crossing that line could backfire (McCants, 2008; Styles, 2006; Hochmuth, 2008; Vickery, 2006).

In the final analysis, the eighteenth-century luxury wars owed their force less to actual consumer behaviour than to ideas and beliefs about that behaviour and its feared effects on social order, public morality, and freedom. J. J. Rousseau traced alienation to the very beginning of civilization. The 'savage', he wrote in his 'On the Origin of Inequality', 'lives within himself, while social man lives constantly outside himself' (Rousseau, 1754/1952, p. 362): appearance and the opinion of others meant everything to him. Emulation and conspicuous display were the wheels of material civilization. But, Rousseau was also clear to point out, some societies were more unequal than others. Commercial societies, he and fellow critics argued, amplified the lust for things and the urge to impress one's superiors. In the process, they spun a new global circuit of slavery and dependence. In the old world, the fixation with novelty and luxury sapped the strength of republics and made the nobility stooges of the royal court. In the new world, Europeans' lust for exotic goods planted slavery.

The luxury wars have been studied in depth (Berry, 1994; Berg and Eger, 2003; Berg and Clifford, 1999). What is worth adding for our purposes is how the *moral* career of luxury was the opposite of that of *material* inequality. By the mid-eighteenth century, rising levels of comfort and the pursuit of novelty were appreciated as sources of economic wealth, national power, and a stronger civil society—David Hume defended them as 'modest luxuries'. Luxury was a far less sensitive topic at the end of the eighteenth century than at its beginning. Inequality in income, by contrast, was much worse in Britain. In 1700 Britain was distinguished by the highest real wages in Europe. By the late eighteenth century, real wages were falling and poverty was rising (Allen, 2009). Luxury and emulative behaviour, then, generated the greatest heat at a time when inequality was historically low. The critique softened just as the gulf between rich and poor reached new extremes.

Anxieties about luxury fever returned with a vengeance around 1900; and nowhere more so than in the United States. The late nineteenth-century 'gilded age' saw an unprecedented concentration of riches. When J. P. Morgan died in 1914, he left behind an estate worth $80 million. 'And to think he wasn't even a wealthy man', J. D. Rockefeller was said to have commented (Rubinstein, 1980, p. 18). In the previous decade, Rockefeller's own wealth had quadrupled from $200 million to $800 million. A million was suddenly small change. Together, the arrival of nouveaux riches and the rising ceiling of wealth gave emulation and status anxieties a fresh boost. This is the era of Vanderbilt mansions and castle-sized holiday homes in Newport, of ever more grandiose yachts and parties. Social scientists know this world through the eyes of Thorstein Veblen, who subjected it to a blistering critique in his classic *Theory of the Leisure Class* in 1899. The new rich were the idle rich who 'wasted' resources in an emulative display of conspicuous consumption (Veblen, 1899/1953).

There are two ways of reading Veblen. We can appreciate Veblen as a primary source which gives us an insight into how concerned observers reacted to the accumulation of riches around them. Here it does not matter especially whether he was original or not. As C. Wright Mills noted in the 1950s, Veblen's ideas were anticipated by John Adams and others in the eighteenth century and might have been little more than 'extended pieces of worldly wisdom, long known and perhaps often stated, but stated by Veblen in a magnificent form and at a time when it could take hold of a literate public' (Mills, 1956, p. 89). Still, as Mills pointed out, his anxieties about 'wasteful' prestige gratification tell us how strong the social ideal of efficiency was in 1900 America, at the time he was writing. The upper classes did not 'work' as far as Veblen was concerned.

Many social scientists, however, have read Veblen as a secondary source, holding out insights that can be applied to other periods and places. The question is: how well does it do? Since 'conspicuous consumption' ranks among the most successful popular exports in the history of the social sciences and today's ideas about luxury fever and emulative behaviour continue to take inspiration from Veblen, this question deserves more attention than it has received.

Veblen did not invent the lavish world of luxury before demolishing it. In the real world, there were those like William C. Whitney who fit the critique well, with his luxurious homes, yachts, and thoroughbred race horses. But Whitney was only one segment of a diverse elite culture. Just as representative was Hetty Green, the 'witch of Wall Street', worth nearly $100 million, mainly from railways and real estate. With her wealth, Green also inherited frugality.

She was the polar opposite of Veblen's conspicuous consumer. Diamonds were not her best friends. Green did not do 'waste'. She wore her clothes until they literally felt apart, lived in cheap hotels, and used her local bank as her office. All resources were fed back into business. Whitney and Green represented two extremes. In between, rich America was composed of a third strand of industrious businessmen with a social mission. For Rockefeller, who grew up in a family of abolitionists, charitable giving was part of his identity from a young age. Similarly, Carnegie, a labour reformer in his youth, gave away some 90 per cent of his wealth (Jaher, 1980). Charity and political engagement were, of course, also markers of distinction but they were hardly the kind of idle leisure singled out by Veblen. Mills had a point when he criticized Veblen for being 'not quite serious enough about status because he did not see its full and intricate importance to power.' 'Veblen laughed so hard... at the servants and the dogs and the women and the sports of the elite that he failed to see that their military, economic, and political activity is not at all funny' (Mills 1956, p. 89). Whitney, for example, boosted the American fleet as United States Secretary of the Navy in the late 1880s.

Veblen did not offer a theory of *the* leisure class but of one particular segment: the nouveau riche. In addition, he was dealing with leisure in a society that did not know either court or old nobility—an odd exception in the annals of history that makes Veblen's theory of limited comparative use. Finally, he was writing at the cusp of a media revolution. When Mills observed the American elite in the 1950s, he did not fail to note a new crop of conspicuous consumers with recognizable Veblenesque traits like the construction tycoon Hal Hayes, whose bar at home was fitted with faucets for Scotch, bourbon, and champagne. Yet, Mills also noted a seismic shift in the gravity of social prestige from conspicuous display to a media-based celebrity culture. The new rich no longer spent their energy and fortune on debutante balls but on being seen with crooners, TV stars, and movie starlets.

This shift was (and remains) of historic significance because it changed the communicative logic of luxury and, with it, the part played by inequality. The 'luxury fever' thesis presumes that what happens at the apex of society is seen and known at the middle and the bottom. This is doubtful. The very rich cannot simultaneously live in a 'self-contained world' (Frank, 2008, p. 3) and be a lodestar for the rest at the same time. Most people would be hard pressed to name a handful of billionaires, other than a few football-owning oligarchs. We may know a lot about the size of a bonus a banker takes home but very little about what he or she spends it on. This should not be a surprise. The very rich are a secretive bunch. Enterprising recent economists managed to identify the occupations of only 17 per cent of the 0.1 per cent top earners in the United States (Rauh and Kaplan, 2010). By comparison, 250 million viewers followed the Latin hit video 'Danza Kuduro' in 2011, in which Don Omar picks up Lucenzo in a BMW Z 4 and enjoys a cruise on a Viking Sport Cruiser V 52 (a 'mere' 56 ft motor-yacht) (Universal Music, 2011). Where the lifestyle of millionaires reaches broader audiences it has had to ape celebrity culture, as in reality tv shows such as *Made in Chelsea* (UK) or *Mulheres Ricas* (Brazil). It is pop stars, film stars, and sport celebrities who define the landscape of luxury with their special edition watches, luxury bags, and sports cars.

11.3.2 *The Diversification of Riches*

If it were true that inequality, via a cascade of luxury, shifts the engine of consumption into a higher gear, we should expect greater equality to shift it downwards. The decades after the Second World War did the very opposite. Affluent societies in the 1950s, 1960s, and 1970s were marked by two developments: a decline in inequality and an unprecedented era of growth and consumption. The tailfins of American cars were getting longer and American homes bigger, as America was becoming more equal. The richest 1 per cent of Americans controlled 17 per cent of income on the eve of the Second World War; the richest 10 per cent secured 45 per cent of income. By 1960 their share of income was down to 8 per cent and 32 per cent respectively.

At the same time, the American elite was diversifying, in background, lifestyle, and identity. The rise of celebrities was part of this, but so were the growing number of mega rich doctors and lawyers and the arrival of an affluent elite of painters, writers, and musicians. Of the top earning 1 per cent, in the early 1990s 2 per cent came from arts, media, and sports; another 5 per cent were professors, scientists, and engineers; lawyers contributed 9 per cent; doctors 20 per cent. Executives and managers made up one third, the financial professions around 10 per cent. The financial profession doubled its share of the top 1 per cent income in the last generation (Bakija et al., 2012).

For the wealthy, reference groups and lifestyles multiplied. Models of luxury fever and emulation focus on trickle-down effects. At least for the American rich, the post-war decades were distinguished by trickle-up dynamics. Some super-rich heirs started to emulate middle-income families and long for the simpler comforts of middle-class family life. Houses in Newport were closed or sold off, debutante parties scaled back, and servants given the sack. Others mingled with artists and writers. Whereas William Whitney had poured his wealth into thoroughbreds, his daughter-in-law, Gertrude Vanderbilt Whitney, in 1931 founded the Museum of American Art named after her. More wealth was being devoted to educational foundations and charity than ever before. On the eve of the 1973 oil crisis, 31 per cent of all estates worth more than $10 million were given to charity (Jaher 1980, pp. 209).

A similar diversification of the elite has taken place in other advanced societies. In the United Kingdom, Benjamin Britten left behind a sizeable fortune of £1.7 million in 1976, unthinkable at the time of Veblen's robber barons. Post-war Britain, too, saw the rise of a café society and a growing proximity between the old elite and new cultural taste makers between Kensington and Soho, Princess Margaret and film and artists—but, in contrast to the United States, also the return of the debutante. Royalty and celebrity made for a special conservative symbiosis (Mort, 2010).

In general, the plurality of competing norms and aspirations among the very rich has undermined the positional power of luxury consumption. Contemporary elites no longer have a single, shared point of reference that the court of Louis XIV provided for the French nobility. Take the German multi-millionaire Oliver Berking, whose family has produced silver cutlery since 1874. While selling to the rich across the globe, Berking's status remains rooted in his local community. His leisure time revolves around his family and the local Rotary club in his home town Flensburg. Instead of buying a 100 metre luxury yacht, Berking's pride is a 20 metre restored, wooden old-timer which he sails with like-minded aficionados in local races. Status is asserted on the Flensburg Fjord in the Baltic, not the Med, let alone the Bermudas. Some 15,000 hours and several hundred thousand Euros went into the restoration of his Sphinx (Rickens 2011, pp. 67–80). This is a very different kind of luxury from the conventional 'conspicuous' model. Value and taste are demonstrated through a commitment of time and an acquisition of competence. As a form of consumption, Berking's is closer to that of serious collectors or enthusiastic hobby practitioners than to a Vanderbilt. The new super-rich in America, similarly, include many 'project addicts' who keep themselves busy with their ranch or designing a home (Frank, 2008, pp. 63–7).

The plurality of elite lifestyles has been accompanied by the segmentation of luxury. The concentration of riches may boost spending on high-end luxury goods but more popular forms of luxury consumption follow a separate logic. A group of economists placed luxury consumption alongside stock returns in the United States. They found that the sales of imported luxury cars fell sharply during downturns in the stock market (1969, 1974, 1990, and 2001). Broader measures of consumption which included more general luxury goods escaped such falls (Ait-Sahalia et al., 2004). The demand for a Porsche is one thing, that for Louis Vuitton bags quite another.

One reason is that the luxury market itself has undergone democratization. The market for luxury goods and services in 2004 was worth 12 per cent of total retail (Boston Consulting Group, 2006). Luxury has outpaced regular retail sales for a number of reasons independent of the pronounced concentration of riches at the very top of society: greater travel and a more cosmopolitan culture of taste; greater disposable income amongst the middle classes; more single professional women with independent incomes; a greater number of affluent elderly. It is the top 30 per cent, not the 1 per cent, that is the main force behind luxury. The preoccupation with the super rich tends to miss the broader forces driving up consumption. Will the considerable drop in the share of income going to the top 1 per cent since the recession—from 24 per cent in 2007 to 18 per cent in 2009 (*The Economist*, 21 January 2012, p. 41)—stem the cascade of luxury fever and lead to a similar drop in purchases of luxury bags, watches, and SUVs? Probably not. The last generation has seen a cultural shift in the meaning and uses of luxury away from one of distinction within national society to one of personal lifestyle and membership in global modernity. For Asian consumers, European luxury goods are less about emulating Asian elites than about sharing in the cosmopolitan taste associated with modern professionals. In the west, a good deal of the luxury trade focuses on interior decor, kitchen, and garden, and aims at creating a 'surround-sound experience of luxury', in the words of the editor of *House and Garden*, Dominique Browning (Danziger, 2005, p. 9). Self-expression is found in assembling the components to document personal taste. As in the case of the yachting German millionaire, luxury in the home is tied to connoisseurship that requires a demonstration of competence. Instead of being hidden in servants' quarters, the luxury kitchen becomes a stage to exhibit technique and taste.

Shifts in tastes, habits, and spending priorities provide little evidence in support of a trickle-down or cascade of luxury fever. Shinobu Majima and Alan Warde have compared the spending patterns of the very rich in Britain (top 1 per cent of income) in 1961, 1981, and 2004 (Majima and Warde, 2008). In the course of this period, some items of distinction disappeared—cars, durable goods, wine, and visits to the theatre. By 2004, the lifestyle of very rich Britons was differentiated from the rest by disproportionate spending on jewellery, holidays, and flights within the United Kingdom. But what distinguished them, too, was high saving and high spending on pensions, education, and home renovation—an investment as well as ostentation—and high consumption of health and leisure services. These changing priorities suggest that, while conspicuous consumption has not disappeared, it is increasingly overshadowed by concerns with comfort, security, health, and an active lifestyle. Theories of emulative behaviour and luxury fever tend to take morally suspect forms of consumption as the natural object of emulation. They fail to explain why groups would choose to copy 'wasteful' aspects of elite lifestyle, to use Veblen's language, but not other more 'rational' and 'productive' ones, such as pensions and savings.

Behind concerns with conspicuous consumption lurks the paternalist idea that the less privileged classes find it difficult to resist the urge to copy the extravagance of their superiors. Greater inequality intensifies that pressure and only helps to plunge the less fortunate deeper and deeper into debt. Such anxieties are as old as commerce and debt themselves. But, however well-intentioned, they need to be appreciated as morality tales, which seek to influence policy and behaviour (Horowitz, 1992) rather than as a description of material reality. Amongst today's propertied middle classes, for example, equity withdrawal has not been used to finance luxury cars and fine living but to fund home improvement, pay off debts, and help families with young children bridge a temporary short-fall in earnings. In the United States, a third of all instalment debt was for education (Federal Reserve Bulletin, 2009, A 46, table 15; Parkinson et al., 2009; Jarvis, 2010). Many poorer Americans accumulated credit card debt to pay for medical bills, food, and rent. British studies have found, if anything, a reluctance amongst poor consumers to incur debt in order to live above their station. Debt and bankruptcy are real and have been on the rise since the 1980s in all advanced societies. But they have been primarily the result of unemployment, ill health, and divorce, not of a desire to copy the luxurious living of the few. Nor are over-indebted consumers confined to inegalitarian Anglo-Saxon countries (Reifner et al., 2003; Kempson and Whyley, 1999).

Diagnoses of 'luxury fever' and 'affluenza' are part of a literature that treats Anglo-American society as the essential consumer society, a tradition that reaches back to Galbraith and anxieties of Americanization in the post-1945 world. But consumer culture has come in a great variety of shapes and sizes. So have strategies of elite distinction. The sociologist Jean-Pascal Daloz has noted their bewildering diversity. In Nigeria, anyone wanting to impress will ensure that his or her car has visible markers of status for everyone else to see, such as indications of engine type and model number on the boot, and, with the help of official support or a bribe if necessary, number plates of 1, 11, or 111, to show one's primacy. In Switzerland, by contrast, such conspicuous marks are deemed vulgar. Anyone worth anything will prefer a sleek, anonymous boot (Daloz, 2010). There is no reason to presume that the United States is any more representative than, say, a country like Germany which has one of the highest concentration of millionaires in the world but also one of the highest saving rates.

It would be fascinating to know the relative propensity towards luxury amongst the super-rich in countries at different levels of development. Presumably, in a more mobile and mediated global world, it matters whether a multi-millionaire turns to his or her own society as a point of reference or looks outside towards a cosmopolitan elite abroad. Are super-rich Russians living abroad more likely to spend on extravagantly furnished mega-yachts than a Swiss millionaire positioning him or herself in Zurich? High net worth individuals in Russia and Brazil spend almost twice as much on luxury goods a year as Americans—$35–40,000 dollars compared to $22,000 by US high net worth individuals (Euromonitor, 2011). Emulation and showing off, in other words, might be directed sideways, across space, to impress established elites rather than downwards at the group sitting on the next rung of the social ladder. Arguably, the portrayal of rich Russians as vulgar in the western media points to the difficulty of such transnational strategies of emulation.

Inequality in income measures money but does not tell us how it is viewed within a culture and whether a display of riches is accepted or discouraged. Development over time might be expected to lower the incentive for luxurious spending once conspicuous display started to appear uncultivated. A democratic culture of equality, on the other hand, might also add to the pressure for distinction. This is what Alexis de Tocqueville concluded from his tour of democratic America in 1831–2, in comparison to his native, more stratified France.

> When inequality of conditions is the common law of society, the most marked inequalities do not strike the eye; when everything is nearly on the same level, the slightest are marked enough to hurt it. Hence the desire of equality always become more insatiable in proportion as equality is more complete.
>
> (Tocqueville, 1994, Book II, chapter 13)

Intriguingly, in France, a rare egalitarian island in the international drift to greater income inequality, the very rich spend more on luxury goods than in the unequal United States and Great Britain—$30,000 per high net worth individual in France, compared to $22,000 by an American and $28,000 by a Briton (Euromonitor, 2011). It is no coincidence that societies that took extreme measures to promote an egalitarian lifestyle, like socialist East Germany and the Soviet Union, were also those where consumer goods mattered most for distinction (Zatlin, 2007).

11.3.3 *Loads of Money, Little Time*

So far our discussion has examined luxury in relation to inequalities in income. But consumption takes time as well as money. What happens if we add a temporal axis of inequality? Forty years ago, Staffan Linder predicted that in affluent society, people would respond to the scarcity of time by shifting from leisure-intensive to commodity-intensive consumption (Linder, 1970). In reality, the educated and professional elite have expanded their possessions *and* their time-intensive leisure practices. The 1997 cultural survey of France, for example, shows that the educated elite owns more audio-visual equipment but also attends a greater number and range of concerts, plays, operas, and exhibitions (Donnat, 1998). Music-making, active sport, and amateur literature and art have all enjoyed rising participation, but especially so among the educated classes. A qualitative case study of households in Bristol in the United Kingdom suggests that the more educated change their activities more frequently (Southerton, 2006).

The growing divide between time poor and time rich in the last two generations cuts across the divide between income rich and poor. High earners are the new temporal proletariat. Busyness has replaced idle, conspicuous consumption as the badge of honour (Gershuny, 2005). Americans today may work longer hours in total than Europeans but in both continents it is the educated who work harder and play harder than ordinary workers. For the purpose of this chapter this is consequential in several respects. In spite of the popular stereotype of an all-corrosive work–spend cycle, ordinary Americans have chosen shorter working hours over greater income, unlike their managers. Surely, if they had wanted to keep up with luxury spending, they should have opted for longer working hours. Secondly, the historical relation between the polarization of riches and leisure is ambiguous. Social surveys already reported higher levels of leisure activity amongst high-income, educated Germans in the early 1970s, in what were the golden years of equality (Nave-Herz and Nauck, 1978). In the absence of comparative time use data before the late 1960s, it is unclear how much this was an older trend although American observers already noticed in the 1950s that managers were more prone to trade in free time for income than workers (Heckscher and DeGrazia, 1959). One interpretation would be that greater equality in income and democratic access to leisure devalued idler, conspicuous forms of consumption for social elites who consequently sought refuge in longer hours at the office and an active lifestyle outside it. Status derived no longer in the display of material extravagance but in the resources required to juggle an active lifestyle: mobility, access to time-saving technologies, the money and discipline to acquire skills and taste. If true, the new era of income inequality since the 1980s inherited a temporal culture of consumption in which material luxury played a less significant role than in earlier eras.

Comparing the balance between leisure and income in more or less equal societies adds one final complication. In a recent study, Goodin and colleagues took on the task of measuring 'discretionary time', that is, the free time people would have if they did just enough paid and unpaid work and personal care to stay above the poverty line (Goodin et al., 2008). 'Necessary time' for unpaid housework, for example, is defined as half the median equivalent of actual unpaid household labour. Anything above that threshold is treated as 'discretionary'. Of course, calculating time in lumps like this is beset with problems. It neither captures people's sense of the quality and quantity of time nor how more or less disposable time depends on how well activities are coordinated. Still, it offers a welcome tonic to the mainly Anglo-American literature by placing time poverty in a comparative dimension and differentiating between choice and constraint for different households. As we might expect, Scandinavian welfare regimes do better at cushioning the loss of discretionary time that follows on raising a child or splitting up than the market-oriented United States. An American mother loses 33 hours of discretionary time in the process of moving from a dual-earner to a single carer household, her Finnish counterpart only loses 23 hours. The move from a single to a double-earning couple without children, by contrast, results in a gain of 12 hours of discretionary time. Whereas for the single mother 'time poverty' is 'genuine', it is 'gratuitous' for the childless double earners. What is interesting for our purposes is the large pool of discretionary time they identify for welfare regimes as well as market societies. In real life, a Swede makes do with 30 hours of spare time, but would potentially be able to enjoy a total of 85 hours if they were to draw on all the discretionary time at their disposal. The potential gain for an American would be smaller; 34 hours of actual spare time and 80 hours of total discretionary time.

In popular American accounts, time poverty like consumer debt appears as a consequence of a consumerist work–spend cycle in a society marked by pronounced and rising income inequality. Here the assumption is that more equal societies, by slowing down the hedonic treadmill, also reduce time poverty (Schor, 1991, 1999). Yet, the figures given here suggest the opposite might be the case. Egalitarian Sweden and Finland have the largest amount of discretionary time but fail to convert it into real spare time. Swedes and Finns spend more hours in paid and unpaid work than absolutely necessary than do Americans. Perhaps, it is time to speak of the *Over-worked Swede* as well as the *Over-worked American*. In short, equality can be as bad (or worse) for leisure as inequality.

11.4 Collective Consumption

Equality and welfare bring us back to an issue central to historians and with which we started: the difficulty of deciding on the appropriate chronology for consumption. For the historian, chronology is an intellectual tool to identify the boundaries of major trends and phenomena over time. All social scientists do this when carving up their subject, though it is often left implicit and sometimes little more than a generic 'past' before the 'present'. For our subject, one of the most influential chronologies has been that of Galbraith's *The Affluent Society*. The mid-twentieth century, in his view, saw a historic break and the emergence of a new social system based on standardized production and geared towards the satisfaction of artificially stimulated private demand. The system produced 'private wants, public squalor' in Galbraith's famous phrase. The United States was its original home. Galbraith built on precursors like Stuart Chase who saw America as a new consumer society in the interwar years (Galbraith, 1958; Chase, 1934). Still, it is the post-1945 privatized market version rather than that of the post-1931 New Deal which is remembered today. Galbraith's chronology has been adapted to fit critiques of neo-liberalism, choice, and growth (Schor, 1999; Jackson, 2009; Schwartz, 2005). Private consumerism and public welfare in this view operate like a see-saw. As the first went up, the latter went down. A commitment to public life and communal goods such as the welfare state is superseded by individual choice and private goods. In this chronology, the expansion of consumption is reduced to choice, individualism, and the power of the market.

In the last generation, historians have recast our understanding of the rise of the consumer. As a social and political actor, they show, consumers entered the stage of history in the nineteenth and early twentieth century in battles over collective provision, such as water and gas, as well as market commodities, well before the 'affluent' 1950s and 1960s. The language of choice was not missing from these earlier battles but, far from prompting a retreat from public engagement into private self-satisfaction, it politicized consumers and invigorated citizenship. Choice and the power of the purse gave voice to women and other groups without a formal vote. Research has focused on buyers' leagues and consumer boycotts, anti-slavery sugar protesters and imperialist housewives, Free Traders and New Dealers (Chatriot et al., 2004; Sklar, 1998; Jacobs, 2005; Cohen, 2003; Trentmann, 2008). What has so far been untouched is the bigger question about the role of collective provision and public welfare in the rise of consumption. Crudely put, the history of consumer society has been written as a story of the market. Collective consumption and provision by the state, if they feature at all, are always on the retreat. Education, health, and housing benefits appear in histories of the welfare state, not of consumption. This is quite misleading, I think. This concluding section sets out programmatically two pieces for a new history of public consumption.

11.4.1 *The Company*

The first concerns consumption at the workplace, such as company housing, leisure, and services. In 1792 Samuel Slater opened a free Sunday school to recruit boys for his cotton mill at Pawtucket, Rhode Island in the United States. It initiated what later would be known as 'welfare capitalism' (Brandes, 1976). The late nineteenth-century company town came closest to creating its own universe of consumption. Pullman, Ill. was a typical artefact, built in 1881 by the Pullman Palace Car Company, complete with hotel, shops, a theatre, and a church, as well as housing for workers. Instead of a saloon, workers got a baseball diamond. Whether free, subsidized, or overpriced, housing, leisure, and company shops were collective provisions, not market choices. They aimed at attracting a skilled workforce, stifling union activism and integrating immigrant workers. France had Le Creuset as a company town, Britain Cadbury's Bournville, Mexico the Compania Industrial Veracruzana. AEG provided vacation homes near Berlin, saunas, kindergarten, and hairdressers. By 1916, 1,000 firms in the United States offered housing for 600,000 employees and their families, an impressive 3 per cent of the total population; for comparison, there were 1.3 million units of occupied public housing in 1989 according to the American Housing Survey. In heavy industries, a company's fortune could hinge on a good canteen. 'A man is not a man unless he can eat his own weight three times a day', a reporter wrote in Mason City in 1939, only slightly exaggerating (Carlson 2003, p. 51). Loggers in the Pacific Northwest received double a soldier's ration. In Holden, the typical worker ate a T-bone steak and 1/3 lb of bacon a day. On the eve of the Second World War, a survey of companies in Indiana found that over three-quarters offered recreational facilities. Bowling, softball, and basketball were most popular. One in ten companies offered camera clubs. On average, companies spent 14 cents a week per employee (Diehl and Eastwood 1940/1992, pp. 1–4). Such services have been mainly discussed as part of human resources and management strategies but they also added up to a considerable slice of consumption.

The historiography follows their expansion in the early twentieth century and suggests a decline in the 1930s and 1940s as the threat of unions retreated and the state offered public services and more housing support, on the one hand, and, in the case of Roosevelt's New Deal, prohibited companies from sending worker representatives to sit on recreational committees, on the other hand. The story, however, may be more interesting than a short-lived rise and fall. During the Second World War, some companies took out the laundry for their employees and even did their Christmas shopping. Company towns were dying in the post-war years but company services were not. In the early 1950s, 30,000 American companies offered recreational programmes worth $800 million for 34 million workers. They no longer limited themselves to sport for the individual employee but provided activities for the whole family. The fashion show was the most popular part of the employee recreation programme. Many companies put on four shows a year. Local department stores happily assisted, 'providing samples of their latest styles and even sending live models to display them' (Anderson, 1955, p. 125). There were dance classes, bridge parties, and discounted theatre tickets and holiday trips. Company stores sold everything from soap and clothing to electrical equipment.

The decline of some of these services in the 1960s and 1970s may have been little more than a blip. Since the 1980s, companies have focused their energies once more on health and leisure. What is different is that it is now called 'human capital'. What may be different, too, is the system of provision. Instead of in-house services, firms increasingly subsidize leisure provided by third parties, in the form of subsidized gym membership, discounted holiday options, or free museum passes. Still, company recreation has not vanished everywhere. A survey of 1990s Finland found 14 per cent of employees exercising in their company (Borodulin et al., 2008). Through their works councils (Comités d'entreprise), Air France, France Télécom, and other large utilities and French companies spend €11 billion a year to send their workers on subsidized ski trips and camping holidays. At its Basel headquarters, the pharmaceutical giant Roche offers sport clubs, jazz concerts, and dry cleaning. In Silicon Valley, some high-tech companies provide on-site massage, yoga, and botox injections (*The Economist*, 26 May 2011; Wharton, 2011). Ask your university what it can do for you!

11.4.2 *The State*

I have earlier touched on the importance of modern ideologies for the expansion of consumption. Taking such 'public' forces seriously provides a challenge to the popular idea that hyper-consumption has been the recent result of a neo-liberal hegemony of 'private' choice, individualism, and markets. Equally significant, public support and spending were decisive for how much and what we consume, and continue to be so. Filling a home with possessions depends on having a home in the first place and a wardrobe to fill. This, in turn, depended on more regular employment and income and on mortgages and consumer credit, which historically would not exist without a helping hand from the state—the Home Owners' Loan Corporation and the Electric Home and Farm Authority during the New Deal in the United States are classic examples (Hyman, 2011).

Just as credit and saving allows individuals to smooth income and expenditure over the life course, so public health regimes spread out well-being. A sick consumer is a bad consumer. Social security reduced uncertainty and smoothed the family budget. For the majority, the cyclical visit to the pawnbroker gave way to the accumulation of goods. The consumer boom in the United States from the 1950s was accompanied by rising public expenditure, not a rolling back of the state. The difference with Europe is one of degree. The OECD measure of 'social spending'—public consumption expenditure on health, education, housing, and unemployment benefits, but excluding defence—gives a helpful indication of its rising share. In 1980, OECD countries on average devoted 16 per cent of GDP to social spending. By 2003 it had crossed the 20 per cent mark; since, it has fallen back to 19 per cent (OECD, 2012) (see Figure 11.3). To put this in historical perspective, Lindert, who has done most to analyse social spending, reckons that as late as 1960 the average was below 10 per cent (Lindert, 1996).

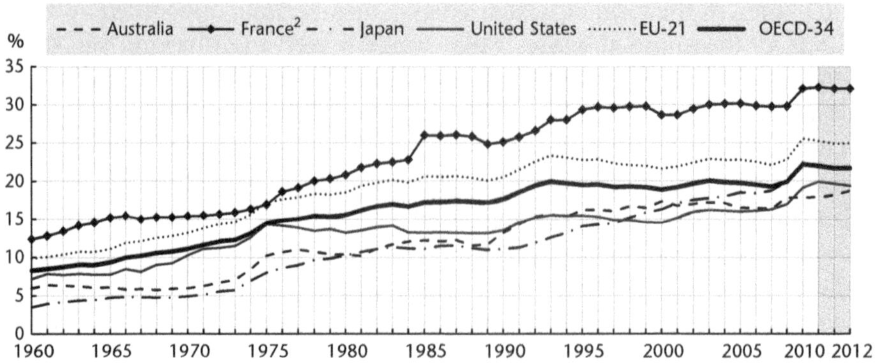

Figure 11.3. Public Social Spending in OECD countries, percentage of GDP, 1960–2012 (note, the figures for 2012 are estimates)

Source: Data from *Public social spending in selected OECD countries, in percentage of GDP1, 1960–2012*, from OECD (2012), OECD Social Expenditure database www.oecd.org/els/social/expenditure

With 28 per cent in 2007, France was well ahead of the rest, but the United States (16 per cent) was only marginally below the OECD average (19 per cent). Public pensions and health have been the main domains of social spending. For comparison, *private* social spending is largest in the United States but even here it amounts to no more than 10 per cent of GDP.

The high share of household consumption as part of American GDP is sometimes used as short-hand for the consumerist orientation of the United States. Clearly, Americans drive a lot of SUVs and carry a lot of debt on their credit cards. Some of the picture, however, involves an optical illusion, which stems from the peculiar balance between private and public social spending. The share of private consumption appears so high not primarily because of greater spending on consumer goods but because of heavy private expenditure on health and education. In the United States, the household consumption rate climbed from 69 per cent in the 1950s and 1960s to 77 per cent in the early 1990s. An analysis of generational effects suggest that a major portion of this came from the rising propensity to consume amongst the elderly; in the early 1960s, the 65+ year olds accounted for 11 per cent of the United States' household consumption but 18 per cent by the late 1980s (Gokhale et al., 1996). A lot involved greater spending on doctors, dentists, and medicines. Similarly, in the United Kingdom, private consumer debt would appear more modest and manageable if the cost of higher education appeared in public accounts as in other European countries and not in private loan statements.

There are few consumption and leisure activities in the developed world today that are not supported by public spending in one way or another. This is a major difference of advanced consumer societies over their precursors in earlier centuries—charitable spending or public feasts organized by local elites fade into insignificance compared to current public outlays. Some of this is indirect. Holidaying would crumble without the supporting infrastructure of roads, trains, and airports. Presumably, eating-out would lose some of its popularity if visitors of restaurants had to worry about public health and hygiene. Other kinds of leisure benefit more directly, such as sport and culture. At the time of the Rome Olympics in 1960, not even one in thirty Italians practised any sport (ISTAT, 2005, pp. 17–19). Today it is closer to one in three. The trend speaks volumes about the thousands of football grounds, swimming pools, and gymnasia built.

I do not want to suggest that public spending leads to a convergence of consumer culture in developed societies—far from it. A consideration of public consumption should heed the lessons learnt from debates about the limits of homogeneization or McDonaldization in the private sector. South Korea, for example, is a consumer society even though it only channels 7 per cent of its GDP into social spending. Equally striking are different priorities in public spending on culture and welfare. In Germany in 1999, each visit to the theatre was subsidized by €89 of public money. The share of theatre's own income has been steadily declining since the 1960s from 26 per cent to 14 per cent (Statistisches Bundesamt Deutschland, 2002, p. 152). In the Hamburg state opera—'opera for the people'—you can sit in the stalls and listen to four hours of Wagner for £25. In the Royal Opera House in Covent Garden, you will not even find a seat in the amphitheatre for that. Surely, there is a connection between public funding for the arts, civic associations that provide popular access to theatre and music, and the level of cultural participation. The success of national football teams points to a similar conclusion. It is difficult to win the World Cup for a country which does not build football pitches for its youngsters. Social spending can make for a more or less democratic culture of consumption.

Such flows rarely feature in critiques of affluenza which treat shopping and shopaholics as symptomatic of consumer society. Our analysis suggests, by contrast, that the interesting story for the late twentieth and early twenty-first centuries might not be so much the shift from welfare capitalism to neo-liberal markets but the intertwined growth of private *and* public consumption. The neo-liberal 1980s may be a far less important paradigm break than often thought. Private consumption expanded with the help of public support. Whether the world recession and current attacks on public spending will reverse this post-1945 trend remains to be seen.

11.5 Conclusion

For the purpose of this multidisciplinary volume, it might be preferable to mix conclusions with some open questions that emerge from this excursion into the historical dynamics of consumption. One is to urge caution about the applicability of general models and make for greater awareness of the moral and ideological baggage that standard explanations have carried with them. The argument of 'luxury fever' did not suddenly emerge in the 1980s and 1990s because of secular spending trends. It draws on a longer intellectual tradition stretching back to republican critiques of commerce and beyond. Such traditions deserve analysis and respect in their own right, but they must not be confused with an understanding of how people actually lived their lives. They, secondly, carry the danger of editing out historical developments and subject areas from the study of consumption. The disregard for the effects of social equality and public spending are two such areas. Putting the state back into consumption raises a host of fascinating questions where the historian could do with a bit of help from colleagues in the social sciences. Keynesian policy debates ponder the issue of crowding out. But in the case of public spending on health, housing, and culture we are dealing with long-term, not short-term, transfers.

Should we see the expansion of private and public consumption as symbiotic, with public spending on social services freeing up households' discretionary income, on the one hand, and greater consumer spending propelling growth forward to pay for greater public services, on the other? Or, are there certain public parts eating into private pockets? How could one model such relationships? Tax transfers have been sometimes more, sometimes less effective. Finally, if public consumption plays a bigger role than is normally recognized, how does it affect debates about sustainability? Presumably, nature is indifferent whether the local government builds and runs a heated-swimming pool or Mr and Mrs Citizen pay to swim their laps in a commercial leisure facility. Company holidays produce carbon just as a private, commercial budget flights do. How much responsibility has the welfare state and rising social spending for making consumer society what it is today?

References

Ait-Sahalia, Y., Parker, J. A., and Yogo, M. (2004) 'Luxury goods and the equity premium', *The Journal of Finance*, 59: 2959–3004.

Allen, R. C. (2009) *The British Industrial Revolution in Global Perspective*, Cambridge: Cambridge University Press.

Anderson, J. M. (1955) *Industrial Recreation. A Guide to its Organization and Administration*, McGraw-Hill Book Co.: New York.

Bakija, J., Cole, A., and Heim, B. T. (2012) *Jobs and Income Growth of Top Earners and the Causes of Changing Income Inequality: Evidence from U.S. Tax Return Data*, available at:

<http://web.williams.edu/Economics/wp/BakijaColeHeimJobsIncomeGrowthTopEarners.pdf>.

Bennett, T., Savage, M., Silva, E., Warde, A., Gayo-Cal, M., and Wright, D. (2009) *Culture, Class, Distinction*, London: University of Chicago Press.

Berg, M. (2004) 'In pursuit of luxury: Global history and British consumer goods in the eighteenth century', *Past and Present*, 182: 85–142.

Berg, M. (2005) *Luxury and Pleasure in Eighteenth-Century Britain*, Oxford: Oxford University Press.

Berg, M. and Clifford, H. (eds) (1999) *Consumers and Luxury: Consumer Culture in Europe 1650–1850*, Manchester: Manchester University Press.

Berg, M. and Eger, E. (eds) (2003) *Luxury in the Eighteenth Century: Debates, Desires and Delectable Goods*, Basingstoke: Palgrave Macmillan.

Berry, C. (1994) *The Idea of Luxury*, Cambridge: Cambridge University Press.

Borodulin, K., Laatikainen, T., Juolevi, A., and Jousilahti, P. (2008) 'Thirty-year trends of physical activity in relation to age, calendar time and birth cohort in Finnish adults', *The European Journal of Public Health*, 18: 339–44.

Boston Consulting Group (2006) cited in: 'The Luxury Market', *The Silver Word* (2006) available at: <http://thesilverword.com/media/pdfs/Luxury%20Market.pdf>.

Bourdieu, P. (1984/1979) *Distinction: A Social Critique of the Judgment of Taste*, Cambridge, Mass.: Harvard University Press.

Brandes, S. D. (1976) *American welfare capitalism, 1880–1940*, Chicago: University of Chicago Press.

Brewer, J. and Porter, R. (eds) (1993) *Consumption and the World of Goods*, London and New York: Routledge.

Carlson, L. (2003) *Company Towns of the Pacific Northwest*, Seattle: University of Washington Press.

Chase, S. (1934) *The Economy of Abundance*, New York: Macmillan.

Chatriot, A., Chessel, M.-E., and Hilton, M. (eds) (2004) *Au Nom du Consommateur: Consommation et politique en Europe et aux États-Unis au XX Siècle*, Paris: Éditions La Découverte.

Chessel, M.-E. (2012) *Histoire de la consommation*, Paris: Presses de Sciences Po.

Cohen, L. (2003) *A Consumers' Republic: The Politics of Mass Consumption in Postwar America*, New York: Alfred A. Knopf.

Csikszentmihalyi, M. and Rochberg-Halton, E. (1981) *The Meaning of Things: Domestic Symbols and the Self*, Cambridge: Cambridge University Press.

Daloz, J.-P. (2010) *The Sociology of Elite Distinction*, Basingstoke: Palgrave Macmillan.

Danziger, P. N. (2005) *Let Them Eat Cake; Marketing Luxury to the Masses—As Well as the Classes*, Chicago: Dearborn Trade Publishing.

Dasgupta, P. (1993) *An Inquiry into Well-being and Destitution*, Oxford: Clarendon.

Davies, J. B., Sandstrom, S., Shorrocks, A., and Wolff, E. N. (2006) *The World Distribution of Household Wealth*, New York: World Institute for Development Economics Research of the United Nations University.

De Graaf, J., Wann, D., and Naylor, T. H. (2001) *Affluenza: The All Consuming Epidemic*, San Francisco, Calif.: Berrett-Koehler Publishers; London McGraw-Hill.

De Grazia, V. (2005) *Irresistible Empire: America's Advance through 20th-Century Europe*, Cambridge, Mass.: Belknapp Press.

De Grazia, V. and Furlough, E. (eds) (1996) *The Sex of Things: Gender and Consumption in Historical Perspective*, Berkeley, Calif. and London: University of California Press.
De Vries (1994) 'The Industrial Revolution and the Industrious Revolution', *The Journal of Economic History* 54, no. 2, 1994: 249–70.
De Vries, J. (2008) *The Industrious Revolution: Consumer Behavior and the Household Economy, 1650 to the Present*, Cambridge: Cambridge University Press.
Diehl, L. J. and Eastwood, F. R. (1992/1940) *Industrial Recreation: Its Development and Present Status*, Ann Arbor, Michigan: UMI.
Donnat, O. (1998) *Les Pratiques Culturelles des Français: Enquête 1997*, Paris: Documentation Francais.
Douglas, M. and Isherwood, B. (1979) *The World of Goods: Towards an Anthropology of Consumption*, London: Allen Lane.
Dyer, C. (2005) *An Age of Transition? Economy and Society in England in the Later Middle Ages*, Oxford: Oxford University Press.
Euromonitor (2011) *Business of Luxury*, available at: <http://www.wisekey.com/en/Press/2011/Documents/Euromonitor_Report_for_FT_Business_of_Luxury_Summit_2011.pdf> (accessed November 2012).
Federal Reserve Bulletin (2009) *Changes in U.S. Family Finances from 2004 to 2007: Evidence from the Survey of Consumer Finances*, Federal Reserve Bulletin.
Fitzpatrick, S. (1999) *Everyday Stalinism: Ordinary Life in Extraordinary Times: Soviet Russia in the 1930s*, Oxford: Oxford University Press.
Frank, R. (2008) *Richistan: A Journey through the 21st Century Wealth Boom and the Lives of the New Rich*, London: Piatkus.
Frank, R. H. (1999) *Luxury Fever: Money and Happiness in an Era of Excess*, Princeton, N.J.: Princeton University Press.
Galbraith, J. K. (1958) *The Affluent Society*, New York: The New American Library.
Gershuny, J. (2005) 'Busyness as the badge of honor for the new superordinate working class', *Social Research*, 72: 287–314.
Gokhale, J., Kotlikoff, L. J., Sabelhaus, J., Bosworth, B., and Haveman, R. (1996) 'Understanding the postwar decline in U.S. saving: A cohort analysis', *Brookings Papers on Economic Activity*, 1: 315–407.
Goodin, R. E., Rice, J. M., Parpo, A., and Eriksson, L. (2008) *Discretionary Time: A New Measure of Freedom*, Cambridge: Cambridge University Press.
Grahn, E. (ed.) (1902) *Die Städtische Wasserversorgung im Deutschen Reiche sowie in einigen Nachbarländern*, Munich: R. Oldenbourg.
Hamilton, C. and Denniss, R. (2006) *Affluenza: When Too Much is Never Enough*, Crows Nest, N.S.W.: Allen and Unwin.
Haupt, H.-G. (2002) *Konsum und Handel: Europa im 19. und 20. Jahrhundert*, Göttingen: Vandenhoeck and Ruprecht.
Hebdige, D. (1979) *Subculture: The Meaning of Style*, London: Methuen.
Heckscher, A. and DeGrazia, S. (1959) 'Executive leisure', *Harvard Business Review*, 37: 6–12.
Hochmuth, C. (2008) *Globale Güter—lokale Aneignung: Kaffee, Tee, Schokolade und Tabak im frühneuzeitlichen, Dresden:* Konstanz: UVK.

Horowitz, D. (1992) *The Morality of Spending: Attitudes Towards the Consumer Society in America, 1875–1940*, Chicago: Ivan R. Dee.

Hunter, R. (2007) 'Globalization, growth, poverty and inequality', in Ravenhill, J. (ed.) *Global Political Economy*, Oxford: Oxford University Press.

Hyman, L. (2011) *Debtor Nation: The History of America in Red Ink*, Princeton, N.J.: Princeton University Press.

Istat (2005) 'Lo sport che cambia', *Argomenti*, 29.

Jackson, T. (2009) *Prosperity without Growth: Economics for a Finite Planet*, London: Earthscan.

Jacobs, M. (2005) *Pocketbook Politics: Economic Citizenship in Twentieth-Century America*, Princeton: Princeton University Press.

Jaher, F. C. (1980) 'The gilded elite, American multimillionaires, 1865 to the present', in Rubinstein, W. D. (ed.) *Wealth and the Wealthy in the Modern World*, London: Croom Helm.

James, O. (2007) *Affluenza*, London: Vermilion.

Jardine, L. (1997) *Worldly Goods: A New History of the Renaissance*, London: W.W. Norton & Co.

Jarvis, H. (2010) 'Housing to manage debt and family care in the USA', in Smith,S. J. and Searle, B. A. (eds) *The Blackwell Companion to the Economics of Housing*, Oxford: Oxford University Press.

Kempson, E. and Whyley, C. (1999) *Kept Out or Opted Out? Understanding and Combating Financial Exclusion*, Bristol: Policy Press.

Lahire, B. (2004) *La culture des individus: dissonances culturelles et distinction de soi*, Paris: La Découverte.

Leigh, A. (2007) 'How closely do top income shares track other measures of inequality?', *Economic Journal*, 117(520): 589–603.

Linder, S. B. (1970) *The Harried Leisure Class* New York: Columbia University Press.

Lindert, P. H. (1996) 'What limits social spending?', *Explorations in Economic History*, 33: 1–34.

Lüdtke, A., Marssolek, I., and Von Saldern, A. (eds.) (1996) *Amerikanisierung: Traum und Alptraum im Deutschland des 20.* Jahrhunderts, Stuttgart: Franz Steiner.

Lury, C. (2011) *Consumer Culture*, Cambridge: Polity Press.

Majima, S. and Warde, A. (2008) 'Elite consumption in Britain, 1961–2004: Results of a preliminary investigation', *The Sociological Review*, 56: 210–39.

McCants, A. (2008) 'Poor consumers as global consumers: the diffusion of tea and coffee drinking in the eighteenth century', *Economic History Review*, 61: 172–200.

MCKendrick, N., Brewer, J., and Plumb, J. H. (1982) *The Birth of a Consumer Society: The Commercialization of* Eighteenth-century *England*, Bloomington: Indiana University Press.

Milanovi, B. (2005) *Worlds Apart: Measuring International and Global Inequality*, Princeton, N.J.: Princeton University Press.

Miller, D. (2008) *The Comfort of Things*, Cambridge: Polity Press.

Mills, C. W. (1956) *The Power Elite*, New York: Oxford University Press.

Mort, F. (2010) *Capital Affairs: London and the making of the Permissive Society*, New Haven, Conn.: Yale University Press.

Mort, F. (1996) *Cultures of Consumption: Masculinities and Social Space in Late Twentieth-Century Britain*, London: Routledge.

Mort, F. (1989) 'The politics of consumption', in S. Hall and M. Jacques (eds) *New Times: The Changing Face of Politics in the 1990s*, London: Lawrence and Wishart.

Nave-Herz, R. and Nauck, B. (1978) *Familie und Freizeit*, Munich: Juventa.

OECD (2011) *Divided We Stand: Why Inequality Keeps Rising*, Paris: OECD.

OECD (2012) Social Expenditure database, available at: <http://www.oecd.org/els/social/expenditure>.

Offer, A. (2006) *The Challenge of Affluence: Self-Control and Well-Being in the United States and Britain since 1950*, Oxford: Oxford University Press.

Parkinson, S., Searle, B. A., Smith, S. J., Stoakes, A., and Wood, G. (2009) 'Mortgage equity withdrawal in Australia and Britain: Towards a wealth-fare state?' *European Journal of Housing Policy*, 9: 365–89.

Piketty, T. (2013) *Le capital au 21e siècle*, Paris: Éditions du Seuil.

Ramey, V. A. (2009) 'Time spent in home production in the twentieth-century United States: new estimates from old data', *Journal of Economic History*, 69: 1–47.

Rappaport, E. D. (2000) *Shopping for Pleasure: Women and the Making of London's West End*, Princeton N.J.: Princeton University Press.

Rauh, J. D. and Kaplan, S. N. (2010) 'Wall Street and Main Street: What contributes to the rise in the highest incomes?', *Review of Financial Studies*, 23: 1004–50.

Reifner, U., Kiesilainen, J., Huls, N., and Springeneer, H. (2003) 'Consumer overindebtedness and consumer law in the European Union: Final report presented to the Commission of the European Communities, Health and Consumer Protection Directorate-General', Brussels: Commission of the European Communities, Health and Consumer Protection Directorate-General.

Rickens, C. (2011) *Ganz Oben: Wie Deutschlands Millionäre Wirklich*, Leben, Cologne: Kiepenheuer & Witsch.

Robinson, J. P. and Godbey, G. C. (2005) 'United States of America: Time-use and cultural activities' in G. Cushman, A. J. Veal, and J. Zuzanek (2005) *Free Time and leisure Participation: International Perspectives*, Wallingford: CAB International.

Rousseau, J.-J. (1952/1754) *A Discourse on the Origin of Inequality*, translated by G. D. H. Cole, Chicago: University of Chicago Press.

Royal Commission on Water Supply (1900) Cd 25, Vol. 38 Pt 1, Final Report.

Rubinstein, W. D. (ed.) (1980) *Wealth and the Wealthy in the Modern World*, London: Croom Helm.

RWE/Archive (1975) Abt. Anwendungstechnik Marketing, June 1975, Bericht über die Haushaltskundenbefragung 1974 im direkten RWE-Versorgungsgebiet.

Sand, J. (2003) *House and Home in Modern Japan: Architecture, Domestic Space, and Bourgeois Culture, 1880–1930*, Cambridge, Mass.: Harvard University Asia Center.

Savage, M. (2011) *Identities and Social Change in Britain Since 1940: The Politics of Method*, Oxford: Oxford University Press.

Schama, S. (1988) *The Embarrassment of Riches*, Berkeley and Los Angeles: University of California Press.

Schor, J. B. (1999) *The Overspent American: Why We Want What We Don't Need*, New York: HarperPerennial.

Schor, J. B. (1991) *The Overworked American: The Unexpected Decline of Leisure*, New York, Basic Books.

Schwartz, B. (2005) *The Paradox of Choice: Why More is Less*, New York: Harper Collins.

Sen, A. (1999) *Development as Freedom*, Oxford: Oxford University Press.

Siegelbaum, L. H. (1988) *Stakhanovism and The Politics of Productivity in the USSR, 1935–4*, Cambridge: Cambridge University Press.

Silverstein, M. J. and Butman, J. (2006) *Treasure Hunt: Inside the Mind of the New Consumer*. New York: Portfolio Penguin Group.

Sklar, K. K. (1998) 'The consumers' white label campaign of the national consumers' league, 1898–1918', in S. Strasser, C. McGovern, and M. Judt (eds) *Getting and Spending: European and American Consumer Societies in the Twentieth Century*, Cambridge: Cambridge University Press.

Slater, D. (1997) *Consumer Culture and Modernity*, Cambridge: Polity Press.

Sorokin, P. (1925) 'American millionaires and multi-millionaires: A comparative statistical study', *Journal of Social Forces*, 3: 627–40.

Southerton, D. (2006) 'Analysing the temporal organization of daily life: Social constraints, practices and their allocation', *Sociology*, 40: 435–54.

Statistisches Bundesamt Deutschland (2002) (Hrsg.) *Datenreport 2002, Zahlen und Fakten über die Bundesrepublik Deutschland*, Bonn: Statistisches Bundesamt Deutschland.

Steigerwald, D. (2006) 'All hail the republic of choice: Consumer history as contemporary thought', *The Journal of American History*, 93: 385–403.

Stiglitz, J. E., Sen, A., and Fitoussi, J.-P. (2009) Report by the Commission on the Measurement of Economic Performance and Social Progress, available at: <http://www.stiglitz-sen-fitoussi.fr>.

Styles, J. (2007) *The Dress of the People: Everyday Fashion in Eighteenth-Century England*, New Haven: Yale University Press.

Styles, J. (2006) 'Lodging at the Old Bailey: Lodgings and their furnishing in eighteenth-century London', in J. Styles and A. Vickery (eds) *Gender, Taste and Material Culture in Britain and North America, 1700–1830*, New Haven: Yale University Press.

Taylor, V., Chappells, H., Medd, W., and Trentmann, F. (2009) 'Drought is normal: The socio-technical evolution of drought and water demand in England and Wales, 1893–2006', *Journal of Historical Geography*, 35(3): 568–91.

Taylor, V. and Trentmann, F. (2011) 'Liquid politics: Water and the politics of everyday life in the modern city', *Past and Present*, 211: 199–241.

Thirsk, J. (1978) *Economic Policy and Projects: The Development of a Consumer Society in Early Modern England*, Oxford: Oxford University Press.

Tocqueville, A. D. (1994/1838) *Democracy in America*, New York: Alfred A. Knopf.

Trentmann, F. (forthcoming) *The Consuming Passion: How Things Came to Seduce, Enrich and Define Our Lives, from the Sixteenth Century to the Twenty-First*, London: Allen Lane/Penguin.

Trentmann, F. (2008) *Free Trade Nation: Commerce, Consumption, and Civil Society in Modern Britain*, Oxford: Oxford University Press.

Trentmann, F. (2009) 'The long history of contemporary consumer society: Chronologies, practices, and politics in modern Europe', *Archiv für Sozialgeschichte*, 49: 107–28.

Trentmann, F. (ed.) (2012) *The Oxford Handbook of the History of Consumption*, Oxford: Oxford University Press.

UC Atlas (2012) University of California Atlas of Global Inequality, available at: <http://ucatlas.ucsc.edu/home.html>.

Universal Music (2011) <http://universalmusica.com/donomar/> (accessed 4 December 2011).

Veblen, T. (1953/1899) *The Theory of the Leisure Class: An Economic Study of Institutions*, New York: The New American Library.

Vickery, A. (1998) *The Gentleman's Daughter: Women's Lives in Georgian England*, New Haven: Yale University Press.

Vickery, A. (2006) 'Neat and not too showey: Words and wallpaper in regency England', in J. Styles and A. Vickery (eds) *Gender, Taste and Material Culture in Britain and North America, 1700–1830*, New Haven: Yale University Press.

Welch, E. (2005) *Shopping in the Renaissance: Consumer Cultures in Italy 1400–1600*, New Haven: Yale University Press.

Wharton (2011) 'A recession for perks? What companies offer and what employees want': Knowledge@Wharton, Philadelphia: University of Pennsylvania , available at: <http://knowledge.wharton.upenn.edu/article.cfm?articleid=2800>.

Wilkinson, R. G. and Pickett, K. (2009) *The Spirit Level: Why Equality is Better for Everyone*, London: Penguin.

Zatlin, J. (2007) *The Currency of Socialism*, Cambridge: Cambridge University Press.

Zelizer, V. (2005) 'Culture and consumption', in N.J. Smelser and R. Swedberg (eds) *The Handbook of Economic Sociology*, Princeton, N.J.: Princeton University Press.

12

Sociology, Consumption, and Habit

Alan Warde

12.1 Introduction: Sustainable Consumption and the Habits of Affluence

The political issue of sustainability is transforming scholarship around consumption. Although the concept of sustainable consumption is little more than ten years old, and despite lack of agreement on what exactly it would mean for consumption to be sustainable, hardly anyone denies its importance. Sustainability is arguably the most pressing political problem of the twenty-first century, a consequence of climate change and environmental degradation and depletion, exacerbated by a predicted massive expansion of the world's population. Existing patterns of personal and domestic consumption constitute a major, perhaps the primary, threat to human well-being on Earth. Now the problem is not insufficient consumption—despite that remaining a problem for a couple of billion people—but excessive depletion or degradation of natural resources, for example water, air, and stable global temperatures.

The preferred response of incumbent political elites is economic growth and technological innovation; that is, business as usual with salvation to be achieved through 'cleaner' or 'greener' technologies whose development will return acceptable levels of profit to capitalist corporations. However, although natural sciences and their technological applications have demonstrated remarkable Promethean powers in the past, one doesn't have to be a chronic pessimist to anticipate that they will be insufficient. Indeed, governments implicitly admit as much by deeming it necessary to address sustainability as a problem of changing personal and collective behaviour.

The term, 'sustainable consumption', which reached politicians' lips about ten years ago, presents a grave political problem. First, no party can propose that material standards of living, whatever their consequence for Earth's natural resources, should fall. Second, such standards probably will be demanded, and morally could not be resisted, everywhere; as economies like those of India, China, Brazil, and Russia expand they will incorporate many of the imperatives of global consumer culture so that popular aspirations converge on western levels. Third, national governments do not have the powers, and nor probably the political will, to intervene authoritatively to determine what can and cannot be consumed. What to do?

Governments have responded ponderously. On the international stage the very existence of Earth Summits to reduce carbon emissions and mitigate their effects on climate confirms that a real problem exists. Internally, in many countries, governments seek some means to change the everyday patterns of behaviour of their citizens: they recognize that current established patterns of consumption are unsupportable. In the UK, the ministry charged with devising policies for mitigating environmental damage, Department for Environment, Food and Rural Affairs (Defra), having noticed that household energy-use, the production and supply of foodstuffs suitable to an acceptable diet for Britons, and established modes of transportation (to mention the most problematic issues) contribute very substantially to carbon emissions, has for some years been attempting to alter the behaviour of individuals and households. It has typically conceptualized the problem as a lack of fit between values and action. Almost everyone, if asked, is in favour of protecting and preserving the environment and slowing climate change. However, people do not appear to act on their values, hence the primary strategy of Defra, to circulate information with a view to changing people's orientations, has so far had little success. Arguably, this failure can be explained by revealing that the principal models of action used in policy-making (and most of social science), also in fields far beyond mere consumption, are flawed.

In this chapter, then, I suggest that the nature of the problem of sustainability reveals gaps and weaknesses in social scientific approaches to consumption. The tools and instruments available do account for and explain some phenomena, and may suggest some robust ways of going about improving or at least maintaining quality of some aspects of collective and personal life, but they mostly do not apply well to the issue of sustainable consumption.

I take here the principal problem of sustainable consumption to be the *relentlessness* of the use of resources which are not merely scarce, but are also either irreplaceable or inherently harmful. Regular, routine, and habitual behaviour, on a global and mass scale—like having a shower every day, driving to work, or eating meat daily—is more the source of the problem than what design of shower, which car, or the price and quality of meat. The problem is a prior one of the normalization of standards of decency, cleanliness, convenience, and taste (see e.g. Shove, 2003). It is mass participation in normal activities, and the manner of use rather than nature of the initial act of economic exchange, which have environmental consequences. Buying greener products is not the solution, or rather not a sufficient solution.

In this regard, recent Sociology has made a promising contribution by focusing attention not just on acquisition, but also on appropriation (as well as on aesthetic appreciation) (Warde, 2010). Schematically, *acquisition* involves exchange (by market and other mechanisms) which supplies the means for personal and household provisioning. *Appropriation* involves practical activities entailing the use of goods and services for personal and social purposes. *Appreciation* covers the myriad of processes giving symbolic and aesthetic meaning to provision and use.

12.2 The Sociology of Consumption

Consumption was identified by sociologists as a topic for systematic investigation only about 25 years ago. For most of the twentieth century, sociological analysis of consumption was driven largely by normative and quasi-political considerations about the threats that mass consumption posed to good citizenship and the good life. As Schudson (1993) observed, consumption was variously condemned for encouraging cultural mediocrity, pandering to status concerns, promoting hedonistic materialism, creating excessive waste, causing privatization, and obscuring the exploitation of labour. However, these normative diagnoses were rarely supported by systematic evidence, the notable exception being investigations into poverty, that condition in which some people consume too little for achievement of socially acceptable standards of physical reproduction and cultural participation.

Social scientists intensified their attention to consumption in response to unprecedented material abundance during the Long Boom. Since then, the social science of consumption has had three broad, partly overlapping, phases of development, each of which has had a distinctive focus. Schematically, emphasis shifted between the three fundamental dimensions of consumption—acquisition, appreciation, and appropriation. In the first phase literature focused on the economic system and its reproduction in an age of mass production and mass consumption. Sociological accounts, revolving around themes from macroeconomics and critical political economy, were 'economistic' in the sense that consumption was subordinate to, and to be explained in terms of, production; the stereotypical instance was the Marxist base and superstructure theorem. Cultural phenomena, like taste, were, if not determined by, heavily steered by the apparatus of industry, for example advertising, and were by-products in capitalist societies of the unequal, usually class-based, distribution of property and income. By implication, welfare provision was a consumption issue. Debates centred on the relationship between needs and wants, and upon the patterns and the justice of the existing distribution of access to goods and services among the population.

Phase two coincided with 'the cultural turn' in the humanities and social sciences in the 1970s. Critical of 'economism', attention increasingly shifted from the instrumental aspects of consumption to its symbolic dimensions, its capacity to convey social meaning. The new discipline of cultural studies was a major stimulus to the sociology of consumption in Europe. It contested not only economistic explanation but also the earlier moral condemnation of consumer behaviour. Not only did mass produced goods and services provide comfort and entertainment, they also expanded cultural experience for many people, supplied materials to be used in personal self-development and self-expression, and, as with the example of gifts, established and consolidated social relationships (Warde, 2002). Consumption was thus re-habilitated—no longer (despite its inevitability) a cause for regret, but rather grounds for celebration. Presented often as a new societal form based on processes of globalization, aestheticization, and commodification, people's aspirations, activities, and possessions were interpreted in terms of the spread of 'consumer culture'. Research, much of it rich in semiotic and experiential detail, focused on style and taste, on sub-cultural expression, on popular culture, on uses of mass media, and on the playful and non-instrumental aspects of life. Increasingly, consumption came to be seen as a means by which individuals and groups expressed their identities through symbolic representation in taste and lifestyle, with their desires focused on symbolic rather than material reward. The associated moral, social, and aesthetic judgements can be treated as part of the process of *appreciation*, which is partly a matter of pleasure and satisfaction and partly related to the meanings attached to different activities, possessions, and their aesthetic representation.

In the mid-1980s, anthropologists began to apply their discipline's insights about non-market exchange and material culture to modern consumption (e.g. Appadurai, 1986; Kopytoff, 1986; Miller, 1987; McCracken, 1990). Sociological and socio-cultural studies of consumption in the third phase subsequently adopted the notion of appropriation to capture the importance of people 'domesticating' mass produced and alien products, endowing them with particular personal meanings and converting them into items to be made use of and enjoyed for their own practical purposes. The idea of appropriation emphasizes use. Consumption serves the practical activities of everyday life.[1]

[1] The concept of consumption has two separate historical roots. One emerged from political economy in the eighteenth century to describe market relationships, whence the distinguishing of consumer from producer. The other, an earlier notion, emerging from Latin into early English, had a negative connotation—to destroy, to waste, to use up. Use, not acquisition, was primary.

Appropriation connotes the personal use of products and services, as in eating food at dinner, receiving therapeutic treatment, wearing clothes that communicate messages to others, making a home, or playing the piano. All these are acts of appropriation through someone making use of material objects. The mode and manner of appropriation will be inflected by both what has been acquired and how it is appreciated—by access and taste—but is reducible to neither. Appropriation, then, refers to the incorporation, adaptation, and using up of items to serve practical purposes.

Ultimately there is no reason not to consider the observations, insights, and perspectives of the work in these three phases as complementary. At least some of the differences are matters of emphasis. Others are the effects of focus, of addressing specific explanatory puzzles. As a matter of historical fact, however, they developed in competition with one another, with lines of division drawn by disciplinary boundaries and contrary theoretical convictions. The history is both complicated and interesting. However, given that the focus of this chapter is upon habit, it is the specificity of the third phase that is important. In sociology it arose in part as a critique of the one-sidedness of the second.

As would be expected, the cultural turn diverted attention away from some empirical phenomena relevant to the analysis of consumption. First, much of the work on the culture of consumption focused on the display for others of symbols of identity, obscuring the fact that most consumption is ordinary or inconspicuous. Those actions which require little reflection, which communicate few social messages, which play no role in distinction, and which do not excite much passion or emotion, were typically ignored. As Gronow and Warde (2001) argued, social scientific investigations typically had concentrated on musical taste, clothing fashions, private purchase of houses and vehicles, and the attendance at 'high' cultural performances like theatre and museums, to the exclusion of everyday food consumption, use of water and electricity and petrol, organization of domestic interiors, and listening to the radio. The latter types of activity are at the core of issues of sustainability and presuppose a different approach and a different set of concepts to understand their social uses, for these are the activities of mundane, everyday life, tools for survival and getting by. The consequence of the cultural turn, perhaps its key defining feature, was a tendency, by contrast, to focus disproportionately on identity, expressivity, and communication. This inevitably downplays the role of instrumental reasoning and action. Postulating the primary role of self-referential symbolic systems means that people's activities are examined from within a web of meanings rather than with reference to

The tension between the two meanings drives public and scholarly debates about modern consumerism.

their capacities for action. As Campbell (1995, 1997) argued, because consumption was presented as a code or language, it was often analysed preeminently as a mode of communication which, according to him, seriously neglects the fact that most action is directed not towards communicating with others but towards the fulfilment of self-regarding purposive projects which presume consumption to involve routine application of items in pursuit of use values.

Second, the earlier core business of the sociology of consumption went into relative decline as earlier accounts of conspicuous consumption directed towards an understanding of class and status became less common. Pronouncements about the end of class and serious questioning of the methodological strategy of seeking statistical associations between social position and hierarchically distributed cultural forms meant fewer studies of resource distribution and the influence of material inequalities. Strategic and competitive consumption, and consumption for the sake of survival, were less in keeping with the temper of cultural analysis, a tension expressed more widely in terms of a shift from class politics to identity politics. In theoretical perspective this shift was associated with the methodological precepts that treat culture primarily as a web of meanings, and a tendency, described by Kaufman (2004), to explain culture endogenously. To emphasize culture was to de-emphasize social structure (Abbott, 2001a), eclipsing distinctive features of the social realm, of social interdependence, and social interaction.

Third, the cultural turn found little place for objects and technologies as material forces. As Reckwitz (2002, p. 202) charged, in cultural theory '[t]he material world exists only insofar as it becomes an object of interpretation within collective meaning structures'. He argued that the main theoretical problem of the cultural turn was that material entities, the copious materiality of mass manufacture and consumer culture, are treated as objects of knowledge and not as material *sui generis*. He envisages correction by way of 'praxeological thinking' which asserts that:

> certain things or artefacts provide more than just objects of knowledge, but necessary, irreplaceable components of certain social practices, that their significance does not only consist in their being 'interpreted' in certain ways, but also in their being 'handled' in certain ways and in being constitutive, effective elements of social practices. (Reckwitz, 2002, p. 210)

Reckwitz proposed that the analyses of Bruno Latour and some of the propositions of Actor Network Theory make possible a suitable break from purely cultural explanation.

Arguably, cultural analysis of consumption contained also a further and deeper set of theoretical weaknesses embedded in its general theory of action.

Despite its internal diversity, primary recourse was to a voluntaristic theory of action, upholding models of an active, expressive, choosing consumer motivated by concerns for personal identity and a fashioned lifestyle. The model of an active and reflexive agent predominated, implying that conscious and intentional decisions steer consumption behaviour and explain its sense and direction. In key respects its model is little different from the sovereign consumer of neo-classical economics, which has always been a bête noire of sociology.[2] For it effectively shares in the dominant and basic template of consumption which presents the process as one where the individual engages in very many discrete events, characterized by personal deliberation preceding personal, independent decisions made with a view to the satisfaction of preferences. The many variants of this model are coming to be known as the 'portfolio model of the actor', a term coined by Hindess and defined by Whitford (2002, p. 325) as one in which 'individuals carry a relatively stable and pre-existing set of beliefs and desires from context to context. Given the situation, they select from this portfolio "those elements that seem relevant and [use] them to decide on a course of action"'.

The model of the expressive individual is contestable on several grounds, but two have been especially challenged in Sociology. First, it mis-defines or mis-specifies consumption—a notoriously chaotic concept of which the active agent model uses only one of the possible definitions, arguably a poor one, precisely because it pays insufficient attention to appropriation. Second, the postulate of the autonomy of the individual and freedom of individual choice is contested (e.g. Levett et al., 2003; Sassatelli, 2007; Southerton et al., 2004). Despite its own (growing) complement of scholars pursuing rational action theory, game theory, principal agent modelling, and the like—part of its shift, in parallel with other social sciences, towards micro-level analysis—the majority view within sociology has always rejected the many versions of utilitarian theory which take individuals pursuing their personal self-interest as the foundation of social action. Consequently, the models used in studies of consumer behaviour informed by economics and some branches of psychology—like the influential theory of planned behaviour and its cognates—have been subject to endless (persuasive to me) critique. There is nothing much new about sociology preaching to other social sciences with a proclivity to methodological individualism that they should take better into account the social, collective, and normative aspects of human conduct. However, sociology alone was never likely to lever the change in approach

[2] Of course, all disciplinary approaches qualify such simple or parsimoniously abstract models of voluntary action, admitting to contextual influences on decisions (income, subjective norms, socio-demographic characteristics, lifestyle groupings). Nevertheless, individual choice is the core presupposition.

that I believe is required. Who listens to sociologists! Now, however, there is a rather general assault on such foundations, across disciplinary boundaries, which perhaps finds its legitimacy and its common core in recent developments in cognitive psychology and neuroscience. A more prestigious body of knowledge (because a form of experimental science applied to individuals), it challenges the portfolio model for its failure to accommodate the automatic, reactive, and habitual aspects of most normal human conduct.

12.3 Thinking Differently: Appropriation and Habituation

The Portfolio Model, which postulates that we typically plan our acts, select goals in the light of our values and norms, and then adduce optimal means to their attainment, has dominated accounts of cultural consumption and has propped up a preposterous model of the consumer. Gabriel and Lang (1995), reviewing current social scientific accounts of consumption, classified approaches in terms of nine different figures of '*the* consumer' in different guises, such as Chooser, Communicator, Explorer, Identity-seeker, and 'Hedonist or Artist?'. The very exegetical strategy for classification, describing alternative characterizations of an individual's orientation towards consumption, betrayed the dominance of individualistic approaches in the field and the entrenchment of the partial models of sovereign and expressive individual. There is much controversy over better alternative frameworks and explanations, with critical accounts within philosophy, cognitive neuroscience, social psychology, cultural sociology, and theories of practice all posing strong critical objections to the Portfolio Model of the actor and the importance of capturing better the less agentic, semi-conscious, non-rational, un-calculating dimensions of action.

There are three avenues wherein recent scholarship has found a renewed interest in habit. The first springs from developments in cognitive Psychology and neuro-science which observes that people do not think as much, as clearly, or as purposefully as previously imagined. It strikes a nail in the coffin of the deliberative properties definitive of Cartesian Mind and undermines key assumptions of the Portfolio Model, though it does not actually discard the decision-making form or element of the latter. Because people do not think much they have to operate on auto-pilot and they tend to repeat (their successes and their mistakes) over and over again. I will illustrate this with reference to Thaler and Sunstein's (2009) work, *Nudge: Improving Decisions about Health, Wealth and Happiness*.

The second type of account, which has several variants on a continuum, gives much greater influence to the external environment in which people act. At one end of the continuum would sit renovated versions of an earlier discarded behaviourist psychology where external cues call up conditioned responses. At the other end would be an account of species-level adaptation to (social) environmental niches within which people tailor their conduct effectively by virtue of inhabiting a familiar space which affords them opportunities to apply their well honed habitual skills. I illustrate two versions of this, Swidler and Noe.

The third approach identifies habits not so much as repetitive acts, but as practical skills or capacities. Most notably in pragmatism, habits—learned ways of effortlessly proceeding through the world—are the bedrock of capacities for more complex activities, including deliberating; but for so long as habits work satisfactorily or have satisfactory outcomes they are implemented without reflection or hesitation. Repetition is not the decisive characteristic, and lack of deliberation, while efficient, is easily reversible. The practice theoretic variant, associated with Pierre Bourdieu, is premised not on command of individual habits; rather he uses the term *habitus* which refers to learned dispositions, constantly modified by experience and trajectory, which offer coherence and direction to everyday actions from which transpire recognizable, repetitious and *socially shared* patterns.

12.3.1 *Mindlessness*

The potentially radical implications of cognitive neuroscience are probably best introduced with reference to work hailing from behavioural economics which is much better known in the context of sustainability and behaviour change, namely the phenomenon of 'nudge'. Thaler and Sunstein (2009) re-iterate claims of cognitive science to the effect that that the brain has two systems generating behaviour, one 'automatic', which is uncontrolled, effortless, associative, fast, unconscious, and skilled, the other, 'reflective', controlled, effortful, deductive, slow, self-aware, and rule-following. The first is far more important. A great deal of behaviour is governed by mental processes which are automatic, intuitive, emotion-driven, and which therefore involve little deliberation or rational thought. The result is said to be biased judgements, difficulties in resisting temptation, and a strong tendency to social conformity. In this account, consumers certainly are *not* rational, calculating, self-aware, independently-minded agents. Hence the advocacy of better 'choice architecture'—default settings, infrastructural design, feedback on the outcomes of actions, and purposefully aligned economic incentives—which will steer people away from the detrimental consequences of their naturally rash behaviour. From the perspective of sociological theory, *Nudge* seems wanting in several regards. It adopts an arbitrary standard of rationality against which to compare actual behaviour. It also fails to consider whether its findings require, imply, or entail a fundamentally different model of action;

behavioural economics seems loathe to extrapolate from its findings to mount a broader challenge to neo-classical axioms and theories (see e.g. Rabin, 2002).[3] That much behaviour bears no relation to the rational action expected in models of the sovereign individual seems to be of major significance but is not registered in theoretical development.

12.3.2 *Environmental Cues*

Sociology has been slow to exploit these new developments but promising new shoots can be found within cultural sociology in the United States in the work of Cerulo, DiMaggio, Lizardo, and Martin. The already strong current of opinion rejecting the value-led model of action associated with the older Parsonian orthodoxy crystallized in Ann Swidler's (1986, 2003) arguments about the primacy of the external social environment in explaining how culture is deployed in action. Drawing upon Geertz's (1973) account of culture as a public property rather than internalized personal knowledge, her basic proposition was that 'Culture influences action not by providing the ultimate values toward which action is oriented, but by shaping a repertoire or "tool-kit" of habits, skills, and styles from which people construct "strategies of action".' (1986, p. 273). As Lizardo and Strand (2010, p. 223) note, 'toolkit theory' puts great stress on the cues and clues provided by the environment in situations of quasi-decision serving to 'offload a lot of the cognitive work that previous approaches inscribed in the mental make-up of the agent outside towards the world of institutions and external structure afforded by the environment in which the actor is embedded'.

By attempting to incorporate new ideas about brain functioning into understandings of human action as ineluctably cultural, the cultural sociologists have further distanced social theories of action from the portfolio model (e.g. Turner, 2002; DiMaggio, 2002; Cerulo, 2010). Among the key features of cognitive science to attract attention have been emphases upon the speed of mental response and the absence of a storage capacity for knowledge of the kind envisaged by orthodox representations of mind and memory. Martin, for example, advances the case that: 'The nature of our conscious processes are such as to lead us to imagine that we use more complex reasoning systems, and have more individuated perceptions, than is the case.' (2010, p. 235). He maintains that people are good at recognizing things, rather than knowing precisely what they are or where they come from, such that, for example, they comprehend the gist of matters readily. They use simple heuristics rather than true calculations; they recognize patterns without knowing the rules or causes.

[3] In addition, in relation to sustainability, it probably has a limited range of practical relevance (Warde, 2011).

Cognitive successes are accomplished not in minds (through mental agility, complex mental processing, extensive thought, etc.) but through attention to the environment. Relevant information is mostly gathered through our senses and used without being aware of having come to judgements: 'Much of our interactional competence is related to our ability to process physical data below the threshold of consciousness.' (p. 239). All in all, Martin maintains that culture lies not in our heads but in material objects and the behaviour of other people. Internally, culture exists as unorganized fragments which can be assembled for particular purposes; culture constitutes 'a set of potentials for experience' but outcomes owe a great deal to the chance matters of 'what is available'. (p. 240).

In such fashion the indirect fallout from cognitive psychology and neuroscience potentially drives stakes through the heart of the Cartesian model of Mind as it has been deployed in social science (Lakoff and Johnson, 1999). Importantly, it seems conducive to the development of a sociological understanding of appropriation, one which needs explanations of recurrent behaviour, habit, and automaticity, and with the implication that there are social standards or norms that govern everything from how often to shower to how to get to work, that practical procedures (how to do things) can be learned so that they may be invoked without deliberation. Actors can understand what is required for accomplishing the flow of everyday life without recourse to scholastic reflexivity, etc. Much depends, however, on how the findings of cognitive neuroscience are interpreted.

Alva Noe's book, *Out of Our Heads: Why You Are Not Your Brain, and Other Lessons from the Biology of Consciousness* (2009), is a critique of a very common (mis)interpretation of the implications of research in neuroscience. Noe insists that the brain does not cause behaviour, but is merely a conduit which offers specific affordances for carrying out action.[4] He suggests that the human brain has evolved in particular environmental niches, such that it facilitates a particular tranche of capabilities. It predisposes people to be creatures of habit whose span of activity is encompassed by the necessity of inhabiting what might be described as their social environment.

Noe's account is consistent with, and owes an acknowledged clear debt to, modern pragmatism. Capacities for deliberation and intellectual endeavour are built upon, and are therefore secondary to, acquired basic habits and procedures. Intellectual fireworks are only possible because of 'confident mastery of the more basic skills' which underpin an activity (he gives the example of solving an advanced mathematical problem).

[4] 'Neural activity enables us to develop the forms of expertise that determine how we deal with the world around us, but the brain is never more than part of the story about how all this works'. (Noe, 2009, p. 127)

> The real problem with the intellectualist picture is that it takes rational deliberation to be the most basic kind of cognitive operation when in fact thinking and deliberating are themselves the exercise of more basic capacities for skillful [sic] expertise. And the hallmark of expertise is its fluency: it is engaged and, precisely, nondeliberative [sic]; the expert eschews just the kind of distanced, careful contemplation that, according to the intellectualist, is definitive of our truest nature. (2009, p. 99)

If true of mental activities this is, *a fortiori*, the case for embodied or bodily habits. Noe makes a more general case against the applicability of portfolio models thus: 'A life without habits would be robotic. Each day would be like one's first day in an unfamiliar country. No familiar pathways or tested strategies for getting things done would be available; no routines would be in place to serve as anchor. We would scan, interpret, evaluate, decide, execute, reevaluate.' But, he continues, life is not like that, 'our presence in a familiar context reduces to a manageable number the choices and degrees of freedom with which we need to concern ourselves.' (p. 119). A distinctive feature of his position is the way in which he relates habits to the situation or environment, as in the section 'The Ecology of Habit' (p. 125):

> Habits are basic and foundational aspects of our mental lives. Without habit, there is no calculation, no speech, no thought, no recognition, no game playing. Only a creature with habits like ours could have anything like a mind like ours. But habits, at least many of them, are situational or environmental.

He elaborates this point when concluding:

> insofar as we are skilful and expert, we are not deliberate in what we do. Our skill enables us to respond appropriately to the world and in an automatic way. If we were to deliberate, we would interrupt the flow and undermine the conditions of our own expertise. We would choke. An appreciation of habit and practical skill in our intellectual life reveals that intellectualism is a misguided conception even of our intellectual capacities. Habit and skills, however, are world-involving. Just as my habitual route to work is shaped in part by the landscape in which I find myself, so in general our habits are made possible by the world's being as it is (even if it is also true that our action shapes the world in turn). (Noe, 2009, p. 127)

The argument against 'intellectualism' has been made in different ways (and of course there have always been externalist accounts). All subscribe to some form of distributed cognition; what is in the environment, beyond our minds and our bodies, is integral to what and how we know. The anthropologist Hal Wilhite (2012) makes a case for a model of distributed agency applied to consumption, which draws especially upon material culture accounts and the scripting effects of technology on action. However, he also emphasizes more the embodied nature of habits, seeing the body as both a source and site of action.

12.3.3 *Habits and Habitus*

Noe is not alone in thinking habit important. Habit may be more or less emphasized. Habit has undergone something of a revival in recent social science. However, despite some obvious affinity with patterns of relentless consumption, it is not readily accepted. Nick Crossley (2010) suggests three powerful reasons for resistance to analysis in terms of habit. First it has strong overtones of the now largely discarded behaviourist school of thought in psychology associated with Skinner. The stimulus-response model, based on conditioning, seems to fit the laboratory psychologist's rat better than the average human. Second, antipathy arises from the hugely influential Kantian philosophical tradition which sought to present humans as different from animals because of the separation of their minds from mere animal bodies. Third, it is hard to find a consensual definition of the term. As Crossley (2010) puts it: ' "Habit" belongs to everyday language, wherein its meaning is variable and imprecise. Where it is used technically, by philosophers, sociologists and others, it is used in different ways and in the context of very different theoretical frameworks'.

In fact, sociologists, including Weber, Durkheim, and Elias, have mostly preferred the term *habitus*, rather than habit, to capture elements of habituation. Of contemporary relevance, both Marcel Mauss and Bourdieu deployed the concept of *habitus*. Mauss (1973), did so most famously in relation to bodily techniques. Bourdieu, also insisting upon the embodied nature of action, used the term in a much broader way, to capture the learned, shared dispositions of members of social groups upon which they draw in everyday situations. For Bourdieu, *habitus* is a central concept, referring to the ingrained perspectives, experiences, and predispositions which one person shares with others in a similar social position. Perhaps his classic definition is:[5]

> The conditionings associated with a particular class of conditions of existence produce *habitus*, systems of durable, transposable dispositions, structured structures predisposed to function as structuring structures, that is, as principles which generate and organize practices and representations that can be objectively

[5] In the earlier book, *An Outline of a Theory of Practice* (Bourdieu, 1977 [1972]), *habitus* is defined as 'the strategy-generating principle enabling agents to cope with unforeseen and ever-changing situations... an acquired system of generative schemes objectively adjusted to the particular conditions in which it is constituted, the *habitus* engenders all the thoughts, all the perceptions, all the actions consistent with those conditions, and no others... an endless capacity to engender products—thoughts, perceptions, expressions, actions—whose limits are set by the historically and socially situated conditions of its production' (1977, pp. 72, 95).

> adapted to their outcomes without presupposing a conscious aiming at ends or an express mastery of the operations necessary in order to attain them. Objectively 'regulated' and 'regular' without being in any way the product of obedience to rules, they can be collectively orchestrated without being the product of the organizing action of a conductor. (Bourdieu, 1990, p. 53)

Bourdieu's version of the underpinnings of a theory of practice is a very clear alternative to the voluntarist theory of action associated with Parsonian orthodoxy. Durable and transposable dispositions generate courses of action without recourse to expressly formulated intentions or calculations. A practical consciousness guides activity such that people respond effectively to the situations in which they find themselves. The model is one of non-deliberative, yet still purposive, action. The concept of *habitus* goes beyond habit in at least two senses. First, people in similar positions will have similar reactions—habits are a predicate of social groups as well as individuals. Second, there is a form of entailment, which is social and practical; emergent properties of repetition go beyond the mere sum of the already performed acts.

Bourdieu's account is controversial among sociologists, and his concept of *habitus* has been heavily criticized on both theoretical and empirical grounds.[6] Nevertheless, there are signs that, once divested of its primary association with social class, it is being rehabilitated.[7] The idea that there might be a mechanism which can 'generate and organize practices and representations that can be objectively adapted to their outcomes without presupposing a conscious aiming at ends' is one that finds echoes in other accounts. It would seem to be potentially consistent with developments in behavioural economics, especially in the latter's critique of neo-classical assumptions about rational action. It might also find support from recent research programmes in social psychology which have developed a post-behaviourist account of habit (e.g. Wood et al., 2002; Wood and Neal, 2009).

[6] *Habitus* is sometimes interpreted as entailing structural determination, in which case it is inconsistent to see it as also a generative mechanism for responding innovatively to new situations; Bourdieu is accused of downplaying agency and the subjective meaningfulness of action. He is also accused of having an overly strategic conception of action—for *habitus* operates to reproduce privilege and disadvantage. Also there is dissatisfaction with the idea that a *habitus* can be collectively shared: Bourdieu's most sustained empirical analysis of *habitus* in modern societies was in *Distinction* (1984 [1979]), a study of cultural consumption, where *habitus* was more or less synonymous with class position—critics suggest that this hopelessly exaggerated class homogeneity, even in France of the 1960s. There is also suspicion that dispositions are often not transferrable across situations, and indeed some hostility to the idea that dispositions and predispositions can serve effectively as elements of a basic psychological foundation for his practice theoretical approach.

[7] Ways of doing things are socially differentiated not only on the basis of socio-demographic aggregate characteristics, but also in relation to histories and biographies of degrees of engagement with different practices. Thus is there differentiation within classes, genders, and generations.

As well as emphasizing practical sense over scholastic reason, Bourdieu, as noted already, puts the typical sociologists' emphasis on the socially shared aspects of practice and consumption. People perform, have preferences and desires, and observe normative standards, of people like themselves, irrespective of whether they have personal contact. Members of collectivities are habituated in similar ways.

Some of those 'collectivities' are very large. Elizabeth Shove (2003) showed how showering became common practice in the western world in a very short period of time. In the UK, the replacement of the weekly bath with a daily, or now twice daily, shower has significant resource implications. As a result of changing standards of bodily cleanliness and of new domestic architecture and infrastructures, new personal habits adjusted to the temporal routines of daily life developed and they have become completely normalized across Europe. The hunch would be that individuals think very little, if at all, about whether to take a shower, and conduct the procedures of washing in a purely repetitive and mindless way. Moreover, they almost certainly do not consider it a form of consumption.

12.4 Discussion: Habits, Practices and the Sociology of Consumption

The emphasis on consumption as appropriation, especially if married to a concept of distributed agency, severely challenges the model of the sovereign individual as a foundation for understanding the conduct of everyday life. At the very least we have to say that models of the sovereign and the expressive individual are only applicable in a very limited number of situations where we might be trying to analyse, or indeed alter, consumer behaviour. The strong position would be that the portfolio model of the actor underlying these accounts of consumption, although currently hegemonic, should be abandoned as misleading.

New models of action raise the question whether customary techniques for the investigation of consumption are appropriate. Surveys, for instance, are widely devised to find out what people do and why, but if people typically can neither reliably remember nor articulate relevant practical knowledge, they may be poor instruments. If the course of action is not the result of a discrete causal sequence then the compromises involved in operationalizing concepts as standardized numeric measures may not be worthwhile. And if context matters more than individual intention and planning (this being a longstanding presumption of sociology) then the typical recourse to linear causal modelling of individual behaviour will miss the point. Each has significant consequences for social scientific method. However, to date, alternative formulations which permit calculation of the probability of individual and collective actions are inadequately developed and diffused. The approaches described in this section still need to be worked up into explicit and useful analytic form.

If consumption is primarily driven by appropriation with a view to practical tasks, and is sustained by means of automatic and repetitive activity, then the categories and concepts of theories of practice perhaps offer some suitable analytic tools (Schatzki et al., 2001). Practices represent the institutionalization of regular conduct, with each new performance acknowledging and reproducing, and sometimes modifying, the practice. This idea of recursiveness, generic to theories of practice, is more amenable to techniques of historical investigation and ethnography than to the causal modelling of individual behaviour (see SPRG, 2012). Habituation through appropriation—the becoming familiar with procedures and equipment through recurrent exposure to similar activities—requires a somewhat more relaxed understanding of habit than would be suitable for modelling techniques in psychology. Sociologists have been attracted to the working definition of Camic (1986, p. 1044), for whom 'the term "habit" generally denominates a more or less self-actuating disposition or tendency to engage in a previously adopted or acquired form of action'. To adopt the concept of 'disposition'—as do pragmatists and Bourdieusians, for example—is to accept greater contingency in relation to the adoption of courses of action and to put more weight on the situational features of a particular event than does blind repetition. Whether the gain from faithfulness to the ontological and experiential characteristics of action outweighs the loss of abstraction, simplification and reduction obtained via precise numeric measurement of operationalized concepts employed in causal modelling is a perennial matter of dispute within social sciences. However, if alternative approaches like that of practice theory and its affines seek to jettison the portfolio model and develop alternatives, they will require measures that span the standard dualisms—internal/external, individual/social, and unit act/sequence of action—in order to develop a level of systematicity with operational measures of concepts and indicators which permit precise description and comparison across cases.

Let me then recommend two avenues which are already reasonably well developed but not widely used, QCA (qualitative comparative analysis) and time-use studies. QCA (see Ragin, 1987, 2000) is a method for use with case studies which offers a different approach to causal analysis from the 'linear model of reality' (Abbott, 2001b). This is not the place to elaborate, except to say that it is designed to address the institutional characteristics of situations of action and to examine configurational rather than linear causation. A key insight is that a particular outcome of interest to the analyst may result from more than one set of social processes or conditions, and that it is the combination of factors, rather than their individual presence, which explains the outcome.

With respect to systematic measurement of individual habitual behaviour there has been some preliminary success using diary data. Wood et al. (2002) had people fill in a diary, at hourly intervals, describing what they were doing, and what they were feeling and thinking. Habitual behaviour (frequently performed, without conscious intention, requiring little if any thought, in stable circumstances) was very common; 'approximately 45% of everyday behaviours tended to be repeated in the same location almost every day' (Neal et al., 2006 p. 198). In the course of habitual behaviour 'participants thoughts wandered from their behaviour during habit performance about 50–60 per cent of the time' (Wood et al., 2002 p. 1293). If this diary method is used in combination with a satisfactorily validated self-report index of habit strength (Verplanken and Orbell, 2003; Verplanken et al., 2005) it becomes possible to envisage a more comprehensive analysis of the role of individual habits in consumer behaviour (Wood and Neal, 2009).

From a sociological perspective, even more interesting is time-use analysis, which is highly compatible with theories of practice. Time-use studies have been carried out in many countries over the last 80 years. They compile data on what people are doing, where, when, and with whom, during the course of several days (see Gershuny, 2000). People record the main activity (and sometimes subsidiary ones) undertaken during each period of time (measured at intervals of between 10 and 30 minutes typically) for anything between a day and a week. Activities are sometimes presented as a list by the researchers, sometimes the subjects describe what they are doing in their own words. That people can usually do this act of recording without difficulty indicates that they are accustomed to thinking in terms of different practices. The method of inquiry, which is fairly reliable and amenable to independent checks, reflects the theoretical premise that everyday life is conducted as a bundle of practices. Regularity and repetition is identifiable at the level of routines, for both individuals and relevant collectivities (see e.g. Southerton et al., 2012). Not only can the extent to which any individual repeats activities at the same time on different days be estimated, but also the extent to which shared temporal rhythms obtain. For example, the regimenting power of meal times is revealed by the proportion of the population eating at any particular time of the day. The technique captures routines and conventions.

Time, besides having the useful property of being measurable in standard units (minutes), is a scarce resource subject to a logic of substitution—to spend more time reading requires me to spend less time doing something else (say driving my car). To the extent that consumption is a matter of appropriation through use of goods and services then, in principle, the environmental cost of any bout of activity can be calculated and compared with alternative activities. (In most respects, the amount of time spent driving is a more strategically significant fact than the environmental performance—miles per gallon, levels of emission, or the cost—of the vehicle). Ultimately, the basic parameters of environmentally sustainable consumption are the number of participants, the intervals between events, and the intensity of resource utilization when engaged in the practice. That provides a basic formula for understanding environmental impact of the practices of everyday life. Thereafter, the information about who else is present gives some measures of network connections (the relevance of the presence of particular types of people to a given activity), and where the activity occurs, supplying information about mobility and locality. In other words, the time-space coordinates give a measure of the situation and environment of activity. In addition, sequences of activities can be analysed, it being reasonable to assume that the order in which activities take place (especially with respect to spatial movement[8]) will impact on resource use.

12.5 Conclusion

The intellectual developments described in section 12.3 raise difficult questions about how best to explain the actions of individuals. Sociology is perhaps a little better equipped than some other disciplines to respond because of its awareness of the collective character of mundane, everyday life with its routine and conventional aspects, especially those which sustain mutual understanding and effective anticipation of the acts of others. The perpetual flows of generally predictable conduct that sociologists conceptualize as institutionalization depend upon extended repetition, by the same individual and by many unconnected individuals over time. To the extent that this transpires as regular accomplishments achieved without deliberation of strategic calculation, innovative explanation is required across the social sciences. Theories of practice offer one option which is currently receiving serious attention (e.g. Shove et al., 2012). The conceptual framework emphasizes doing rather than thinking, habits rather than decisions, embodied procedures and the affordances of material equipment rather than deliberative acts, collective guidance over individual choice—all moves that enhance the understanding of processes of appropriation in ordinary consumption (Warde, 2005). From such considerations are emerging new and alternative recommendations for ways to intervene in order to render consumption less unsustainable (Spurling et al., 2013).

[8] A trip to the supermarket by car in advance of every meal would be less sustainable than a once monthly visit.

So finally, if consumption is driven in the manner postulated (as appropriation by virtue of the need to establish habits for traversing and inhabiting one's social environment) then policies for changing consumer behaviour require re-examination. There is already some cognizance of this, at least in the United Kingdom, where the potential for exploiting the arguments of *Nudge* have entered high up in the policy chain (see Dolan et al., 2010). Whether in its current formulation its injunctions could have the necessary range of impact is in considerable doubt (Warde, 2011), but there is no reason why more radical and far-reaching policies to deal with the facts of automatic, repetitive, and mindless conduct might not be considered. Indeed practice theory has now entered the policy-makers' frame of reference having been engineered as a potential tool for engendering behavioural change (Darnton et al., 2011). Strategically, it puts much greater emphasis on changing the social and material environment of action rather than the beliefs or intentions of individuals, a move to be welcomed precisely because policies aimed at getting individuals to change their own behaviour are so rarely successful and because the scale and urgency of the problem of sustainable consumption is unprecedented.

References

Abbott, A. (2001a) *Chaos of Disciplines*, Chicago: University of Chicago Press.

Abbott, A. (2001b) *Time Matters*, Chicago: University of Chicago Press.

Appadurai, A. (ed.) (1986) *The Social Life of Things: Commodities in Cultural Perspective*, Cambridge: Cambridge University Press.

Bourdieu, P. (1984 [1979]) *Distinction: A Critique of the Judgment of Taste*, London: Routledge.

Bourdieu, P. (1990 [1980]) *The Logic of Practice*, Cambridge: Polity Press.

Bourdieu, P. (1977 [1972]) *Outline of a Theory of Practice*, Cambridge: Cambridge University Press.

Camic, C. (1986) 'The matter of habit', *American Journal of Sociology*, 91(5): 1039–87.

Campbell, C. (1995) 'The sociology of consumption' in D. Miller (ed.) *Acknowledging Consumption: A Review of New Studies*, London: Routledge, pp. 96–126.

Campbell, C. (1997) 'When the meaning is not a message: A critique of the consumption as communication thesis, in M. Nava, A. Blake, I. MacRury, and B. Richards (eds) *Buy this Book: Studies in Advertising and Consumption*, London: Routledge.

Cerulo, K. (2010) 'Mining the intersections of cognitive sociology and neuroscience', *Poetics*, 38: 115–32.

Crossley, N. (2010) 'Habit and habitus', mimeo, University of Manchester.

Darnton, A., Verplanken, B., White, P., and Whitmarch, L. (2011) *Habits, Routines and Sustainable Lifestyles: A Summary Report to the Department for Environment, Food and Rural Affairs*, AD Research & Analysis for Defra: London.

DiMaggio, P. (2002) 'Why cognitive (and cultural) sociology needs cognitive psychology', in K. Cerulo (ed.) *Culture in Mind: Towards a Sociology of Culture and Cognition*, London: Routledge.

Dolan, P., Hallsworth, M., Halpern, D., King, D., and Vlaev, I. (2010) *Mindscape: Influencing Behaviour through Public Policy*, London: Cabinet Office/Institute for Government.

Gabriel, Y. and Lang, T. (1995) *The Unmanageable Consumer: Contemporary Consumption and Its Fragmentation*, London: Sage.

Geertz, C. (1973) *The Interpretation of Cultures*, New York, Basic Books.

Gershuny, J. (2000) *Changing Times: Work and Leisure in Post-Industrial Society*, Oxford: Oxford University Press.

Gronow, J. and Warde, A. (2001) *Ordinary Consumption*, London: Routledge.

Kaufman, J. (2004) 'Endogenous explanation in the sociology of culture', *Annual Review of Sociology*, 30: 335–57.

Kopytoff, I. (1986) 'The cultural biography of things: commoditisation as process', in A. Appadurai (ed.) *The Social life of Things: Commodities in Cultural Perspective*, Cambridge: Cambridge University Press.

Lakoff, G. and Johnson, M. (1999) *Philosophy in the Flesh: The Embodied Mind and its Challenge to Western Thought*, New York: Basic Books.

Levett, R., Christie, I., Jacobs, M., and Therivel, R. (2003) *A Better Choice of Choice: Quality of Life, Consumption and Economic Growth*, London: Fabian Society Report.

Lizardo, O. and Strand, M. (2010) 'Skills, toolkits, contexts and institutions: clarifying the relationship between different approaches to cognition in cultural sociology', *Poetics*, 38: 204–27.

Martin, J. L. (2010) 'Life's a beach but you're an ant, and other unwelcome news for the sociology of culture', *Poetics*, 38: 228–43.

Mauss, M. (1973) 'Techniques of the body', *Economy and Society*, 2: 70–89.

McCracken, G. (1990) 'Diderot unities and the Diderot effect', *Culture and Consumption: New Approaches to the Symbolic Character of Consumer Goods and Activities*, Bloomington: Indiana University Press, pp. 118–29.

Miller, D. (1987) *Material Culture and Mass Consumption*, Oxford: Basil Blackwell.

Neal, D., Wood, W., and Quinn, J. (2006) 'Habits – a repeated performance', *Current Directions in Psychological Science*, 15(4): 198–202.

Noe, A. (2009) *Out of Our Heads: Why You Are Not Your Brain, and Other Lessons from the Biology of Consciousness*, New York: Hill and Wang.

Rabin, M. (2002) 'A perspective on psychology and economics: the Alfred Marshall lecture', *European Economic Review*, 46: 657–85.

Ragin, C. (1987) *The Comparative Method: Moving Beyond Quantitative and Qualitative Strategies*, Berkeley: California University Press.

Ragin, C. (2000) *Fuzzy-Set Social Science*, Chicago: University of Chicago Press.

Reckwitz, A. (2002) 'The status of the "material" in theories of culture: from "social structure" to "artefacts"', *Journal for the Theory of Social Behaviour*, 32(2): 195–217.

Sassatelli, R. (2007) *Consumer Culture: History, Theory and Politics*, Oxford: Berg.

Schatzki, T., Knorr Cetina, K., and von Savigny, E. (eds) (2001) *The Practice Turn in Contemporary Theory*, London: Routledge.

Schudson, M. (1993), *Advertising, the Uneasy Persuasion: Its Dubious Impact on American Society*, London: Routledge, postscript to 2nd edition.

Shove, E. (2003) *Comfort, Cleanliness and Convenience: The Social Organization of Normality*, Oxford: Berg.

Shove, E., Pantzar, M., and Watson, M. (2012) *The Dynamics of Social Practice: Everyday Life and How it Changes*, London: Sage.

Southerton, D., Chappells, H., and van Vleit, B. (eds) (2004) *Sustainable Consumption: The Implications of Changing Infrastructures of Provision*, Cheltenham: Edward Elgar Publishing.

Southerton, D., Diaz-Mendez, C., and Warde, A. (2012) 'Behaviour change and the temporal ordering of eating practices: a UK-Spain comparison', *International Journal of the Sociology of Agriculture and Food*, 19(1): 19–36.

Spurling, N., McMeekin, A., Shove, E., Southerton, D., and Welch, D. (2013) *Interventions in Practice: Re-Framing Policy Approaches to Consumer Behaviour*, Sustainable Practices Research Group, available at: <http://www.sprg.ac.uk/uploads/sprg-report-sept-2013.pdf>.

SPRG (Sustainable Practices Research Group) (2012) *Researching Social Practices and Sustainability: Puzzles and Challenges, SPRG Discussion Paper 2*, Sustainable Practices Research Group, available at: <http://www.sprg.ac.uk/uploads/practices-and-methodological-challenges.pdf>.

Swidler, A. (1986) 'Culture in action: symbols and strategies', *American Journal of Sociology*, 51: 273–86.

Swidler, A. (2003) *Talk of Love: How Culture Matters*, Chicago: University of Chicago Press.

Thaler, R. and Sunstein, C. (2009) *Nudge: Improving Decisions about Health, Wealth and Happiness*, Harmondsworth: Penguin.

Turner, S. P. (2002) *Brains/Practices/Relativism: Social Theory after Cognitive Science*, Chicago: University of Chicago Press.

Verplanken, B., Myrbakk, V., and Rudi, E. (2005) 'The measurement of habit', in T. Betsch and S. Haberstroh (eds) *The Routines of Decision Making*, Mahwah N.J.: Lawrence Erlbaum, pp. 231–47.

Verplanken, B. and Orbell, S. (2003) 'Reflections on past behaviour: a self-report index of habit strength', *Journal of Applied Social Psychology*, 33: 1313–30.

Warde, A. (2002) 'Changing conceptions of consumption', in A. Anderson, K. Meethan, and S. Miles (eds) *The Changing Consumer*, London, Routledge, pp. 10–24.

Warde, A. (2005) 'Consumption and theories of practice', *Journal of Consumer Culture*, 5(2): 131–53.

Warde, A. (ed.) (2010) *Consumption* (*Volumes I–IV*), London: Sage, Benchmarks in Culture and Society Series.

Warde, A. (2011) 'The power of nudge', *Food Ethics*, 6(1): 20–1.

Whitford, J. (2002) 'Pragmatism and the untenable dualism of means and ends: why rational choice theory does not deserve paradigmatic privilege', *Theory & Society*, 31: 325–63.

Wilhite, H. (2012) 'Towards a better accounting of the role of body, things and habits in consumption', in A. Warde and D. Southerton (eds) *The Habits of Consumption*,

COLLeGIUM: Studies across Disciplines in the Humanities and Social Sciences, Volume 12, Helsinki: Helsinki Collegium for Advanced Studies, Available at: <http://www.helsinki.fi/collegium/journal/volumes/volume_12/index.htm>.

Wood, W. and Neal, D. (2009) 'The habitual consumer', *Journal of Consumer Psychology*, 19: 579–92.

Wood, W., Quinn, J., and Kashy, D. (2002) 'Habits in everyday life: thought emotion and action', *Journal of Personality and Social Psychology*, 83: 1281–97.

13

The Body in Consumption

Perspectives from India

Harold Wilhite

13.1 Introduction

Despite their conservative and transformative effects on many forms of consumption practices, body and flesh have been largely absent from mainstream theory about consumption. The predominant focus in the study of consumption has been on mental states, meaning, cognition, and rational choice. In the academic discipline which dominates consumption studies—economics—every consumption act is treated as if it were 'immaculately conceived', in the words of Brewer and Trentmann (2003, p. 3), stripped of its cultural and collective history. For economists, consumption is a rational exercise done by a fully reflexive consumer who deploys a weighing of costs and benefits in making consumption choices. Psychologists share with economists the view that consumers are sovereign, and that consumption is a reflexive exercise, though they add values, attitudes, and motivations to consumer decision-making. By contrast, many sociologists and anthropologists are sceptical of theories of consumption that dismiss the importance of social context, the material world and the consumer's personal and societal history that are present in concepts such as culture, habit, and practice.

In this chapter I align myself with those who acknowledge the role of history and social context in consumption. I assert that bodies are cultural and historical repositories of information important to consumption and explore the importance of body as a locus of global and local consumption trajectories in India. I draw on the work of Marcel Mauss, Pierre Bourdieu, and Michel Foucault, who in differing ways have brought bodies to an understanding of human action. In anthropology, Mauss was a pioneer in proposing that the body was an important repository of knowledge which is relevant to behaviour or action (1935). Bourdieu (1977, 1998) drew on the work of Mauss in his theory of *habitus*, in which body is postulated as a source of predispositions for action. Both Mauss and Bourdieu conceived bodies as reservoirs of knowledge acquired through 'historical inscription'. They were interested in how this knowledge becomes agentive in practices (Crossley, 1996, p. 100). They postulated that the experiences of the body in a socio-cultural space form a reservoir of pre-dispositions for future performance.

Aside from Bourdieu's development of a theory of *habitus*, body was side-lined in mainstream anthropology until its revival in the 1980s in theories of identity, communication and sense making (see Halliburton, 2002; Csordas, 1990, and 1994 for reviews, as well as contributions by Roseman, 1991; Stoller, 1989; Jackson, 1989; Turner and Bruner, 1986). More recent work such as that of Crossley (1996) and Csordas (2011) revisits and builds on the work of Mauss and Bourdieu on embodied knowledge, as well as on the work of Foucault and his followers, who examine bodily action through the lens of governmentality and discourse (1977). Foucault was more interested in the body as a mirror of changes in discursive formations regarding appearance, sexuality, race, and so on (Csordas, 2011). These discourses have multiple sources, including government policies and regulations, institutional norms, and commercial advertising. Theories of *habitus* and discourse both give attention to body–world interactions and both emphasize the importance of a historical perspective; yet, they differ in their weighing of the directionality of agency. To put it simply, Foucault discounted encultured predispositions, or the agency in bodies, while Bourdieu emphasized that bodies were agentive in practices (Ortner, 1999). Of course, the distinction is not clear cut. Bourdieu opened for a dialectic in which agency is actually two-directional: embodied predispositions have a conservative effect on bodily practices, but nonetheless practices change through exposure to changes in individual life experiences and to changes in the socio-material contexts of action. While Foucault discounted the importance of material agency, Bourdieu acknowledged the ways that the social world is manifested in the material, although he was never specific about the ways that the material world impacts on practices. Mauss had been clearer about this in his theory of body *habitus*, which he wrote is 'ingrained through our interactions with objects' (1973, p. 73).

In this chapter I draw on this re-emerging theory of body and action, exploring the ways that body has figured into changing consumption in India. I apply the body theories of Mauss, Bourdieu, and Foucault to the interpretation of stability and change in body-centred consumption practices such as eating, dressing (clothing and cosmetics), and the execution of household chores. I argue that these perspectives are relevant to understanding changing bodily practices in India, where discourses promoting consumption have entered India in full force after the opening to global capitalism in the 1990s, but where distinctive cultural practices, many of them anchored in the body, have figured into a dialectic of changing practices. My intention is to use the Indian example as a way to demonstrate how the body has figured into trajectories of change in a non-western context and, theoretically, to draw out the relationship between bodies, culture, and things in shaping patterns and forms of consumption. I will explore how the Indian body has been both a cultural reservoir and political symbol through several phases of globalization, from its exposure to colonial authority and discourse from the eighteenth to the twentieth century, through the Gandhian re-invention of the Indian body as a symbol of resistance to western-based development, and further into the period of rapid economic globalization after the 'opening' of India in the early 1990s, where bodies have been important subjects of commodification.

13.2 The Indian Context

In order to set the stage for an analysis of changing body and consumption in India, some minimal knowledge of Indian political and social life is necessary. In this brief chapter, I cannot possibly do justice to the complexity of India's cultural, economic, and political diversity across its regions. I will focus mainly on south India and the state of Kerala, which was my research focus over a period of four years from 2000 to 2004. Kerala is unique in several ways. First, while Kerala is one of the most densely populated states in India, there are no megacities in Kerala that can compare with the northern megacities of Mumbai, Calcutta, and Delhi. Second, Kerala is one of two Indian states (the other being Bengal) with a Marxist-socialist dominated political history from its creation in the 1950s. Most importantly from a consumption perspective, Kerala was the highest consuming state in India from the mid-1990s to the mid-2000s in spite of having one of the lowest economic growth rates during that period.

Any analysis of body in India must address the role of caste. Body and self are closely related in Hindu ontology, and these are in turn highly structured by caste (Donner, 2011). For most of India's history, caste has been determinative of many bodily practices, from the physical spaces one could occupy, to the things one could touch and how one dressed. In Kerala, caste ranking and influence has been somewhat different than that of other parts of India. The population of high caste Brahmin has declined in Kerala over the past couple of centuries. The caste which has been most populous and influential in social and political life is the upper caste Nair (Nayer). Among the various denominations of Kerala Christians, which make up about 30 per cent of the Kerala population, the Syrian Christians constitute an elite whose status is comparable in many ways with that of the Hindu Nair. The Nair and Syrian Christians have dominated the positions of land-owners, business executives, and politicians, as well as key positions in the Indian civil service and military. For lower caste Hindus, late Christian converts, and those considered outside the caste system (vadasis and tribal peoples), their caste has been virtually totally determinative of work as unskilled labourers. Despite decades of reforms, until very recently, the social and physical spaces into which these low and non-caste peoples could move, their dress, and even what, and who, they were allowed to touch was caste-determined. However, religious, social, and political reforms have weakened the importance of caste. From the mid-twentieth century, members of the lower castes were permitted to own land and to enter temples. From the late 1960s, land reforms granted land ownership to lower caste agricultural workers. The majority of participants in the extensive Kerala work migration to Gulf countries are members of lower castes who have repatriated income, improved their socio-economic situations, and built homes in Kerala. My survey of middle-class households in Trivandrum (Kerala's capital) in 2002 indicated a near economic and educational parity between the upper caste Nair and lower caste Eshava. This socio-economic change has contributed to the diminishment of the importance of caste for bodily practices. The extended family has emerged as the strongest social institution in disciplining the bodies of its members. While there has been a gradual partitioning of the extended family into nuclear household units over the course of a century, the extended family continues to be a source of control, obligations, and intergenerational decision-making, both social (such as choice of marriage partners) and economic (work and consumption). As I will explore in this chapter, senior family members in the extended family play an important role in the disciplining of dress and comportment of young women.

Aside from caste and family, another important contextual point in an analysis of consumption is Kerala's geographical position on the Gulf of Oman and its long history of trade and contact. In the pre-colonial period, trade brought with it new goods which influenced what people produced, the ways they dressed, and what they ate. Looking outward, Kerala's spices, agricultural products and crafts had a profound effect on eating and dress practices in places around the Gulf of Oman and further afield in Europe and East Africa.

13.3 Independent Bodies

Though only one of the three former kingdoms which were merged to form Kerala was directly under colonial rule, all of them were affected by colonial governance, which imposed exploitative forms for political control and trade. The penetration of British industrial goods during the colonial period disrupted local industries and had a particularly devastating effect on local cloth production (Boddy, 2011). In the nineteenth and early twentieth centuries, India was flooded with cheap imports of industrially produced British cloth. These imports became a target of Indian resistance not only due to its deleterious effects on labour and jobs, but also because cloth is considered a 'biomoral' substance in India in which its texture, colour, and porosity 'combine with the moral substance of a particular person and transform it' (Bayley, 1986, p. 287). Thus draping the body with a foreign substance was seen as a transformation of body. Not only did colonial trade bring a change of substance, but also a change of styles and designs. The skirt-like garments worn by Indian men were characterized as effeminate and Indian elite men began to emulate British dress styles (Haynes, 2011). By the early twentieth century, the preferred dress of members of the Indian civil service, Indian business leaders, lawyers, and academics was western-style business suits, top hats, neck ties, and starched shirts. Mahatma Gandhi (Figure 13.1) was no exception.

The changes in male bodies wrought by colonialism were targeted by Gandhi and other independence activists as examples of an abrogation of

Figure 13.1. Mahatma Gandhi in 1906

Source: Mahatma Gandhi wearing western clothes. India, 1893 (Photo by Mondadori Portfolio via Getty Images). Reproduced with permission

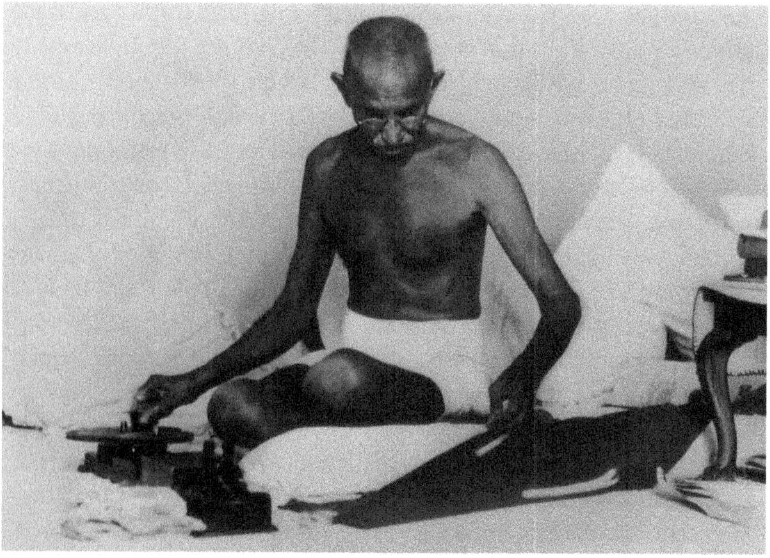

Figure 13.2. Mahatma Gandhi in 1925

Source: The Mahatma Gandhi spinning the Indian typical fabric called 'khadi' by a 'charka'. India, 1920s (Photo by Mondadori Portfolio via Getty Images). Reproduced with permission

Indian control over Indian identity. A series of boycotts of British goods in the early twentieth century focused on cloth. The boycotts were intended to protect Indian industry, but equally importantly to re-establish control over bodies. When Gandhi returned to India after a stay in South Africa, remaking body, cloth, and dress styles were central to his strategy to reclaim Indian control over its destiny. He redefined Indian identity and development in Indian terms, a strategy he called *swadeshi*. Gandhi used his own body as example. He adopted the practice of making his own clothing on an Indian spinning wheel and wearing it in the most formal of settings, including sessions of the Indian parliament (Figure 13.2).

Despite initial scepticism and reticence among elites to wearing Gandhi-inspired clothing in formal settings, such as state parliaments and in court, Gandhi and other *swadeshi* activists were eventually successful in changing male clothing norms and in strengthening the Indian weaving industry. These changes were important to the post-independence consolidation and development of the independent Indian identity. Politically, Nehru, Ghandi, and the other contributors to the new India were intent on nurturing that which had been threatened by colonial interference and on developing a political strategy which protected India from excessive influence from the emerging global economic and political power of the west. This strategy embraced *swadeshi* and *swaraj* (self-reliance), both of which contributed to India's aim to be an independent force in global affairs. A new Indian identity was consolidated in which the Indian body figured in a number of ways.

In line with Indian politics of Indian development on Indian terms, western commodities and western consumerism were held at bay by early Indian governments. This began to change in the mid-1980s under Prime Minister Rajiv Gandhi. He initiated a drift away from post-independence development policies and made consumption an integral part of India's economic development strategy. His most visible consumption-oriented project was support for Indian automobile production. A cooperative agreement was established between India and Japan, in which the Japanese company Suzuki would assist in the production of an Indian car affordable for the Indian middle class. The first Indian Marutis were produced in the late 1980s. Within a decade, the middle class transport of choice began to change from the body-active bicycle to the body-passive motorcycle and automobile. My research showed that 20 years after the first Maruti was produced, 46 per cent of middle-class households in Trivandrum, Kerala, owned at least one car and 50 per cent owned a motorcycle. Bicycling has come to be a stigmatized form of transport amongst the middle class and very few middle-class Malayalee (natives of Kerala) use them.

A landmark year for India's relationship with the global economy was 1991. The government fully abandoned its indigenous development strategy and opened its economy to transnational capital, goods, and media. The ensuing 30-year period witnessed a rapidly expanding economy, growing affluence among a relatively small segment of the population and an overwhelming influx of goods and supporting images from elsewhere. My research revealed that most people embrace this access to global markets and products. Western goods have lost the stigma of the post-independence era (Wilhite, 2008). This is reflected in the Indian political landscape. Only a handful of Indian nationalists and Ghandian socialists regard the aftermath of the 1991 liberalization as detrimental to India.

13.4 Beautiful Bodies

The post-1991 wave of transnationalism has had a massive focus on female beauty and dress. Transnational and Indian companies viewed the gap between Indian and western female appearance ideals as constituting a potentially huge market for the cosmetic, soap, clothing, and dieting industries. At the same time, however, Indian women, their bodies, and their appearance continue to be regarded by both men and women as repositories for Indianness. Thus Western body ideals and practices, which had shattered Japanese body *habitus* in short order in the 1960s and initiated a rapid assimilation of western styles (Wilhite et al., 1997), faced a formidable source of resistance in the Indian female body, which has become a site of contestation between local and global representations. Women should, on the one hand, exemplify Indian values and Indian culture; on the other, they should signal their cognizance of new, global fashions and their capacity to challenge established norms through the subtle use of western dress and cosmetic products. This contest between Indian and western body practices is most evident in the lives of women of marriageable age. While young women in the pre-bridal period, up to around 17 years old, wear jeans and western style blouses without much risk of stigmatization, as women approach marriageable age, they wear more Indian clothing in order to project their willingness and capacity to assume the role of Indian wife and mother. What has emerged is a heterogeneous mix of Indian and international appearance norms the composition of which varies by age and by social situation. A western–Indian dress style, the *churidar-kurta*, is one example of this hybrid. It is made from Indian fabric yet incorporates features of western beauty styles. It supplants the *sari (mundum neriyathum)* which covers the torso and hips in layers of cloth which obscure

Figure 13.3. Woman in *chirurdar*

Source: © v.s.anandhakrishna via Shutterstock. Used with permission

the shape of those parts of the body. The *churidar-kurta* uses Indian cloth yet reveals the body shape and uncovers the arms (Figure 13.3). It is rapidly becoming the dress style of choice for young south Indian women.

As in the case of clothing, a cosmetic hybrid is developing which draws on Indian and western beauty ideals. The cosmetic ideal has been fair skin, with little or no facial colour, and oiled hair (rather than shampoo). From the early nineteenth century Kerala women have used powders, creams, and treatments to lighten their skin. Since 1991, transnational soap and cosmetic corporations have come up with a wide range of fairness oriented powders, creams, and oils. Both Indian and foreign-based fairness products are some of the most heavily advertised on Indian television. Beauty salons offer 'fairness treatments' based on chemical bleaching of the skin, most of the clients being women of marriageable age. Kerala, with 2 per cent of the Indian population, consumes 40 per cent of fairness products.

An Indian cosmetic symbol, the *bindi* is a splash of red applied to the foreheads of married Hindu women. Exposure to western beauty ideals has led to interest in the *bindi's* cosmetic potential. Unmarried Hindus and even Christians are now wearing the *bindi* as a cosmetic which is colourful yet Indian. Cosmetic marketers are well aware of this interest in creating a new Indian beauty hybrid which draws on local and western ideals. Advertising is replete with images which show how products fulfil what Mazzarella (2003) calls 'close-distance', the basis for a very successful marketing strategy for the introduction of new products in India. People want foreign goods but they want them to be adapted to Indian culture and tastes. The bodies of Indian models and actresses provide a perfect bodyscape for the creation of a new, close-distant Indian style and they are used extensively in advertising by both transnational and local beauty and fashion companies. Among younger women, the use of western cosmetics such as lipstick, nail polish, and shampoo is growing. Figure 13.4 shows the use of these cosmetics by age group.

The bottom line in beauty is that a dialectic that took form 20 years ago with the opening of India to foreign beauty products is contributing to the emergence of a new Indian beauty *habitus* which draws on both international discourses and historically-anchored Indian and western practices.

13.5 Clean Bodies

In south India, cleanliness is intimately related to godliness. Neither one's body nor one's home will be inviting to the gods, nor will personal communication with gods be possible, if domicile and body are not clean. Thus cleaning bodies and cleaning homes have both practical and spiritual

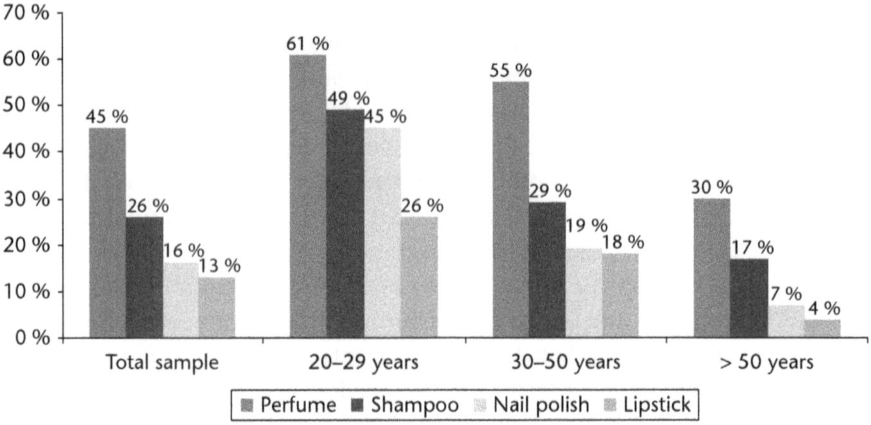

Figure 13.4. Percentage of women using selected beauty or cosmetic products more than once a week, based on a survey of 408 households in four Trivandrum neighbourhoods
Source: Wilhite (2008)

purposes. This dual purpose is manifested in the *puja*, in which homes are ritually cleaned both physically and spiritually. Periodically, women of the house clean, sweep, and wash the home in preparation for a visit by a priest or holy man who spiritually cleanses the home with prayers and smoke from a pot of burning incense.

There is not much use of soap in either ritual or day-to-day cleaning of home or bodies. Hand washing before and after eating is accomplished with little or no soap. Body techniques around eating have developed to accommodate this. Food is only touched with the right hand, which is thoroughly cleaned with water before eating. Since natural bodily smells have not until recently been regarded as a problem, the de-odorant quality of soaps has not been relevant. As in the case of beauty cosmetics, the lack of relevance of soap for cleanliness and de-odorizing constitutes a huge market for soap companies. Soaps, perfumes, and cleaning products have been heavily marketed. In advertising, subjects such as 'B. O.' (body odour, invented as a target of soap by Lever Brothers) and 'germs', invented in western advertising, are posed as targets for soap. The use of soaps is increasing, with the fastest growing sales in perfumed soaps. The 'fragrance' market, consisting of perfumes, perfumed soaps, and body creams grew at 15 per cent per year in India in the early 2000s. Even the Gandhi-inspired local self-help groups, which generate work for mainly poor, rural women, have understood the commercial potential for soap and are making soaps by hand from local ingredients and selling them door-to-door.

At the other end of the local–global scale, the World Bank has been pushing soap in Kerala. In 2002 it introduced its global 'hand washing campaign' in Kerala in alliance with soap multinationals. The campaign was eventually stopped mainly due to heavy criticism from non-government organizations (NGOs) which posed the question why Malayalee should use more soap given Kerala's excellent hygiene record. The association of soap with cleanliness and good smells has created a strong discursive regime used to promote soap in North America (Vinikas, 1989), Latin America (Colloredo-Mansfeld, 1999), Africa (Burke, 2003), and India. In Kerala, increasing soap use puts an extra strain on household budgets and on the local environment. Most household runoff is not treated, so that soapy wastewater ends up in Kerala waterways.

13.6 Bodies and Things

The ways in which women accomplish housework are changing rapidly as household appliance technologies become available. In households where chores are accomplished through intensive labour and simple tools, such as brooms, washcloths, and kerosene stoves, the promise of a technology which can significantly reduce labour and time is attractive. As prices for appliances have declined and new financing schemes become available, which require minimal initial payments, households are buying appliances such as electric kitchen mixers, washing machines, and refrigerators in order to help women manage stressed time schedules which include the accomplishment of all household cleaning and cooking chores as well as primary care of children and older family members. Additionally, Indian women are increasingly entering the work force, leaving less time available to accomplish chores related to home and family. This time squeeze was earlier alleviated in part for middle-class women through the employment of domestic house help. However, for various reasons, fewer women are willing to work as domestic labourers. At the same time, housework remains strongly gendered and women do virtually all of the work associated with home and family. Household appliances such as the washing machine and refrigerators offer mechanical relief.

My survey of consumption in rural Kerala communities revealed that the appliances most sought, after homes are connected to the electricity grid, are the electric iron, the electric kitchen mixer (mixi), and the television. The purpose of the latter is obviously for amusement, entertainment, and connectedness, but there is no doubt that the relatively inexpensive iron and mixi are bought in order to save time and hard work. Ironing without an electric iron involves building a fire, heating the iron on a stove, and tending the fire.

The electric iron saves time and drudgery. Women are buying mixis to save time in meal preparation. Preparing Kerala curries for three meals a day involves hours of grinding, chopping, and mixing spices and condiments. The mixi accomplishes many of these tasks in a few minutes. Its popularity is testified by the fact that it is owned by 98 per cent of the middle-class households surveyed in 2002 (Wilhite, 2008). The washing machine is another work and time reducer, though it is not affordable for most housewives in lower socio-economic groups. Washing a household load by hand takes around two hours and is physically demanding. The clothes must be soaked, soaped, rinsed, and beaten to dislodge dirt. A washing machine eliminates these tasks and provides flexibility as to when the clothes can be washed. They are especially sought out by families in which wives are working. The results of the 2002 survey showed that 68 per cent of middle-class households with working wives owned a washing machine, compared to 49 per cent in households in which the wife was not working (Wilhite, 2008).

Women's bodies must accomplish more with less time and household appliances provide the capacity for reducing physical work and saving time. From a body perspective, one could say that household appliances provide the possibility for a material innovation on a stressed household *habitus* which is anchored in deeply seated gender divisions of labour. These have been reinforced in discursive regimes put forward by both government and commercial marketing. From the early twentieth century, modernist and feminist reformers have associated the modern Indian woman with qualities such as assertiveness, orderliness, thrift, and intelligence (Jain and Rajan, 1996). Nonetheless, women should retain their traits of 'chastity, obedience, self-sacrifice, adaptability, modesty, nurturance, domesticity, and being "home-loving"'; and should not forget 'the importance of social appearance, and social conformity... while discouraging independence or pursuit of individual goals' (Mukhopadhyay and Seymour, 1994, p. 4). The qualities of thrift and intelligence were reinforced in educational reforms for women in the early and mid-twentieth century. Home management was added as a favoured subject for women's education (Bannerji, 1991). Women reformists supported these changes. Reformer K. Das (cited in Bannerji, 1991, p. 58) wrote, 'Running a home requires controlling family affairs, maintaining order and accuracy, hard work, thrift, frugality, skill and judgment, all of which will be improved with education.' In the post-1991 opening of Indian media for international advertising, appliance marketers have deployed this discourse, emphasizing the use of appliances as evidence of a modern, efficient housewife (Wilhite, 2008; Donner, 2011). As in the case of soap advertising, this discourse is not new, but is rather a retread and adaptation of the message that characterized appliance marketing in North America in the 1930s and 1940s

(Cowan, 1989), in Japan in the 1960s and 1970s (Wilhite et al., 1997), and elsewhere in Asia, notably China, from the 1990s (Hooper, 1998).

As household appliances, cosmetics, and soaps become integrated into beauty and household practices, the *habitus* is altered. Bourdieu has referred to this process as 'the internalization of externality', the result of a dialectic between internalized pre-dispositions and changing external circumstances (1977, p. 72). However, to my knowledge, Bourdieu was never specific about the ways in which things, once integrated into practice, bring with them a potential to be change agents. A simple illustration of material agency is life in a building. The practice of leaving and entering the building or moving from room to room is structured by the placement of doors. But material scripts for practices can be less obvious and lie dormant until a change in social context activates them (Akrich, 2000). The best example of a latent script from my Indian research is the refrigerator. In a hot climate, a cold cabinet is replete with potentials for altering practices, even in a place like southern India where bodies have an uneasy relationship with cold foods, both ideologically and physically. The imbibing of cold foods and drinks is considered by most Hindus and many Christians to be bad for the body. Furthermore, after food is prepared it should not be stored, but rather imbibed right away in order to avoid the accumulation of 'bad' substances which can cause bodily imbalances. For these reasons, the refrigerator's latent potential to provide storage for left-over foods remained unexploited over at least a generation for Hindu families as well as many Christians. However, over that same period there have been important changes in women's situations. Women who work must get up very early every morning to make food from scratch for the day's three meals before they leave for work. The refrigerator's cold storage script provides time relief in the form of storing batches of food which can be reheated for meals later in the day or week. As this potential has been exploited, new food preparation practices have taken form and a changed *habitus* is emerging in which the association between health, cold, and storage of food is dissipating. The refrigerator has also provided a space to store pre-made convenience foods. It has altered the ways that people shop, decreasing the number of trips to local markets and increasing the demand for supermarket refrigerated foods. In short, the refrigerator has significantly affected food preparation, food shopping, and the landscape of food provision.

13.7 Conclusions

The refrigerator is just one example of the massive influx of household technologies into India over the course of a single generation. These enter into practices with bodies and in the interaction the *habitus* of consumption is transformed. This interaction involves a 'double vector' of agency, 'pointing in opposite and reciprocal directions between our bodies and the world that we inhabit and that inhabits us' (Csordas, 2011, p. 138). A disembodied theory of demand, such as that of market economics has no chance of capturing these dynamics of change. Consumption theorists need to give attention to bodies, or to put it succinctly, to embody demand. In the words of Locke 'an understanding of the body is needed in which it is not just subject to external forces mediated through society, but in which it can be seen as simultaneously an agent in world construction' (1993, p. 89). A robust theoretical engagement with bodies, things, and contexts will be essential to understanding the impacts of globalization, to developing new perspectives on consumption–environment interactions and to the discussion on the increasing displacement of know-how from bodies to technologies in the execution of simple household tasks. The ontology of consumption is undergoing a significant transformation everywhere. Bodies are becoming managers of complex technologies, the workings of which are opaque to them. An understanding of this transformation is crucial to a robust theory of consumption and to the reframing of policies aimed at ameliorating its social and environmental impacts.

References

Akrich, M. (2000) 'The de-scription of technical objects', in W. Bijker and J. Law (eds), *Shaping Technology/Building Society*, Cambridge, Mass.: MIT Press.

Bannerji, H. (1991) 'Fashioning a self: Educational proposals by and for women in popular magazines in Colonial Bengal', *Economic and Political Weekly*, 26(43): 50–62.

Bayley, C. A. (1986) 'The origins of swadeshi (home industry): Cloth and Indian society, 1700–1930', in A. Appadurai (ed.) *The Social Life of Things: Commodities in a Cultural Perspective*, Cambridge: Cambridge University Press.

Boddy, J. (2011) 'Bodies under colonialism', in F. E. Mascia-Lees (ed.) *A Companion to the Anthropology of the Body and Embodiment*, Chichester: Wiley-Blackwell.

Bourdieu, P. (1977) *Outline of a Theory of Practice*, Cambridge: Cambridge University Press.

Bourdieu, P. (1998) *Practical Reason*, Cambridge: Polity Press.

Brewer, J. and Trentmann, F. (2003) 'Introduction: Space, time and value in consuming cultures', in J. Brewer and F. Trentmann (eds) *Consuming Cultures, Global Perspectives: Historical Trajectories, Transnational Exchanges*, Oxford and New York: Berg.

Burke, T. (2003) *Lifebuoy Men, Lux Women: Commodification, Consumption and Cleanliness in Modern Zimbabwe*, Durham and London: Duke University Press.

Colloredo-Mansfeld, R. (1999) *The Native Leisure Class: Consumption and Cultural Creativity in the Andes*, Chicago and London: University of Chicago Press.

Cowan, R. (1989) *The Ironies of Household Technology from the Open Hearth to the Microwave*, London: Free Association Books.

Crossley, N. (1996) 'Body-subject/body-power: Agency, inscription and control in Foucault and Merleau-Ponty', *Body & Society*, 2(2): 99–116.

Csordas, T. J. (2011) 'Embodiment: Agency, sexual difference and illness', in F. E. Mascia-Lees (ed.) *A Companion to the Anthropology of the Body and Embodiment*, Chichester: Wiley-Blackwell.

Csordas, T. (1990) 'Embodiment as a paradigm for anthropology', *Ethos*, 18: 5–47.

Csordas, T. (1994) *The Sacred Self: A Cultural Phenomenology of Charismatic Healing*, Berkeley: University of California Press.

Donner, H. (2011) 'Gendered bodies, domestic work and perfect families: New regimes of gender and food in Bengali middle-class lifestyles', in H. Donner (ed.) *Being Middle Class in India: A Way of Life*, New York: Routledge.

Foucault, M. (1977) *Discipline and Punish: The Birth of the Prison*, New York: Pantheon.

Halliburton, M. (2002) 'Rethinking anthropological studies of the body: *Manas* and *Bodham* in Kerala', *American Anthropologist*, 104(4): 1123–34.

Haynes, D. E. (2011) 'Masculinity, advertising and the reproduction of the middle-class family in Western India, 1918–1940', in H. Donner (ed.) *Being Middle Class in India: A Way of Life*, New York: Routledge.

Hooper, B. (1998) '"Flower Vase and Housewife": Women and Consumerism in post-Mao China', in K. Sen and M. Stivens (eds), *Gender and Power in Affluent Asia*, London and New York: Routledge, pp. 167–95.

Jackson, M. (1989) *Paths Toward a Clearing: Radical Empiricism and Ethnographic Inquiry*, Bloomington: Indiana University Press.

Jain, P. and Rajan, M. (1996) 'Introduction', in P. Jain and R. Mahan (eds) *Women Images*, Jaipur and New Delhi: Rawat Publications.

Lock, M. (1993) 'Cultivating the body: Anthropology and epistemologies of bodily practice and knowledge', *Annual Review of Anthropology*, 22: 133–55.

Mauss, M. (1973 [1935]) 'Techniques of the body' trans. B. Brewster, *Economy and Society*, 2: 70–88.

Mazzarella, W. (2003) *Shoveling Smoke: Advertising and Globalization in Contemporary India*, Durham and London: Duke University Press.

Mukhopadhyay, C. C. and Seymour, S. (1994) 'Introduction and theoretical overview', in C. C. Mukhopadhyay and S. Seymour (eds) *Women, Education and Family Structure in India*, Boulder, San Francisco and Oxford: Westview Press.

Ortner, S. B. (1999) '"Thick Resistance": Death and the Cultural Construction of Agency in Himalaya Mountaineering', in S. B. Ortner (ed.) *The Fate of 'Culture': Geertz and Beyond*, Berkeley: University of California Press, pp. 136–65.

Roseman, M. (1991) *Healing Sounds from the Malaysian Rainforest: Temiar Music and Medicine*, Berkeley: University of California Press.

Stoller, P. (1989) *The Taste of Ethnographic Things: The Senses in Anthropology*, Philadelphia: University of Pennsylvannia Press.

Turner, V. and Bruner, E. M. (1986) *The Anthropology of Experience*, Urbana: University of Illinois Press.

Vinikas, V. (1989) 'Lustrum of the cleanliness institute, 1927–1932', *Journal of Social History*, 22(4): 613–29.

Wilhite, H. (2008) *Consumption and the Transformation of Everyday Life: A View from South India*, Basingstroke and New York: Palgrave Macmillan.

Wilhite, H., Nakagami, H., and Murakoshi, C. (1997) 'Changing patterns of air conditioning consumption in Japan' in P. Bertholdi, A. Ricci, and B. Wajer (eds) *Energy Efficiency in Household Appliances*, Berlin: Springer.

14

Consumer Cultures Past, Present, and Future

Richard R. Wilk

14.1 Introduction

In this chapter I discuss some of the unique strengths and weaknesses of an anthropological approach to consumption, concentrating on conceptual issues, rather than methodological approaches. Anthropology came extraordinarily late to the study of consumer culture, because for many years the discipline defined itself as the study of the non-modern. As Miller says 'modern consumer culture was used as the very definition or boundary of what anthropologists would not study, because consumer culture was not considered culture on a par with that of tribal or village societies' (2012, p. 62). More recently, anthropologists have joined with historians and archaeologists in seeking a broader understanding of how human culture has evolved over time to have a greater and greater impact on the planet, primarily from extracting and processing resources and then disposing of wastes. As I will discuss, this broad brush and time depth can be very useful in framing contemporary issues of sustainability, recognizing that there are many different kinds of consumer culture with variable environmental footprints, and many paths towards different ecological futures.

The second part of the chapter seeks to use anthropological understandings of consumer culture to problematize some of the dichotomies that have become commonplace in the literature on sustainable consumption. Terms that are laden with moral connotations like thrift and extravagance, saving and spending, work and play, are given some historical and sociological context. The chapter seeks to better define these terms using the anthropological concept of a 'folk model' or a 'cognitive schema'. In cognitive linguistics and anthropology the folk model is a representation of how people think the world works, usually consisting of named entities and relationships between them. Since everyone in a cultural group shares the same model, it is grounded in everyday 'common sense', which can be elicited through interviews and participant observation. Many anthropologists argue that understanding how people behave, particularly in such a complex arena as consumption, requires that we have a thorough knowledge of how they understand and interpret their own actions (Strauss and Quinn, 1997; Holland and Quinn, 1987).

The particular folk models of contemporary consumers in the United States, I argue, are *not* driven by a desire for more and more goods, by greed, or insatiable need, as some would have it. Instead I suggest that the desire for *balance* and *virtue* usually has the effect of driving a lifelong career of expansive consumption. From this perspective, urging people to moderate their consumption for the sake of the planet is missing the basic point of why they are consuming in the first place, and is therefore likely to fall on deaf ears. Making people feel guilty about their consumption could even have the perverse effect of increasing the kinds of wasteful practices we seek to curtail.

14.2 Consumption Theory in Anthropology

Anthropologists have tried a number of times to define the things that make an anthropological approach to consumption unique, in my opinion without a great deal of success.[1] Partially this is because anthropologists are latecomers to the study of consumption and consumer culture and the topic remains marginalized in the discipline in a number of ways. Consumption is an uncomfortable topic for anthropologists because it seems to be a term based on the singularity of the modern west, a foundation that the discipline treats with deep ambivalence and distrust.

The social science that comes to us from the enlightenment began with the assumption that the western tradition of thought and governance had a unique capacity for rationality, economic and technological advancement, and civilized manners. The material abundance of the civilized countries, the superiority of their goods and their 'standard of living', was therefore both the substance and the evidence of their pre-eminence in the world.

Material abundance and consumer culture were therefore central to the way European science looked at the rest of the world, classifying people and apportioning them to different specialized branches of science. Sociology studied 'modern' (acquisitive) people, and was therefore a form of reflection. Anthropology on the other hand was more like a natural science, akin to zoology and geography, devoted to the comparative study of the primitive

[1] Early attempts include Appadurai (1986) and Orlove and Rutz (1989). Miller (2006) is perhaps the best of the recent reviews.

and 'natural' state of humanity. Rousseau (1950) stated this division clearly, when he posited a long human history in which people got their satisfaction from sociability, and had few needs, easily satisfied (see also Illich, 1977). This assumption turned all the less-civilized peoples into vestiges of history, past stages of humanity that could be arranged in chronological order (see Fabian, 1983; Latour, 1993). Since consumption was by definition a quality of modernity, the topic had no relevance for anthropology, except as one of the many forces that were in the process of corrupting and destroying the 'primitive world'.

This early charter for the discipline was restated and reinforced in twentieth-century anthropology under the influence of the economic philosopher Karl Polanyi, who collaborated with anthropologists and archaeologists at Columbia University, resulting in the work 'Trade and Markets in the Early Empires' (1957). His argument was that there was no market economy before modern capitalism, and therefore the pre-modern peoples studied by anthropologists organized their economic lives in fundamentally different ways from those in the contemporary west. They circulated goods in socially-embedded ways like gift-giving and reciprocity, which restrained individual desire to accumulate. They were not in any way consumers, because their goods had religious, magical or ritual meanings, quite different from *utility*. Possession was a social relation, so goods were not fungible or freely transferable, since they were tied to particular ranks and roles. These assumptions became axiomatic through the work of Marshall Sahlins (1968, 1972) and his archaeological collaborator Elman Service (1960), structuring anthropology and archaeology textbooks to this day and forming the foundation of the still-dominant 'substantivist' position in the sub-discipline of economic anthropology.

Archaeologists therefore continued to assume that mass consumer society was a recent invention of western Europe, so if they found evidence for large-scale consumption in the past, they had to explain it in some other way, as 'feasting' or 'ceremony' or 'sacrificial ritual' (Pyburn, 1998). In prehistoric and non-western cultures, only members of small elite classes were acquisitive of self-interested, and archaeologists assumed that most people followed relatively narrow paths through life, with most actions and consumption prescribed by culture and custom. Based on ethnographic studies of highly-competitive and acquisitive indigenous societies on the Pacific Coast of North America as well as Polynesia and Melanesia, archaeologists defined a category of 'prestige economies' where people competed for social status and rank through lavish feasts and ceremonies, which often entailed giving away large amounts of wealth. As the surrealist George Bataille said in *The Accursed Share*, the goal in these societies was spectacular public waste, which was converted into rank and status (1991). Here, thought anthropologists, was the very antithesis of a modern society where people sought to accumulate goods for their own sake.

This perspective in effect made an anthropology or archaeology of consumer culture impossible. The predominant goal of the anthropology of the time was a kind of rescue mission to record the 'pristine' pre-modern cultures before they disappeared entirely. As late as 1983, the flagship anthropology journal could still refuse to review a paper on consumer culture because it was 'not an anthropological topic'.[2]

By the 1980s, however, most anthropologists could no longer deny that the people they were studying, even far off in the most isolated parts of the world, were becoming deeply involved with consumer culture and mass media. Three other linked changes in the discipline led to the rapid emergence of consumption as a legitimate and important category in anthropology.

First, under the influence of world systems theory, anthropologists began to recognize that people they had thought of as isolated remnants of an ancient world actually had long and deep historical engagements with global capitalism (Wolf, 1982). The radicalization of anthropology in the 1980s and 1990s brought ideas of exploitation and neocolonialism into the discipline, helping people think about how the category of the 'primitive' indigene had been created to serve economic and political purposes. This in turn connected with the historians' project of rethinking the 'invention of tradition' (Hobsbawm and Ranger, 1983). For similar reasons, the discipline stopped accepting cultural boundaries and ethnic divisions as 'natural' units, and began to think about how and why specific cultural units and designations historically emerged as part of the process of conquest and colonization.

Second, starting with the work of French Marxist anthropologists in the 1970s, the discipline began to recognize that rather than being a monolithic entity, capitalism itself had a history, and it took many forms (Lapegna, 2009; Pred and Watts, 1992). Consumer capitalism based on Fordist assembly line production as found in the United States, for example, was not at all like state paternalist consumer capitalism in South Korea (Nelson, 2000), or the peripheral capitalism of West Africa (Meillassoux, 1981). Anthropologists began to look more closely at wealthy countries with growing economies, and, as the academic job market declined throughout the 1980s, more and more anthropologists began to find applied jobs in developed countries, in industry and other settings that were far from the isolated villages of the disciplinary tradition.

Third, archaeological discoveries, along with flourishing historical research on consumption, revealed that what were once considered hallmarks of

[2] This was the experience of the author and Eric Arnould when submitting a paper on this topic.

consumer culture, practices like branding, packaging, and advertising, extended far back into prehistory (Wengrow, 2008). Even before the emergence of Homo sapiens about 40,000 years ago, our ancestors were travelling long distances to get pigments for self-decoration, selecting stone for tools on aesthetic grounds, and making jewellery and other adornments. Rather than being static and determined by biological needs, consumption expanded, changed, and multiplied for thousands of years before the emergence of capitalism as people invented entire categories of material culture, and eventually settled down in permanent homes where they could accumulate possessions and pass them along to their descendants. The ancient Greek philosopher Epicurus lamented the continuing growth of peoples' needs, arguing that unhappiness was the result of needing too much rather than having too little (cited in Sanne, 1998; see also Seneca cited in Armstrong, 1998, p. 515).

It should therefore not surprise us that religions preached against greed, envy, and avarice more than 5,000 years ago. Dissatisfaction is not a modern invention at all, nor are planned obsolescence, fads and fashions, or public controversy over a younger generation that is held to have life too easy and take wealth for granted. As Grant McCracken points out, historians have been unable to find the dividing line between traditional and modern consumption, and the origin of a modern 'mass consumer' society cannot be located in a single time or place (1988, pp. 9–30).

These three trends have had a mixed cumulative effect on the way anthropologists approach consumption. By giving up the 'primitive' as our exclusive subject we have lowered the intellectual boundaries around anthropology.[3] Yet the deeply historical and broadly comparative approach of anthropology gives the discipline some unique strengths in understanding the present moment, and particularly issues of sustainability and responses to global problems like climate change (Crate and Nuttall, 2009).

14.3 Consumer Cultures at the Margins

Since the publication of Said's *Orientalism* (1978) anthropologists, like many other scholars, have questioned the way world history has been written. In particular, the anthropological principle of cultural relativism leads us to question why the history of modern consumer culture has been written almost exclusively from the standpoint of the middle classes of western

[3] Losing our sole focus on the 'primitive' leads some to react defensively or seek an exclusive theoretical core, while others are happy to abandon ship and move into flourishing interdisciplines like cultural studies, evolutionary psychology, social informatics, and material culture studies (Segal and Yanagisako, 2005).

Europe and North America. Along with other anthropologists studying the growth of the world-system, I would argue that this position misses some of the most important interactions that led us to our present condition. Instead of emerging first in Europe and then spreading around the world, we should look at consumer culture as it developed in many places as part of the interaction between several competing mercantile empires, and a variety of prosperous Asian, American, and African cultures with their own consumption economies. Historically, this pushes the lineage of what we now think of as 'western' consumer culture as far back as the fifteenth century. Rather than originating on continents, we would probably do better to place different kinds of consumer cultures in the oceans and littorals, so there would be a Mediterranean and later an Atlantic consumer culture, one in the Indian Ocean, and yet another in the South China Sea.

To illustrate what I mean as interaction between areas, consider the eighteenth-century colonial trade in raw materials to Europe. Imports like coffee, tea, spices, tobacco, chocolate, rubber, bird of paradise feathers, beaver hats, mahogany, and hundreds of others were paid partially with a counter flow of manufactured items like mirrors, lamps, iron tools, knives, guns, beads, cloth and clothing, hats, perfume, alcohol, soap, processed food, and thousands of other items. These fed into slave-trading consumer cultures in Africa, extractive consumer cultures in the Atlantic world, and state-managed consumer cultures in the Indian and western Pacific oceans. The tastes of the consumers in these areas were quite specific, and were notoriously fickle and hard to predict. They often took a manufactured product meant for one purpose, and adapted it to a novel local purpose; for example, substituting petroleum jelly for shea-nut butter as a skin-softener (Burke, 1996).

More fundamentally, the path towards global consumer culture involved social reorganization, part of a programme of cultural imperialism on the part of mercantile powers, Catholic, Protestant, and Islamic. The diverse people at the margins of the Atlantic and Indian Ocean were converted to Christianity and Islam in huge numbers. All three religions (and Buddhism) strongly disapproved of wealth and lavish consumption. This disciplining of consumer culture went along with a reorganization of family life and gender roles, and the institution of concepts of sin and redemption through public acts of generosity. But notably, these attempts at shaping diverse local cultures on a European model were met with resistance, and even in times of success they were uneven and partial. In many places consumer culture and new cash economies proved immensely corrosive to social relations, leading to social dissolution, chaos, and conflict. Often indigenous political systems founded on kinship and gender distinctions collapsed when traditionally subservient groups found new sources of status and income (Wolf, 1982). Consumer culture often had seriously corrosive social and political effects long before European colonists arrived in any numbers.

Historical and comparative study shows that consumer culture is not founded in a single group, institution, or class (*contra* Veblen), or on stable social hierarchies. Instead consumer culture thrives in situations of instability and contradiction, on social disruption and individual mobility. In my own research, I have argued that we can find some elements of modern consumerism on the margins of the expanding system of mercantile capitalism, and even in areas that were dominated by debt-servitude and other forms of non-free labour. In this I am following work by other social scientists who have worked in the Caribbean, both contemporary and historical. In the Caribbean ethnographers identify two modes of consumerism linked to different forms of labour; in one the worker is a mobile individual, and in the other he or she is part of a household that pools resources. To illustrate, let me give an example from my present research site on the southern coast of Belize.

When I first met Paul three years ago, he was introduced to me as a 'failed Mennonite'. He had grown up in one of the German-speaking conservative Mennonite communities in the northern part of Belize, with a mostly religious education, and had learned mechanical skills on the family farm. After fleeing the religious colony as a teenager, for reasons he does not want to discuss, he found work as a mechanic in several places around the country before ending up as our neighbour, employed on the staff of a real-estate development.

At the time he was living by himself rent-free as the caretaker of an abandoned bar, eating his meals in the 'camp' where single men working for the development had a communal kitchen. Like a lot of young men in Belize, Paul lived paycheque to paycheque. Twice a month on Friday he would take his pay to town, buy some supplies, and then spend the rest of his money in bars and clubs, drinking and trying to meet women. Sunday would usually see him dragging back to camp, hung-over and broke. When I asked why he spent all his money instead of saving it, first he said he was having fun. Then he explained he had nothing else to spend it on. He was never going to save enough money to buy a house, a pickup truck, a boat, or even the tools he would need to set up his own business. When I asked his co-workers about his behaviour, one thought that the way he was acting was a response to his restrictive upbringing in the Mennonite colony; now he was just acting like a *leggo beese* (Kriol for 'let-go beast'). But this kind of behaviour is typical of many young men, and some young women, in rural Belize, particularly around the banana, citrus, and shrimp farms.

A few months ago Paul did some work for me, and when I paid him I asked him, jokingly, if he was going to spend it all in town that night. He looked at me seriously and said, 'I don't do that stuff no more.' He got one of his girlfriends pregnant and they were expecting the baby in a few weeks. They had bought a small house in a nearby town with a loan secured by his employer, and everything he earned went towards paying off the loan and supporting his wife. He was working late evenings and weekends fixing machinery at a shrimp farm to bring in extra cash, and was planning to open his own shop in the future.

In a matter of months, Paul went from being a *grasshopper* living for the pleasure of the moment, to being an *ant*, saving and investing for the future, deferring his immediate gratification and thinking about his responsibilities. In the anthropology of the Caribbean we have a vocabulary for the two kinds of behaviour; the grasshopper is seeking *reputation* in a 'street' peer culture which values drinking, free sexuality, and conviviality. The *ant* pursues *respectability* through domesticity, formal position in community institutions like the church, and through hard work and saving. There is an extensive literature on reputation and respectability, which originally cast the two as gendered performances, as stages in the life-course, then as class-based value systems, and as colonialism and resistance (Austin, 1983; Besson, 1993). Instead, following Daniel Miller, I see these two not as opposites, but as closely related movements that work together to drive contemporary consumer societies (Miller, 1997, 1998b). Furthermore, contemporary capitalism *requires us* to move back and forth between the poles of grasshopper and ant, saver and spender, selfish hedonism and selfless sacrifice. The two movements appear rhetorically as polar opposites, but when combined they create a dynamic that explains some of the central contradictions of life in consumer capitalism. They provide the power that drives the 'ratchet effect' of ever-rising standards of living (Shove, 2003). No matter how well we are doing on one scale, we are always falling short on another. Each time our standard of living rises, we find ourselves once more spending everything, without achieving contentment.

This lack of contentment is connected to one of the central contradictions in consumer society identified by Georg Simmel in 1902; that in a fashion system, people are always balancing the desire to fit in with everyone else against a need to stand out from the crowd. Conformity is a respectable goal; we make obeisance to the values of others and quell our individuality in order to fit into a social role. Standing out, on the other hand is a matter of individual reputation; no matter how subtle, nonconformity always tests individual status, since it risks rejection. Standing out is competitive and challenging. As with reputation and respectability, most people find some way to combine the two, saving and spending, asserting their own position while falling back into the comforting safe anonymity of community standards.

There is certainly something universal and timeless about the moral fable of the grasshopper and the ant, which emphasizes the element of choice and responsibility, echoing the teachings of the major world religions. But the two caricatures also have historical specificity, when they were linked to two very different social forms, one homosocial and the other conjugal, each with its own mode of consumption, both founded in the heterogeneous and contradictory qualities of capitalism (Wilk, 2006).

14.3.1 *Grasshoppers—Male Crew Culture*

I have done comparative research on what I call the 'binge economies' that surrounded most extractive industries starting in the eighteenth century when the all-male work gang became the dominant form of labour in the far-flung corners of an expanding mercantile-capitalist system.[4] I argue that the gang and the 'crew culture' (Belich, 1996) it developed, was an inexpensive and malleable form of labour, often more so than slave labour because the men required a minimum of supervision doing hazardous and arduous kinds of work in very difficult locations. The crew was also cheap to maintain, because it could be fuelled with bulk rations of grain flour, pulses, and salted meat or fish, and because it operated as its own training system, taking raw recruits and putting them through an arduous initiation process. Placer mining, forestry, commercial hunting/fishing/trapping (including whaling), and long distance sailing employed large gangs of men, most of whom severed their ties with households and families, often for the rest of their lives.

Instead gangs typically developed strong bonds of male solidarity that were cemented through rituals of consumption in extended binges. Most of the men's working life was spent outside the cash economy, and their daily routines were organized around rations, and practicing the kind of close trust, discipline, and interdependence that was required for managing dangerous equipment, and long periods of arduous labour, usually in difficult environments. The work often marked their bodies, so, for example, sailors and cowboys could be distinguished by their gait, loggers by their missing digits, and most gangs also adopted distinctive dress; red checked shirts and hobnail boots for loggers, long braided hair and tattoos on sailors, distinctive hats among cowboys and Gauchos.

[4] So far my work has concentrated on the well-documented crew cultures of men, while the lives of unattached women were much more varied; a huge proportion worked in domestic service, but some historians have suggested that the number of women employed in prostitution was equal or greater than the number of men working in extractive industries.

When they were paid off, typically at the end of a season or voyage, they did not invest their often-substantial earnings in property or banks or find some way of escaping their occupation. Instead they dissipated their earnings quickly on fancy finery, expensive dining, prostitutes (notorious for stealing their money), and drinking bouts that often ended in brawls and other kinds of public disorder. By the middle of the seventeenth century most coastal cities had entire districts, often called 'sailortowns', devoted to the binge economy, and the same kind of settlements marked the location of expanding colonial frontiers in the Americas, parts of Africa, and Austronesia.

Fortunes were made both by employing work gangs and by catering to their crew culture. Men could be further exploited by running commissaries and company stores where they could buy addictive luxuries like tobacco or drug-laden patent medicines, as an advance against wages. In practice many men were bound by debt to their employers, as they borrowed against future labour in order to binge. Men were also cheated out of their pay, or abandoned by employers, and they often faced unemployment due to changing markets, or new technologies which made their skills irrelevant.

From a subjective standpoint, the most interesting thing about gang labour was the way it exploited social interactions as a means of profit, in a way far different from serfdom or slavery. Men in work gangs took immense pride in their work, and competed with one another; at the same time that they hated its disciplined and exploitative nature. They engaged in feats of almost incredible heroism and endurance, though it brought them little profit. Their labour was ostensibly about earning money, but when they had money in their pockets they were uncomfortable and unsure of themselves. They relished their binges, and experienced them as a sort of freedom, even as they knew that bingeing perpetuated their bondage.

Though gang labour and the binge economy were just small portions of the machinery of mercantile and then industrial capitalism, they had a major lasting influence on consumer culture in many places. Beginning in the eighteenth century, the figure of the pirate, and later the sailor, cowboy, miner, and logger were romanticized in fiction and popular culture (Linebaugh and Rediker, 2000). These mythologized images were caught up in the 'crisis of masculinity' that overtook the European and English-speaking worlds in the late nineteenth century, a widespread fear that urban men engaged in office work were becoming effeminate and weak (Mosse, 1998). Rather than being seen as a form of exploitative labour, the work gang was associated with nature and antiquity, and the figures were exalted as 'real men'. This firmly identified binge consumption with working class masculinity, and set up the enduring polarity that Bourdieu found so pervasive in French society even in the late twentieth century (1984). The aesthetics of working class consumption, he found, were based in concepts like simplicity, directness, and experience, valuing hedonistic embodied sensuality, and a lack of foresight and planning. The dominant cultural classes and institutions were the opposite.[5]

So, even though there are very few extractive workers still engaged in gang labour today, their styles of consumption, their values, and their images are pervasive in consumer culture. Today binge consumption may be confined to a life stage (typically young adulthood), or it may emerge into dominance at particular times of the year (consumption holidays like Carnival or Halloween), and it may also be identified with unemployed people, gamblers, day labourers, truck drivers, the homeless, and other marginal subcultures. Most often, however, the impulse to splurge, to spend without forethought on experiences that engage the body (to experience thrill), is internalized and seen as one component of every individual personality (see Stromberg, 2010). It can be repressed and modified, but it is still heavily associated with nature through the essentialized concepts of urges, instincts, and hormones.

14.3.2 *Ants—Domesticity*

In a book called *Conversations in Columbia*, anthropologists Rivera and Gudeman travel through rural areas talking with smallholder farmers, trying to understand the economic models that guide their actions (1990). The Colombian farmers believe that the only true increase in wealth comes through farming and raising stock. Their goal is to preserve their house and farm (their 'base'), to feed their families and livestock, and to return any increase from their farm back into the base. The economy is symbolically organized around the central metaphor of a house, and their strategy is to 'keep the base within the doors'. This mental model, say Gudeman and Rivera, accounts for behaviour that often seems, from the outside, irrational and conservative. The peasants do not value their labour in monetary terms when they work 'inside the house' (on their own farm), so they work long hours for much less return than they would get working for wages. The farmers concentrate on ways to save and be thrifty instead of figuring how to invest outside the house for future returns. They value increases in their livestock (inside the house) much more than the equivalent value in money earned from selling things or from wages. The anthropologists say that the Colombian peasants' ideas are really very similar to those of early physiocratic European economic theorists, who

[5] Bourdieu, on the other hand, did not identify the working class aesthetic with a specific history, but thought of it as being set up in *opposition to* the dominant values of the cultural elites. See also Levine (1989) and Featherstone (1991, pp. 55–7) on the distinction between high culture and mass culture. Anthropologists have documented other cultural groups and subgroups scattered across the world that also place a high value on 'living for the moment' spontaneously instead of acting like thrifty ants (Day et al., 1999).

believed the only real profits came from the earth through 'natural increase', branding profits from trading or rent as immoral and insubstantial.

Thrift and savings, reinvested in the household economy, are central to the survival strategies of rural people all over the world (Netting, 1993). Nothing could be further from the logic of the gang labourer, since smallholders constantly forgo the pleasures of immediate consumption in favour of long-term investments in a collectivity. The key to making this kind of enterprise work is that the household must be what anthropologists call a *corporate unit*, meaning that it holds property in common, and pools money and labour. There may be rules for the dissolution or fission of corporate households, but usually they continue for many generations.

Not all kinds of households work this way. In many places the domestic group is constituted by rules of exchange and sharing, what I have called non-pooling households (Wilk, 1994). Each adult member of the household keeps their own accounts, and donates specific amounts of labour, resources, and money for particular expenses and tasks. In urban Kumasi (Ghana), for example, husbands are expected to provide cash for food and part of the expenses of raising and educating children, but women own their houses (often with their brothers and sisters) and provide most of the domestic labour, or pay for service with their own income. Every item in the house itself has an individual owner (Clark, 1989).

In my research in Belize I contrasted villages that had corporate households with those where households held no property in common (Wilk, 1984, 1989). Corporate households accumulated property and invested in appliances, vehicles, and other goods that were used and enjoyed by all household members. Individuals living in non-pooling households, on the other hand, tended to spend their money instead on clothing, jewellery, and tools or implements to save labour and intensify their own productive activities. In comparative work, it is clear that corporate households are associated with stable communities with regular and predictable forms of livelihood, secure land tenure, and an absence of public or state-sponsored insurance, pension, and disability systems. The household groups are held together over time by *implicit contracts* between generations, and research has demonstrated both the flexibility of corporate households in the face of rapid economic change, as well as the causes of their failure and dissolution (Wilk, 1990; Creed, 2000).

The contrast between types of households is particularly clear in Belize, where some parts of the country are dominated by Mennonite, Hispanic, and Mayan-descended people who live in corporate households, while other areas are settled by Garifuna and Creole populations where the borders between households are difficult to define (Wilk and Miller, 1997). In these communities a man may sleep in one house, take meals in two or three others, and leave his laundry elsewhere, while sending money to two or three women for child support. Common-law unions are much more common than formal marriage, and migrants often do not send remittances home, in sharp contrast to migrants from Hispanic and Maya communities.

For many years there has been debate among social scientists more widely on whether or not this kind of non-corporate house-holding (sometimes glossed as 'matrifocal') is an adaptation to poverty, or the cause of it (as in the well-known literature on the 'culture of poverty'). Elsewhere I have suggested that the predictability and overall stability of the household economy, and the importance of land and other capital goods, may be more important than absolute income or ethnicity in explaining the distribution of corporate and non-corporate households (1990). The problem remains complex and contentious and cannot be resolved here, outside of the historical context of each specific case, and in the absence of good comparative data. As far as I know, there is no systematic comparison of the consumer expenditures of corporate and non-corporate households. Such a study would be considerably complicated by urban/rural differences, mobility, and crosscutting distinctions of wealth, class, and ethnicity.

My own survey of consumer preferences in Belize in 1990 found few strong associations between any social variables and the structure of taste and preference, though distastes proved much more informative than tastes and preferences (Wilk, 1997). Instead I argue that the present consumer culture in Belize and elsewhere incorporates both respectability and reputation—the legacies of gang labour *and* domesticity. As I have suggested, the movement back and forth between the two, and the tensions they generate, are essential in driving the 'consumer revolution' we are seeing in places like China, Indonesia, and India, and among the middle classes everywhere. The polarity takes different forms in every place, but it builds upon a general contrast between what are seen as socially constructive legitimate forms of consumption, and those considered destructive. In many cultures the cash economy is considered amoral and antisocial, while gift economies based on reciprocity or sharing are constructive and virtuous (Sahlins, 1968, 1972). The opposition between selfishness and generosity is a related moral issue that seems to emerge in consumer cultures, giving the act of shopping a social significance far beyond the utilitarian purchase of luxuries and necessities (Wilk, 2001, 2004; see also Miller, 1998b).

14.4 A General Cultural Framing of Consumerism

The argument in section 14.3 is typically anthropological in that it moves across time and social scales quite freely, from the distant past to the present, and from the individual to the level of national culture. National-level studies of consumerism by anthropologists and other social scientists have identified different balances and interactions between what I have glossed here as reputation and respectability. In Korea, for example, government incentives, public education, and the high cultural value of familism have led to high savings rates and a great reluctance to use credit to purchase consumer goods, values of thrift, which the Korean government now sees as a drag on economic development (Nelson, 2000). On the other hand, the authors of chapters in an edited volume on 'People who live for the moment' identify a whole series of cultures and subcultures from around the world which value spontaneity and a willingness to give away or share resources widely, and among whom planning for the future is actively censured (Day, Evthymios, and Stewart, 1999).

These are relatively extreme cases. The high-level of consumption in western Europe and North America is better characterized as a kind of precarious balance between equally strong culturally-mediated impulses towards both frugality and indulgence, saving and spending. This becomes very clear in studies of attitudes and behaviour towards food, particularly in diet culture and eating disorders that have become increasingly common, along with ever-increasing weight and associated health problems.

Mark and Mimi Nichter are medical anthropologists who have studied both normal eating and dietary disorders among children and teens in Arizona. They found that the children, like their parents, show a great deal of anxiety about their eating, and almost half the children have been on one kind of diet or another by the time they are eight years old. A majority are dieting and worrying about their weight by the time they turn ten. The paradox is that dieting does not actually lead to thinner kids—instead dieting and binge eating go together. More concern and anxiety does not lead most people to actually cut down on their average diet. Instead, explain the Nichters, people get in a cycle; eating is considered sinful but enjoyable, and it leads to guilt, and atonement through dieting. The guilt eventually fades, and the cycle begins again when the person feels that they have suffered enough to deserve a reward. In other words, they are constantly in ethical motion, propelled by sin, guilt, virtue, and reward (Nichter and Nichter, 1991; Nichter 2001).

The Nichters suggest that this sin–guilt cycle is a fundamental part of consumer culture in contemporary capitalism, simultaneously maintaining discipline in working life and high levels of consumption in leisure time. The rhythm of restraint and release marks time in the lives of consumers; every day is divided into periods of work and breaks to consume coffee, lunch, snacks, and tobacco. Work is followed by leisure, during the day and in the week in the form of the weekend break. Years have work time and holiday time, and even our lives have a rhythm where the hard work and discipline of our working years leads to the relaxation of retirement. This cycle connects our consumption to work in a direct way, and is based on a moral scheme in which the pleasures of consumption are earned through the pain and the sacrifice of unrewarding, disciplined labour.

The Nichters' work suggests that consumption is always in motion, and that the expansive dynamic of consumer culture comes not from the extremes of self-indulgence and discipline, but from the movement between the two. Can we broaden this insight to understand how consumption engages with the logic and routines of everyday life? Most social science disciplines assume that the routines and rhythms of everyday behaviour are completely structured by habits, customs, and the environment, leaving almost no room for decision-making. Economics is unusual in depicting each person's day as a long sequence of calculated decisions, each one determined by an algorithm that weighs costs with benefits. Adding the insights of economic psychology and prospect theorists reduces the burden of choice by adding in the cost of information, and allowing people to use rules of thumb and other heuristics to simplify choices.

My argument here is that consumption is rarely motivated by immediate practical goals or ends. Instead it forms part of a social and personal discourse, akin to the *practices* defined by Warde in Chapter 12 in this volume, that define a person's social and individual identity, and particularly their status as a moral person. The same fundamental idea emerges in the influential work of George Lakoff in cognitive linguistics, particularly his *Moral Politics* (1997). Recent work in consumer psychology has also identified behaviour among consumers that has been labelled 'compensatory ethics' in which consumers keep track of the moral valences of different goods, and try to compensate for the 'bad' (polluting, energy-intensive) by consuming more of the 'good' (organic, fair trade, etc.). Others writing on sustainable consumerism have discussed similar 'moral licensing' effects (Eskine, 2013) as well as 'moral balancing', a theme that also emerges from Miller's influential theory of shopping, where consumers strive to make shopping moral through saving and sacrifice, but then give themselves and others treats and rewards. All of this work can be seen as part of a more general revival of interest among social scientists in the role of morality and values in everyday life (e.g. Browne and Milgram, 2009; Oxfeld, 1993; Hartman, 2011; Barr and Gilg, 2006).

I have begun a pilot research project with undergraduate students at my own institution, asking specific questions about moral accounting. I began with the idea that food was a relatively autonomous field of decision-making, and that, following other research, I would find that students were trying to balance food intake with exercise. Most nutritionists and dieticians in the United States teach that weight is entirely determined by caloric balance; the only way to compensate for high-calorie foods is to burn more calories with exercise and in the process improve overall fitness and health (though

Guthman points out there is almost no actual scientific research basis for this dogma, 2011).

Instead, to my surprise, the moral field of food and exercise also included good and bad sexual behaviour, school work, liquor, drug consumption, and social events like parties and study groups. Refusing to do something bad, resisting the temptation to go to a party to drink heavily for example, is an act of virtue on a par with eating well or going to class on time. Eating a heavy calorie-filled desert is not as sinful as having unprotected sex, but the guilt produced by both acts can be mostly ameliorated by studying hard all week. This work is still in very early stages—I still have not found out which kinds of sin fades over time, and which kind typically 'festers' and get worse. The rules of transitivity and exchange are still unclear, and we do not know how people deal with acts or goods that have mixed valences, like organic snack foods and sweets, or fair trade coffee in a disposable plastic cup. Do people edit and block information that might change the values of the things they consume? Are there events that 'clear' the registers, and, if so, does one start over with a positive or negative balance? All of these questions must be answered in order to flesh out the folk model of consumption operating here, a model that is used to rationalize behaviour after the fact, and may also play a major role in guiding and shaping that behaviour.

At a larger social scale the idea of moral balancing can help us understand how people's efforts to consume in a more sustainable and greener way may actually lead to an increase in total consumption, an opinion echoed in Monbiot's column entitled 'We cannot change the world by changing our buying habits' (2008), as well as a good deal of literature on 'rebound effects' in sustainable consumption (Potts and Burns, 2011). This is much the same as the Nichters' discovery that when people diet they tend to gain weight, that all they do is intensify the swings back and forth between deprivation and indulgence. When we encourage people to consume 'green' products, or encourage them to buy more efficient appliances, we may actually be promoting increased total consumption, particularly if we look at entire households, rather than individuals over a short period and their spending in a single domain such as food, heating, or transportation.

In households there is a whole new level of complexity in achieving balance. Wilhite (Chapter 12) and I once did a project on household energy consumption in California (1984), where we found that married couples polarized each other, so that one became the 'spender' and the other the 'saver'. But there was no clear gendered pattern, and some divorced people had been the saver in one relationship and the spender in the next. Of course, we also saw couples who avoided conflict over what to spend their money on by buying everything that any family members wanted, leading to serious household debt. There is also a literature on the role children play in household spending, which suggests that sometimes parents compete with each other to provide expensive treats, burdening children with guilt and more material possessions than they can ever use, wear, or learn to play with. Children also compete with each other, and parents may give them money and goods to try to achieve balance, in ways that also fuel cycles of expansion in consumption.

14.5 The Future

If we think about consumption in the most general possible way, we can see that it plays the role of 'reward' in an economic system that divides everything up into costs and benefits, plusses and minuses. The incentives for work, creativity, skill, and education are mostly things that use energy and have environmental costs and externalities. Going far back into human history, the cost of a growing number of people who could consume luxuries and complex products has been covered by exploiting non-renewable and renewable natural resources and subordinate groups of people, and externalizing waste disposal. People may lament the consequences of the system, but the general acceptance of concepts such as comfort, freedom, leisure, quality of life, and standards of living, rests on the assumption that owning and consuming little is poverty, and the opposite is wealth; that poor people have few options and the rich have freedom to choose what they want. Choice is essentially for sale in this system, so it should not surprise us that it has been commoditized; supermarkets rent out their shelves to the highest bidder, determining which groceries the customer can choose from, and similar transactions take place at every level of the consumer economy. Choice itself has become a super-commodity.

Expanding our analysis to the economy as a whole, we can see how the combined efforts of millions of households to change their consumer behaviour, to be more frugal and 'sustainable,' can lead to paradoxical effects on total consumption. Even when money appears to be standing still, it is actually moving. If people would follow our advice and spend less on their own consumption, that means they will save more, but it does not mean the money they have saved is going to become inert. Invested or put in a retirement fund or bank, it just moves to someone else's anonymous hands and may be used to finance a gas pipeline or offshore oil drilling. If I spend the money on weather-stripping or solar panels, I am also putting that money into further circulation; my building contractor may use it to go out and buy a jet ski or snowmobile.

Those pursuing green consumer choices try to get around this by patronizing green and local businesses and buying organic, fair trade, or other goods that promise that their money will be used to good purpose. The problem remains, however, that when I spend money, even on the greenest of goods, I am contributing to circulation that provides the lifeblood of capitalist expansion. As a consumer careful choices can lower negative impacts, but being 'less bad' is not the same as contributing to sustainability by reducing overall consumption. The recognition of the problem of circulation lies behind the recent explosive growth of the 'slow money' movement in the United States, where investors take a pledge to put a percentage of their money into local green businesses and farms (Tasch, 2010).

If there is just no way you can save, or spend in a way that helps the environment more than not spending anything, then the only solution is to earn less. A sustainable economy would require that we act like Max Weber's peasants. Beyond a certain level of income, we would have to increase our leisure time, rather than take an increase in pay that might lead to more consumption. And we would have to spend that leisure time using as little energy and material as possible.

I am not suggesting that the economy is a zero-sum game, or that we should return to the physiocratic thinking from the Middle Ages. Some resources, like the sun and the supply of iron and silicon in the Earth are for practical purposes inexhaustible. We can learn to do a lot more with less, but we cannot keep expanding the 'more' apace with our savings because at the global level we still have the task of bringing three to five billion people into the scope of essential services like housing, water, electricity, and public transport. We have to grow our economies, but not in the direction of infinity, as Schor says in her book *Plenitude* (2010). But this is going to require a very different kind of human being, and a society willing to accept something akin to the 'maximum wage' that the occupy movement has brought back into public discourse (Pizzigati, 1992). Sumptuary laws once regulated consumption and determined what people of different ranks and occupations were allowed to own and consume. The onrush of consumer capitalism and the collapse of old regimes of social ranking have swept most of these regulations away. But in the face of the clamouring demands of eight or even ten billion people for their fair share of the wealth of consumer society, we may have to find a way to dig through the dustbin of history and recycle an updated version of sumptuary law.

Until we think about the limits of wealth, a sustainable consumer culture remains an oxymoron, and sustainable consumption a term that allows science to say one thing and the public to hear another. North Americans take their freedom to consume very seriously and they don't like it when people suggest that they are going to have to give up some comforts and luxuries. If the concept of sustainable consumption actually does begin to threaten to have an economic impact, or serious restrictions akin to rationing ever become part of a serious public discussion, I would expect a vicious and effective counterattack from the advocates of free markets, personal freedoms, economic individualism, and infinite growth. In this the USA is merely an extreme case of a more general dilemma. The freedom to consume according to wealth, in a highly stratified society, combined with political regimes that require the consent of the majority, is a recipe for an unsustainable expanding consumer culture.

References

Appadurai, A. (ed.) (1986) *The Social Life of Things: Commodities in Cultural Perspective*, Cambridge: Cambridge University Press.

Armstrong, R. (1998) 'Insufficiency and lack: Between consumption and production in a longhouse economy 1909–1996', *Journal of the Royal Anthropological Institute*, 4(3): 511–30.

Austin, D. (1983) 'Culture and ideology in the English-speaking Caribbean: A view from Jamaica', *American Ethnologist*, 10(2): 223–40.

Barr, S. and Gilg, A. (2006) 'Sustainable lifestyles: Framing environmental action in and around the home', *Geoforum*, 37(6): 906–20.

Bataille, G. (1991) *The Accursed Share*, trans. Robert Hurley, New York: Zone Books.

Belich, J. (1996) *Making Peoples: A History of the New Zealanders*, Honolulu: University of Hawaii Press.

Besson, J. (1993) 'Reputation and respectability reconsidered: A new perspective on Afro-Caribbean peasant women', in: J. H. Momsen (ed.) *Women and Change in the Caribbean*, London: Jas. Currey.

Bourdieu, P. (1984) *Distinction: A Social Critique of the Judgment of Taste*, Cambridge, Mass.: Harvard University Press.

Browne, K. E. and Lynne Milgram, B. (eds) (2009) *Economics and Morality: Anthropological Approaches*, Boulder: Altamira Press.

Burke, T. (1996) *Lifebuoy Men, Lux Women*, Durham: Duke University Press.

Clark, G. (1989) 'Separation between trading and home for Asante women in Kumasi central market, Ghana' in R. Wilk (ed.) *The Household Economy: Reconsidering the Domestic Mode of Production*, Boulder: Westview Press.

Crate, S. A. and Nuttall, M. (eds) (2009) *Anthropology and Climate Change: From Encounters to Actions*, Walnut Creek: Left Coast Press.

Creed, G. (2000) 'Family values and domestic economies', *Annual Review of Anthropology*, 29: 329–55.

Dame, K. (2009) 'The duality of desire', *Patterns*, 1: 1–2, available at: <http://patterns.ideo.com/>.

Day, S., Evthymios P., and Stewart, S. (1999) *Lilies of the Field*, Boulder: Westview Press.

Eskine, K. J. (2013) 'Wholesome foods and wholesome morals? Organic foods reduce prosocial behavior and harshen moral judgments', *Social Psychological and Personality Science*, 4(2): 251–4.

Fabian, J. (1983) *Time and the Other*, New York: Columbia University Press.

Featherstone, M. (1991) *Consumer Culture and Postmodernism*, London: Sage.

Gudeman, S. and Rivera, A. (1990) *Conversations in Colombia: The Domestic Economy in Work and Text*, Cambridge: Cambridge University Press.

Guthman, J. (2011) *Weighing In: Obesity, Food Justice, and the Limits of Capitalism*, Berkeley: University of California Press.

Hartman, L. (2011) *The Christian Consumer*, New York: Oxford University Press.

Hobsbawm, E. and Ranger, T. (eds) (1983) *The Invention of Tradition*, Cambridge University Press.

Holland, D., and Quinn, N. (eds) (1987) *Cultural Models in Language and Thought*, Cambridge: Cambridge University Press.

Illich, I. (1977) *Toward a History of Needs*, New York: Pantheon

Lakoff, G. (1997) *Moral Politics: What Conservatives Know That Liberals Don't*, Chicago: University of Chicago Press.

LaPegna, P. (2009) 'Ethnographers of the world . . . united?', *Journal of World-Systems Research*, XV(1): 3–24.

Latour, B. (1993) *We Have Never Been Modern*, Cambridge, Mass.: Harvard University Press.

Levine, L. (1989) *Highbrow/Lowbrow: The Emergence of Cultural Hierarchy in America*, Cambridge, Mass.: Harvard University Press.

Linebaugh, P. and Rediker, M. (2000) *The Many-Headed Hydra*, Boston: Beacon Press.

Meillassoux, C. (1981) *Maidens, Meal and Money: Capitalism and the Domestic Community*, Cambridge: Cambridge University Press.

Miller, D. (1997) *Capitalism: An Ethnographic Approach*, Oxford: Berg Publishers.

Miller, D. (ed.) (1998a) *The Dialectics of Shopping*, Chicago: University of Chicago Press.

Miller, D. (1998b) *A Theory of Shopping*, Ithaca, N.Y.: Cornell University Press.

Miller, D. (2006) 'Consumption', in C. Tilley, W. Keane, S. Küchler, M. Rowlands, and P. Spyer (eds) *Handbook of Material Culture*, London: Sage.

Miller, D. (2012) *Consumption and its Consequences*, Cambridge: Polity Press.

Monbiot, G. (2008) 'We cannot change the world by changing our buying habits', available at: <http://www.guardian.co.uk/environment/georgemonbiot/2009/nov/06/green-consumerism> (accessed 20 February 2112).

Mosse, G. (1998) *The Image of Man: The Creation of Modern Masculinity*, New York: Oxford University Press.

Nelson, L. C. (2000) *Measured Excess*, New York: Columbia University Press.

Netting, R. Mc. (1993) *Smallholders, Householders: Farm Families and the Ecology of Intensive, Sustainable Agriculture*, Tucson: University of Arizona Press.

Nichter, M. (2001) *Fat Talk: What Girls and Their Parents Say about Dieting*, Cambridge Mass.: Harvard University Press.

Nichter, M. and Nichter, M. (1991) 'Hype and Weight', *Medical Anthropology*, 13: 249–84.

Orlove, B. and Rutz, H. (eds) (1989) *The Social Economy of Consumption*, Lanham, Md.: University Press of America.

Oxfeld, E. (1993) *Blood, Sweat and Mahjong: Family and Enterprise in an Overseas Chinese Community*, Ithaca, N.Y.: Cornell University Press.

Pizzigati, S. (1992) *The Maximum Wage: A Common-Sense Prescription for Revitalizing America By Taxing the Very Rich*, Denver: Rowman & Littlefield Publishers.

Polanyi, K., Arensburg, C., and Pearson, H. (eds) (1957) *Trade and Market in the Early Empires*, New York: Free Press.

Potts, M. and Burns, C. (2011) 'The "rebound effect": A perennial controversy rises again', *Solutions Journal*, Spring, available at: <http://blog.rmi.org/Blogs/Solutions+Journal>.

Pred, A. R. and Watts, M. (1992) *Reworking Modernity: Capitalisms and Symbolic Discontent*, New Brunswick, N.J.: Rutgers University Press.

Pyburn, K. A. (1998) 'Consuming the Maya', *Dialectical Anthropology*, 23: 111–29.

Rousseau, J. J. (1950[1755]) 'A discourse on a subject proposed by the Academy of Dijon: What is the origin of inequality among men, and is it authorized by natural law?' in G. D. H. Cole. (ed.) *The Social Contract and Discourses*, New York: E. P. Dutton.

Sahlins, M. (1968) 'Notes on the original affluent society' in R. Lee and I. Devore (eds) *Man the Hunter*, Chicago: Aldine.

Sahlins, M. (1972) *Stone Age Economics*, Chicago: Aldine.

Sahlins, M. and Service, E. (1960) *Evolution and Culture*, Ann Arbor: University of Michigan Press.

Said, E. (1978) *Orientalism*, New York: Vintage Books.

Sanne, C. (1998) *The (Im)possibility of Sustainable Lifestyles*, Australian National University Working Paper No. 63: Canberra.

Schor, J. B. (2010) *Plenitude: The New Economics of True Wealth*, London: Penguin Press HC.

Segal, D. A. and Yanagisako, S. J. (eds) (2005) *Unwrapping the Sacred Bundle: Reflections on the Disciplining of Anthropology*, Chapel Hill, N.C.: Duke University Press.

Shove, E. (2003) *Comfort, Cleanliness and Convenience: The Social Organization of Normality*, Oxford: Berg.

Simmel, G. (1902) 'Fashion', *International Quarterly*, 10: 130–55.

Strauss, C. and Quinn, N. (1997) *A Cognitive Theory of Cultural Meaning*, Cambridge: Cambridge University Press.

Stromberg, P. (2010) *Caught in Play: How Entertainment Works on You*, Stanford: Stanford University Press.

Tasch, W. (2010) *Inquiries Into the Nature of Slow Money: Investing as If Food, Farms, and Fertility Mattered*, White River Jct.: Chelsea Green Publishing.

Wengrow, D. (2008) 'Prehistories of commodity branding,' *Current Anthropology*, 49: 7–34.

Wilk, R. (1984) 'Households in process: Agricultural change and domestic transformation among the Kekchi Maya', in R. Netting, R. Wilk, and E. Arnould (eds) *Households: Comparative and Historical Studies of the Domestic Group*, Berkley: University of California Press.

Wilk, R. (1989) 'Houses as consumer goods: Social processes and allocation decisions.' in B. Orlove and H. Rutz (eds) *The Social Economy of Consumption*, Lanham, Md.: University Press of America, pp. 373–406.

Wilk, R. (1990) 'Household ecology: Decision making and resource flows', in *The Ecosystem Approach in Anthropology: From Concept To Practice*, E. Moran (ed.) Ann Arbor, Mich: University of Michigan Press.

Wilk, R. (1994) 'Inside the economic institution: Modeling household budget structures', in J. Acheson (ed.) *Anthropology and Institutional Economics*, New York: University Press of America.

Wilk, R. (1997) 'A critique of desire: Distaste and dislike in consumer behavior', *Consumption, Markets and Culture*, 1(2): 175–96.

Wilk, R. (2001) 'Consuming morality', *Journal of Consumer Culture*, 1(2): 245–60.

Wilk, R. (2004) 'Morals and metaphors: The meaning of consumption' in K. Ekström and H. Brembeck (eds) *Elusive Consumption*, Oxford: Berg.

Wilk, R. (2006) 'Consumer culture and extractive industry on the margins of the world system', in J. Brewer and F. Trentmann (eds) *Consumer Cultures: Global Perspectives*, Oxford: Berg.

Wilk, R. and Miller, S. (1997) 'Some methodological issues in counting communities and households', *Human Organization*, 56(1): 64–71.

Wilk, R. and Wilhite, H. (1984) 'Household energy decision making in Santa Cruz County, California', in B. Morrison and W. Kempton (eds) *Families and Energy: Coping with Uncertainty*, East Lansing, Mich.: Michigan State University, College of Human Ecology.

Wolf, E. (1982) *Europe and the People Without History*, Berkeley: University of California Press.

Index